Understanding Infancy

A Series of Books in Psychology

Editors:

Richard C. Atkinson
Jonathan Freedman
Gardner Lindzey
Richard F. Thompson

Understanding Infancy

Eleanor Willemsen

With the assistance of Louise Nicholson

W. H. Freeman and Company
San Francisco

Cover photograph: Emilio A. Mercado.

Chapter Frontispieces: 1, Emilio A. Mercado; 2, copyright © Suzanne Arms/Jeroboam, Inc.; 3, copyright © Suzanne Arms; 4, copyright © Suzanne Arms; 5, copyright © Hank Lebo/Jeroboam, Inc.; 6, copyright © Suzanne Arms; Appendix, Emilio A. Mercado.

Sponsoring Editor: W. Hayward Rogers; Project Editor: Pearl C. Vapnek; Manuscript Editor: Linda Chaput; Designer: Gary A. Head; Production Coordinator: Linda Jupiter; Illustration Coordinator; Batyah Janowski; Compositor: Holmes Composition Service; Printer and Binder: The Maple-Vail Book Manufacturing Group.

Library of Congress Cataloging in Publication Data

Willemsen, Eleanor Walker, 1938–
    Understanding infancy.

    (A Series of books in psychology)
    Bibliography: p.
    Includes index.
    1. Infant psychology. I. Title.
BF723.I6W5   155.4'22   78-21181
ISBN 0-7167-1002-1
ISBN 0-7167-1001-3 pbk.

Printed in the United States of America

9 8 7 6 5 4 3 2 1

For Mike and Karen

Contents

Preface

Until recently, babies have been somewhat mysterious. How does the world appear to them? Do they recognize and like us? What is the best way to care for them? How can we help them to grow up to be healthy adults?

The answers to these questions depend upon the age of the baby. Thus, *developmental psychology* is the study of how children develop through time. Researchers in this field seek the facts about the changes in babies' abilities and behavior that relate to age, and, more important, they seek an understanding of how those changes occur. This book, written from the viewpoint of a developmental psychologist, is a survey of the facts and insights we now have about babies.

You can learn from this book how babies gather information from the world around them and how they react to what they perceive. You can also discover what we know about babies' relationships with other people and about the uniqueness of their personalities. We also carefully trace the changes over time in babies' abilities and behavior.

We have written this book for people who are interested in research about the psychological development of babies—an audience that includes students, pediatricians, parents, and all others who care for and about babies. For this reason, we have tried to keep the language as nontechnical as possible. The book should be appropriate for undergraduate courses in human development (not only during infancy and childhood, but throughout life), family life, education, and related disciplines. The book should also prove useful to graduate students just beginning research in infant development, and to pediatricians preparing to work with infants. Parents and other caregivers will find the book particularly useful: Throughout the book, we apply what is known about babies' development to the problems that arise in everyday caregiving situations.

We draw on the research literature of the last 15 years (with selected references to important earlier studies) to review the important aspects of psychological development from the beginning of life to just before children begin talking in sentences. In Chapter 1, we discuss the experiences of the mother and the fetus from conception through birth. In Chapter 2, we describe the skills and limitations of newborns, focusing on their perceptual, motor, and mental abilities. Chapter 3 traces the changes during infancy in how babies perceive and learn. In Chapter 4, we examine the factors that influence early mental growth and their effects on babies' developing perception, learning, memory, and motor behavior—a diverse topic we (and many others) call *cognitive development.* Chapter 5 considers social and emotional growth: We explore babies' relationships with their families and other companions and their reactions to strangers. In Chapter 6, we turn to the intriguing subject of the baby's personality: How do babies differ from one another, and what does this imply for their future development?

We have included the Appendix for readers who are interested in using professional techniques to observe infants—an enlightening experience for both parents and students. The Appendix is a handbook of methods by which to observe infants, from the informal anecdotal record to highly structured psychological tests. The Appendix may be quite helpful for students doing an observational project or a research study. Instructors, too, may find the Appendix useful in planning observational projects.

About the pronouns *he* and *she.* . . . Although we wished to avoid referring to every baby as *he,* we were then caught on the other horn of the dilemma: When should a baby we were writing about be a *he,* and when a *she?* We tried to solve the problem by writing *they* when describing general facts about babies. When we described single babies, we alternated between male and female examples. We hope the reader will not be confused or jarred by our attempt to emphasize the humanity of babies.

Each writer contributed her part to the endeavor of this book. Eleanor Willemsen, the author (and the "I" in the book), is the psychologist and is completely responsible for the research, the organization, and the writing of the first draft. Louise Nicholson rewrote the entire manuscript to clarify the diction and added explanatory material, such as the examples. A number of other people have been helpful to us along the way. Mary Jane McTighe took on the herculean task of collecting the research bibliography and abstracting some of the sources. At various times the manuscript has been read by James Booth, Joe Campos, Shirley Feldman, Bernadette Fong, Diane Dreher, and Jeff Zorn. Their comments have been truly helpful and have enabled us to improve the book in many important ways.

We are particularly appreciative of the dedicated and professional help we have received from the staff at W. H. Freeman and Company. The encouragement and assistance of psychology editor W. Hayward Rogers has been invaluable to E. W. over the years of our association, and especially throughout the preparation of this book. Linda Chaput, the manuscript editor, has patiently and professionally used her many talents to improve the manuscript immeasurably. The attractive design of art director Gary Head has added to our pleasure in working on the book.

Throughout the several years required to put together a book amid other diverse duties, our families, friends, and colleagues have been at various moments incredulous (that we could undertake such a time-consuming project), unbelieving (that we would ever finish), bewildered (by some well-meant but ponderous academic prose in the first draft), and—best of all—personally encouraging in various ways. Particular recognition for emotional support is hereby given (with heart-felt thanks) to Michael and Karen Willemsen; Mary Jane McTighe; Diane Dreher; and Thomas, Katherine, Anne, Eugenie, and Lisa Nicholson, who were all valued advisers. For patience and perseverance in typing the manuscript in its various drafts, we are grateful to Paula Davidson and Lois Strand. While we are most appreciative of the help of all those people, responsibility for the final product, with whatever imperfections it may have, is ours.

During the work on this book, we have been inspired not only by the interest of others but by the fascinating insights we have had about babies and their lives. We are enthusiastic about passing this information on to you, for we think it will make a difference in your lives.

Eleanor Willemsen
Louise Nicholson

November 1978

Understanding Infancy

Chapter 1

Beginnings of Life

Babies spend many months getting ready to enter the world, an event that can affect them both physically and psychologically for the rest of their lives. During the months before birth many of the infant's individual characteristics are being developed according to a uniquely personalized set of genetic messages. At the same time the special environment in which the unborn baby lives—the mother's body—is exerting its influence over the course of growth and development. These influences, heredity and environment, work together in a highly complex way that raises many questions about their relative importance and duration. What part of our identity is determined by heredity and what part is determined by environment? What happens to a baby whose mother has had a poor diet during pregnancy? What can be done for babies who have been born with a handicap?

To answer these questions, let us start by considering the biology of conception, pregnancy, and birth. Once we have done so we can discuss how these processes affect a baby's development, later behavior, and psychological experiences. (For example, how does the period between conception and birth affect the baby after birth? How do environment and heredity interact in causing birth defects? How do drugs, alcohol, cigarettes, hormones, infections, and even the mother's emotional state affect an unborn child?) Next, we will consider prematurity—what it is and how it affects an infant's physical and psychological condition.

Finally, in the last section, we will discuss the term "at risk," which is coming to be widely used to describe babies who have the potential to develop serious physical or psychological problems. Use of the term has advantages and disadvantages that we should consider.

The Biology of Conception, Pregnancy, and Childbirth

The Mechanisms of Heredity

Every cell in the human body contains information that directs both the cell's own reproduction and its manufacture of proteins. This information is coded in the structure of molecules of deoxyribonucleic acid (DNA). The

DNA molecules are in the *chromosomes*—long, thin, threadlike bodies in the nucleus of the cell. A chromosome can be thought of as a long sequence of segments, called *genes,* arranged like beads on a string. A specific piece of genetic information (like eye color or height) may be contained in a single gene or in an interacting combination of genes.

During somatic cell division, or *mitosis,* which is constantly going on in your body, chromosomes and their genes are exactly duplicated so that your new cells are exactly like the ones they are replacing. In this way, eye color, hair texture, and other characteristics retain their distinctive aspects throughout life.

Almost every cell in a person's body contains 46 chromosomes, in 23 matched pairs. Each pair consists of one chromosome from the person's mother and one from the person's father. Everyone has some specialized reproductive cells, called *germ cells,* that divide to produce ova (eggs) in women and sperm in men. Germ cells divide by a process called *meiosis,* in which the pairs of chromosomes are separated, and each new germ cell contains one chromosome from each pair. Thus, each egg and each sperm contains only 23 chromosomes. When a sperm unites with an egg, the resulting fertilized egg contains a new combination of genetic information that differs from the combination possessed by either parent. In meiosis, the chromosomes of each pair can exchange genes. Further, the pairs separate in a random way: each egg cell contains some chromosomes from a woman's mother and some from her father; likewise, each sperm cell contains a mixture of chromosomes from a man's mother and father. Thus, it is practically impossible for any two sperms, or any two eggs, to be exactly alike. The multitude of possible sperm and egg combinations makes for a truly enormous variety in the possible genetic makeups of the offspring of each man and woman. This is what makes each person unique.

Sometimes one trait—say, blond hair color—will be dictated by the mother's gene on a certain chromosome, while a different one—say, brown hair color—will be dictated by the father's gene on the matching chromosome. This conflict is usually resolved by one of the genes being *dominant* over the other; that is, its trait prevails. The nondominant gene is called *recessive.* A recessive trait is not exhibited in a person who has both a recessive and a dominant gene for that characteristic, but of course the recessive gene is nevertheless present in that person's cells. Consequently, his or her offspring will exhibit that recessive trait if the offspring inherits another recessive gene for that characteristic from the other parent.

One of the 23 pairs of chromosomes that human beings have is the pair determining, among other things, their sex. In this pair, there is at least one X chromosome, which is the same size as all the other chromosomes. Females have a second X chromosome, which determines their sex. Various other traits carried by genes in the X chromosomes of women are expressed or suppressed by the principle of gene dominance. Males, however, have an X chromosome and a Y chromosome, which is much smaller and carries very few genes. For most genes on the X chromosome, there is no corresponding gene on the Y chromosome. Thus, a recessive gene on a woman's X chromosome can be suppressed by a dominant gene on her other X chromosome, but both dominant and recessive genes on a man's X chromosome will be exhibited as traits. A man inherits these X-linked traits only from his mother, from whom he receives his X chromosome. Most X-linked traits are normal, but some of them, unfortunately, are illnesses or handicaps.

Once in a great while a gene is altered, either spontaneously or because of environmental factors. Such a change, a *mutation,* gives rise to a heritable trait different from the one formerly determined by the particular gene. The trait may be superior to the original, but more commonly it is a disease or a handicap.

Conception

A woman's ovaries release an egg about once every 28 days. It takes about a day or two for the egg to travel down one of the fallopian tubes to the uterus. The egg is susceptible to penetration by the sperm during only a fraction of this time. If during this time sexual intercourse occurs, conception is possible. If the egg is not fertilized, it disintegrates and passes out of the body.

At least 100 million sperm cells are released in a single ejaculation, and one in ten is capable of fertilizing an egg. Once the sperm cells are deposited in the vagina, they begin making their way upward, through the cervix into the uterus and fallopian tubes, in one of which they may encounter the egg. The moment a sperm penetrates an egg cell *fertilization* occurs, and processes instantly begin in the newly fertilized egg to prevent other sperms from penetrating. Within 12 hours after penetration, the 23 chromosomes from the father and the 23 chromosomes from the mother have formed a nucleus in the center of the ovum. The newly formed cell, the *zygote,* with its 46 chromosomes, now contains all of the genetic information necessary for the development of a human being.

Prenatal Development

Beginning very soon after conception, the zygote divides repeatedly by mitosis until it becomes a tightly packed ball of similar cells called a *blastocyst.* The blastocyst, which has been moving down the fallopian tube, enters the uterus on the third or fourth day following conception. Around the end of the first week after conception it embeds itself in the lining of the uterus, which, since the moment of conception, has been thickening and becoming engorged with new blood vessels in response to chemical products produced by the developing blastocyst. At this point, the first week of human development, the *germinal period,* has come to an end, and a six-week period called the *embryonic period* is about to begin.

Once the blastocyst is embedded in the uterine lining, its cells begin to differentiate, and then to form various tissues. Those on the outside gradually become the *placenta* and the *chorion membrane.* The placenta, a spongy mass of tissue, is connected to the uterine lining on one side and to the *embryo* on the other by means of the *umbilical cord.* Once it has developed, the placenta will take care of almost all of the needs of the fetus: it will deliver nutrients and oxygen from the mother's blood and remove wastes and carbon dioxide from the fetus's blood. These vital materials are exchanged between the blood supply of the mother and that of the fetus in the placenta: there is no mixing of maternal and infant blood.

The inner cells of the blastocyst become the umbilical cord, the amniotic membrane that forms the sac that contains the embryo, and the embryo itself. After the initial differentiations occur, the nervous and circulatory systems develop, followed by limb buds, the digestive tract, and rudimentary eyes and ears. The placenta and umbilical cord do not function fully until the development of the embryonic period is nearly complete. Until then the nourishment of the embryo is provided by the contact between small projections of the blastocyst and pools of maternal blood contained in the uterine lining.

During the second lunar month (28 days) the embryo grows in size. The nervous and circulatory systems continue to be refined and they begin to function. The skeleton and muscles develop enough to give some form to the embryo. Finally, the glandular systems of the body begin to function. When all the basic bodily structures are present the embryonic period ends—usually at about the end of the second lunar month after conception.

The *fetal period* of prenatal development lasts from the beginning of the third lunar month until birth. At the beginning of this period the fetus is about 4 centimeters (1½ inches) long (from the crown to the rump), and weighs about 3½ grams (⅛ ounce). The fetus will grow during the next seven months until it is about 50 centimeters (20 inches) long and weighs a little more than 3 kilograms (7 pounds).

During the third lunar month of pregnancy the fetus begins to move about in its watery environment, but its early movements are not usually felt by the mother because the fetus is so tiny. The facial features and the external genitalia continue to develop during this third month. By the fourth month, bones begin to harden, nails become evident, and the fetus's

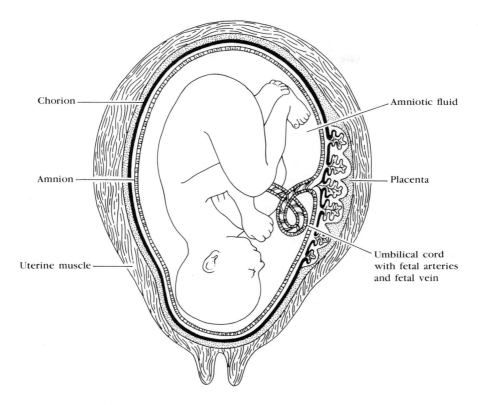

Chorion

Amniotic fluid

Amnion

Placenta

Uterine muscle

Umbilical cord
with fetal arteries
and fetal vein

Figure 1-1. *A mature fetus and placenta.*

movements are vigorous enough to be detected by the mother. If a stethoscope is placed on the mother's abdominal wall, the fetal heartbeat can be detected.

During the fifth and sixth lunar months, the fetus continues to grow rapidly. It becomes covered with a temporary coat of hair called *lanugo,* which is soft, fine, and silky, and with a protective waxy substance, *vernix.* Few fetuses are capable of surviving if they are born at this time: although they look well developed, they simply do not have enough tissue to regulate temperature and facilitate all of the other vital processes.

During the last three lunar months the development of the fetus consists mainly in growth of existing tissues. The fetus acquires the layers of fat, the muscle, bones, and other tissues that it will need to survive in the external world where temperature shifts, senses have to react, and it must breathe unassisted. At the end of these months, the infant is better equipped to survive the stresses of birth.

We do not know what starts the processes of labor and birth. One theory is that, as the placenta matures, it begins to produce hormones that signal the mother's body to eject the baby. Another possibility is that the mother's body comes to regard the baby's body as a foreign object—perhaps through some chemical transaction that takes 38 weeks to complete. Scientists have identified hormonal substances secreted by the fetus that might signal the mother's body to initiate labor. By whatever means, the mother's body begins an orderly process of ejecting the fetus about 266 days after conception.

The smooth muscles of the uterus occasionally contract in an irregular manner in all women, pregnant or not; but when these contractions become regular, recurrent, and strong in a pregnant woman, *labor* has begun. Each uterine contraction moves and straightens the body of the fetus. Its head is thus pushed down hard into the bony pelvic ring at the opening of the uterus into the vagina. The tissue surrounding this opening, the *cervix,* begins to stretch and widen the opening in response to the pressure of the descending fetus. This dilation process continues as labor proceeds.

The fetus's head is soft and pliable because the bones of the skull have not yet grown firmly together. Thus it can be molded by the uterine activity until it is elongated enough to pass through the cervical ring into the mother's vagina. The period between the onset of labor and the start of the movement of the fetus through the cervix is the *first stage* of labor. For women giving birth for the first time, the first stage typically lasts from 9 to 18 hours, although in later births its duration is usually shorter. During the *second stage* of labor the baby passes through the mother's vagina and into the world. During this stage, which lasts from 10 to 90 minutes, powerful contractions occur that can be assisted by the mother's voluntary efforts.

Immediately after the baby is born, the attending physician, midwife, or nurse ties off or clamps the umbilical cord, and from that moment the baby must then sustain its own life. The mother's uterus continues to contract and in a few minutes the placenta is expelled in the *third stage* of labor. An infant's general bodily functioning and condition are evaluated immediately after birth according to a system developed by Virginia Apgar (1953), which is described in Chapter 2.

Early Influences on a Baby

Although babies enter the world at birth, they are not untouched by the influences of that world during gestation. Throughout the sequence of conception, pregnancy, and birth, a baby is affected by genetic influences and by the environmental influences of the mother's body: the chemistry of her blood; such foreign substances as toxins, drugs, or infectious agents; and the

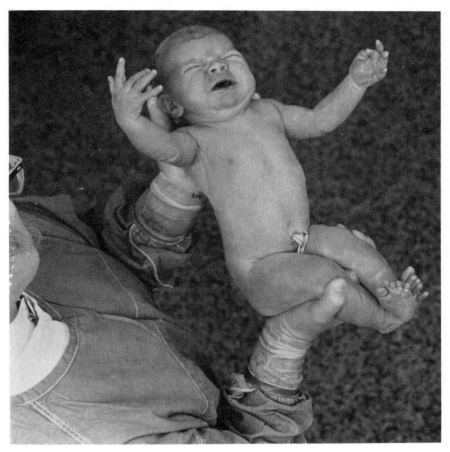

Figure 1-2. *A newborn baby, shortly after birth. (From LIFE Science Library/Growth. Published by Time-Life Books Inc.)*

size and position of her uterus and vagina. One of the most significant influences is the change in a baby's environment during labor and the baby's subsequent birth. However smoothly birth proceeds, the baby experiences an abrupt change from a dark, uncomplicated environment to one containing many bright, complex, and changing stimuli, many of which require a response.

In considering influences on development that arise before and during birth, keep in mind that they may be due to environment, heredity, or an interaction between the two.

Any anomaly in a gene or in an entire chromosome is usually called a *genetic defect.* Most of these defects are inherited because they existed in the reproductive cells of one or both parents. Other defects result from some alteration in the gene that happens during the time the parent's body produces the sperm or egg cell. Such alterations are *mutations,* and they can be thought of as *environmentally* produced events. Thus genetic defects can be either inherited or environmentally caused.

Prenatal environmental influences that act on the baby include the chemicals contained in the mother's reproductive tissues and in her blood and also the way in which her tissues and blood function. Anything that induces a change in the mother's physical state after the moment of conception but before the onset of labor can be considered a *prenatal environmental* influence. Some important prenatal environmental influences are maternal diet, chemicals such as drugs that the mother takes, infectious agents (and the resulting antibodies), and various emotional or physical stresses that the mother experiences that cause chemical changes in her body.

During the birth process, the baby is subjected to events that have a great impact on its later development. Almost all defects that are caused at birth can be attributed to the fetus's lack of oxygen at some crucial point. Length of labor affects the fetus's supply of oxygen because the placenta gradually loses its ability to supply oxygen as labor continues. An unusually long labor may be caused by some other complicating factor. For example, the position of the fetus in the uterus, the position of the placenta, and the size and shape of the mother's birth canal can each complicate the birth and interfere with the oxygen supply that the fetus receives through the placenta during birth. Use of excessive quantities of pain-relieving drugs by the mother during delivery may depress the newborn's reflexes—one of which is the reflex to begin breathing—and thus decrease its oxygen supply after birth as well.

Finally, defects may be caused when genetic and environmental influences interact. For example, a reproductive cell may mutate when it is exposed to some unusual biochemical factors because it has inherited the tendency to do so. The fetus may inherit the tendency to shift frequently in the uterus and may thereby adopt a position that will hinder its own birth. Although the exposure of a mother to psychological stress is an environmental event, how intensely and quickly she reacts to it (which may change the chemical composition of her blood) may be an inherited characteristic.

We know that some environmental influences such as virus infections do not affect the fetus much if they occur at one point in the prenatal period but that they have a powerful effect if they occur during another. The time when a fetus's development will be affected by presence of a factor is called the *critical period,* and fetuses probably inherit the program for when the critical periods occur. All fetuses are more susceptible to the effects of rubella in the first three months of pregnancy, for example, but whether the fetus is exposed to rubella depends on the mother's environment. *Thus heredity and environment constantly interact.*

Consequences of Harmful Influences

A substantial majority of pregnancies and births are entirely free of any harmful influences. But, rarely, abnormal influences do occur, and sometimes their effects are permanent. We should discuss the abnormalities for several reasons. First, by studying what happens when development somehow goes awry we can better understand how the various influences work. Prospective parents should understand genetic defects for another reason as well. Many abnormal genetic conditions can now be detected early in pregnancy by a procedure known as amniocentesis. In this procedure a small amount of amniotic fluid is withdrawn (through a needle inserted through a woman's abdominal wall and into her uterus) and is then analyzed. Through amniocentesis prospective parents can learn of genetic problems and can decide whether to continue a pregnancy or to terminate it. The decision to terminate a pregnancy through abortion is unacceptable to many people and the choice has to be made in relation to the values of the people it concerns directly. So although the invention of amniocentesis has given us information that can be beneficial, it has also created moral dilemmas that simply did not exist before. When does life begin? What is the role of "defective" persons in society? These issues are not going to be resolved in a psychology textbook, but we owe it to ourselves and to society to be aware of them.

Genetic Defects

One hundred birth defects are known to be caused when some gene fails to function normally. Let us consider several of the most common genetic defects: classical hemophilia, sickle-cell anemia, cystic fibrosis, diabetes mellitus, and Rh disease.

Classical hemophilia is a disease characterized by delayed clotting of the blood. The gene responsible for it is recessive and is on the X chromosome. Females can carry the gene but they rarely have the disease themselves because they have two X chromosomes. Both of a woman's chromosomes would have to carry the recessive gene for her to have the disease—she could inherit it only from a hemophiliac father and a carrier mother. It would be much more likely that the daughter of a hemophiliac father would receive from her mother a dominant gene that would counteract the recessive gene that she received from her father. However, females can transmit hemophilia to their sons, who have no corresponding gene on their Y chromosome to counter the effects of the gene that carries the disease.

Sickle-cell anemia is a disease characterized by an inability of the red blood cells to carry sufficient oxygen. It is caused by a recessive gene that is common among inhabitants of tropical countries and among people with ancestors in tropical countries—for example, blacks. Many of the red blood cells of those who have sickle-cell anemia assume a sickle shape in the presence of low concentrations of oxygen. The affected cells mass together, obstructing small blood vessels and eventually larger ones. Tissues depending upon the obstructed vessels for oxygen die because they do not receive enough oxygen. If a child receives a recessive gene for this disease from each parent, he or she will develop sickle-cell anemia and will require treatment with frequent blood transfusions in order to survive.

Cystic fibrosis, another disease carried by a recessive gene, is a metabolic error that affects the exocrine glands, which produce saliva, sweat, and mucus. The lungs of an affected person produce a sticky mucus that clogs the air passageways. Mucus also blocks the pancreas and thereby drastically interferes with the digestion of food. The symptoms can be partly controlled by managing the diet, by administering a pancreatic enzyme, and by preventing respiratory infections through the use of antibiotics. Because of these treatments, more and more children are surviving the disease into adulthood.

Diabetes mellitus is an apparently genetic defect in the way the body processes sugar. Either the pancreas does not produce enough insulin, or it produces the wrong kind, so that sugars and starches are not converted into the form of glucose that the body can readily use for energy. Severe forms of diabetes mellitus can be controlled by diet and by administration of insulin. But diabetes varies in severity, and some instances of it are not apparent until middle adulthood. Because of this and because of studies that indicate a relation between national diet and incidence of diabetes mellitus, there is controversy about whether the disease is entirely hereditary. It may turn out to be the result of an interaction between heredity and environment.

Rh disease, another genetically transmitted defect, is caused by a blood characteristic called the Rh factor, after the Rhesus monkeys in whom it was first identified. People who have the characteristic are called Rh positives; those who do not are called Rh negatives. If the mother is an Rh negative and the father an Rh positive, their second child and those following will probably have the disease. This is because a few of the first child's Rh positive blood cells cross the placental barrier into the mother's bloodstream during gestation. More such cells enter her bloodstream during childbirth as the placenta (which has the baby's blood characteristics) disintegrates. The mother's Rh-negative blood reacts by manufacturing antibodies to destroy the foreign cells. These antibodies will not affect this first baby. But they will remain in her system to destroy Rh-positive blood and thus will affect any subsequent children. If she conceives another child, its blood cells may be attacked by the antibodies circulating in her blood. The destruction of the fetus's blood cells can be moderate, causing only a slight anemia at birth, or severe, causing death.

Babies born with Rh disease can be saved by an exchange transfusion in which all of their blood is removed and replaced by new blood right at birth. The invention of this transfusion procedure has meant that an Rh-negative woman and an Rh-positive man can safely plan for more than one child if they choose.

Chromosomal Errors

Some inherited conditions are due to chromosomal abnormalities that arise in meiotic cell division rather than to genetic defects.

Down's syndrome (also called "mongolism") is the result of an extra chromosome. Affected persons grow slowly, have several characteristic facial features, and, almost without exception, are severely mentally retarded. Children who have Down's syndrome differ widely in their ability to respond to special educational efforts and to medical treatment. Some are able to master the most elementary skills and to live to adulthood. Others can learn little and die before reaching adulthood.

As you will recall, normal women have two X chromosomes, and normal men have one X chromosome and one Y chromosome. Males who have an extra X chromosome, giving them an XXY pattern of sex chromosomes, have *Klinefelter's syndrome.* They fail to develop sexually and the likelihood of their being mentally retarded is much higher than in the general population. Because most males with Klinefelter's syndrome are sterile, they do not pass the syndrome on. There is no cure for Klinefelter's syndrome, but sometimes its effects can be lessened by treatment with hormones.

Persons with *Turner's syndrome* have only one sex chromosome, an X chromosome. They have many recognizable female sex characteristics, but they generally lack ovaries and have underdeveloped uteruses. Other symptoms include a webbed neck, shortness, and certain distinctive facial features. The cause of this syndrome is somewhat unclear because some people who have either an XX or XY chromosome pattern also have these characteristics.

Males who have an *XYY chromosome pattern* do not exhibit dramatic physical symptoms. It has been found that the frequency of this pattern is higher among male prisoners than among the male population in general. In the prison populations studied, from 3 to 4 percent of the prisoners have an extra Y chromosome. This finding has led some people to argue that the extra Y chromosome is somehow related to being violence prone. However, the evidence for a direct cause and effect is slight, and the matter is highly charged with controversy.

The Effects of Maternal Diet

Because a developing fetus receives all of its nutrients from its mother's blood, the mother must have a good diet if the fetus is to develop normally. Pregnant women whose diets don't supply enough calories and essential nutrients tend to experience more difficulties than women whose diets provided sufficient nutrition: more of them have premature deliveries, more have infants with low birth weights, more have complications such as anemia and toxemia, and more experience prolonged labors (Drillien, 1964). Sufficient protein is particularly important for the growth and development of an infant's nervous system. One study conducted in the United States compared 57 infants whose mothers had not eaten enough protein with 57 other infants who were similar in most respects except that their mothers *had* eaten enough protein while they were pregnant. The children were tested on the Bayley scales (a standard test of infants' psychological development) at eight months, given a neurological examination by a physician at 1 year, and scored on the Stanford-Binet IQ test at four years of age. It was found that those who had not received sufficient protein before birth experienced more developmental difficulties (Rosenbaum et al., 1969).

Research with animal subjects shows even more decisively that protein deficiency causes damage to the central nervous system. One important study examined three generations of rats and demonstrated that if the grandmother does not have enough protein during her pregnancy her grandchildren can be affected, even if their mother has adequate protein in her diet (Zamenhof, Van Marthens, and Gravel, 1971). Clearly protein is essential for growth before birth as well as after it.

The Effects of Drugs and Other Chemicals

Most Americans accept taking drugs as a matter of course, and many women use alcohol, cigarettes, tranquilizers, and sleeping pills throughout their pregnancies without thinking that they may affect their unborn children. Yet the use of these has been associated with the incidence of birth defects; consequently, many doctors caution their pregnant patients not to take any unnecessary medication. The relation of drugs to birth defects is particularly difficult to verify because mothers of babies who have birth defects may not remember what chemicals they used and when they used them during pregnancy. Furthermore, certain defects can be caused by any one of several events during pregnancy, so it is hard to say precisely which is responsible for the defect.

Sometimes an "outbreak" of deformed babies occurs. In 1961, for example, when pregnant women who had been using a popular mild tranquilizer called Thalidomide gave birth to infants with missing or malformed limbs, the connection was relatively easy to demonstrate. But although it is suspected that a connection exists between birth defects and many other psychoactive drugs—including some sleeping pills, antidepressants, and tranquilizers—the connection has not been clearly demonstrated. Possibly, tranquilizers interact with other factors and do not affect all developing embryos adversely.

Research has definitely shown that fetuses are adversely affected if their mothers drink or smoke heavily: infants born to alcoholic mothers are more prone to have various problems adapting to sights, sounds, temperature changes, and other demands of the environment than are those born to mothers who drink moderately or not at all during pregnancy. Women who smoke heavily during pregnancy have infants who weigh less than normal for some months and who therefore are more susceptible to a variety of health problems. Many offspring of heroin addicts are born addicted to heroin, and they may suffer from withdrawal, which can be fatal (Apgar and Beck, 1974). Unfortunately, the major effects of drugs and other chemicals that cause birth defects occur during the embryonic period—the earliest stage of pregnancy—when many women may not even be aware that they are pregnant. Thus, in order to prevent birth defects in their children, women who have reason to believe they might be pregnant should avoid using any drug without inquiring into its possible effects on the fetus.

Research concerning hormones administered to pregnant animals demonstrates clearly the powerful impact on the fetus of chemical changes in the mother's body during pregnancy. In general, research with rats has shown repeatedly that, if rats are injected with hormones during pregnancy, their offspring respond differently to hormone stimulation later in life than do the offspring of rats that received no injections. Indeed, male rats that for any reason do not have a normal supply of male hormones during birth fail to develop the normal behavioral responses to male hormones injected later in life (Beach, Noble, and Orndoff, 1969). Too, if rats receive hormone injections right at birth their behavior is altered by it. Thus, since the timing of and reason for hormone fluctuations in a developing animal both have an influence, the cause of behavioral fluctuations must be complex (Kornetsky, 1970). These experiments clearly support a cause-and-effect relation between chemical changes in the mother's body during pregnancy and the behavior of her offspring. Although it has not been proven, many people believe that many of the chemicals that are commonly taken by pregnant women affect their children's behavior.

Researchers have carefully examined the effects on babies of drugs that are administered during labor and delivery. The most recent review of these studies indicates that commonly used obstetrical medications affect a wide variety of behaviors and functions of the newborn child. Many of the off-spring of mothers who received medication during labor exhibit one or more of the following symptoms: (1) they do not begin to suck as quickly and consequently are slow to start nursing, (2) they give fewer of the automatic smiles that are part of normal newborn behavior, (3) they exhibit a slow habituation rate, which means that they are slower to remember repeated stimuli, (4) the pattern of electrical waves (EEG) from their brains is different from that of other babies, (5) they do not pay as much attention to their surroundings and they react less to all stimuli, (6) they have poorer muscle tone, and (7) they are in greater danger of experiencing *anoxia,* or lack of oxygen, which can result in permanent damage to the brain that is manifested in motor defects. These effects may not become apparent until up to three days after birth. The effects become more pronounced the larger the dose of the drug and the closer to the time of actual delivery it is administered (Alexandrowiz, 1974). Clearly the mother and her doctor must carefully consider whether she will use medication during delivery and, if so, its kind and amount. Even short-acting, seemingly harmless, drugs may affect an infant's behavior at birth. Through interaction with their caregivers babies may continue these altered patterns of behavior.

Women who are aware of the dangers of obstetrical drugs and who wish to participate more fully in the birth of their children are turning to various techniques for reducing the pain and tension of childbirth. Most com-munities have classes for expectant mothers and fathers to teach them to control pain in childbirth through exercise, hypnotism, or psychological training.

Infections

As you know, certain exchanges take place between the fetus and the mother during pregnancy: the fetus receives nutrients from the mother, who in turn disposes of its waste materials. (As you will recall, this is accomplished by diffusion. There is no mixing of maternal and fetal blood.) It is not surprising, therefore, that some infections pass from the mother's to the fetus's blood. How seriously this affects the fetus depends upon when it happens and upon what virus, bacterium, or other agent is responsible for it. The best-known viral infection that can affect a fetus is *rubella,* or Ger-

Figure 1-3.   *In recent years more women are turning to means other than drugs to help them through the process of birth. Here a pregnant woman does stretching exercises to prepare her body for childbirth. (Photo copyright © Suzanne Arms.)*

man measles. About 12 percent of the fetuses who are exposed to the rubella virus in the first three to four prenatal months will develop one or more of several defects: blindness, deafness, heart malformation, and mental retardation (Mussen, Conger, and Kagan, 1974). Rubella itself is a mild disease, and the mother may not even realize that she has it or that she has been exposed to someone who does. Obstetricians are especially careful to warn expectant mothers to avoid contact with anyone who has rubella or has been exposed to it. But all women should be immunized against rubella before they become pregnant; in some communities, this immunization is a requirement for a marriage certificate. A final danger of rubella is that a baby who has contracted the disease shortly before birth from its mother may be born with it and may spread the infection to nurses and others who may expose even more pregnant women.

Syphilis is another infectious disease that can cause profound damage to a fetus. This disease, caused by a small organism known as a *spirochete,* is transmitted through sexual contact. The genital sores typical of the disease may disappear in a few weeks, but unless the syphilis is treated the spirochetes will continue to multiply in the body and to cause extensive damage. If a woman who has the disease is pregnant, her unborn child may be affected. The spirochetes can multiply rapidly within the fetus and invade all of its organs, so that it may be born with an enlarged liver, impaired hearing, or abnormal skin. The disease may be latent for years but may eventually cause a child to have brain damage, bone and joint problems, and loss of vision and hearing. The long-term effects of the disease can be averted by treating an infected child with antibiotics. Apparently fetuses under four months of age are not susceptible to congenital syphilis, so it may be prevented if the mother is treated with antibiotics during those months. But the disease can only be treated if women know that they have been exposed to it. This is one reason why in the United States, state health departments attempt to record all incidences of syphilis and to inform the sexual partners of those known to have the disease.

It is thought that many other infectious diseases cause birth defects and congenital illnesses. And yet many such diseases seemingly do not affect the embryo because the number of problem births is small compared with the number of viral infections that pregnant women have in the course of their daily lives. Some scientists think that other factors—perhaps hereditary ones—determine whether a given viral infection will be transmitted from a mother's blood to that of the fetus. A great deal of research remains to be done before we will be able to understand how microorganisms affect an unborn child.

Emotional Stress During Pregnancy

Professional opinions have varied over the years on the question of whether a mother's emotional state during her pregnancy can affect the well-being of her baby. Because the nervous systems of mothers and their fetuses are entirely separate, the reactions that take place in a mother's nervous system are not directly transmitted to her child. However, the mother's nervous state could influence the baby by means of several mechanisms. First, when a person is upset or under stress, the glands of the body increase their output of certain hormones, such as adrenalin. During times of stress the amount of those hormones in the mother's blood increases. Through the diffusion process that transfers oxygen and nutrients from the mother's blood to that of the fetus, the hormones can also be transferred. Then, as they circulate in the bloodstream of the unborn child, they can stimulate the same physical changes that they cause in the mother—changes in heart rate, respiration, and blood pressure.

Second, the fetus may be able to detect changes in the rate of its mother's heartbeat. Evidence indicates that infants can do so (Sontag, Steele, and Lewis, 1969). Third, prenatal and birth-related events can interact. The mother who is emotionally distraught may have a more difficult labor and delivery than a calm mother. She may have a longer labor, for example, or one characterized by irregular contractions. These differences in the birth process may lead to irregularities in the baby's oxygen supply or can constitute a kind of stress that will consequently affect how the baby behaves after birth. For instance, babies born after prolonged labor may be slower to adjust to the stimulation around them. They may also be irritable.

Experimenters have studied rats to measure the relation between mothers' anxiety during pregnancy and the emotionality of their offspring. In these studies investigators made pregnant rats anxious by exposing them to stimuli that they had been taught to associate with stressful electric shocks. The researchers then measured the emotionality of the pups by observing how frequently they moved about and defecated. They found that a mother's anxiety in pregnancy definitely led to higher emotionality in her pups (Thompson, 1957). Some evidence indicates that hormonal changes in the mother's body cause this effect (Lieberman, 1965). Experiments with rats have also shown that if a mother rat is anxious during her pregnancy, the nonmaternal female rat who cares for the pup after birth (as part of the experimental design) is also affected (Dennenberg and Whimbley, 1965). Thus anxiety has both physiological and psychological effects.

But what about human infants? An important study published in 1964 demonstrates a clear connection between a mother's anxiety during pregnancy and the condition of her newborn child. In this study the mothers answered a standard questionnaire on anxiety every three months during their pregnancy. Then, when their babies were born, their weights, their activity during their first days, and the time they spent crying were measured. The offspring of very anxious mothers cried more before feeding and were more active than those of less anxious mothers (Ottinger and Simmons, 1964). A similar finding was reported in one other study (Davids, Holden, and Gray, 1963). But many more studies must be done, with more subjects and better controls, before we will understand fully the effects of maternal anxiety on infants.

Anoxia During Birth

Many events that can occur during the birth process can cause a baby to be deprived of oxygen. As you may recall from our earlier discussion, this lack of sufficient oxygen is called anoxia. Anoxia can occur if a baby is born feet first (rather than head first, as most babies are). This sort of delivery is called a *breech delivery* and it may cause labor to be prolonged and difficult. During labor the placenta gradually loses its ability to supply oxygen, so if labor is lengthy the fetus may have insufficient oxygen during part of the birth process. Also in a breech delivery the placenta or the umbilical cord may become wedged between the uterine wall and the baby's body in such a manner as to place abnormally heavy pressure upon them. If this occurs, the placenta may not function properly.

Anoxia can also result immediately after birth when the umbilical cord is cut, and the baby is no longer connected to the mother. Once the baby is detached from the placenta a complex of physiological and chemical events stimulates it to breathe on its own. Anything that interferes with the capacity of the respiratory center in the brain to respond to these signals—drugs given during delivery, deprivation of oxygen during birth, or brain hemorrhage caused by any shock to the baby's head during birth—can lead to anoxia.

There are now obstetrical procedures that can prevent all of these events from occurring, or can at least lessen their tendency to produce anoxia. Fetal heartbeat, circulation, brain activity, and sometimes even makeup of blood can now be monitored. If the fetus is having difficulties doctors can speed delivery by inducing labor or by performing a Caesarean section. Such procedures carry their own risks, of course, and choice of the best course requires careful clinical judgment. But even though anoxia is a serious threat to an infant's well-being and survival, it usually can be prevented.

What happens if anoxia does occur? Any lack of oxygen damages the brain: if the deprivation is extreme, the damage will be severe. Anoxia is likely to cause damage to the brain stem, which results in motor defects. Some of these defects are: cerebral palsy (a condition of insufficient muscle control); minimal brain dysfunction, or *MBD,* which is characterized by abnormally high levels of activity and difficulty with concentration; epilepsy, a disease of convulsive seizures; and mental retardation.

As you probably know, all of these conditions can result from brain damage, which has many causes other than anoxia: for example, it can be the result of genetic defects or shocks to the baby's head before birth. And, of course, brain damage after birth can also cause these conditions.

Many of the complications of childbirth that cause anoxia and the defects that result from it are more common to the lower economic class than they are to the middle class. This is simply because poor diet and daily stress during pregnancy—conditions that increase the chances of prolonged labor and diseases—are more common problems of lower-class mothers. Also, unhappily, few lower-class mothers can afford the high-quality medical care and advanced techniques that can lessen the effects of anoxia (MacMahon and Feldman, 1972).

Prematurity

Newborns are considered *premature* if they are born less than 37 weeks after conception. However, because the date of conception cannot always be determined precisely another measure of prematurity is needed. So doctors commonly use a baby's birth weight as a rough indicator of *gestational age,* the length of time between conception and birth. Infants weighing less than 5½ pounds at birth are considered premature, and those weighing less than 4 pounds are considered to be severely premature and therefore especially vulnerable to some of the difficulties that we will discuss in this section. Babies born between the 28th week and the normal delivery time of the 38th week have a strong chance of surviving if they weigh at least 2½ pounds and if they are given oxygen, are isolated, and are put in a temperature-controlled place.

Physical Condition of the Premature Infant

Premature infants come into the world with serious physical problems. Because they are underweight, they cannot control their body temperature as well as full-term babies and they lack reserve energy supplies. Most premature infants have unstable respiratory and circulatory patterns that must be continually monitored to insure that they continue to function. The brains and nervous systems of premature infants are not fully developed, so the infants are physically irritable and their reflexes are weak or absent. Because of their shorter gestation, premature infants have received fewer antibodies from their mothers by the time they are born; thus, they are very susceptible to infections. They also have difficulties digesting formula feedings. Thus premature infants present a challenging task to their parents and the hospital staff who care for them: that of insuring their survival by giving them the care they need while working to minimize the harmful effects of that care.

Behavior of Premature Infants

Premature infants behave differently from full-term infants in several ways. First, they suck less strongly and less efficiently than full-term infants and therefore do not receive as much nourishment; this, of course, hinders their growth (Barrett and Miller, 1973; Dobignon and Campbell, 1969). In addition, when premature infants are born, their reflexes are poor because of the effects of prolonged labor and use of drugs, which accompany most premature births. These difficulties sometimes make it necessary to feed them intravenously. Also, because sucking is one of the first behaviors that babies learn to modify, and because they learn about many objects in this

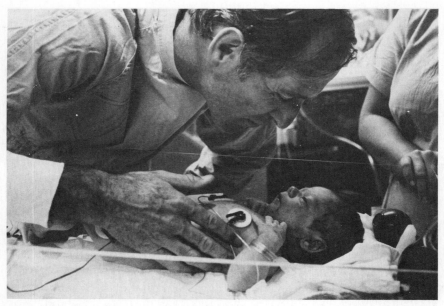

Figure 1-4. *Touch is one of the most important experiences for premature as well as full-term infants. Here a father touches and talks to his half-hour-old son in a high-risk nursery. (Photo copyright © Suzanne Arms.)*

way, the sucking problems of premature babies may cause them to get a poor start in learning.

Premature infants do not habituate to repeated stimuli as reliably as do full-term infants, something we can tell from their failure to stop reacting strongly to repeated "stimuli" (Barrett and Miller, 1973; Eisenberg, Coursin, and Rupp, 1966). When they are awake premature infants are startled by low sounds that full-term infants treat with interest (Bench and Parker, 1971; Schulman, 1969).

Studies have shown that babies do most of their learning when they are awake and quiet, but research on premature infants indicates that their sleeping and waking cycles may be indistinguishable. Two studies have reported stable, predictable differences between sleeping and waking states of premature infants (Goldie et al., 1971; Frank and Chase, 1968), but two others report no clear distinction between the two states (Dreyfus-Brisac, 1974; Sterman and Hoppenbrouwers, 1968). Another extensive study of newborns reports that premature infants show nervous system discharge in grimaces or smiles more frequently than full-term infants (Emde,

McCartney, and Haron, 1971). Apparently the immature nervous system of prematurely born infants makes them especially vulnerable to internal stimulation and less likely than other newborns to be capable of the learning that babies do when they are fully awake but quiet. It would seem that premature infants can only take in events within their bodies. But the evidence for any statement about learning in premature infants is not strong.

Effects of Prematurity on Later Behavior

Illnesses, physical handicaps, and psychological problems occur more often among premature infants than among full-term infants. You may ask why these effects accompany prematurity. The same genetic or congenital defect that caused the baby to be born prematurely can cause permanent damage.

The causes of prematurity are varied; some are unknown. For example, prematurity is common in babies who have congenital rubella or another viral illness. (You will recall from our earlier discussion that rubella can also cause birth defects.) Some abnormal condition within the mother's system can cause the placenta to stop functioning before normal gestation is over. Also, a prematurely born child is especially vulnerable to the birth complications that result in anoxia, and thus is susceptible to its effects. Prematurity is also more common in poor mothers with inadequate diets and poor prenatal care (Wortis et al., 1963).

Sometimes the care premature infants receive hinders them as much as it helps them. Most premature infants are cared for in specially equipped nurseries according to a nursing regimen that greatly increases their chances for survival by protecting them from life-threatening infections. However, this regimen isolates the infants not only from infectious agents but also from much of the environmental stimulation that other newborns receive. Premature infants experience less temperature variation, tactile stimulation, variation in light and sound, and human handling than full-term infants do. The unusual environment may be responsible for some of the instances of developmental retardation that occur among premature infants.

Besides being handled less than full-term newborns, premature infants have much less contact with their mothers in the first days of life. Premature infants and their mothers are separated immediately after birth, and, although mothers are later allowed to see their babies, generally they cannot touch or hold them.

There is evidence that the care that is given to premature infants may cause them to develop psychological problems. Studies of people who were born prematurely indicate that they have a greater tendency than people born at term to become emotionally disturbed; perhaps early isolation is a cause (Rothschild, 1967). Some of these consequences of care for premature infants can be prevented. One study found that when prematurely born infants heard tape recordings of their mothers' voices in their early days they adapted much better than prematurely born infants who did not hear recordings (Katz, 1971).

Many parents fear that if premature babies are treated differently from normal babies, their later behavior may be affected by it. Anxious parents fear that because they are so impressed with the fragility and vulnerability of their new charges they may treat them too carefully, hesitating to pick them up as often as they otherwise would. Because they believe that sleep is important for a premature baby, they may be quieter than usual. They may turn away solicitous friends and relatives who come to call out of fear that the baby will become infected with some disease. They may continue to regard a premature child as especially weak even after any signs or symptoms of weakness have disappeared. Of course, this excessive care would deprive a baby of needed stimulation, but, so far, there is only scanty evidence that premature babies are "pampered" any more than normal babies are. One study indicates that there is no difference between how mothers of premature babies and those of full-term babies behave toward their babies (Smith et al., 1969).

Long-Term Follow-Up Studies of Prematurely Born Persons

Several investigators have conducted long-term studies of prematurely born babies to evaluate their physical and psychological health. Their results make clear the lasting effects of prematurity. In one famous study Drillien observed 72 Scottish infants born between 1948 and 1960 (Drillien, 1964). He found that by their fifth birthdays the prematurely born children differed from the full-term children (controls) in several ways: they were physically smaller than the controls and their average IQ score was clearly below that of the controls. Indeed, only one in 11 of them had an IQ over 100 whereas half of normal children would be expected to have IQs over 100. Seventy percent of the children who had been born prematurely had a learning problem. Drillien noted that more premature children had congenital defects and that more of their mothers had had complications in previous pregnancies as well. These factors may relate to why they were born prematurely in the first place.

A number of studies have shown that prematurely born children have cognitive skills that are inferior to those of children who were carried full-term (Lubchenco et al., 1963; Engleson, Rooth, and Thornblom, 1963; Cutler et al., 1965; Braine et al., 1967; Wiener, 1968). The perceptual abilities and motor coordination of premature children are also impaired

(Wiener, 1968; Cutler et al., 1965). These problems appear to persist until premature children are at least 10 years old (Lubchenco et al.,1963). Several investigators note that females seem to be less vulnerable than males to the effects of prematurity (Braine et al., 1966). But the evidence indicates that prematurity is accompanied by some degree of retarded development that persists over a period of time.

Prematurity and Socioeconomic Class

Most of the factors that lead to premature childbirth are more common among lower-class families than among middle-class families. As we discussed earlier, a poor mother is less likely to have an adequate diet during pregnancy. She is also less likely to receive regular medical care, and if her infant's birth begins early she is less likely to be able to obtain the high quality of emergency care that is required to prevent or minimize the impact of premature birth on her child's development. The result is that the frequency of both premature births and of their drastic long-range consequences is higher in the lower economic classes than it is in the middle class (Wortis et al., 1963).

Remedying the Effects of Prematurity

Some infants escape the most harmful effects of prematurity, whereas others do not. Too little is known about why this happens, but several investigations have yielded promising information about methods for minimizing the damaging effects of prematurity. One team of investigators demonstrated that five prematurely born newborns who were frequently stroked by their nurses in the hospital were healthier, more active, and more advanced in motor skills than were five prematurely born infants who were treated identically except that they were not stroked (Solkoff et al., 1969). Another investigator designed a vigorous program of in-hospital stimulation of prematurely born infants followed by a program of home visits for one year to encourage mothers to stimulate their infants. Infants who participated in this program developed more rapidly (as measured by the Cattell Infant Intelligence Scales and the Brazelton Scales; see the Appendix) than premature infants who did not (Scarr-Salapatek, 1973). A recent program in which infants were massaged vigorously has also reported very good results (Rice, 1976).

Granted, these are rather small projects, but their results are very encouraging. They suggest that, with regular patterned stimulation in the first year, the worst effects of prematurity can be overcome. Widespread education on prematurity for parents and for those who plan to become parents is the key to reducing the psychological damage associated with premature birth.

The differences among social classes in the seriousness of the results of premature birth may reflect in part the fact that middle-class families have a greater opportunity relative to lower-class families to give their infants personalized, patterned, and regular stimulation. Lower-class families have more children and smaller space in which to live, and are more often headed by busy single mothers, factors that are not conducive to personalized care for infants. Although relative poverty and its effects cannot be altered by any simple program of parent education, knowledge about the importance of stimulation for premature infants could help all parents to remedy some of the harmful effects of prematurity upon their infants.

A Note on the "At Risk" Concept

The medical community has in recent years made greater efforts to identify as early as possible children who have or will have psychological or learning handicaps. Clinicians are doing this in response to the accumulating evidence that, the earlier they intervene to help a child, the better the chances of lessening these problems. The generic terms "at risk" and "perinatal stress" have been coined to refer to all babies whose histories contain any factors known to be related to psychological or educational handicaps. The term "at risk" implies that there is some greater than average chance that the infant so designated may later have cerebral palsy, mental retardation, psychosis, learning disabilities, or any of a host of other handicaps. But the term does not indicate that the infants so labeled will inevitably develop a handicap. It simply implies that a child's history—the parents' genetic make-up, the mother's pregnancy, and the birth process—contains one or more factors that have appeared in the histories of children who have these handicaps more often than in the histories of normal children.

The primary advantage of labeling a baby "at risk" is that it alerts the baby's doctor and parents to watch for signs of any problem. Also, there are now programs for babies "at risk" that attempt to prevent the problems from developing. A large-scale study of all the children born on the Hawaiian island of Kauai in the year 1955 was recently completed (Werner and Smith, 1977). Children who were classified as having "perinatal stress" did indeed turn out to have more than their fair share of psychological problems and early intervention was indeed helpful to many of them. So these labels serve to designate those infants who might benefit from special programs. Another use for the labels is that researchers can use them to choose appropriately when they wish to study only "normal" or average babies or only "at risk" babies.

Using a term like "at risk" carries with it all of the problems associated with any diagnostic labeling. Labeling infants "at risk" can unjustly lead their caregivers, doctors, and later their teachers to expect certain behavior from them. Infants "at risk" are expected to develop slowly, to perform poorly, and to learn with difficulty. Like premature babies, "at risk" babies may not be given the challenge of stimulating problems; when they make mistakes that all normal children make, their behavior may be misinterpreted as backward or sick. Adults must be aware of the labeling problem and must take steps to prevent themselves from being too influenced by the label.

Summary

The beginnings of life have a profound influence upon the rest of human development.

Many of our characteristics are determined by the unique set of genes that we receive from our parents at the time of fertilization. The genes are contained in our 46 chromosomes, 23 of which we receive from each parent. The mixing of genetic material that is brought about by sexual reproduction accounts for the great variety of human characteristics, even among offspring of the same parents.

During the 38 weeks from conception to birth, a human being develops from a single fertilized egg cell, a *zygote,* into a baby that is capable of surviving the influences of the outside world. Throughout this period of development, or *gestation,* the developing fetus is nourished by its mother through the placenta and the umbilical cord, two temporary organs that are shed at the time of birth.

There are three distinct stages of birth: first, the baby moves through the cervix; second, it passes through the vagina and into the world; third, the placenta and umbilical cord are expelled.

Throughout gestation the development of a fetus is affected by genetic influences and by such environmental influences as the mother's diet, the chemistry of her blood, and any infection she may contract. Fetuses are also affected by the amount of oxygen they receive during birth.

Most pregnancies are entirely free of serious harmful influences. But such influences can occasionally produce permanent damage. A number of conditions, such as classical hemophilia, sickle-cell anemia, cystic fibrosis, diabetes mellitus, and Rh disease, are attributable to genetic defects. Others, such as Down's syndrome, Klinefelter's syndrome, Turner's syndrome, and the XYY chromosome patterns, are due to chromosomal abnormalities. Poor maternal diet can also exert a negative influence upon a fetus's development, as can drugs and a mother's anxiety.

Prematurity is a condition that can have serious negative consequences. Premature babies are underweight, have immature reflexes, and have fewer antibodies than full-term babies, so they may learn less in their early days than full-term infants. Certain studies show that prematurity is often associated with reduced cognitive abilities and impaired motor coordination. But it appears that regular patterned stimulation may foster normal development of premature babies.

The medical community has recently attempted to identify "at risk" infants, or infants who may have psychological or educational problems when they are older. Although caregivers, doctors, and teachers should avoid expecting certain behavior from children who have been determined to be "at risk," the term does alert them to possible difficulties that sometimes can be averted through special programs.

Chapter 2

The Newborn Human Infant

The average person's image of the newborn infant is not especially flattering. Most of us think of babies as being fragile, helpless, and completely lacking anything that resembles intelligence. I remember my experience with my only child. My daughter and I spent eight days in the hospital after she was born and I inspected her in the nursery at every opportunity. Much to my surprise, she looked just like all the other babies—wrinkled, wet, and downright ugly. But she seemed so fragile and helpless that I felt a deep responsibility to help and protect her.

This "automatic response" of many parents to a fragile infant perhaps serves to foster an extremely important caregiving bond. But this sense of the infant's need for our care may also limit that bond by exaggerating the difference between the baby and ourselves. How terrible to be so helpless! How glad we are to have left this experience of infancy long behind us! Many of us suspect that we ourselves could never have been *that* fragile and incompetent. Many of us take on the responsibility for our newborns with a feeling of relief that at least we are not in their predicament. Such spontaneous feelings are quite natural, but they can inhibit the growth of empathy between caregiver and baby.

In this chapter, we explore what is known about the basic psychological processes of newborns. As a first step in our exploration let us briefly review the history of developmental theories about babies. Interestingly, the attitudes of many theorists reflected the belief that a newborn child was something less than human. In an introductory psychology text, William James (1890) said that babies perceive the world as a "blooming, buzzing confusion." Early psychoanalytic theory considered the behavior of newborns to be entirely dominated by biological drives. It was believed that the infant's personality consisted simply of an adaptive ego, that counseled sensible behavior and emerged only through experience. Behaviorism in the mid-1900s considered newborns as passive creatures who developed stable behavior patterns that were molded by certain events that occurred in their lives. Indeed, a glance at the literature on developmental psychology in the United States in the 1930s, '40s, and '50s reveals that very few investigators studied the behavior of newborns. According to the prevailing professional view during those years, newborns were biological phenomena that adapted to their environment by purely physical mechanisms.

However, some theorists—especially Jean Piaget, the famous Swiss psychologist—regarded babies as something more. Work influenced by his ideas was going on during the '30s, '40s, and '50s as well (see Flavell, 1963). Finally, around 1960, American psychologists began to seriously consider Piaget's view that infants are active human beings who initiate and organize the events that take place around them. Researchers began to investigate the means by which babies exercise their initiative. Accordingly, a large and growing literature on the behavior of newborns has emerged in the last 15 years.

In these recent studies, psychologists have been concerned with a question that is of great interest: Are essential psychological functions of older children and adults also present in newborns, and, if they are, do the functions of newborns differ from those of older people? The question gives rise to many others, some of which we consider in this chapter. How are babies equipped at birth to adapt to their new environment? Are newborns conscious beings, and, if they are, what states of awareness do they experience? How do newborns interpret the events that go on around them? Are they capable of remembering and learning? Are they capable of sharing communication with those who care for them? The answers to these questions will apply to the concerns caregivers have about caring for babies' needs and fostering their proper development.

Finally, some of us are drawn to the study of these very youngest people in the elusive hope that they, being newly arrived and as yet little affected by their cultures, can show us human nature in its nascent and most essential form.

One recurrent philosophical controversy about the nature of human beings seems especially appropriate to consider here: Are people basically the product of their inborn nature, or are they the product of experience?

Innate Adaptive Behavior

Birth poses an enormous challenge to infants, for it is the severing of their physical bonds with their mothers. For the entire gestation period, she has been not only a source of nourishment but also a buffer against the outside world. Beginning at birth an infant must learn to take care of its own needs and to meet the demands of the environment: it must *adapt*. And as you will

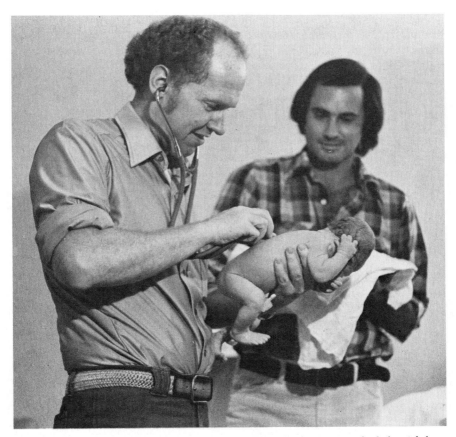

Figure2-1.   *An obstetrician conducts a routine physical examination of a baby girl, born 30 minutes earlier, as her father watches nearby. (Photo copyright © Suzanne Arms/ Jeroboam, Inc.)*

see, humans are prepared at birth to do just this—to learn from their experiences.

Biological Adaptation

At birth infants are ready to begin the essential life functions of respiration, digestion (of simple foods), circulation, and elimination. Because they have received antibodies from the mother's blood during gestation, they begin life immune to many common infections and their immunity may last several months.

In hospitals throughout the civilized world babies are tested immediately after birth to determine how well they can survive in their new environment. Their physical condition is assessed according to a procedure developed in the 1950s by Virginia Apgar (1953). The procedure consists of ratings in five categories: skin color (apparent circulation), heart rate, reflexes (gauged by a baby's response to a tap on the sole of the foot), activity, and respiratory effort. Babies are rated on the basis of careful but nontechnical observations that can be made by a delivery-room nurse or an anesthesiologist. Infants are scored 0 to 2 (the larger numbers indicating superior condition) in each category, and the sum of the five scores is the Apgar score. It is measured immediately after birth and again five minutes later. The majority of newborns have Apgar scores in the 7-to-10 range at 60 seconds after birth, and those who score 8 or above are considered to be in satisfactory health. Most newborns who have scores below 4 are not breathing and they may show no pulse: this means that vigorous efforts will be required to keep them alive.

The Apgar test is very useful for several reasons. First, it accurately predicts a baby's chances for survival in early infancy and, second, a low score may warn of severe damage to the nervous system (Apgar, 1953, pp. 63–64). (Also, because of the relation between the proper functioning of the nervous system and the development of basic mental processes such as learning and perception, psychological researchers often exclude infants who had low Apgar scores from their experiments.)

Reflex Behavior

Reflexes—like the backward jerk that protects your finger from getting too close to a flame—are automatic responses to certain stimuli. They are essential to human survival. Babies are born with a set of reflexes that psychologists believe evolved to help them adapt to the world. For example, a baby *by reflex* will grasp anything placed firmly in his palm, will begin to suck on any nipple-like object that is placed gently into his mouth, will withdraw his foot if it is pricked, and will blink when a light is flashed in his eyes.

Some of a baby's reflexes are more complex, for they consist of several responses to several stimuli. For example, consider the Moro reflex. Whenever the position of an infant's head changes abruptly—for example, if he is lowered quickly after being held aloft, face up—his arms flail out and back from his body and his mouth may open and close. Another more complex reflex is the Babkin reflex: if you touch a baby's cheek near his mouth, he will turn his head toward that side. Table 2-1 lists various reflex behaviors that pediatricians usually test when they give a newborn a neuro-

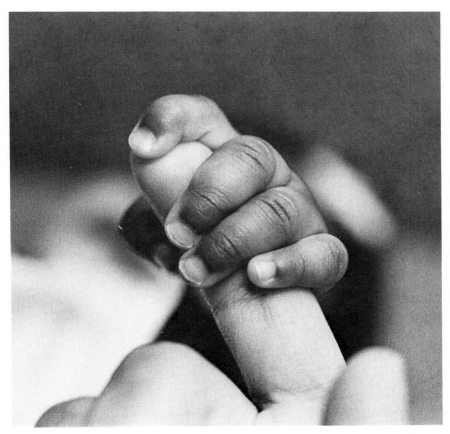

Figure 2-2. *Infants begin life with certain reflexes, involuntary responses to stimulation. Here an infant demonstrates the grasp reflex, in which she closes her hand tightly in response to the pressure of her father's finger. (Photo courtesy of George B. Fry III.)*

logical examination. The absence or weakness of any of these reflexes is a sign of possible nervous system defect, which must be further investigated.

Many of these reflex behaviors disappear several months after birth if a baby's growth is proceeding properly; their disappearance generally is considered a sign of normal development. These automatic stereotyped responses are gradually replaced by more flexible and self-directed responses. For example, babies will abandon the rigid, involuntary fingers-into-palm grasp and will instead grasp objects voluntarily, using their thumbs and fingers.

Table 2-1   Reflexes of the Newborn and the Stimuli That Produce Them

Effective Stimulus	Reflex
Tap upper lip sharply	Lips protrude
Tap bridge of nose	Eyes close tightly
Shine bright light suddenly into eyes	Eyelids close
Clap hands about 18 inches from infant's head	Eyelids close
Touch cornea with light piece of cotton	Eyes close
With baby held on back, turn face slowly to right side	Jaw and right arm on side of face extend out; left arm flexes
Extend forearms at elbow	Arms flex briskly
Put fingers into infant's hand and press his palms	Infant's fingers flex and enclose finger
Press thumbs against the ball of infant's feet	Toes flex
Scratch sole of foot starting from toes toward heel	Big toe bends upward; small toes spread
Prick sole of foot with pin	Infant's knee and foot flex
Tickle area at corner of mouth	Head turns toward side of stimulation
Put index finger into mouth	Sucks
Hold infant in air, stomach down	Attempts to lift head; extends legs

SOURCE: From *Child Development and Personality,* 4th edition, by Paul Henry Mussen, John Janeway Conger, and Jerome Kagan. Copyright © 1974 by Paul Henry Mussen, John Janeway Conger, and Jerome Kagan. By permission of Harper & Row, Publishers, Inc.

Reflex behaviors of newborns are significant because of their apparent adaptive nature. Some reflexes serve as protection—babies blink to shut out overly bright light or to prevent a foreign particle from entering the eye. Other reflexes are related to feeding, which is vital to survival. Because infants automatically suck any soft nipple-like object that enters their mouths and respond to being touched near their mouths, they have a better chance of getting food.

Not only do babies have these reflexes, but they can learn to modify them according to the need. Consider the sucking reflex. Objects other than the mother's nipple or the nipple of a nursing bottle invariably make their way into the mouths of infants; indeed, during the mid-1960s some psychologists spent much of their time placing tubes and such into the mouths of newborns (see, for example, Dubignon and Campbell, 1969; Kaye, 1966; Sameroff, 1970). They found that the reflex to suck an object placed in the mouth is a highly adaptable response, which increases in strength with the softness of the tubing (Dubignon and Campbell, 1968), the temperature of the room (Elder, 1970), and the degree of quiet (Semb and Lipsitt, 1968; Kenn, 1964). The sucking response decreases in strength as sucking continues (Levin and Kaye, 1966; Sameroff, 1967). Infants also quickly distinguish between sucking a tube that supplies a nourishing sugary solution and sucking an empty tube (Kaye, 1966).

Most psychologists agree that these changes in sucking mean that babies learn to adjust what began as an automatic response triggered by the presence of an object in their mouths until their responses reflect their experiences—both in strength and pattern. During this learning process the baby has modified an inborn response to fit specific circumstances. Babies also adjust their grasp gestures, their patterns of crying, and other responses as well. Thus, it seems that human beings are born with reflexes that enable them to survive with care. As they grow, they develop through adaptation ways of behaving that are more efficient and flexible. Adaptation, however, implies only that one has learned to adjust a natural response to fit changes in environmental sensations. Adaptation is not the creation of a new response and thus many psychologists do not regard it as a form of learning. In any case, it shows that babies can deal with moderate changes in their circumstances. (I will return to the topic of learning in a later section.) Wolff (1968) disagrees with the notion that babies modify their reflexes because of their experiences. He thinks that their unlearned responses change when their nervous systems mature and create a new set of unlearned responses, which then interact with the ones that preceded them. So according to Wolff, changes in behavior do not reflect learning.

States (of Awareness?)

In the last section we discussed babies' behavior, which offers essential and easy-to-observe answers to many of our questions about their nature. But anyone who has spent time watching a newborn infant begins to wonder: Can they make any sense of this noisy, colorful, complex world? If they can, what are their impressions? Can they distinguish one person from another? Can they remember what happens from one day to the next?

These questions bring us immediately to one of the ultimate philosophical dilemmas: *How can we ever know the mind of another?* Especially, how can we know the mind of someone who does not yet use language, and who seems to be so different from us in so many ways? Caregivers wonder how they can possibly achieve empathy with these small, wrinkled, apparently unconscious creatures. Developmental psychologists have sought to answer these questions, but because babies are incapable of verbal communication they must be studied by a more indirect means. For example, researchers can change the stimuli that babies receive and then observe the effect of this on their physical responses. In the course of many such observations, investigators have found what most parents already know—that babies do not always react the same way to a given stimulus. Instead, reactions to any stimulus will vary dramatically depending on whether a baby is physically active, calm and receptive, or drowsy and nearly asleep. Researchers must take account of these variations in order to make accurate conclusions about what infants perceive and learn.

The alertness and attentiveness of adults will also vary according to their state of consciousness. In addition to normal waking attentiveness, adults are capable of experiencing many other states of consciousness—quiet and active sleep, meditation, hypnotic trance, feverish delirium, and drug-induced alterations of perception (Hilgard, Atkinson, and Atkinson, 1975). Adult subjects are much easier to study than babies because they can describe their experiences to investigators as they are taking place (although experiences during sleep—dreams—have to be reported later). By comparing these reports to physiological and observational data, researchers can gain a better understanding of the various states of consciousness. But this term is not applied to infants because, although their physical activity and apparent attentiveness vary, it is inappropriate to refer to their consciousness when there is no way of measuring their experiences. Instead, researchers refer to infant *states*, which are defined according to infants' behavior and, sometimes, their physiological condition.

A Description of Newborn States

Developmental psychologists are immensely indebted to Peter Wolff, an English pediatrician who spent many hours observing in detail the daily behavior of a number of newborns. He has described seven states that can be identified by careful observation (Wolff, 1966).

1. *Regular sleep.* During regular sleep babies lie quite still with their eyes closed and unmoving. Their respiration is even, and their skin is pale.
2. *Irregular sleep.* During irregular sleep babies' muscular response to pressure is stronger than in regular sleep. Babies jerk, startle, and grimace spontaneously. The eyes are clearly closed but sometimes they move. The skin may be flushed, and breathing is irregular.
3. *Periodic sleep.* Periodic sleep is a combination of regular and irregular sleep: it consists of bursts of rapid breathing, jerks, and startles, followed by spells of quiet.
4. *Drowsiness.* During drowsy states babies are moderately active. Their eyes open and close intermittently, and they look glazed. Respiration is regular but more rapid than in regular sleep.

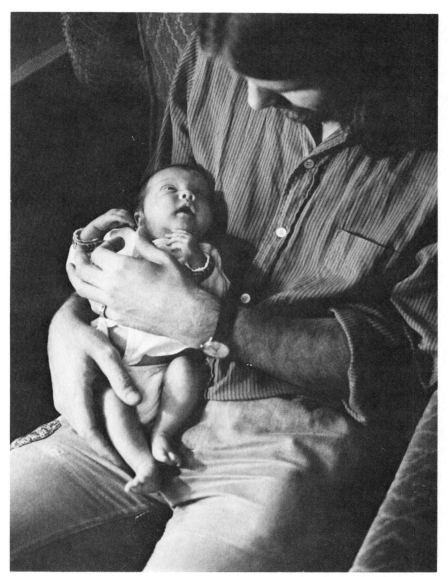

Figure 2-3.   *An eight-week-old baby looks at his father's face with interest. Apparently, babies learn most about their environment when they are in the alert inactive state. (Photo copyright © Suzanne Arms.)*

5. *Alert inactivity.* Alert, inactive babies are awake. Their eyes are open and shining, and they look at their surroundings with interest. Babies' bodies are relatively still, and their respiration is rather fast and irregular.
6. *Waking activity.* During waking activity babies are awake but their eyes focus less often, and they have spurts of vigorous activity. During these random spurts they move their legs and arms and twist their torsos. The length and intensity of these activity spurts vary.
7. *Crying.* During crying states infants engage in vigorous activity. Their skin is flushed and they cry (although without tears yet).

Several other researchers have devised systems for classifying infant states that are similar to Wolff's descriptions (for example, Prechtl, 1961).

Although one might be inclined to attribute states to babies' reactions to changes in their own nervous systems, the evidence does not support this interpretation: the physiological functioning of an infant's body is not clearly different from one state to another (Ashton, 1971b). However, as we shall see shortly, if their environment changes while they are in the waking states, babies' behavior also changes. Lewis (1972) has suggested that the *state* of infants is best thought of as a mediator between them and their environment. Being newly arrived in a world of many diverse and complex stimuli, infants protect themselves from being overwhelmed by simply not processing much of this stimulation. According to Lewis, they absorb most information about the environment during the waking alert state. When the amount of such information becomes too much for them to absorb they disengage by becoming more active or by going to sleep. It is not clear what determines their course of action, but some sort of self-pacing mechanism allows babies to regulate their stimulus load by tuning out when they have had enough.

This information can be of great help to caregivers, who can learn to respond to the needs of infants. Many mothers do this unconsciously; if their baby abruptly becomes uncomfortable or active they respond to what experience tells them their baby needs—whether to be held or simply given some peace and quiet. The distinctness and clarity with which babies demonstrate the various states they experience can vary widely (Korner, 1972), so the success of this "caregiver–infant dialogue" varies as well.

Determinants of the Time Spent in the Various States

To most observers, it seems as if newborn infants spend most of their time asleep. And research verifies this impression. A well-planned observational study of 50 newborns during their first four days of life produced the following estimates of the percentages of time they spent in several states:

asleep (all forms) 67 percent, drowsy 7 percent, awake alert (Wolff's alert inactivity) 10 percent, fussy (similar to Wolff's waking activity) 11 percent, and crying 5 percent (Berg, Adkinson, and Strock, 1973). The observers paid special attention to the alert inactive state, in which babies take in their environment. During their observations, which took place between one and just over three hours after a feeding, the investigators counted the number of times infants were in an alert inactive state that lasted for two or more minutes. Some babies never experienced the awake alert state, whereas others experienced it as many as eight times; the average was 5.47 times. From this we can infer that some newborn infants never stay in this maximally receptive state long enough to take in very much about their surroundings, whereas others may absorb a great deal of information about the environment.

Can the awareness states of a baby be altered? Can fussy newborns be made to sleep for several hours so that those who care for them can get some rest? Or, on the other hand, if we wanted to show a baby something special, could we arrange to put him into the alert inactive state to insure that he noticed it?

One investigator deliberately exposed his newborn subjects to environments that would be expected to alter the length of their sleep time and perhaps influence their waking states as well. He placed one group of babies in a room similar to the normal hospital nursery except that the lights were dimmed to lower the intensity of a major source of stimulation. The room for a second group was lit like the normal nursery but was noisier. A third group of newborns were placed in a normal nursery and they served as *control* subjects. (In experiments, investigators observe a control group, whose experiences are not changed to see what happens in the normal situation. They then compare the controls' reaction to that of the experimental group.) These changes in the environment had no detectable effect on the daily cycle of states for the infants (Ashton, 1971).

General studies do suggest that a brief transition from one state to another can be caused by certain events. Korner and Thoman (1970) report that if infants are lifted from a prone position to being held upright on their caretaker's shoulder this stimulation often promotes their going into the alert inactive state. In their experiment Korner and Thoman used controls to pinpoint what caused the change in state. They found that if crying babies received vestibular stimulation (the sensation mediated by organs in the internal ear that tells you when your body's position changes) they usually became alert and inactive whereas sleeping babies frequently did not. It would seem to follow that crying infants who are picked up from their cribs and carried about on their caregiver's shoulders will cry less and may be more aware of their environments than those who are infrequently picked

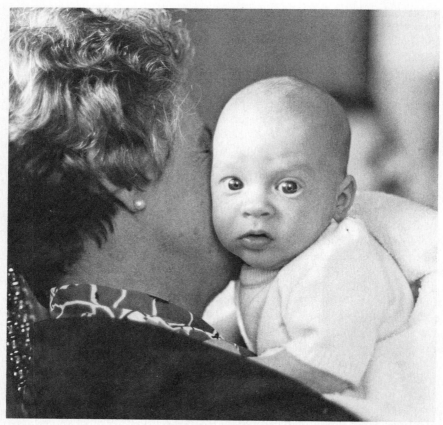

Figure 2-4.   *Changing a baby's position can change his disposition by producing vestibular stimulation. Only moments before the picture was taken, this baby was lying on his back, crying; now he rests, alert but quiet, upon his grandmother's shoulder. (Photo courtesy of Gary Head.)*

up, but, because so little is known about changes in state of infants, this is largely conjecture.

Evidence also indicates that when babies are aroused (that is, when they are crying or fussy) they can be quieted by any stimulation that is continuous and unchanging for some minutes (Brackbill, 1970). Because this has obvious practical implication for caregivers, we will discuss this research fully later in this chapter.

To sum up what is known from caregiving experience and from research about states and the environment: Continuous stimulation and vestibular stimulation will quiet excited babies, whereas the sudden stimulus of movement will awaken them. At this writing, no study has shown yet that babies' daily pattern of states can be altered by changes in noise or lighting.

Sleep Patterns in Newborns

A great deal of attention has been devoted in recent years to the study of sleep. Although the question of why we sleep has not yet been answered, researchers have discovered that sleep consists of two distinct phases: one that is characterized by rapid eye movements, REM sleep, and one in which eye movements are absent, non-REM sleep. REM sleep is also characterized by occasional muscle twitches and jerks, fast brain waves (which are indicative of brain activity), and definite darting movements of the eyes. Non-REM sleep is characterized by slower brain waves and greater muscle tone (without the quick, jerky motions characteristic of REM sleep). Most adults begin their cycles of sleep with non-REM sleep, which alternates with cycles of REM sleep. In studying sleeping patterns of adults, experimenters found that when awakened during REM sleep, nearly all of the adults reported that they had been dreaming. Thus, it seems safe to say that when adults are experiencing REM sleep, they probably are dreaming.

Figure 2-5 shows the average percentage of total sleep time that persons of different ages spend in REM sleep. An examination of it suggests some important questions about infants and their sleep states. Newborn infants are in REM sleep nearly 60 percent of the time they are sleeping; premature infants, 85 percent. Are they dreaming all of this time? One fact has led researchers to believe that this may not be the logical conclusion. Their sleep cycle takes a course that is opposite to that of adults: infants first enter REM sleep which then alternates with non-REM sleep. REM sleep may have some different functions for infants than it has for adults. In fact, some researchers have concluded that REM sleep performs some very primitive nervous system function that helps in the physical and mental development of infants. Let us consider other evidence related to this idea, which has not yet been established.

Some psychologists suggest that REM sleep is a form of self-stimulation by the brain (Roffwarg, Muzio, and Dement, 1966). Perhaps stimulation, alternating with periods of rest from stimulation, is required for brain organization. Indeed, research has shown that immediately after being circumcised, male infants experience shorter periods of REM sleep (Emde et al., 1971; Spitz, Emde, and Metcalf, 1970). The circumcision may be thought of as an abrupt increase in stress (stimulation), and the subsequent reduction in time spent in REM sleep as a compensatory mechanism. No work with other comparable stress experiences has been published, and therefore this discussion is only very speculative.

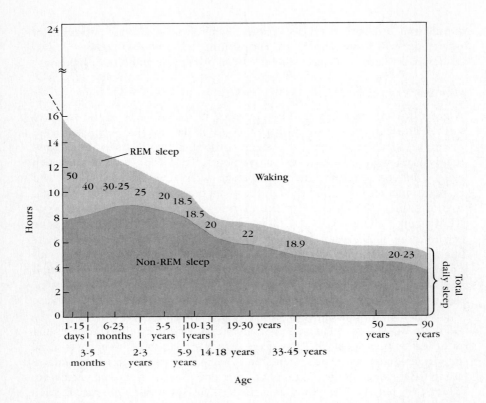

Figure 2-5. *Changes with age in total amounts of daily sleep, daily REM sleep, and percentage of REM sleep. Notice the sharp diminution of REM sleep in the early years of life. REM sleep falls from 8 hours at birth to less than 1 hour in old age. The amount of non-REM sleep throughout life changes less dramatically; it falls from 8 to 5 hours, and in fact remains undiminished for many years. Although total daily REM sleep falls steadily during life, the percentage rises slightly during adolescence and early adulthood. This rise does not reflect an increase in amount: it is due to the fact that REM sleep does not diminish as quickly as total sleep. Data for the 33 to 45 and 50 to 90 year groups are taken from Kales et al. (1967), Feinberg et al. (1967), and Kahn and Fisher (1969), respectively. (Updated since original publication in "The ontogenetic development of the human sleep-dream cycle," by H. P. Roffwarg, J. N. Muzio, and W. Dement.* Science, *1966, 152, 604–619. Copyright 1966 by the American Association for the Advancement of Science.)*

The percentage of sleep time an infant spends in REM sleep begins to drop off rapidly at about three days of age (Minard et al., 1968). By three months of age, only 40 percent of an infant's sleep is REM sleep (see Figure 2-5) and infants no longer begin their episodes of sleep with REM sleep (Emde and Metcalf, 1968). Infants' brain wave patterns during sleep also become more stable over the birth-to-three-months period. At birth the wave patterns change frequently and abruptly, and even some infants who are awake have patterns that would be indicative of REM sleep in an older infant or an adult. By three months, these abrupt changes are less frequent, and the waking REM patterns have disappeared (Emde and Metcalf, 1968). These changes suggest that large amounts of REM sleep support an organizational process that is going on in the brain during the first three months. The fact that premature babies, whose nervous systems are not well developed, spend more time than normal babies in REM sleep also supports this conclusion.

Researchers have observed that babies rarely have severe sleep disturbances in the first year (Nagera, 1966). However, newborns whose mothers received major tranquilizers—those used to control psychotic symptoms—during pregnancy reportedly experience an increase in REM sleep during the first few days of life (Emde et al., 1971). This sparse evidence would seem to suggest that infant sleep cycles are automatically regulated by some organic process and that abnormal sleep patterns probably result from physical causes. When sleep problems do occur in the first year, in many instances it is later discovered that the child has other malfunctions of the nervous system (Bernal, 1973).

I have speculated here that the function of the large amounts of REM sleep in the newborn has to do with the developmental organization of the brain. But a great deal of work in developmental psychophysiology must be done before anyone can offer a clearer picture of the function of sleep, let alone its significance for infants.

The Relation of Infants' States to Their Behavior

As I have said, the state of newborns affects their ability to process information about the environment. Let's look at the evidence that supports this conclusion. Several investigators have presented auditory stimuli such as simple tones to newborn babies in various states (Wolff, 1966; Ashton, 1971; Korner, 1972). Their findings indicate that babies' behavior changes in response to these stimuli—for example, their heart rate decreases (indicating attention)—only when they are in the alert inactive state. It is also known that newborn babies in sleeping states respond differently from those in waking states to tactile sensations (Lewis, Dodd, and Harwitz, 1969), but no one has studied yet how babies' responses to tactile stimuli differ in the various waking states or the two main sleep states. Although Wolff mentioned that his neonates paid more attention to visual stimuli when they entered the alert inactive state, no more systematic studies have been done. In sum, what evidence we have consistently indicates what may seem obvious—that newborns react with greatest attention to sensations that occur when they are in an alert inactive state. But much more evidence on the degrees and definitions of attention is needed before this generalization can be considered fact. Indeed, one of the authors whose work contributed to the tentative generalization has come to consider the concept of "state" inadequate (Ashton, 1974).

Psychologists have attempted to discover whether newborn infants can respond—as children and adults do—to *classical conditioning.* In other words, can they learn to connect a new stimulus (a *conditioned* stimulus) to an inborn response? If a baby began sucking when she saw her mother enter the room with a bottle rather than after she felt the bottle in her mouth, it would mean she had learned to do so by classical conditioning. In this instance the mother entering the room with a bottle would be the *conditioned stimulus;* the sensation of a bottle in the infant's mouth, the *unconditioned stimulus.* Several studies of classical conditioning in newborns indicate that this learning—the forming of new connections between stimuli—occurs reliably only if the infants are in the alert inactive state (see reviews by Papousek and Bernstein, 1969; Korner, 1972). As you can see, classical conditioning requires that a person notice the conditioned stimulus: otherwise, it would be impossible to make the connection between unconditioned stimulus (feeling the bottle) and the conditioned stimulus (seeing the mother bring the bottle).

One investigator has explored the influence of state on several motor reactions and on the sucking reflex. He found no relation, which indicates that state does not affect all of a newborn's responses. However, because variations in an infant's state do affect some rather important responses related to perception and learning, it is important to observe the states of babies and to relate their states to the conclusions we draw about the behavior we are studying. Also, because the pattern of changes in states varies widely from one newborn to the next (Berg, Adkinson, and Strock, 1973), we can safely infer that babies differ markedly in the amount that they find out about the world during their first days. Those who are more frequently in the alert inactive states (perhaps because they are more often picked up and carried about) learn a great deal about their surroundings, while other babies, who for various reasons are rarely in that state, learn little. These individual differences must have profound implications for the babies' further development, but so far no long-term study that has followed different groups of babies as they develop specifically looks at this matter.

Why Newborns Cry

What person who has cared for a baby has not wondered what can make it change in moments from a smiling, gurgling delight into a raging, red-faced bundle of anxiety. In the course of Wolff's studies of infant states (Wolff,

1966), he tried to discover what caused each episode of crying that his subject (and he) endured. He concluded that newborn infants most commonly awake crying because of spontaneous nervous system discharge that is not caused by any obvious external stimulus. The other leading causes of crying were pain (for example, from a pinprick) and exposure to cold, according to Wolff, who said that newborns cried for a variety of reasons—not only wet diapers or hunger.

Wolff also observed that brain-damaged infants have a characteristic shrill cry that, with appropriate electronic equipment, can be distinguished from the normal newborn's cry, an observation that has been validated by one other, perhaps more systematic, study (Fisichelli, Karelitz, and Haber, 1969). In sum, newborns have a variety of cries, each of which means something different from every other. Careful study of these cries are rendering them even more useful as indicators of the infants' needs and state.

Sensation and Perception in the Newborn

The philosophers' problem of epistemology is concerned with the question of how we know reality. One way we know reality is through perception, so when we study newborn perception we are finding out how human beings first come to know reality. The study of perceptual development deals with how we become conscious of a three-dimensional environment organized in a particular way and containing solid objects with space between them. Psychology originally emerged as a discipline seeking scientific answers to questions such as "Is reality what it appears to be?" So sensation and perception, studied together, were the original problems of scientific psychology. Sensation refers to the process by which the sense organs transmit information from the environment to the brain. Thus, *sensations* are such experiences as colors, sounds, smells, and pressures on the skin. *Perception* refers to the processes that give sensations their meaning: it is the integration of sensory impressions. From the standpoint of sensation, my clipboard resting on this desk in front of me produces merely an array of visual impressions of various colors and brightnesses. But perception tells me that my impressions can be separated into several distinct objects, one on top of another and both in front of another object—me. Perceptually, I can enjoy Beethoven's *Fifth Symphony,* but as sensation it is simply noise.

Although many studies have been done on sensation and perception in very young infants—enough to provide material for most of an entire chapter in this book (see Chapter 3)—only a small number of these investigations study newborns. However, these few address one of the most crucial questions in psychology: Are human beings born with perceptual abilities that allow us to organize sensations? Can babies gain any meaningful impression of the world, from birth, or are they born into a confused jumble of sensations that they learn to interpret only gradually?

When William James described the newborns' impressions of their environment as a "blooming, buzzing confusion," he was expressing the then-popular view that a newborn is capable of sensation but not perception. Earlier, in central Europe, the opposite notion of Immanuel Kant had enjoyed a wide following. Kant, a nativist, argued that we are born with certain innate perceptual processes, which he called "categories of the understanding" (see Boring, 1929). He believed that the newborn can perceive and thus can experience a meaningful world of objects, located in space and organized in some coherent pattern. On the other hand, empiricists, like James, believed that some period of experience with sensation is necessary before senses become organized into meaningful patterns: according to them, one must learn how to perceive.

But none of the nineteenth-century philosophers such as James ever studied the reactions of newborn infants to stimuli, even though potential subjects for such observation were available. They did not think of observing babies because the epistemology of the day was unempirical. Here we use the term "empirical" to mean founded on observation. One of the fascinations of the psychological study of newborns is that it provides an empirical approach to this most basic of all philosophical problems.

Sensory Capabilities of Newborns

The study of newborns' senses indicates that all of the human senses are functioning in some form at birth. In studying newborns' sensations, researchers generally present to infants a series of stimuli that differ from one another in some obvious way. They then record the babies' responses, most often the changes in their heart rate and general activity. Because there is so much debate about the influence of methods on results, I advise readers to turn to the appendix for a more lengthy discussion of methods. Here I simply review the findings.

Vision.   Vision, the sense upon which human beings depend the most, is present and functioning fairly effectively at birth. Newborn babies can distinguish the details of what they see, and, for example, can discriminate between solid gray patterns and those composed of five gray stripes (Dayton et al., 1964). In fact, babies see effectively enough to pick out a variety of patterns (Fantz, 1963). However, newborns cannot focus upon objects that are farther than about 7½ inches away, (Haynes, White, and Held, 1965), so they may not see much of the detail of their environments. Not only are objects at varying distances from the baby (as they are from us all), but they also move. Newborns probably experience more "blurred" images than do babies several months of age, who have by then become capable of operating their eyes together to adjust to the changing distance of the objects. Newborns can follow a moving object with their eyes when that object is moved in a plane (provided it is at the right distance for them to focus on it). Their eye movements are more jerky and irregular than those of older children and adults, and their normal following process is more tenuous, but they are born with the ability to follow (Greenman, 1963).

Besides being able to distinguish the details of an object at the proper distance for focusing, newborns are sensitive to changes in illumination (Porges, Stamps, and Walters, 1974). They are probably sensitive to color differences as well, but this capacity has been less well researched. We do know that infants exhibit different brain wave patterns in response to being shown different colors (see, for example, Lodge et al., 1969). Newborns look for a source for sounds that they hear, which may indicate that they do integrate the experiences of different senses (Turkewitz, Birch, and Cooper, 1972b).

Hearing.   Newborn infants react to all the major aspects of auditory stimulation—that is, pitch, loudness, timbre, and pattern (rhythm) (Eisenberg, 1970). However, some evidence indicates that they cannot detect a pure tone, which has a single definable pitch, and that they respond only to tones that are combinations of pure tones (Turkewitz, Birch, and Cooper, 1972a; Turkewitz, Birch, and Cooper, 1972b; Hott et al., 1968).

Newborns react more consistently to longer or continuous sounds than they do to shorter or intermittent sounds (Ling, 1972); this may mean that they do not experience successive separate sounds as being related. Thus, for example, the notes in a melody may seem to them to be unrelated noises.

Newborns seem to respond most to sounds whose pitch is within the range of the human voice (Webster, Steinhardt, and Senter, 1972). In one study newborns paid attention to sounds within a frequency range typical of many everyday sounds and their heart beats sped up (usually a sign of fear) at sounds outside of this range (Kearsley, 1973). If they were particularly attuned to the sounds made by their human caregivers, newborns would have a definite adaptive advantage, but further research must be done to establish whether they are.

Anyone who has ever dropped a pan around a resting newborn can verify that babies are sensitive to the loudness of the sounds they hear. Indeed, the research bears out this informal observation. Babies' hearts beat faster in response to loud sounds, increasingly so with the increasing loudness of the sound (Steinschneider, 1966; Steinschneider, 1968; Bartoshuk, 1964).

Clearly, newborns can hear quite well at birth, and they appear to be aware of a variety of sounds. They may be especially aware of the human voices around them, but as yet the sounds lack the meaning that will transform them into language.

Smell.   The ability of newborn infants to detect different odors (Engen, Lipsitt, and Kaye, 1963; Self, Horowitz, and Paden, 1972) is relatively weak immediately at birth, but it develops during the first three days of life (Lipsitt, Engen, and Kaye, 1963). By varying the intensity of the odors presented to infants, experimenters have shown that newborns can discriminate differences in intensity (Rovee, 1969). Because newborn infants can discriminate among many odors, investigators use their responses to odors in studies of learning, which we will discuss shortly.

Taste.   Newborns can clearly detect the difference between plain water and sugar water (Kobre and Lipsitt, 1972; Desor, Maller, and Turner, 1973) and, in one study, they even distinguished among various types of sugar solutions (Engen, Lipsitt, and Peck, 1974). Although researchers have not studied other tastes, it seems likely that newborn infants would be able to detect them as well. Some evidence exists that infants respond to variations in the intensity of sugar concentration (Engen, Lipsitt, and Peck, 1974), but more research on taste remains to be done.

Touch.   In reviewing the research on newborns, I have found no study that dealt specifically with the reactions of infants to tactile stimuli. However, infants' reflexes and the experiences of their caregivers clearly show that their sense of touch functions adequately from birth. Further investigation is needed to pinpoint the range of tactile stimuli to which newborn babies respond and their differing responses (if any) to various sources of tactile sensations.

Other Sensations.   As you will recall, babies respond to the *vestibular sensation* caused by bodily movements (Korner and Thoman, 1972). They also are sensitive to pain, although perhaps not to the same extent as adults (Stone and Church, 1973, p. 19). My experience with babies would suggest that they can detect at least the extremes of heat and cold, but few of the details of their reactions to temperatures have been documented.

Perception

Human beings apparently are born into the world with functioning senses. As newborns, we have the means to acquire the raw data of color, of sound patterns, of odors, and the rest—to construct some coherent impressions of a meaningful world. But do newborns do this? Do they perceive objects located in space, each with its individual properties? Although a great deal of research has been done on the perception of young infants just past the newborn period (and we review this information in the next chapter), only one of the studies I have mentioned used truly newborn babies. Although many investigators generalize from their data to include the newborn, strictly speaking it is uncertain whether newborns experience their sensations in meaningful patterns that bear any resemblance to the perceptual experiences of children and adults. But we do know something about how they divide their attention among the various sensations, and from this we can make some guesses about their perceptions.

Attention.   Because babies cannot talk, they are incapable of articulating what they see, hear, or smell. But it is safe to infer that, like adults, they do not process all the stimuli that come to them, but rather perceive selectively. Here we meet the problem of *attention*. Given that only a small part of the stimuli from the environment ever reaches our conscious awareness, what rules govern the selection of which ones we will notice?

Indicators of attention.   Being above all curious creatures, human beings are very likely to notice any new sensation that comes their way. We display the *orienting reflex*—our bodies make definite physiological changes that indicate that we are preparing to receive further sensations. We may also focus our eyes deliberately or show other external signals of paying attention as well. The external signs of a newborn infant's orienting reflex are not as well defined as those of an adult. But when researchers present novel experiences to newborns, they experience several observable behavioral and physiological changes that researchers use to indicate that the babies are paying attention.

Some investigators consider a change in heart rate to be indicative of attention to an experience (see, for example, Bower, 1966). However, controversy has arisen about whether a decrease in an infant's heart rate reliably indicates that the infant is paying attention (Schacter et al., 1971; Porges, Stamps, and Walter, 1974; Lewis, Bartels, and Goldberg, 1967). First, heart rate is highly variable in newborns, and thus it is hard to make a definite connection between a change in it and any stimulus. Second, babies may be interested in stimuli within a certain intensity range but may show fear and avoidance toward those that are too intense. The speeding up of a heartbeat can show fear. Because they do not know very much about what range of stimulus intensity newborns find tolerable, many investigators accidentally use stimuli that startle or frighten their subjects—and cause their heart rates to increase. In another investigation with similar, but less intense, stimuli, a baby may show interest and may make an orienting response (including heart-rate decrease). The problem is further complicated because newborns' reactions to a given stimulus depend upon their state. Because of all of these difficulties, studies that use only heart-rate changes to indicate newborn attention are difficult to interpret, and one study may yield findings that are inconsistent with those of another. Nevertheless, some investigators still use heart-rate decrease to measure attention.

To study attention to visual stimuli, many investigators simply observe whether, and for how long, an infant looks at various stimuli. Fantz (1963) has developed a special looking chamber, which is shown in Figure 2-6. The infant is placed on a reclining chair similar to those commonly used in the United States to carry infants. The reclining infant is then slid into a chamber with dark sides and slanting roof. Slides of various stimuli can then be shown on a screen that is on the roof of the chamber, and an observer can look through a small opening in this screen to determine what the infant is looking at. The length of time that babies hold their eyes steady while looking at an object, the *fixation time,* is commonly used as a measure of attention. By comparing fixation times for several stimuli (which are all presented for the same length of time), investigators can gauge the babies' interest in each of them.

Newborns also indicate attention by interrupting their sucking. An infant who is sucking on a nipple will stop briefly if a light suddenly flashes within view (Haith, 1966). Researchers have studied whether babies also interrupt their sucking when they hear sounds, but the results are not conclusive (Semb and Lipsitt, 1968; Kaye, 1966; Kaye and Levin, 1963).

Older babies will laugh, smile, and vocalize if their interest is captured, but newborns have not mastered these responses yet. So the least ambiguous method to test whether they are paying attention to visual stimuli is simply to watch where they are looking. However, to study their other senses, researchers generally measure their heart rates and any subtle but reliable changes in their behavior.

Stimuli that attract a newborn's attention.   Most of the work on newborn attention has concentrated on vision, because it is the dominant human sense. Fantz has reported (1963) that newborns can detect the *contrast* between light and dark, as between the edge of a dark figure and a white

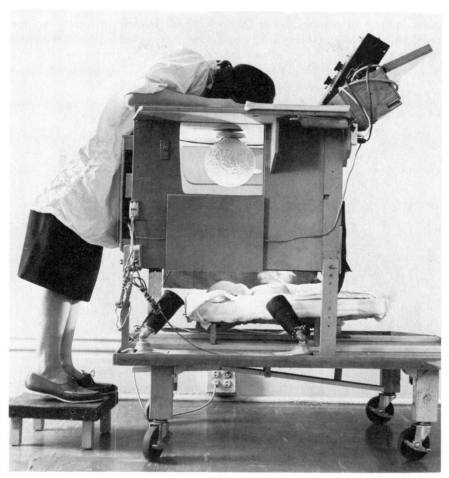

Figure 2-6.   *The looking chamber used by Robert Fantz to test the visual interests of babies. (Photo courtesy of David Linton.)*

background. Salapatek (1968) and Haith (1968) have demonstrated, by observing how infants scan a pattern, that newborns concentrate on *contours*. Because moving lights have such obvious contrast and motion, infants respond strongly to them (Haith, 1966; Kagan, 1972). Infants pay more attention to a several-angled polygon than to one with only a few angles or with very many angles, which indicates to some observers that they prefer shapes of intermediate complexity (Munsinger and Kessen, 1964). (In Chapter 3, I discuss the controversy about how infant preferences among these random polygons should be interpreted.) Clearly, *movement* and *contrast* attract the newborn's visual attention. In Chapter 5, we will see that, as development proceeds, attention is determined more and more by the *meaning* of the stimulus to the infant and less by its absolute, sensed properties.

Remembering and Learning Capacities of the Newborn

Learning is broadly defined as relatively permanent changes in behavior that result from experience; the extent to which it occurs in humans distinguishes them from all other forms of life. But does it begin at birth? Can newborns profit from their experiences? We will see in subsequent chapters that very young infants do understand some important things about their worlds. This fact brings us to a question: Could they have learned these things during the newborn period—that is, can newborns learn? Even when it is demonstrated that they sometimes can learn, this fact does not prove that a specific concept or behavior change was learned. Even though all of us can learn, we may acquire some concepts in other ways. It may be that some are the product of maturation alone. But once we know that babies can learn, then we can test whether they have learned a specific concept or gained it as part of maturation.

The answer has practical as well as philosophical implications. If we as caregivers believe that babies can learn, we are far more likely to try to facilitate that learning. Evidence shows that many mothers of young infants believe them to be incapable of much learning (Tulkin and Kagan, 1970). With this belief, they are probably unlikely to try to stimulate their babies. Indeed, they may follow the folk wisdom that says newborns should be kept in a quiet, dim room away from much stimulation. I suspect that our estimate of newborns' learning capabilities would influence the style of "dialogue" we have with them through looking, touching, and speaking.

In the discussion that follows, let us consider the evidence on newborn learning.

Habituation

A novel stimulus is likely to get our attention and perhaps our overt response. When we go to a friend's house, we immediately notice the hum of the old clock, the staccato of rain on the roof, the soft music they have on their record player. But after we have spent some time sitting in this room with our friends, we will no longer be aware of these new sounds; we will have ceased to hear them. Psychologists refer to our lack of response after prolonged exposure to a sensation as *habituation*.

Researchers use the following method to study habituation in babies. A stimulus such as a tone, light, or odor is produced over and over again in a series of separate presentations called trials. The researchers then observe whether babies pay attention to the stimulus on each trial. This can be measured by their visual fixations, a change in their bodily activity, or some psychophysiological reaction such as a change in their heart rates. Habituation is said to have occurred if the intensity of their responses declines with successive trials. For instance, suppose I turn a slide of an attractive geometric design on and off repeatedly for ten trials. Ordinarily, infants will look at it intently for quite a few seconds during the first trial. But in each successive trial they will become less interested until, finally, they are not looking at all.

Habituation indicates that an elementary memory process is taking place. If an infant startles to a sudden loud noise, but shows no sign of having heard the sixth steady repetition of that same noise, we must infer that he knows it to be the sound he has heard before. On this basis, the habituation is considered evidence for the existence of a primitive memory process.

Several investigators have studied habituation in newborn infants. A popular research design in the 1960s called for the experimenter to present to newborns tones loud enough to cause them to respond with a heart-rate increase that indicated a defensive reaction. Several studies found that the cardiac response of infants decreased over trials: habituation occurred (Bridger, 1961; Bartoshuk, 1962a; Bartoshuk, 1962b; Stratton, 1970; Field, 1967). These investigators reported that some infants did not seem to habituate to the stimulus. The infants' state was shown to be a factor in one study (Campos and Brackbill, 1973), in which the smoothest habituation was found to occur when infants were asleep. Another factor that can determine the rate of habituation for infants is the duration of the tone. Some evidence indicates that, if a sound lasts less than two seconds, an infant's heart rate will continue to change when it is repeated. However, not only do sounds that last more than two seconds bring about habituation, but infants still are unsurprised at the sounds 24 hours later, which indicates that they remember it for 24 hours (Keen, Chase, and Graham, 1965).

When investigators compared the reactions of a group of babies to auditory and tactile stimuli, they found that the babies habituated more quickly (in fewer trials) to what they felt than to what they heard. The same investigators demonstrated that responses of skeletal muscles, such as startle reactions or changes in activity, ceased to occur sooner than autonomic responses such as heart rate during habituation (Moreau, Birch, and Turkewitz, 1970).

A series of studies in the early 1970s examined how rapidly newborns become accustomed to visual stimuli (Friedman, Carpenter, and Nagy,

1970; Friedman, Nagy, and Carpenter, 1970; Friedman and Carpenter, 1971; Friedman, 1972; Friedman, Bruno, and Vietze, 1974). In these studies newborns in the alert inactive state were shown checkerboard designs. The investigators recorded how long the infants looked at the pattern and then added up their total fixation time. They discovered that, over the course of a few trials, the infants looked less each time. They also found that newborns three or more days of age usually habituated faster than those in the first three days of life.

The one important criticism of habituation studies is that the gradual lessening of the response could possibly be caused by the sense receptors becoming fatigued. The nervous system does tire until finally it fails to react to stimulation (Hilgard, Atkinson, and Atkinson, 1975, pp. 117–118). One way of resolving the question is to present a series of novel stimuli to babies. For example, after ringing a doorbell until infants became habituated to it, a researcher might switch to a small toy bell and observe whether they pay attention to the new sound. If they react (with heart-rate increase, bodily quieting, or whatever) to the new stimulus, it can be assumed that their previous lack of response represents real habituation and not inability to respond. The work of the early 1970s on visual fixation in newborns includes tests with a second stimulus. But some of the studies on heart-rate response to sounds do not use this check, so their results are open to more than one interpretation.

So although some evidence indicates that newborns have early memory traces that make habituation possible, only two types of stimuli and a very few responses have been studied. Some methodological problems exist as well. Thus, researchers are cautious in drawing conclusions about the ability of newborns to habituate. They believe that habituation may play some role in the development of infants during their first days, but that much remains to be known about it.

Classical Conditioning

In the earlier discussion of infant states, I pointed out that newborns are capable of learning through classical conditioning when they are alert but inactive. You should remember that classical conditioning results in the formation of new links between two stimuli that previously were experienced as unrelated. Young infants appear to know that their bottles are connected with the sensations of milk, and that the sight of the faces of those who care for them means they are about to receive pleasant ministrations. These learned connections between stimuli are instances of the classical conditioning process.

In order to demonstrate classical conditioning, experimenters begin with some unlearned connection between a stimulus and a response—this might be a reflex such as blinking in response to a blast of air on the eye. The stimulus in the unlearned connection is called *unconditioned stimulus* (or US) because the response to it is automatic, not conditioned: in our example, the US is the air blast. The experimenters' goal is to cause a subject to make a connection between the air blast and some other stimulus that has no inherent relation to it. This second stimulus is called the *conditioned stimulus* (or CS) because subjects learn to respond to it only by conditioning.

During the experiment—a series of conditioning trials—a blast of air is administered to the subject on each trial just an instant after the tone is sounded. At first the subject will show no reaction to the tone alone, but he will blink at every air blast. After several trials, the subject begins to blink *before* the air blast but just *after* the tone. Now the tone is eliciting the blink response, so we can infer that our obliging subject has associated the tone and air blast. Thus, he has responded to classical conditioning.

In a classical conditioning experiment the timing of the stimuli is crucial. The CS (here, the tone) must come before the US (air blast) in order to demonstrate that the CS, and not the US, causes the response. However, if the CS comes too long a time before the US, conditioning will not take place. Research shows that, in the optimal plan, the conditioned stimulus occurs about one-half second before the unconditioned stimulus (Hilgard, Atkinson, and Atkinson, 1975, p. 197). Most well-planned conditioning studies include several kinds of control groups to determine whether the new occurrence of the response in the presence of the CS is caused by the US-CS pairing and not some characteristic of the CS itself (or any other irrelevant factor).

Now, let us get back to newborns. Although several studies of classical conditioning with infants have been done (see Chapter 3), relatively few of these have included newborn subjects. Lipsitt and Kaye (1964) reported the successful classical conditioning of infants' sucking response. They said that an association had been learned by the babies they studied between the sensations from a nipple in the mouth (US) and a tone (CS). Connolly and Stratton (1969) also reported successful classical conditioning of infants using the US of pressure applied to the babies' palms and two CSs: a tone and the raising of their arms.

But these studies have been met with criticism. In a discussion of these and other similar studies, Sameroff (1972) has argued that the classical conditioning of newborns was not established by them. He has criticized the studies because they did not include the proper control groups. After testing six groups of babies (three control groups and three experimental groups), he reported that one supposedly conditioned stimulus was probably an unconditioned stimulus that automatically triggered the response. Therefore, he argued, the results of the earlier studies did not prove that subjects were classically conditioned (Sostek, Sameroff, and Sostek, 1972). Other reviewers have argued that studies that examine infants' states find some classical conditioning among the alert inactive infants. Apparently, these positive results are canceled out by the negative results from studies that do not consider state. The evidence for classical conditioning in newborns thus appears to be inconclusive. Variations in the states of newborns make classical conditioning difficult to demonstrate. Also, most classical conditioning experiments require that subjects relate stimuli that affect two different senses—an ability that may require subjects to have nervous systems that are more mature than those of newborn infants (Sameroff, 1971). Therefore, more well-controlled studies must be concluded to determine whether classical conditioning of newborns is possible. Probably it is under certain experimental circumstances, but these may be rare in everyday life. In any case, classical conditioning probably does not play an important role in the newborn's emerging understanding of the world.

Operant Conditioning

Operant conditioning produces associations between responses and their immediate consequences. Every parent is familiar with the idea of rewarding desirable behavior in order to insure that it will occur again. Psychologists are interested in this form of learning because it produces straightforward proof that learning has been brought about by experience. If newborns can be operantly conditioned, it would prove that experience is an important teacher for them. Let us consider a brief example of operant conditioning. An infant sucks on a tube that happens to contain a sugar solution and then sucks again. The starting place for the operant conditioning process is some response (R) whose frequency can be measured. Unlike the responses of classical conditioning, the operant response is not *caused* by a stimulus. The chosen response is simply followed with a stimulus that is pleasurable or that satisfies a need of the subject.

If R (sucking the tube) results in a reinforcing stimulus S^+ (a good taste) on a number of occasions, and if S^+ rarely occurs without R, then S^+ is said to be *contingent* on R: it only occurs if R occurs first. This contingency between behavior and its reinforcing consequences is the essence of operant conditioning. (As you will learn in later chapters, an important part of infants' development is their realization that they can influence their environment.) When R causes S^+ many times, the subject learns to make the R response more frequently because the R-S^+ relation has proven dependable. In our example, the baby sucks the tube again.

Our example is not a far-fetched one, because when researchers study babies they use the sucking response as R. Most babies suck rather slowly and inefficiently on laboratory tubes. However, if the tubes contain a sugar solution, the babies rapidly become efficient suckers, so we can infer both that the sugar solution is reinforcing to them and that they probably can learn by operant conditioning. But to be sure that they are in fact responding according to the laws of operant conditioning, it must be demonstrated that, when the contingency between sucking and receiving sugar is removed, their sucking rate will decline. If this happens, we know that the babies changed their sucking rates because the sucking was not met with reinforcement.

One study demonstrated that sucking rate of newborn infants can be increased by the delivery of sugar and decreased by its removal. The experimenter sounded a buzzer when tubes would deliver sugar; when the sugar was not forthcoming, the buzzer did not sound. He found that the babies sucked more when the buzzer sounded (Kron, 1966). The design of this study, like many operant conditioning studies, includes a combination of the operant conditioning model (the babies increased a response because of the sugar) and the classical model (two previously unrelated stimuli—the buzzer and the sugar—were connected).

The other investigators have reported the successful operant conditioning of newborns' sucking responses. One study reported that infants learned a more efficient sucking style in order to get sugar reinforcement than they used when they didn't receive a food reward (Bosack, 1973). In this instance, the form of their response as well as its rate was modified through learning. The other study (Lipsitt and Kaye, 1964) found that access to a regular rubber nipple rather than to a blunted one could reinforce the babies' sucking rate.

Hanus Papousek has developed a procedure for conditioning newborns that has become quite popular in American laboratories (Papousek, 1967). His procedure also brings about a combination of operant and classical conditioning. Papousek works with babies' rooting reflex (babies respond to a stroke on the cheek by turning their heads in the direction of the stroke: this is the rooting reflex) in an effort to teach them to make it in response to a bell. Classical conditioning would occur if this result were obtained by exposing the baby to a series of trials in which the bell preceded the stroking. But, as you will recall, the results of classical conditioning of newborns are inconclusive. So Papousek rewards any head turns that do occur by placing a sugar solution where infants can reach to suck and receive it if their heads are turned. This aspect of the procedure—reinforcing head turns—is operant conditioning.

There is strong evidence that newborns learn using the Papousek procedure (Papousek, 1967; Siqueland, 1968; Papousek, 1969; Clifton, Siqueland, and Lipsitt, 1972; Clifton, Meyers, and Solomons, 1972). Older infants learn more quickly than newborns (Papousek, 1967), perhaps because newborns' states are unpredictable and rapidly changing. One group that has taken account of infant state in its work reports that the efficiency of conditioning newborns with the Papousek procedure clearly depends on the subjects' state. According to their results, conditioning is most effective when the babies are awake and alert (Clifton, Siqueland, and Lipsitt, 1972; Clifton, Meyers, and Solomons, 1972).

Newborn infants can be conditioned, and they can learn complex schedules of reinforcement (Papousek and Bernstein, 1969; Bosack, 1973; Siqueland, 1968), but they probably do not learn as efficiently as they will when they are older. They are obviously *able* to order their experiences, and some psychologists believe that they actually do so.

Imprinting

Imprinting is a very simple type of early learning that depends heavily upon unlearned reactions to moving stimuli. It is the basis for a young animal's attachment to its parents. Imprinting is an important process because it plays an intimate role in social development. For example, the newly hatched duckling begins to follow the first moving object it encounters during the first day or so after hatching; normally, but not always, this object is the duckling's mother, and the following behavior helps keep the immature animal near the caregiving mother. Ducklings' imprinting processes have been extensively studied by the ethologist E. H. Hess (Hess, 1972), who has successfully imprinted ducklings on himself, wooden hunting decoys, and various other moving objects. Sheep, dogs, guinea pigs, and various species of birds that walk upon hatching imprint as well.

Imprinting qualifies as learning because it is a change in behavior—the start of the following behavior—as a result of experience—the exposure to a particular moving object. Research has established that imprinting can be altered by altering the first moving object that a naive newborn encounters. However, imprinting differs in an important way from conditioning because if imprinting does not occur within a certain interval during the newborn period, it will never occur. If a newly hatched duckling is kept caged for the first two days of life, and thus sees no moving object, it will never imprint. The crucial interval of time, called a *critical period,* seems to be specific to each species.

Human babies form attachments to their regular caregivers, and I will discuss these extensively in Chapter 5. But nothing as specific and inflexible as the following response of ducklings happens during the human newborn period. Some researchers have speculated that human infants imprint before birth to some aspect of their mother's biological being such as her sleep cycles (Anders, 1968). However, evidence for an imprinting process in human newborns is inadequate.

The Significance of Learning in Newborns

It is clear that babies are born with some capacity for learning, which means that they probably are making some connections between sounds and sights and such reinforcing events as feeding. Babies also probably make connections between their behavior and its reinforcing consequences. Perhaps they even detect the relations (although not as consistently) among the various stimuli that they passively experience. Because of this, apparently they do experience a meaningful world: the old model of the "blooming, buzzing confusion" is simply wrong.

Given that newborns learn better by operant conditioning than by classical conditioning, it seems safe to conclude that they most easily connect events in which they are participants. We will see in subsequent chapters that this excitement of "making things happen" is a powerful influence on learning and development of infants.

The success of operant conditioning in newborns has another implication: If babies can influence their reinforcing outcomes through their own acts, they probably do so often. The behavior of caregivers—perhaps even as investigators—is unconsciously modified in response to infants' behavior. If a baby stares intently at a display of bright, moving objects that happens to be a patio windchime, his father may move it indoors near his crib so that he may see it often. If he quiets from a vigorous fuss when his mother rocks him gently, she may begin to hold and rock him routinely at any sign of restlessness. On the other hand, if he stiffens uneasily when he is held for a long time, his family may do so less often. Caregivers learn through a baby's responses as he learns through theirs. This reciprocity is a cornerstone of the relationship of mutuality between newborns and their principal caregivers.

The learning process in newborns offers advantages to psychologists as well. Psychologists study how the infant's behavior changes in the presence of the stimuli they are using in their experiment. Babies' reactions to a stimulus tell us whether they can see (or otherwise sense) a given stimulus and can discriminate between two stimuli. For instance, we might condition a newborn's head-turning response to a flashing light stimulus according to the Papousek model. In a sense, her head-turning response is a form of communication: it communicates to us that she sees a certain stimulus. We can then substitute a dimmer light and observe the rate of head turning. If the infant continues to turn her head, we infer that she detects no difference between the two light stimuli. If she fails to turn her head to the dim light, we can infer that she detects a difference. Thus newborns' capacity for learning can become a tool for studying what they perceive. This is especially important for studies of perception in young infants who cannot give us any verbal indication of their perceptions.

The fact that newborns have a capacity for learning leads many caregivers to wonder what to teach them. Countless harassed parents have attempted to train their newborns' crying patterns. In fact, some parents tell themselves that if they ignore the crying of their child it will stop for lack of reinforcement. However, research has shown that crying is *not* readily stopped by this procedure (Bell and Ainsworth, 1972) because the causes of newborns' crying are complex, and many. As you will recall from Wolff's studies, babies sometimes cannot control their crying because it has a physiological cause. When their crying has a physiological cause, the most effective soothers are continuous vestibular stimuli—like rocking or wrapping in a blanket—that alter the functioning of their nervous systems in some way.

Crying notwithstanding, newborns do learn, and thus it would be possible to teach them some connections. But this seems premature, given that they are learning all the time in the natural course of events. By the time they are two or so, children from different socioeconomic classes show differences in many learning skills such as language and problem solving. Programs designed to reduce these differences abound, many of them aimed at older infants. Inevitably some will advocate that learning programs start for younger and younger children until even newborns will be enrolled as pupils. However one may feel about the controversy of "infant education," it must be acknowledged that the possibility of newborn education follows from the fact that newborns learn.

Communication Between Newborn and Caregiver

Newborn infants and their caregivers do not yet play the back and forth smiling and vocalizing "game" that will begin a month or two later. Most observers can judge whether a newborn's emotions are positive, negative, or neutral but can make no finer distinctions than that. Immediately after birth, an infant gives little evidence of feeling any real affection toward people or things. In general, the feelings of newborn human beings are an enigma to those around them.

One might conclude from this that caregivers cannot have any empathy for infants during the first crucial weeks of life. Indeed, many new parents are distressed by their lack of feelings for their newborn child. Other parents, however, respond to their infants enthusiastically and seem to feel a deep sense of comradeship with them. To some extent, difficult parental experiences arise from the parents' own needs and unrealistic expectations. But other possibilities should be considered as well. Do babies give cues about their feelings through their behavior that some parents can interpret whereas others cannot? Do some babies have an unusual means of giving signals about their needs—one that makes them difficult or impossible to discern?

These questions have not really been attacked by any concentrated program of research. However, some evidence exists that newborns may communicate with their caregivers through the unique quality of their cries. One study has found that about half of the mothers tested could distinguish their infants' cries from others during the first two days of life; after two days, all the mothers could do so (Formby, 1967).

Even though their cries are unique, the ability of newborns to communicate is limited. Although caregivers have a greater ability to communicate, they may be insensitive—especially in their first experiences with infants—to whatever clues their infants give about their feelings. An active dialogue does develop between most caregivers and infants in the second month. Because the newborn period is a challenging time for parents as well as infants—especially first-time parents—it would be valuable to have the best communication possible.

Individuality

Almost all of us have wondered at one time or another when our individual uniqueness as human beings starts. Parents search their babies' faces, bodies, and behavior for signs of family inheritance and special characteristics, yet each believes that his or her child is like no other. What is the reality?

Traits

So far in this chapter we have concentrated on behavior and characteristics that babies have in common. But babies are not entirely alike. Several studies have identified ways in which newborn infants differ from each other; from these Bee (1975) has made a list of the following six characteristics:-

1. *Vigor of responding.* Some infants react with forceful movement and crying to many stimuli. Others respond only to very intense stimuli.
2. *General activity.* Some babies are very active: they swing their arms, turn their heads, and twist their bodies. Others move little but appear to be very observant of their surroundings.

3. *Restlessness during sleep.* Some infants move quickly into a quiet, apparently deep sleep with little motion. Others wiggle and appear to sleep lightly.
4. *Irritability.* Some infants cry often for unknown reasons and are difficult to soothe. Others cry infrequently and are comforted readily.
5. *Habituation rate.* Newborns and young infants differ in the number of repetitions of a stimulus they customarily require before they stop responding. Presumably the fast habituators are better at focusing their attention on a particular experience.
6. *Cuddliness.* Some newborns like to be cuddled; other do not. Those who do not, remain still and appear unresponsive when they are picked up.

And I would add a seventh: newborns differ greatly in the amounts of time they spend in various states; this fact has profound implications for learning (Korner, 1971; Brown, 1964). Those newborns who have relatively long periods (several minutes) in the alert inactive state must learn more, and thus their experiences must have more meaning than those of infants who have few or short alert inactive periods. We have seen that babies react differently to stimuli depending on their state. All newborns have similar physical makeups, but they can respond very differently to stimuli. Some babies seem much more capable of restoring and maintaining a resting level of physiological functioning, whereas others show prolonged changes in heart rate and respiration when they react to stimulation (Crowell, 1967; Richmond, Lipton, and Steinschneider, 1962).

Korner has said that the underlying characteristic of an infant's individuality seems to be the ability to take in and integrate sensory stimuli. Some babies are fast stimulus processors whereas others are slower, in her view, and a very active baby may also process stimuli quickly, while a less active baby processes stimuli more slowly (Korner, 1971). This view has not been proven, but it is known that all infants have some method for handling stimulus "overload." Some cry; some fall asleep; some shift their attention.

Bee's list illustrates only some of the traits that are part of the "trait approach" in infant psychology. The main assumption behind this approach is that differences in behavior among infants are the product of the infants' own dispositions. If this assumption of personal dispositions is valid, individuals should maintain characteristic patterns as they mature. Some evidence does show that babies retain their individual characteristics beyond the newborn stage (Korner, 1971). Several other studies of infant personality begin when the infants are over one month of age and thus do not really prove the maintenance of personality traits beyond the newborn period (Bee, 1975, pp. 83–87).

Group Differences

Psychologists specializing in personality often look at patterns of traits that seem to clearly differentiate people according to groups. Commonly studied groups are the sexes, subcultures and races, and socioeconomic classes. When members of these groups consistently behave differently, there are two possible interpretations: (1) there are genetic differences between the groups that lead to the observed differences; (2) there are different patterns of experiences that lead to the differences between groups. Because newborn infants have had such a brief time to have any experiences outside of the womb, group differences are especially interesting.

Reliable sex differences in the newborn period are few. Females seem to mature physically at a faster rate than males; thus, at birth, various indicators of nervous system maturation show them to be more fully developed than male newborns. Males are bigger and heavier and they have a greater proportion of muscle tissue in their bodies than females. There is a greater incidence of birth complications before and during birth among males than among females. Many studies indicate that males are more active than females, and it is possible that this difference reflects physiological differences due to the males' greater experience of birth complications—in studies that do not eliminate subjects with birth complications (Maccoby and Jacklin, 1974). Few differences that exist between males and females seem to be biological in nature. However, since research has clearly shown that mothers treat male and female newborns differently during the first few days of life (Moss, 1967), we cannot rule out the possibility that these differences are learned.

Known socioeconomic-class differences in newborn infants are almost entirely a result of the higher incidence of stress before and during birth in lower classes. The apparent differences in functioning that do exist involve the level of maturation in the nervous system and muscular system as well as the reflex reactions. Examples of behaviors that appear to be more slow to develop in nonwhite races and lower-class infants are lifting the head from a prone position and using the two eyes in coordination (Bee, 1975). The birth stresses that lead to these problems are often associated with inadequate nutrition and care of the mother during pregnancy. Although the possibility of genetically based group differences cannot be summarily dismissed, race and class differences very likely relate to these prenatal environmental differences.

Freedman and Freedman have reported findings that seem to indicate differences among infants that could be attributed to race. They compared Chinese-American and Caucasian newborns on several behavioral and neurological signs and found that the Caucasian babies were more changeable in their moods and less easily soothed than the Chinese-American babies. Chinese-American infants' habituated more rapidly to a light shone in their faces. When a cloth was placed over their faces, Chinese-American babies were impassive, whereas the Caucasian babies thrashed about in an attempt to rid themselves of it (Freedman and Freedman, 1969). But how should these results be interpreted? Although the biological functioning of Chinese-American newborns *may* differ from that of Caucasian newborns, we do not have proof that a difference exists. We also do not know whether the mothers of the two groups treat their newborns differently. As yet there is little other information about race comparisons for newborns, although some findings are available for older infants (see Chapter 6). In general, when differences between groups show up in the absence of any clear theory or any replication with other samples, they should be interpreted cautiously.

Environmental Arrangements for the Newborn

New parents are very aware of a newborn's patterns of sleeping and waking and eating. For one thing, their own sleeping and eating patterns are usually quite disrupted by the arrival of their first child. Also, the time they must devote to satisfying the basic biological needs of a newborn serves to emphasize the importance of this new member of the family. Naturally, parents are concerned about caring for their babies day to day and they wonder what they can do to insure their comfort. Do babies prefer noise or quiet, light or darkness, and so on?

Stimulation Level

In my earlier mention of individual differences, I said that most newborns do something to regulate the amount of stimulation they receive. All babies habituate to stimuli as they become familiar with them. And, as you may recall, some simply fall asleep when stimulation becomes too much for them, whereas others fuss until they tire or someone removes the stimulation. Although the arrangement of a room probably does affect babies, the presence of noise, clutter, and light is not nearly as disruptive to their sleep as many people suppose. On the other hand, a sharp change in stimulation—which occurs, for example, when an infant is taken from a noisy party into the silence and darkness of the bedroom—may cause fussing.

An example of the effects of changing a baby's stimulation level is an incident that occurred when my husband and I brought our newborn home

Figure 2-7. *An infant dozes placidly, oblivious to the activity going on around him. (Photo courtesy of Emilio A. Mercado.)*

to a relatively quiet apartment. She had spent some days in a noisy, brightly lit hospital nursery with different people coming and going frequently, and, when we placed her in a quiet bedroom of our apartment and turned off the light, she started to bellow. After she had cried for two nights, I realized that the very quiet we had created for her was probably the problem. We brought her out to the well-lit living room, where the television was on and the neighbors were visiting, and there, amid the general clatter, she abruptly fell asleep. Thereafter we always allowed her to fall asleep in the living room and then carried her to her room.

Those infants who react to increased stimulation by waking and fussing may prefer quiet, dim sleeping quarters, but most infants will adapt to the stimulation of their surroundings, provided that it is consistent day to day.

Thus, parents need not feel concerned if they can't give the baby a quiet, private room in which to sleep. This is a luxury that most of the world's families do not have and that babies do not require.

Number of Caregivers

There is increasing emphasis in our society on the right of women to pursue a life apart from raising a family if they choose. The question of how the new patterns of living that many women are choosing affect older infants is discussed extensively in Chapter 5. Many working mothers decide to continue their work uninterrupted except for those days actually required for childbirth. This means that their newborns are being cared for some of the time by their fathers, other relatives, or hired caregivers. Very little is known about how these care arrangements affect newborns' development. We do know that babies are not attached at birth to their mothers, as they will be later. It is also clear that newborns are not afraid of strangers (see Chapter 5). Most newborns seem to progress normally if they are cared for by others rather than by their biological mothers. Although the long-range effects of such arrangements are not known, there is no evidence that they are harmful. Keeping the care arrangements reasonably stable seems to be more important to babies' welfare than their number of caregivers. Clearly, research is needed to explore more fully the effects of various care arrangements on newborns.

Scheduling

Parents are confronted immediately after the birth of their baby with the question of how to plan the care that it will need. Should they try to figure out when the baby is hungry, tired, wet, or overstimulated? Or should they try to teach the baby to adopt a regular schedule of sleeping and eating? Is one way better than another for an infant's biological needs? Most current books that give advice on caring for babies suggest that babies be allowed to establish their own cycles and that caregivers try to adhere to them (see, for example, Spock, 1976). Because most parents have responsibilities apart from those of raising children, a compromise usually must be made that satisfies their needs as well as those of their children.

Gaensbauer and Emde (1973) studied how the scheduling of feedings affected the cycle of states in the newborns—theirs was an especially important study because states influence learning. They found that the total time spent in the alert inactive (or, in their words, awake-alert) state was no different for 30 newborn babies fed according to a four-hour schedule than for 30 fed on demand. However, the babies' patterns of sleeping and waking differed. Schedule-fed babies were awake and alert just before, during, and for a short time after feeding, whereas babies fed on demand were drowsy or asleep at feeding time and active before feeding. Demand-fed newborns were awake and fussy during the hour before feedings. Although the authors did not report this as a conclusion, it appears that the schedule-fed infants were in the fussy state less often than the demand-fed infants.

A regular schedule that fits a baby's general cycle seems thus to be most advisable. In this way, caregivers can prevent their baby from experiencing the long periods of frustration that lead to high states of arousal. They also can avoid the practice of waking a sleeping baby abruptly for feeding because babies will adapt their waking and sleeping patterns to a relatively consistent schedule. Babies fed in this way will probably be awake during the feeding time and thus will be able to interact more with their caregivers.

Soothing a Fussy Baby

Crying is babies' first social communication with those around them, and a great deal of caregiving effort seems to be devoted to interpreting it and satisfying the need that it communicates.

Most people think that a crying newborn must be either hungry or in pain. As I mentioned earlier, Peter Wolff (1966) reports these two causes among the most common ones for the episodes of crying he observed in his extensive study of four newborn infants in their own homes. Wolff also describes a spontaneous cry that occurs periodically and awakens the infant. Wolff attributes this to "nervous system discharge." Being too hot or too cold is a fourth cause for babies' crying. Research in the pediatrics field indicates that these causes of crying may lead to different types of cries—something mothers have long suspected.

Stopping the Crying.   Whatever the cause of the crying, how to stop it is of major concern to most parents. This problem has been studied by a number of researchers, whose findings agree with the informal lore that caregivers of many cultures have drawn on for centuries.

Babies' crying can be soothed in two ways: by being picked up and by receiving some form of continuous stimulation. We will consider them in turn.

Most crying newborns will quiet both their loud cries and their agitated movements if they are picked up. Studies by Korner and her associates demonstrate that putting crying infants to the caregiver's shoulder is very effective in causing them to stop crying: this action produces vestibular stimulation, which promotes visual alertness and thus may make them more aware of the environment (Korner and Grobstein, 1966; Korner and Thoman, 1970).

Many parents are afraid that, if they pick their babies up every time they cry, they will create spoiled children who are unable to tolerate frustration. The evidence does *not* justify this common concern. Researchers have found that the infants who are not comforted in the opening weeks of life are those who become fussy when they are a year old and beyond (Bell and Ainsworth, 1972).

Continuous stimulation soothes babies by keeping one of their senses constantly active. In many cultures, newborns are routinely swaddled (wrapped in cloth), so that they receive continuous all-over tactile stimulation. Many Americans find swaddling a distasteful notion because restriction of a baby's movement seems to be a limitation of his freedom and, therefore, an invasion of his humanity. However, swaddling is an effective technique that appears to comfort infants (Stone and Church, 1973, p. 17).

Brackbill has studied continuous stimulation of crying newborns under controlled conditions. She has reported that, the more senses that receive continuous stimulation at the same time, the calmer babies become. If babies are swaddled they become soothed; if at the same time they hear a steady tone, they are soothed even more, and so on. The infants' heart rates slow and they stop crying, which further reveals the calming effect of the stimulation (Brackbill, 1970, 1975). But the stimulation must be continuous and regular to be effective. Intermittent stimulation—like a randomly flashing light or a recorded symphony—is not as effective. It has also been found that the low tones are more effective than higher ones (Bench, 1969). Brackbill has speculated that the continuous stimulus is so soothing because of some innate reaction by the nervous system to it.

Nature, Nurture, and the Newborn: A Summary

At the beginning of this chapter I told you that there are philosophical reasons as well as practical ones for studying newborns. Now that we have looked at some scientific and practical matters, I would like to return to more philosophical matters. Psychologists generally agree that most of human behavior is a product of complex interaction between inborn forces (nature) and the experiences our environments provide (nurture). Interaction means, not only that both nature and nurture play important roles, but also that one influences the other. Thus, an infant may be born with an unusually high activity level, but her experiences may determine whether she channels her energy into developing athletic skills, managing a demanding business, or having learning problems that are followed by antisocial aggression. Another infant may grow up in a home and community environment rich in sources of stimulation, but, if he lacks enough inborn capacity to learn from such a resource, it may not have much impact.

You may well be wondering why I am writing about the nature-nurture controversy if I regard it as a pseudo-problem. However, I think that a discussion of it can bring the information that we have about newborns into better focus. Sometimes the extreme either/or phrasing of an issue helps us discern the implications of what we know to be true. Let us see how this works for the material contained in this chapter.

First, consider what the newborn infant would have to be like if either extreme, nature *or* nurture, were correct. If human behavior is primarily the product of nature, then we would expect to see evidence of this at birth. We also would expect a person to remain uninfluenced by experience throughout life. Individual differences should be discernible at birth and should be demonstrably related to individual differences observed at later ages. Newborn behavior should be predictable from some aspect of the makeup of family members. If, on the other hand, newborn behavior is primarily the product of nurture, then newborns should be very much alike, and it should be demonstrable that they can be influenced by their experiences. As you have probably concluded already, the evidence partly supports both sides.

Newborns are remarkably alike in some ways. They all have good sensory capacities and a repertoire of reflex behaviors. These reflex behaviors are somewhat less flexible than the learned versions acquired later. Thus, for example, the reflex grasp looks much the same from baby to baby, whereas the voluntary grasps of older infants reflect a range of personal grasping styles. All newborns get their nourishment through sucking in some fashion. By the last third of the first year, however, they obtain nourishment in a tremendous variety of ways and show personal styles as they do so. The variety in their behaviors increases as infants mature.

Despite the apparent similarity among infants, their activity levels and reactions to stimuli show clear individual differences. These differences are probably inborn because they are apparent long before nurture could have time to have any effect. Further, these initial differences in temperament do much to mold infants' later environmental experiences.

This interplay between (apparently) inborn characteristics and the baby's environment illustrates the interaction of nature and nurture. We have seen evidence of interaction throughout this chapter. Babies are apparently born with the capacity to learn when they are sufficiently alert and inactive. However, they differ widely in the amount of time that they are in this alert inactive state and, thus, in how much they actually learn. Another example applies to caregiving. Although evidence is inadequate, I would expect that those newborns who are cuddly are cuddled more than those who are not. These labels of "cuddly" and "uncuddly" may create a pattern of interaction between caregiver and infant that persists for years. Still another example is the possible relation between speed of physical maturation and alternate ways of perceiving the environment. A baby who cannot yet crawl may end up spending more time staring at, and thus learning about, interesting objects in his surroundings than will his crawling contemporary who moves about too fast for this. An important theme is found in all these examples. Inherited tendencies can be changed because their ultimate influence is dependent on the environmental response they receive.

In sum, infants enter the world with some definite characteristics. From the start they can learn through experience, and, in fact, we should presume that they do. Although their immature bodily functions begin with irregular cycles, they become more regular until babies establish somewhat predictable routines. Babies are strongly influenced by their state. When they are alert and inactive, they are most responsive to environmental events, but they are much less so when they are either more or less aroused than this.

Chapter 3

Learning and Perception

This chapter is about babies' knowledge of the world. We will discuss several aspects of *perception,* the process by which we find out about our surroundings using information that comes to us through our sense organs. When we find out what babies are aware of, we naturally question how much of it they remember, what types of connections they can make between one thing and another, and whether what they know can have an effect on their world. These are questions about *memory* and *learning.* As you will recall from Chapter 2, newborn babies possess enough perceptual and learning skill to give them a great deal of information about the world and to help them learn from it. This chapter deals with how these basic processes develop over the course of infancy.

The chapter begins with a review of what is known about attention, the most basic of perceptual processes. The next section takes up the elementary memory process of habituation. Then, in the three succeeding sections we will discuss the infant's capacity for learning by three different processes: classical conditioning, operant conditioning, and discrimination learning. On the basis of this information, we will attempt to draw conclusions about how infants subjectively experience the environment and events that surround them. Finally, we will consider modeling, a more complex form of learning.

While reading this chapter, you should try to keep in mind the questions that are addressed by the studies I am summarizing. What do babies notice and what do they ignore? To answer this question researchers have tried to learn how characteristics and movements of objects influence a baby's attention. Armed with this information, they have turned to the question of whether babies can remember their experiences and whether they can apply them to their future experiences.

As you will discover, there are no absolute answers. *Some* babies make *some* connections *some* of the time between *some* events, and many of the

75

studies upon which this chapter builds are attempts to specify the "somes." For example, what types of objects, timing, and environmental contexts will foster accurate perception and successful learning? Are some babies better at some of these processes than others?

Researchers have tried to discover how infants view their surroundings as well. Is the visual world an organized field of objects set into backgrounds and spread out in space? Do objects retain their familiar identities as they move? Can babies organize their memory stores to accurately retain the sequence in which things happen? Are babies aware that much of what they see is outside their control? We will be interested to find the ways in which an average baby's view of the world is the same as that of an older child or an adult.

Attention

Before we can seriously consider what infants know about the world, we have to know what aspects of it attract and hold their attention. Clearly, no one absorbs all of the information that is to be had from the environment; instead we pay attention to some things and ignore others, and thus are aware of only a part of what goes on around us. Our knowledge of the world is based on the information we get from this small part of the world.

How well we understand the objects and events that surround us depends heavily on our attention to the details that clarify their nature. Some meaningful details are divisions between objects and the space that surrounds them, cues that tell us how far away various objects are, and any changes in stimulation that might alert us that our environment is changing. If we discover what attracts and holds infants' attention, then we will know the elementary material upon which they are building a concept of their surroundings. The problem of attention thus qualifies as the best starting place for a study of the infant's perceptual development and ability to learn.

What Interests a Baby: Indicators of Attention

Interest in the problem of attention immediately raises the question of how to discern what babies are aware of at any given moment. When psychologists study attention in adults, they rely on the adult subjects to report what they see and hear; the psychologists then relate their impressions to the physiological indicators of attention (for example, where were they looking when their heart rate sped up). But babies cannot report their impressions. So their attention is measured by *indicator responses,* which are any responses the baby gives only while paying attention to a stimulus. Like the adult's word or phrase, these responses tell the observer that something has captured the baby's attention.

Researchers use several indicator responses in their studies of infant attention. A popular indicator for studies of visual attention is *fixation time.* The observer watches the infant's eyes to see when some stimulus is reflected in them. Because this happens only when the infant's eyes are focused on that object, it reliably indicates attention. Researchers can use a timing device to accurately measure how long the infant focuses on the stimulus and thus record the fixation time. This has proven to be a relatively reliable and highly convenient measure in studies of visual attention (see, for example, Fantz, 1963; Kagan, 1970).

Many infants signal their excitement when they are processing new information by smiling and making a brief one-syllable utterance or two. Thus, if the babies are placed in a fairly confined experimental situation where they can experience only one stimulus at a time, the investigator can equate vocalizing and smiling with the baby's fascination with the stimulus. Attention has been measured very successfully in this way (McCall, 1972). However, babies respond to complex stimuli (which take some time to comprehend) with a period of sober regard before smiling or cooing. Researchers have interpreted this to mean that an infant is absorbing or making sense of the stimulus before signifying recognition with a smile and delighted sound (Schultz and Zigler, 1970).

Until they are about four months of age, young infants cannot look or listen intently while they are sucking on a breast, bottle, or other object. Instead they will briefly pause or interrupt their sucking if an interesting object captures their attention. Researchers use this interruption of sucking as a measure of attention (Sameroff, 1970). But sucking interruption best pinpoints the moment attention is captured rather than the prolonged information processing that may occur next (Mendelson and Haith, 1975). Indeed, this distinction between the momentary capturing of babies' attention and the time that passes while they process the information is an important one, to which we will return.

The most controversial indicator of attention is a momentary change in heart rate. Adults and older children experience a momentary *decrease* in heart rate when they focus their attention on a specific source of stimulation, such as a tone or a visual display (Lewis et al., 1966). However, the heart rate of most newborns *increases* when their interest is captured by a stimulus. Some investigators have concluded that the human response to a new stimulus changes over the course of the first weeks of life from a defensive reaction to an active processing of information (Clifton and Meyers, 1969; Berg, 1974). Others have concluded that because heart rate varies greatly from one person to another it is difficult to establish a clear, unambiguous relation between heart rate and any psychological process (Porges, Arnold, and Forbes, 1973; Porges, Stamps, and Walters, 1974).

Despite the problems of interpretation, a slowing of heart rate has been considered a sign of attention in several studies of babies past two weeks of age. There are some good reasons for this. First, this measure does not require the judgment of an observer and is thus more objective than some other alternatives. Second, in some studies heart-rate deceleration is reliably associated with presentation of a stimulus (Lewis et al., 1966; Meyers and Cantor, 1967; Clifton and Meyers, 1969; Brotsky and Kagan, 1971; Berg, 1972; Moffitt, 1973; Sameroff, 1973; Berg, 1974). A third advantage is that heart rate can be measured in studies directed at any of the senses, and this facilitates useful comparisons.

Heart rate and fixation time to visual stimuli are the two most frequently used indicators of attention, although smiling and vocalization are occasionally used as well. Other attention indicators include the changes in the dilation of the pupils (Fitzgerald, 1968), galvanic skin response (Stechler, Bradford, and Levy, 1966), and changes in brain wave pattern (Karmel, Hoffmann, and Fegy, 1974).

It is important to distinguish between babies' first response to a stimulus, and their continued interest in it. In initial orienting responses, a baby may be surprised or even startled. The startle response usually indicates that the infant is processing information about the stimulus and will respond in a more reflective (rather than reflexive) manner. Some studies carefully differentiate babies' reactions to the onset of their awareness of a stimulus from their continuing reactions; other studies do not. Because these two processes may have different causes, this distinction is important: ignoring it may account for inconsistencies in findings (see Cohen, 1973).

The Determinants of Visual Attention

Now that we know what signals a baby's interest, let us consider visual attention in infants: What characteristics of objects and events capture and hold their interest? These characteristics are important because they constitute a baby's first picture of the world and are the first step toward learning.

Contour, Contrast, and Movement.   During their first months of life babies are attracted most to such definite contours as corners and other changes in direction of geometric figures (Spears, 1964; Nelson and Kessen, 1967; Salapatek, 1969; Karmel, 1969a; Bond, 1972). Babies scan geometric figures from angle to angle and along the edges, a pattern of viewing that would identify these figures as familiar or novel shapes to an adult (Salapatek, 1969). Experiments have demonstrated that babies younger than four months look most at the edges of dark figures printed on light background—possibly because of the contrast between the dark edge of a figure and its lighter surroundings. Some investigators suggest that babies find definite contours interesting simply because, like those of all human beings, their mental patterns encourage them to process visual information about the environment that has high contrast (Karmel, 1969b). Whatever the reason for this preference, it may have adaptive value. When babies pay attention to a series of contours that—taken in sequence—will outline the shape of an object, possibly they are aware of that object *as an object* and not merely as a jumble of unrelated impressions. But because babies cannot report their impressions, researchers must be satisfied with a reasonable and defensible conjecture: when young babies look around, they are most aware of objects and shapes—such as those in the patterns of wallpaper, clothing fabrics, mobiles, toys, and ordinary household objects.

Results of some studies indicate that infants prefer to look at forms with curved lines rather than those with sharp angles (Lang, 1966; Fantz and Miranda, 1975). But other evidence indicates that babies focus on angles while they are scanning objects (Salapatek, 1968). Taken together, the evidence suggests that young babies examine their environments in a manner that includes first picking out the forms with some angles, and then, once a visual field containing various forms is defined, "processing" those with curved outlines to a greater degree than those with angular outlines. But as yet no study has established this.

Movement is another visual feature of the environment that intrigues infants. Even newborns can briefly focus on and follow a moving object (see p. 49). This skill improves rapidly over the first few weeks; by the second month infants are skilled at following moving lights and seem to derive great pleasure from doing so (Vietze, Friedman, and Foster, 1974). This awareness from birth of motion in the environment has obvious survival value: the infant is immediately alerted to possible threats. This trait also gives babies valuable information about how people and objects move, which helps to develop their understanding of the environment.

One glance at the brightly colored toys for babies would cause us to assume that color influences their attention. But so far this question has been studied very little, and results of one study indicate that color has no effect on infants (Spears, 1966).

In sum, young infants are interested in moving objects with definite forms. They examine objects and events by an active scanning process that focuses on the informative details in the environment (Haith, 1968; Salapatek and Kessen, 1966). They rapidly shift their attention from some details to others, and this may help them to notice similarities and differences in the details of the objects around them (Ruff and Turkewitz, 1975). Babies could not make these comparisons if they had to reflect slowly on any one detail because their memories are not developed sufficiently to enable them to remember details for the lengthy stretches of time that this process would entail.

The Role of Novelty.   As they develop, infants begin to be drawn to objects that differ from those they have experienced. This attraction toward novel objects rather than familiar ones has been demonstrated in several studies of infants ranging in age from two to twelve months (e.g., Fantz, 1965; Schaffer and Perry, 1969; Weizmann, Cohen, and Pratt, 1971; Wetherford and Cohen, 1973).

Why is a novel object more attractive than a familiar one? Apparently, for babies familiarity breeds boredom. Their awareness of novel objects around them is very beneficial because it causes them to learn connections between the objects they know and those they discover. How well they do so is the topic of subsequent sections.

But babies do not begin life with this preference for the new over the old. Babies younger than two months of age seem to prefer familiar stimuli to novel ones (Hunt, 1970; Weizmann, Cohen, and Pratt, 1971), and prematurely born infants continue to prefer familiarity for a longer time than full-term infants do (Miranda, 1970). This characteristic of both young babies and premature babies suggests that some built-in process that is made active by biological growth may orient us toward novelty. But the process is not yet known. The sequence of preferences, first for familiarity and then for novelty, may monitor how much stimulation we receive. It may be that initially, when almost everything is entirely new, infants ward off excessive stimuli by favoring the familiar. With experience, they may come to sense the characteristics of the normal environment, and novelty may become more interesting. Several studies suggest that older infants prefer not only novel visual experiences but also novel physical experiences as well. When confronted with a variety of toys or other objects, babies in the last half of the first year reach for, crawl to, and manipulate the more novel ones (Hutt, 1967; Ross, Rheingold, and Eckerman, 1972; Ross, 1974).

But what defines novelty for a baby? It appears that a novel event can be a new situation or simply a new arrangement of previously encountered elements that counters the baby's expectations. For example, a baby is quite accustomed to hearing his mother's voice as he sees her move her lips. Aided by electronic equipment, one investigator set up a situation in which the mother's voice seemed to come from a stranger's face while the stranger's voice seemed to come from the mother's face. The babies' attention was captivated by these incongruous events (Bower, 1965b). So, as you can see, novel combinations of familiar stimuli hold interest for infants.

Jerome Kagan has presented an integrated overview of infant attention that takes account of the changes that occur over the first eighteen months of life (Kagan, 1969, 1970). According to his view, in the first two months biology directs the baby's visual attention. The young baby enjoys watching objects and events that change frequently (for example, objects that have an obvious light-dark contrast), that move, and that have definite contours (which are apparent because of the contrast). Kagan says that this attraction to contrast, contour, and movement is a property of the developing central nervous system.

In his view, after some months of experience, infants develop *schemas*— simplified mental representations of situations that they have experienced repeatedly. To form a schema, the baby abstracts the most basic sensory elements of a frequent experience. For instance, a schema for the human face would be an outline sketch of two eyes, a nose, and a mouth. Once they have formed these schemas for familiar events, babies direct their interest according to schemas: they come to prefer to look at events that differ moderately from their schemas. Kagan believes that babies direct their attention to events that offer interesting changes *from their schemas* rather than simply attending to changes of any kind.

However, the schema does not copy the stimulus as a photograph would. Instead the schema reduces the stimulus to the basic elements that identify it—for example, a bottle might be seen by an infant simply as a hard object that gives milk. The existence of schemas cannot be proven because they cannot be observed by anyone except the baby who devises them. Kagan postulated the existence of schemas to explain some of his findings. He had discovered that babies' interest in objects depends, not simply upon an object's strangeness, but rather upon how different it is from a *familiar* object. How much the new object varies from a familiar schema is called its *discrepancy from schema.* The discrepancy hypothesis suggests that babies older than two months of age prefer to look at objects according to their dissimilarity to an established schema.

Kagan initially developed this hypothesis to explain why babies in the middle of the first year choose to look at a picture of a slightly irregular human face rather than at either a completely regular face or one that is severely distorted. Kagan used experimental crib mobiles to test his theory more generally. Each of over 100 babies was exposed to a standard mobile at home for 30 minutes a day, so that the baby would create a schema for it. When the babies went to Kagan's laboratory, they were shown another mobile that was either identical to or different from the one they saw at home. There were varying degrees of difference: some babies saw a mobile that was almost identical to the first, some saw one that was somewhat different, and so on, with some babies seeing mobiles that were radically different from the first. Kagan found that the babies did look more at mobiles that were moderately different from their familiar mobile than they did at those that were either identical to or drastically different from it.

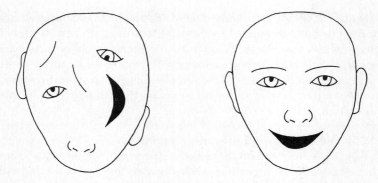

Figure 3-1.   *At six months of age, babies prefer to look at a picture of a slightly irregular human face rather than one that is regular (right) or extremely distorted (left). Changes in infants' attention that occur with age have been studied extensively by Jerome Kagan. (Adapted from "The Determinants of Attention in the Infant," by Jerome Kagan.* American Scientist, 50, May 1970. Used by permission.)

For their first year of life, babies continue to prefer moderately discrepant events, but the total length of time they look at these events declines and then increases again. The reason for decline, Kagan says, is that the relevant schemas are becoming more and more familiar so that more discrepancy is required before an object seems novel. But, as the first birthday approaches, babies' developing cognitive abilities encourage them to try to interpret the discrepant events they encounter. Thus, according to Kagan, they increase their looking time to ponder the meaning of the discrepant event. Infants probably are wary or distressed when they are exposed to markedly incongruous stimuli for which they have no interpretive context because, despite their efforts, they cannot understand them (Kagan, 1974; Perry, 1973).

Thomas (1973) presents major criticism of Kagan's discrepancy hypothesis: he asks, if babies prefer a moderately unusual event, why do so many babies pay attention to either very unusual or very familiar events instead? He argues that, although Kagan's hypothesis may account for how long most babies will look at objects with certain characteristics, it fails to predict whether a particular baby would always prefer all moderately discrepant events. According to Thomas, too many babies prefer either the least or the most discrepant stimulus instead of the moderately discrepant stimulus, and recent data support this position (Jones-Molfese, 1972).

This controversy is sure to continue because babies' awareness is crucial to our understanding of them. Kagan's hypothesis is appealing because it can organize many findings. However, perhaps the process babies follow when they pay attention to one stimulus rather than another is not that clear-cut. Possibly different babies prefer to look at different things. Indeed, wide individual differences in attention patterns exist, so our efforts to make clear generalizations about the causes of attention face many complications.

Other investigators have studied face stimuli similar to those used by Kagan. One interesting study used a discrimination learning situation to find out what features of a face were most essential to an infant's recognition of it. Eyes were found to be the most important feature (Caron et al., 1973). Another experimenter used photographs to acquaint infants with the various angles at which a face can be seen and found that infants four months old had difficulty recognizing the face later (Cornell, 1974). These findings suggest that young infants' recognition of human faces depends on very specific and concrete characteristics that are clearly apparent to them from their first encounter with a face.

Infants ordinarily experience the faces of those who are important to them in animation: their parents smile and talk to them or respond enthusiastically to their behavior. It is reassuring, then, that results of studies using moving human faces indicate that infants attend to them more than they do to still photographs (Wilcox and Clayton, 1968; Carpenter, 1974). Babies also discriminate between their mothers' faces and those of manikins, which is understandable: mothers are familiar and manikins are not. Possibly because of the strangeness of manikin faces, babies look longer at them (Carpenter, 1974). Whether Kagan's interpretations of infant attention are correct or not, it is clear that all kinds of faces are interesting to babies.

The Complexity Controversy.   Another major hypothesis in the study of infant attention relates to the complexity of objects and events. Although complexity of a given stimulus is difficult to define, most psychologists agree that it is determined by the number of elements in a patterned experience, the number of contrasts, and the predictability inherent in the pattern of organization (Fantz, 1965; Brennan, Ames, and Moore, 1966; Thomas, 1965; Greenberg, 1971; Moffett, 1969). Some evidence from studies done in the mid-1960s to the early 1970s seemed to indicate that infants past the first month look most at stimuli that are relatively complex, and that they grow to appreciate complexity more over the first half year of life (Brennan, Ames, and Moore, 1966; Greenberg, 1971; Greenberg and Weizmann, 1971; Greenberg and O'Donnell, 1972). The results of one study indicate that this preference for increasing complexity can be predicted by a baby's age from conception (Miranda, 1970).

Other researchers have tried to find out what specific details of stimulus displays make them attractive to babies. Both the number of elements and the number of angles in geometric patterns have a demonstrated influence on babies' preferences. Babies prefer objects with more elements (Moffett, 1969) and an irregular polygon with an intermediate number of angles (Hershenson, Munsinger, and Kessen, 1965). Still other studies show that babies' apparent preference for complexity might be related to their preference for unpredictability (Collins, Kessen, and Haith, 1972; Charlesworth, 1966), or number of directions of a line (Ruff and Birch, 1974), or amount of contour (Karmel, 1974; Greenberg and Blue, 1975), or element size (Fantz and Fasan, 1975). These varied findings suggest that the complexity concept needs more careful study. Thomas (1973) suggests that we would understand babies' attentional preferences better if we focused more on specific characteristics of stimuli rather than on what we think these characteristics add up to.

This discussion about which characteristics of a stimulus attract the infant's attention raises a related question. How many characteristics of a stimulus can infants attend to at once? For some types of complex learning, one must recognize the combination of characteristics that defines a stimulus as a member of a larger group—for example, we learn that all human beings have certain characteristics. Thus, before we can assert that infants can do such complex learning, we must establish that they can attend to separate characteristics and combinations of characteristics. One study that separated stimuli by their number of dimensions demonstrated that, as babies age, they prefer objects with increasingly more characteristics (Jones-Molfese, 1972). Results of another study indicate that operant conditioning (see Chapter 2) can be used to train babies to attend to more than one aspect of a stimulus (Watson and Danielson, 1969). Both learning and maturation seem to play a part in the baby's developing preference for objects with an increasing variety of characteristics.

Before we leave the subject of visual attention, let us briefly consider two other important points. First, the qualities that cause infants to look at a stimulus initially may differ from those that will hold their attention. One researcher attempted to measure attention-getting and attention-holding separately and found that they did indeed have different determinants (Cohen, 1972). Probably many studies of fixation time that intend to find answers to questions on attention-holding are actually gathering data about attention-getting. Research that explores that distinction is clearly needed. In the meantime, you should keep the difference in mind as you consider the diverse findings about what attracts babies' attention.

Second, various aspects of the environment may affect infants differently depending on their state of awareness. (We have discussed this idea in relation to newborns in Chapter 2.) It has been found that infants who have just been fed or who are alert and inactive are willing to look at novel stimuli longer (Giacoman, 1971; Wolff, 1965). Newborns' attention time is clearly shortened if their mothers received medication during pregnancy; it also is shortened by any other obstetrical event that results in their having lower Apgar scores (Stechler, 1964; Lewis et al., 1967). One experiment has established that the amount of time some one- and three-month-old infants spent each day in the waking alert state could predict the total time they would spend looking at stimuli (Moss and Robson, 1970).

The fact that babies (and all human beings as well) have different patterns of paying attention has important implications. First, researchers must make an effort to assure that the infants they study are alert when they receive stimuli to which they are expected to respond. Second, the wide variation in patterns of attention probably means that babies also differ in how much they learn from experience—partly because they are taking in different amounts of information from their experiences. Finally, because most experimenters in recent years have disqualified nonalert babies from their studies, their data clearly do not apply to all babies. After considering this possibility, two psychologists have recommended that data be gathered for both the alert and the nonalert babies (Lewis and Johnson, 1971).

Attention in the Auditory and Other Senses

The work done on infant attention has been heavily weighted toward visual experiences, so little is known about what engages infants' other senses. Some evidence shows that 4- to 11-month-old infants prefer complex sounds composed of several frequencies to simpler sounds (Mendel, 1968). One study also indicates that five-month-old female infants favor a sequence of tones moderately different from a sequence they have heard over the familiar sequence itself *or* a very different sequence (Melson and McCall, 1970). These findings suggest that babies may find the same types of sights and sounds attractive. But we would be premature to conclude that such a parallel really exists until much more research has been done.

Several studies clearly demonstrate that between one and six months of age babies learn to tell speech and nonspeech sounds apart and to discriminate among various speech sounds such as vowels, consonants, and phonemes (Morse, 1972; Eimas et al., 1971; Moffit, 1971; Trehub, 1973). Although this information does not directly apply to the problem of attention, we can reason that, if two sounds can be discriminated, they must first be singled out and attended to as entities. It makes sense to suppose that attention is selective and focused in the auditory sphere just as it is in the visual. But only extensive research can answer the question of how this selection is made.

Summary of Attention

What aspects of their environments are babies most aware of? A survey of the studies on infant visual attention reveals that young babies notice a difference between objects and background and that they notice changes. Initially they concentrate on familiar objects, noting only such dramatic changes as the sudden movement of an object. Soon, however, they begin to compare familiar objects with new objects that bear some sort of similarity to the familiar ones. Then, as babies mature, they enjoy more and more novelty, probably because they can use their past experience to understand the newer experiences. Their nervous systems also are developing, so they are becoming capable of experiencing several aspects of a stimulus simultaneously.

These generalizations tell us something about what babies are aware of, but they do not tell us how babies put this information together or how well they remember it. In the next sections we will consider these questions.

Habituation

If a stimulus is repeated over and over again in a short time period, we tend to stop reacting to it: for example, we soon stop hearing the annoying ticking of a new clock, the unfamiliar sounds of a strange place. As you will recall from Chapter 2, this reaction to a repeated stimulus is called *habituation*. In Chapter 2, we learned that some investigators have reported habituation in newborns. In the weeks beyond the newborn period, the efficiency and reliability of the habituation phenomenon increases. This section is about the details and the meaning of this change.

Most commonly, habituation is interpreted as a rudimentary memory (Miller, Turnure, and Cohen, 1970; Mussen, Congor, and Kagan, 1974; Pancratz and Cohen, 1970). It is thought that, if a baby stops responding to a repeated stimulus in the way he did when it was first presented, he must have come to recognize the sound, light flash, or other event as being the same as some earlier event. This implies that he has retained a representation of the earlier event—a memory. A baby who no longer reacts to the tenth repetition of a sound must be comparing it to the earlier repetitions of the sound to know they are the same.

If habituation implies a memory process, then it ought to follow the ordinary laws of memory. In particular, if a second stimulus is presented to babies during the repetitions of the original stimulus, the new stimulus should interfere with their memory of the first and should cause them to forget the first. Then, when they encounter the first again, they should respond to it as if it were new. One study demonstrates that this interference process does occur with visual geometric stimuli (Miller, Turnure, and Cohen, 1970), but more work of this kind is needed.

As we discussed in Chapter 2, habituation is a process of "getting used to" a repeated stimulus and, as such, is evidence for the existence of a rudimentary memory. However, habituation must not be confused with mere fatigue of the receptor organs, which causes failure to respond as well. When fatigue is the cause of failure to respond, introduction of a novel stimulus will still not cause the organ to respond. However, with habituation, if we change the stimulus, the organ immediately reacts—a process which has the inelegant title of *dishabituation.*

Researchers often use dishabituation to determine whether babies can discriminate between two similar but not identical stimuli. They repeat the first stimulus until the baby habituates to it and then introduce the second. If the baby reacts to the second, researchers conclude that the baby experiences the second stimulus as different from the first. A study using this technique demonstrated that infants in the second month discriminate between familiar and unfamiliar voices (Horowitz, 1974). Other studies demonstrate that infants can make a variety of subtle discriminations among stimuli (Horowitz, 1972).

Environmental Influences on Habituation

Wendell Jeffreys has suggested that the more a given sense experience stands out, the more it commands a person's attention, and thus the more rapidly babies habituate to it than they do to less noticeable experiences. Some evidence supports this hypothesis (Miller, 1972). Perhaps an unlearned mechanism insures that once a baby's attention has been directed toward an important feature of the environment, habituation will occur and his attention will quickly be redirected toward other significant features. This mechanism would cause the baby to notice several aspects of any complex situation, and thus become able to identify objects with many characteristics.

The environment where habituation takes place would seem to be an important determinant of the rate at which it occurs. One would expect background noise, distracting sights, or disturbing smells to compete for attention with the central stimulus being repeated. A quiet environment with little going on seemingly would permit more rapid habituation. However, surprisingly few researchers have explored this. Several reports having methodological problems relate to the baby's state, which undoubtedly is influenced by stimulation from their surroundings (e.g., Sostek and Anders, 1975).

The stimulus that is being repeated is an important factor in habituation. Researchers have studied habituation to a wide variety of stimuli, including light flashes (Cohen, DeLoache, and Rissman, 1975), visual displays of slides (McCall, 1973), odors (Lipsitt, Engen, and Kaye, 1963), patterned papers (Cornell and Strauss, 1973), and tones (Lester, 1975). But they have not yet reached conclusions about the limits of the stimulus properties to which babies can habituate.

Characteristics of Infants in Relation to Habituation Rate

Babies differ in their rate of habituation to stimuli, which apparently is associated with other characteristics. For example, infants who habituate rapidly also have the strongest preference for stimuli moderately discrepant from a familiar one, whereas slower habituators prefer either no discrepancy or extreme discrepancy (McCall, 1973). Some evidence suggests that the relation between preference for moderate discrepancy and habituation rate is different for males than for females, but we do not yet understand why this difference exists. Additional work has shown that the relation between habituation rate and stimulus discrepancy from a standard is further complicated by the familiarity of the stimulus in the babies' every-day experiences (McCall, 1973). Two other studies find a direct relation between preferring complexity and habituating rapidly (Greenberg, O'Donnell, and Crawford, 1973; Brown, 1974). Another finds a relation between one-year-old girls' preferences for a familiar toy and their rapid habituation rates (Fenson, Sapper, and Minner, 1974). Babies' habituation rates clearly relate in some way to their cognitive processes. But we must understand why the sex differences as well as individual differences exist before we can develop a general theory to integrate habituation and cognitive development.

Sex differences exist in overall rate of habituation as well as in the characteristics associated with habituation rate. Several studies of habituation in young infants show that female babies do not respond or respond less to repetition of stimuli, or require more repetitions before they stop reacting (Meyers and Cantor, 1966; Cornell and Strauss, 1973; Cohen, DeLoache, and Rissman, 1975). Perhaps rudimentary memory is less adequately developed in females than in males, but that seems unlikely. It is known that the nervous systems of females are generally more mature at infancy than those of male babies, so one function of their nervous systems would not be likely to function poorly. Another possibility is that males and females differ in the level of novelty they prefer, so that even though they are equally able to notice that the repeated stimulus is just like the first one, they differ in their reactions.

Another characteristic of infants that relates to habituation rate is their temporary state of arousal. (In Chapter 2, the various states are defined in detail. They include deep sleep, drowsiness, alert inactivity, awake activity, and fussiness.) Habituation seems to occur only when babies are in a waking, alert, but inactive, state (Berg, 1972; Lewis and Goldberg, 1968). Apparently, motor activity disrupts the organized functioning of the nervous system in young infants. Studies of habituation in infants up to four months of age are likely to be successful only if the infants are tested when awake, alert, and inactive. But because babies vary tremendously in how often and for how long they experience any state, research observing only alert inactive subjects creates a sampling bias. Perhaps young infants who remain in the alert inactive state for lengthy periods do habituate, whereas those who are in the state only briefly do not habituate. From the research literature, which is based on studies of infants who remain alert and inactive long enough to be tested, we may be drawing the erroneous conclusion that all young infants habituate readily to a variety of stimuli. You will do well to remember that many of the generalizations that are made here may apply principally to infants who are often awake and alert.

Studies reveal that babies who were improperly nourished during gestation or who suffered birth complications do not habituate as early as normal infants to repeated events. They also require more exposure to stimuli in order to become accustomed to it (e.g., Barrett and Miller, 1973; Lester, 1975). This supports the hypothesis that habituation rate reflects the maturity of the organism (and it may also relate to the shorter attention spans of malnourished infants). The increase both in number of babies showing habituation and the rate of those who do so during the first several months of life is also consistent with this view. Because babies spend more time in the alert inactive state as they get older, the relation between this and their faster habituation rate also contributes to the hypothesis that habituation is affected by maturation.

Classical Conditioning

Classical conditioning was defined and discussed in Chapter 2. You will recall that through classical conditioning we learn to connect two stimuli that we experienced before as unrelated. After we have repeatedly experienced the first stimulus closely preceding the second (going to a certain room to take an exam), we react to the first stimulus (going to the room) just as we originally reacted to the second (taking the exam).

Can Older Infants Be Classically Conditioned Effectively?

We have seen in Chapter 2 that classical conditioning is a fragile process in newborns, who learn better with a procedure that combines classical and operant methods. Babies past the newborn period can be classically conditioned, and the associations formed this way significantly add to their view of the world. Their ability to link one event or object to another allows them to build a more coherent "world view" from these fleeting images of objects as they move and change.

Although some of a baby's responses cannot be conditioned, evidence indicates certain lessons can be learned through classical conditioning by infants younger than four months of age. Thus they can, and probably do, relate environmental events to their reflexive behavior and also they probably experience the sounds, tactile experiences, and visual displays around them as being related.

Through studies of conditioning, Brackbill and her associates have shown that a baby can use the passage of time as a cue to give a conditioned response (Brackbill, 1967; Fitzgerald, Linz, and Brackbill, 1967). This finding has several important implications. First, babies' awareness of the passage of time probably explains how they learn to adapt their sleeping, waking, hunger, and thirst cycles to family routines. Although it is neither wise nor feasible to put babies on schedules that differ greatly from natural biological rhythms, it is possible to place them on a relatively convenient schedule that will deviate only several hours at most.

Temporal conditioning very likely alerts babies to daily sequences of eating, playing, going out, and sleeping as well. We cannot observe this directly, but we can suppose that an infant's view of the surroundings does include schedules. Babies' awareness of time possibly indicates that they are developing a pattern of response to the rhythms of their surroundings. However, because some attempts at temporal conditioning of babies have failed (Abrahamson et al., 1970), we should not assume that all of their responses are equally responsive to environmental rhythms. Infants past the newborn period can learn by classical conditioning to connect various stimuli and also to increase or decrease their heart rate depending on the stimuli that are presented to them (Fitzgerald and Porges, 1971). But it is likely that the lives of most babies are more similar to the combined classical and operant conditioning set-up of Papousek (see p. 59) than they are to a pure classical conditioning set-up. Very likely, young infants learn many important connections between events in their worlds but few of them can be understood in terms of classical conditioning.

Operant Conditioning

In Chapter 2 we discussed operant conditioning and newborns. You will recall that to study operant conditioning we begin by identifying some interesting response that occurs occasionally because of the organism's biology or that is elicited by the environment. We then make sure that the response is followed whenever it occurs (or on a regular schedule) with a stimulus that reinforces it. This has the effect of increasing the frequency of the response.

As every parent knows, the usual way to increase a response is to follow it with a reward. For example, if we follow every smile of a three-month-old baby with a responsive smile of our own, with cooing, and with a friendly jiggling of his tummy, we find that he soon begins to smile more often. We infer that the baby considers tummy-jiggling a reward, because when we repeatedly show him that if he smiles we will jiggle his tummy, he smiles more in hopes of getting the reward. In psychological parlance, we would say that our social response (tummy-jiggling) reinforces the baby's smile (increases its frequency). Note that in this situation tummy-jiggling is *contingent* on the baby's smile: he has to smile before he receives our playful response.

In our play with the baby, we followed every response with reinforcement. However, we can change how frequently the baby smiles by varying our reinforcement schedule and only rewarding every second, third, or fourth response. We can even reinforce the responses irregularly. Variations in reinforcement schedules are known to affect the rate of learning in adults, older children, and animals, but how do they affect infant learning?

The first step in showing the effect of a reinforcement schedule on a baby is proving that the baby is changing how frequently he responds simply because he is receiving reinforcement, rather than for some other reason. We know that our actions are reinforcing if the response increases in frequency when we give the reward after it is made, but drops back to its original level if we do not reinforce it (it is "extinguished"), and if the rate of the response increases again if we begin reinforcing it again.

In the section that follows, let us consider which of an infant's responses can be successfully influenced by operant conditioning procedures and what reinforcers are most effective. We will also discuss how the baby's surroundings and character affect operant conditioning.

The Facts About Operant Conditioning of Infants

After studying the motor responses of infants two to four months of age, researchers have reported that operant conditioning can increase how often babies turn their heads, smile, look at an object, babble, give other vocalizing responses, and suck (Levison and Levison, 1967; Siqueland, 1964; Zelazo and Komer, 1971; Weisberg, 1963; Watson, 1968; Koch, 1967; Todd and Palmer, 1968; Ramey, Hieger, and Klisz, 1972; Bloom, 1974; Brossard and Goiń-DeCarie, 1968; McKinnon, Koeske, and Apland, 1971; Siqueland and DeLucia, 1969; Lipsitt, Pederson, and DeLucia, 1966). Cairns (1979) points out that all of these responses belong to several fixed patterns of action that are thought to be unlearned and controlled by the same processes that control the baby's maturation. So the many findings imply, first, that young infants can learn to modify varied forms of behavior and, second, that the behaviors most subject to change may be part of important instinctive patterns. However, before we could accept this generalization fully we must see the results of efforts to condition responses that are clearly not part of innate patterns. If these efforts were less successful than those with innate responses, we could be more confident of the validity of the generalization that innate responses are most readily conditioned.

Let us now look at the stimuli that have been used as reinforcers in studies of operant conditioning of infants. Rewarding a baby with food was found to increase the rate of sucking (Hillman and Bruner, 1972) and vocalizing (Haugan and McIntyre, 1972). Results of one study indicated that kinesthetic sensations (such as those you experience if someone pulls or shakes your arm) reinforce babies' smiling (Brossard and Goïn-DeCarie, 1968). It was also found that making an interesting display of slides brighter increased the rate of sucking in some infants (Siqueland and DeLucia, 1968). Babies responded to the tactile stimulation of being rubbed by vocalizing more (Haugan and McIntyre, 1972). The auditory stimulation of a pattern of tones apparently reinforces female babies more effectively than males (Watson, 1969).

Babies' social and nonsocial behavior is strongly affected by the vocal and facial responses of the adults around them. If an adult smiles, coos, and says something whenever a baby smiles, that baby will begin to smile much more frequently (Bloom, 1974; Weisberg, 1969; Brossard and Goïn-DeCarie, 1968; Zelazo and Komer, 1971). Babies will also vocalize and babble more if their actions evoke an approving response from the experimenters (Ramey, Hieger, and Klisz, 1972; Weisberg, 1963; Todd and Palmer, 1968; Haugan and McIntyre, 1972). This exchange seems to be a particularly important interaction between baby and caregiver. Cairns (1979) has speculated that human beings are innately disposed to attend closely to the social and emotional reactions of others and to adapt their own communications to communicate better with others. Thus, these early learning encounters can foster an important bond between the caregiver and baby.

Countless parents have wondered why their baby, who has been observing them quietly, suddenly starts to gurgle with delight for no apparent reason, when a few seconds before she was totally unmoved by the sight of brightly colored toys? They will be interested in the findings of two recent investigations that attempt to isolate the exact features of the caregivers' behavior toward the infant that are reinforcing. In one study an experimenter established four positions from which it was easier or more difficult for babies to see her eyes. The results showed that eye contact must occur for babies to be reinforced by the appearance of a human face in front of them (Bloom 1974a, 1974b). Another study found that, although face-to-face interaction was more effective, a taped recording of the experimenter's voice would cause babies to vocalize more than they would without stimulus (Todd and Palmer, 1968). Another study demonstrated that taped voices of males and females were equally effective reinforcers (Banikiotes, Montgomery, and Banikiotes, 1972). Young babies are possibly selectively tuned to the human voice and to eye contact. It may be that they try to stay close to their caregivers because they find these adult reactions reinforcing (see Chapter 5).

Much of operant learning in children and adults works through the effect of *secondary reinforcement.* A secondary reinforcer is a stimulus that acquires the ability to reinforce through repeated pairings with stimuli that are innately reinforcing. For example, we may learn to work hard for the reward of money because we have learned that with it we can buy things that please us. A large literature in the learning field shows the circumstances under which a stimulus acquires reinforcing properties.

But do babies respond to secondary reinforcers? The suggestion of Yarrow, Rubenstein, and Pederson (1975), Cairns (1979), and others that social stimuli are *innately* reinforcing (and therefore are primary reinforcers) is substantiated by studies with animals, in which social stimuli and feeding occur separately (see Cairns, 1979). This separation means that the social contact must be reinforcing for some reason other than its temporal association with feeding. It appears, however, that infants can be influenced by secondary reinforcers. Silverstein has demonstrated that a tone can come to have reinforcing properties through its association with food. According to his findings, after experiencing the pairing of a tone with food, infants learned to change their position when doing so would evoke the tone (Silverstein, 1972; Silverstein and Lipsitt, 1974).

Another phenomenon that occurs in operant conditioning of older babies (as well as children and adults) is *reinforcer satiation.* For example, in a study using various slides as novel visual events to reinforce head turning of infants 3½ months old, researchers found that the rate of responding would first increase and then decline: the babies gradually lost interest. This effect was strongest in girls (Caron, Caron, and Caldwell, 1971). One other study also revealed that when babies became familiar with a novel reinforcing event they no longer found it as reinforcing (Siqueland, 1969). However, this satiation has not been studied extensively in infants, so the importance of its role in day-to-day learning is not known. In everyday life, reinforcement does not usually occur after every response. When we greet people, they often, but not always, smile back at us. Sometimes our hard work receives not even a verbal pat on the back, let alone monetary rewards. Yet, despite the irregular reinforcement of our behavior, we systematically change it in hopes of receiving a reward. Can babies be similarly affected? Little systematic research on the various schedules of reinforcement has been done with infants less than one year old. But we do know that infants respond to consistent reinforcement, and so we can reasonably suppose that reinforcement plays a role in their natural learning experiences. What remains to be known is how *changes* in the schedule of reinforcement might influence learning.

A question that is part of scheduling reinforcement is, "What happens to learning where there is a delay between the response and its reinforcement?" Thanks to the efforts of Millar and his associates, we know something about how babies react to delayed reinforcement. In an extensive monograph, Millar (1972) reviewed the results of several studies in which four- to seven-month-old infants would pull a hand and receive a novel visual display as reinforcement. When the babies received the reinforcement immediately, their rate of responding was very high. One to two seconds of delay between the hand-pull response and reinforcement produced some increase in the baby's original rate of hand-pulling, but significantly less than the immediate reinforcement. If a delay of more than three seconds separated the hand-pulling and the reinforcement, the babies' rate of hand-pulling did not increase. In a study of conditioned vocalization, similar results were found (Ramey and Ourth, 1971): immediate reinforcement was demonstrably more effective than delayed reinforcement.

Millar also studied babies who had previously been exposed to noncontingent reinforcement (the babies could not be sure that their behavior would bring reinforcement). These babies learned better with a delay of one or two seconds before reinforcement than did those who had not already experienced delayed reinforcement. Apparently because the former group of babies had learned to recognize that the reinforcing events would occur, they could tolerate the wait better. However, even these babies did not continue to wait for more than a few seconds. Clearly infants' ability to learn by operant conditioning is somewhat limited compared with that of preschool children, who continue to expect rewards after longer delays (Mischel, 1976).

Millar and Schaffer (1973) have studied the effect on babies of a change in distance between them and the reinforcement. They set up an appealing visual display off to one side of infants who were lying in plastic containers. Although six-month-old infants did not learn when the reinforcement was in this less noticeable position, nine-month-old babies learned just as effectively as they did when the reinforcement was in front of them. In the opinion of Millar and Schaffer, distant reinforcement poses more of a challenge to selective attending skills than does the delay in reinforcement (Millar and Schaffer, 1973).

The Importance of Contingent Stimulation

One aspect of the reinforcement used in operant conditioning studies that deserves special note is *contingency*. Recently, contingent stimulation has been singled out for discussion as a possible primary reinforcer in itself (McCall, 1972; Watson and Ramey, 1972). Possibly the experience of making something happen is very rewarding to babies; it clearly is for other human beings.

To study contingency, two investigators designed special crib mobiles to use at the homes of infants two to three months of age. The mobiles were powered by electric motors that were triggered by the infants' movements. Whenever the infants moved their heads or their crib pillows, the mobile designs would move, and, when the babies stopped moving their heads, the mobiles would stop moving. The babies quickly learned to turn their mobiles on and off, and, more important, they became very attached to them. Mothers reported that the toys were effective baby sitters, but some mothers worried that the toys engaged the babies' attention too effectively (Watson and Ramey, 1972). Two control groups were used, one for whom the mobiles were not movable at all, and one for whom the mobiles moved, but not in response to the baby's behavior. The babies became nowhere near as attached to their mobiles as did the group who could cause their mobiles to move. Apparently, the contingency of the movement of the mobile upon the babies' action was much stronger reinforcement than the novelty of the mobile itself.

Other evidence exists for the power of contingent stimulation. In one large-scale study of 7- to 11-month-old infants, it was found that the babies played longest with toys that responded to their manipulation with "contingent feedback" (McCall, 1974). An example of such a toy is the familiar jack-in-the-box, which pops up when a box lid is opened. Another example is a colorful round disk that plays a recorded song when its string is pulled. Similar findings were reported from an earlier, smaller-scale study done in homes (Leuba and Friedlander, 1968). Related evidence shows that infants 8 to 14 weeks old learn to look longer at stimuli when their motor behavior can cause the stimulus to appear and then to look when those same stimuli appear noncontingently (Foster, Vietze, and Friedman, 1973).

Are babies pleased to discover that they can exert control? Unfortunately, the answer to this question is not yet clear. One result of the experience of exerting control may be that babies gradually gain an awareness of themselves as being independent of the objects that surround them. This

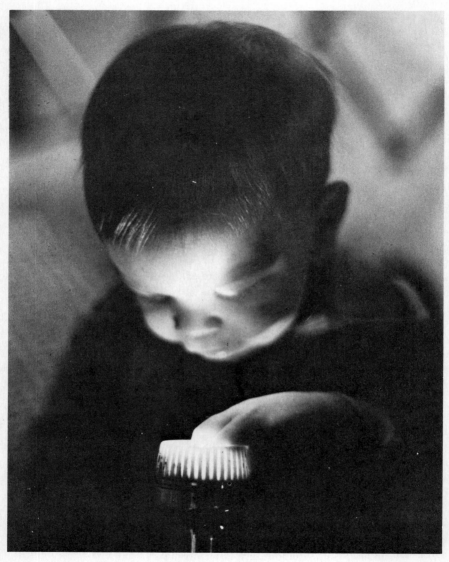

Figure 3-2. *Babies derive seemingly endless delight from objects that respond to their manipulations. Here a baby boy seems absorbed by the contingent stimulation offered by a flashlight. (Photo courtesy of George B. Fry III.)*

was suggested both by Piaget and by Freud. But we do not yet have evidence sufficient to prove that contingent stimulation is a primary reinforcer. This could only be established by separating the stimulation itself from its contingent aspect. Nevertheless, because of its importance, contingent stimulation will continue to receive attention from researchers.

One form of contingent stimulation plays a role in the daily caregiving activities of a family. Loving and interested parents look at, talk to, pat, and smile at their babies as they go about feeding, changing, and bathing them. At about the third month, a baby discovers that he can produce these social behaviors in his caregivers. He smiles, and his mother smiles; he gurgles, and his father laughs; he laughs, and his brother tickles his stomach; he laughs some more, and his sister picks him up. Watson (1973) has named this exchange "The Game." The baby's early recognition of and preference for the human face and voice may arise from the fact that they are the most consistent contingent stimulation he receives in the early weeks.

Two investigators have taken a different look at the role of contingent stimulation. They used a procedure they called "synchronous reinforcement," in which an interesting slide becomes brighter as a baby's rate of sucking increases. The infants' heads were left unconfined in this study. But to see a clear image of the interesting slide, they had to suck more on a device that resembled a pacifier and at the same time focus their eyes on the visual display. Gradually, through trial and error, they learned to coordinate the process of changing their responses until they found the effective suck-and-look sequence. The researchers considered the behavior of their 5- to 12-month-old subjects more consistent with a problem-solving model than an operant conditioning model (Kalnins and Bruner, 1973) because the subjects learned to vary their responses toward a fixed end. In contrast, during operant conditioning responses do not change; rather, they increase in frequency after repeated reinforcement.

Reinforcement of Crying

As you may recall from Chapter 2, the crying of newborns is generally a biologically based response to various events within their own bodies. Adults can be sensitive to the meaning of individual cries and thus the newborns' cries serve to insure that they receive care. As infancy proceeds, crying takes on a more complex significance as part of a developing dialogue between infants and those who care for them. Infants may learn to cry in certain circumstances. One question of concern to caregivers is whether to comfort a crying baby. According to the psychoanalytic theory of Erik Erikson, infants' emotional security and sense of "basic trust" in their world develops out of their experiences of having their needs met (Erikson,

1950). The psychoanalyst John Bowlby, who has been influenced greatly by the naturalistic behavior studies of animals done by ethologists, argues that a baby's cry is a signal alerting the mother that her infant has an unmet need (Bowlby, 1969). Both Bowlby and Erikson would argue that when crying babies are given care and attention their feelings of security and well-being improve, so that, in the long run, a pattern of comforting a crying infant would lead to a more secure infant who cries less.

An opposing view would be based on a strict operant conditioning analysis: If the caregiving activities of adults are reinforcing to infants and if, as we discussed before, making them contingent on the baby's behavior makes them even more reinforcing, then it would follow that babies who are comforted when they cry will learn to cry more. One study tested the contradictory predictions of the psychoanalytic and operant conditioning views. The investigators measured how much babies cried and how much comforting they received in response to their crying during the first quarter of the first year of life. At the end of the first year, the amount of crying was again measured. The results indicated that crying babies who were comforted cried the least at the end of the year. But the babies who had been left alone when they cried were crying the most at the end of the year (Bell and Ainsworth, 1972). This study seems to support the view that comforting reduces a baby's distress. But the findings can be interpreted in another way. It may be that crying and lack of comfort are related, not to each other, but to an event or influence that is as yet unknown. Only carefully controlled studies can reveal whether a connection exists between babies' crying and the comfort they sometimes receive. Results of one brief study indicate that two infants who were problem criers cried less when reinforcement for it was withdrawn (Etzel and Gewirtz, 1967). This finding underscores the need for further study.

Discrimination Learning

Most operant conditioning that takes place outside of the laboratory is complex. We do learn not that we get approval for being quiet, but rather that *some* people approve of us *sometimes* if we are quiet. We learn to recognize certain events as *cues* for when and how our behavior will be rewarded. For example, an infant may learn that, if her mother makes sounds at the stove, she soon may be receiving milk. She may then begin to whine in a low voice when she hears the familiar sounds because she knows that her whine is sometimes rewarded by the fast arrival of her bottle. However, the hoped-for bottle appears only if the sound she heard actually was that of food preparation. The preparation noises are said to have *stimulus control* over the murmuring response, which the milk then reinforces.

Figure 3-3. *Psychologists disagree about the long-term effects of comforting a crying baby. Some argue that comforting makes babies more secure, which will cause them to cry less in the future. Others insist that comforting simply reinforces the tendency to cry. (Photo copyright © Suzanne Arms.)*

When the cue (the preparatory noises) has repeatedly preceded the reinforcement (the arrival of the bottle), the events become associated in the baby's mind. Thus we can use a classical conditioning model to explain how the baby learned to associate the two events. Meanwhile, we can label the relation between murmuring and milk as operant conditioning because the baby's response is followed by reinforcement. As you can see, when babies learn to respond to a cue stimulus, they have experienced a complex process that contains both an element of classical conditioning and one of operant conditioning. Many everyday happenings in the life of a baby eventually become cues that certain responses will be reinforced if they occur. Thus, most of an infant's learned responses are under the control, not only of reinforcement, but also of these cue stimulus events. The responses are under stimulus control.

In laboratory studies of learning, investigators employ a complex extension of stimulus control. Researchers condition babies to respond differently to two cue stimuli. For example, an older infant may be rewarded for pushing a certain response panel or lever if a bright light is on but not if a flashing light is on. This is called *discrimination learning,* because the baby must learn to discriminate between the two lights.

What Can Babies Discriminate?

Some time ago, Harlow conducted a series of discrimination learning studies with human infants and other primates. He reported that most human infants in the first half year of life were able to learn to discriminate among different elementary shapes or spatial positions. However, the learning of a series of such discrimination problems did not seem to help them generalize a principle that would help solve the next problem (Harlow, 1959). We would have to conclude from this that babies can make discriminations but that this skill is much less developed than it will be when they get older.

Work with infants 6 to 12 months old suggests that they are much better at making discriminations than younger infants are. They learn to respond differently to different complex visual patterns and sequential light displays as well as to different simpler forms (McKenzie and Day, 1971; Gibson, 1969; Sheppard, 1969; Weisberg, 1969). Results of one study indicated that infants could discriminate between novel and familiar stimuli, a finding implied by the fact that they choose to pay more attention to novel events than to familiar ones (Schaffer and Parry, 1970; Fagan, 1977). In another study one-year-old infants learned to discriminate between red and blue (Simmons, 1964). In general, as babies age, they learn to discriminate between objects more quickly and to identify their qualities more precisely.

Let us briefly consider the relation of discrimination to what we know about infants' patterns of attention. As you may recall from the earlier discussion, results of many studies of attention indicate that even very young infants form clear preferences for one visual or auditory event over another; the implication usually drawn from this is that these infants can discriminate between them. Learning to discriminate requires more, however. Babies must make obviously different responses to the different stimuli, which requires more coordination than is required to simply look or not look at a stimulus. It may be that discrimination among various objects and happenings in a baby's life proceeds in steps. Perhaps first the baby picks out various identifying features of the stimuli (and can thus be said to be telling them apart). Second, the baby behaves in a certain way only when one of these stimuli is present: this is stimulus control. Finally, the baby may learn to behave one way in the presence of one of the stimuli and another way in the presence of the other.

Consider, for example, the process of discriminating between a small plastic cup with a spout (which generally is used to teach babies to drink from a cup) and a nursing bottle. A baby of two months may spend more time looking at the bottle than at the cup. This difference, or "attentional preference," probably shows that the baby sees the difference between the objects. A little later she may try to suck both of these objects in the same manner and discover that she will receive the reward of milk only from the bottle because cups do not function as bottles do. She quickly will learn to suck only from the bottle but still will not know what to do with the cup. At this point sucking has come to be under the stimulus control of the bottle. Finally, she will learn to drink from the cup as well as to suck on the bottle. She will have learned not only to distinguish between the stimuli but also to respond appropriately to them. In short, she adapts by means of her ability to discriminate.

The Infant's Perceptual World

You now have some very specific information about babies' patterns of attention and their ability to remember and learn from their experiences. What conclusions about the world that infants experience can we draw from this information? Any attempt to answer this question takes us into the realm of speculation. As you can imagine, psychologists hesitate to draw conclusions about perception even when they are studying adults, who can describe their feelings and experiences. So our conclusions about infants are even more tenuous.

Despite the problems of studying the subjective experience of other people, psychologists understand the perceptual worlds of adults and older children fairly well. Much of our understanding is based on research dealing with vision, especially as it pertains to characteristics in our immediate environment that most of us perceive as constant. In this section, I will discuss some similar work that has been done with infants in an effort to discover what features of the world have constancy for them. Then I will propose what I consider a reasonable picture of what the world looks like to infants.

Unlike Alice in Wonderland, we live with confidence that the objects around us will not suddenly grow or shrink: our visual world has *size constancy*. However, when you move about your living room at home, for example, the images of familiar objects—pieces of furniture, books, and rugs—change in size on the retinas of your eyes. As you walk away from an object, your retinal image of it becomes smaller and smaller; similarly, as you approach an object, your retinal image of it enlarges. Chaos would rule if your impressions of the size of the objects around you depended directly on the size of your retinal image of them: the things that make up your surroundings would shrink or grow with your every movement. Fortunately, objects have a fixed size for children and adults, even when motion changes the distance from which we view them.

But do young babies experience size constancy? This question is important for two reasons. First, it is useful to know whether babies experience the world as other human beings do or instead confront a Wonderland where objects grow and shrink as they move. Second, it would be interesting to know whether the experience of size constancy is inborn or acquired.

Even in a controlled experiment, it is quite a challenge to figure out what babies experience when they are confronted with various objects. In a study of adults, objects are generally placed at various distances, and subjects are asked to identify them or to compare their sizes with a standard object. Although babies cannot tell us in words what they see, their nonverbal responses serve as a kind of language for experimental purposes. T. G. R. Bower has used an operantly conditioned response to an object to indicate how similar that object and other objects appear to be to babies (Bower, 1972).

Bower's technique was to place four cardboard cubes each in one of two sizes at either of two distances from the baby's eyes. The four combinations (of the two cube sizes with the two distances) yielded the retinal image sizes that are shown in Figure 3-4. You will notice that the large cube placed farther from the baby has the same retinal image size as the smaller cube placed nearer to the baby. Bower reasoned that, if the babies lacked size constancy and were using retinal image as the only cue to object size, they would respond to the large distant cube in the same manner as they did to the small near cube. On the other hand, if they were responding to the actual sizes of the objects—if they did perceive size constancy—they would respond quite differently to these two events.

Bower used a conditioned head-turning response as a substitute for the verbal response of the adults. The small near cube was used as the standard stimulus to which the babies were trained to make the head-turn response. Whenever they turned their heads in the presence of the standard, they were reinforced by an animated social response from an experimenter. When the babies had learned this response well, Bower continued the experiment by presenting the standard cube and the other three in a planned sequence but without any further reinforcement. He found that the babies made the smallest number of head-turning responses to the large distant cube, an intermediate number of responses to the small distant and the larger near cubes, and the greatest number to the standard. Because their response to the large distant cube was clearly different from the response to the small near cube—even though their retinal image sizes are the same—Bower concluded that babies must experience them differently.

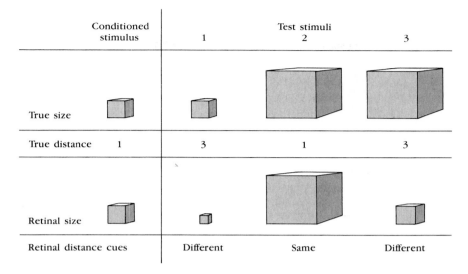

Conditioned stimulus	Test stimuli 1	2	3
True size			
True distance 1	3	1	3
Retinal size			
Retinal distance cues	Different	Same	Different

Figure 3-4. *Bower investigated size constancy by placing cubes of different sizes at different distances from the infants. The conditioned stimulus was 30 centimeters on a side and one meter away, test stimuli 30 or 90 centimeters on a side and one or three meters away. The chart shows how test stimuli were related to the conditioned stimulus in various respects. (From "The Visual World of Infants," by T. G. R. Bower. Copyright © 1966 by Scientific American, Inc. All rights reserved.)*

Apparently, infants two months old use information other than the size of retinal images and they do experience size constancy.

Bower went on to study in detail the cues employed by babies in their perception of objects. He developed technical means to remove one by one the cues normally used by adults in making judgments about size and distance. He found that the most important cue responsible for the size constancy in infants was *binocular parallax,* the phenomenon whereby nearby objects seem to be moving at a faster rate than those that are farther away if we look at them while we are moving our heads (Bower, 1965a). He found that young infants are able to sense the constant shape of objects when those objects are turned at various angles that cause them to produce distorted retinal images (Bower, 1965b). Other investigators have noted that infants one to six months old are able to recognize an object when it is turned at various angles that make it look far different than it would if it were looked at upright (Watson, 1966; McGurk, 1970, 1972). Other investigators have not been able to replicate the work of Bower, so some controversy exists about its implications.

Because infants experience both size and shape constancies, their visual worlds probably consist of discernible objects that move about rather than objects that grow and shrink with the infants' movements. Because Bower has not used newborns in his studies we cannot be sure that these constancy mechanisms are inborn. And although Bower considers it unlikely that a sense of constancy is learned or acquired in the first few weeks of life, it may be.

Another important characteristic of the visual world is the sense of "drop-off" (or depth effect) one experiences when approaching a stair or a platform edge, or when standing on the edge of a cliff. This perceptual impression of depth has been named the *visual cliff* by investigators who built a special apparatus to study it in human and other infants.

Gibson and Walk originally used the visual cliff to study how infants of different species reacted when they were placed on the see-through side of the cliff. They found a relation between the age at which animal infants first were able to move without their mothers and the age at which they first showed fear upon being placed on the see-through side of the cliff. This would seem to indicate that fear of depth is an adaptive response that emerges after development (Gibson and Walk, 1960).

The work done with human infants and visual cliffs shows a similar pattern. Infants under six months of age generally do not seem to become afraid when they are placed on the see-through side of the visual cliff. Instead they have several reactions that are indicative of attention: their heart rate slows, they stare intently, and their motor activity stops. During the next several months of life, this reaction of attention changes to one of obvious arousal and fear (Schwartz, Campos, and Baisel, 1973; Campos, Langer, and Krowitz, 1970). Although younger infants two to three months of age do not show fear of depth, they can discriminate between the two sides of the visual cliff (Schwartz, Campos, and Baisel, 1973).

If we consider both Bower's findings on size constancy and the results of the visual cliff studies, it seems that infants acquire the ability to discriminate between depths in space long before they begin to fear depth. Their fear of the visual cliff seems to imply that they associate the drop they see with the possibility of harm. Another fear that is more directly related to depth and distance is fear of an object that appears to be approaching your face and about to strike it. We can only judge how rapidly the object is approaching us if we have a sense of distance. Several investigators have remarked that objects that rapidly approach or loom toward babies can arouse instantaneous fear. Bower and a student studied these reactions in detail, and found that babies two to five weeks old showed fear of illusory objects (created by light and filter arrangements) that appeared to be coming right at them, whereas they did not fear those same objects if it seemed

Figure 3-5. *Visual cliff, used by Gibson and Walk to test the depth perception of babies. The baby in this photograph has just been asked by his mother to crawl to her across the see-through side of the platform (where the cliff appears to drop off). He pats the glass, but, despite the tactual evidence that the cliff is a solid surface, he refuses to crawl across it. (Photo courtesy of William Vandivert and Scientific American, Inc.)*

the objects would not hit them. The babies continued to show fear on repeated trials when the fact that they had not been hit by an object should have told them that they were not really in danger (Ball and Tronick, 1971). In writing about this study, Bower suggested that human beings have an innate adaptive fear reaction to looming objects (Bower, 1974).

Infants two to three months of age apparently discriminate among distances and degrees of depth. We know little about how they make these discriminations and whether they use the same type of information as do older subjects. Bower's results and those of other studies on the visual cliff are at odds regarding the role of binocular vision. According to Bower, binocular parallax is the important cue to size constancy, which is achieved through a size and distance relation. But results of two studies where babies used only one eye (and thus could not gauge depth by means of two-eye cues) indicate that babies seemingly do not use depth when they react to the visual cliff effect (Walk and Dodge, 1962; Walk, 1968). Much remains to be understood about the role played by various features of the visual field in helping a baby to develop depth perception. Nevertheless, we can conclude with confidence that babies can perceive depth to some degree by the second month of life.

What does the world seem like to a baby? By now we have considered enough evidence to begin some speculation about it. Apparently, objects still maintain their identifying size and shape even as they move about in space. The immediate visual field of babies has more than two dimensions—they are aware of depth and distance—but it may be quite different from that of adults. Probably babies use definite visual features—edges, object contours, motion—to separate the object at which they are looking from the background of the visual field. This does not require coordination of two eyes.

Another question remains to be answered. How do babies perceive the sounds and tactile sensations they receive in relation to their visual experiences? Can babies combine sight, sound, and touch into a conception of a single object? Does a baby recognize that the sound of his mother's voice, the outline of her face, and the feel of her skin all belong to the same object—mother? Experiencing different sensations from the same object as parts of a whole is called *perceptual unity.*

Psychologists disagree about the question of whether perceptual unity is innate. The evidence that exists indicates that infants one month to six weeks old associate sight and sound of familiar objects. One group of investigators found that infants became upset when electronic equipment created the impression that the voices of their mothers, who were standing in front of them, were coming from somewhere else (Aronson and Rosenbloom, 1971). The investigators concluded that the babies perceived the auditory and visual information as being combined in a single experience. However, results of a study in which babies were made to feel an object that was hidden from view indicate that even babies 6 to 12 months old will not look for an object that they can feel but not see (Gratch, 1972). It seems that the tactile sensations do not necessarily lead babies to expect to see an object—that is, the tactile and the visual do not "go together." Results of other work examining the responses of babies to moving objects suggest that their visual impressions of an object both in motion and at rest do not reflect an awareness that they are looking at the same object (Bower, 1974).

Given the little information that we have, it seems safe to generalize that babies' perception is more fragmented than that of adults. Because the object that is felt but not seen is not the same to babies as the object that is seen, and the moving object is not the same as the object at rest, the infant's world seems to contain many more objects than the world of adults. Babies probably understand objects they can both see and touch better than objects they only see or only touch. We have little evidence that young babies reflect much on all this; they appear to accept the complexities of their perception at face value. In Chapter 6 we will consider the cognitive processes of babies in more detail.

How Perception Changes with a Baby's Development

As babies develop, some aspects of their perceptions change, whereas others remain the same for life. For example, the cortex of the brain is not fully mature at birth. This will change as the baby develops and with it the perceptual functions it controls. We can find adequate explanations of all of the facts about attention and perception in the newborn without assuming cortical functioning (Bronson, 1974). Early in infancy babies tend to scan the periphery of a stimulus rather than looking at the center of it (Bronson, 1974). There are great differences in how babies organize their attention, and babies' individual patterns of attention remain unchanged by maturation (Barten and Ronch, 1971). This suggests that the organization of attention is a very basic characteristic that develops over time but is present in some form very early in life, perhaps even at birth. Certain aspects of this attentional organization must be possible without cortical activity because we know this is absent at birth. At this time, we know so little about the development of the cortex in relation to specific perceptual skills that it is impossible to make a useful generalization about it.

A Note on Imitation

One very important form of learning in older children and adults is learning through imitation of others. Bandura has pointed out that imitation—which he calls modeling—requires coordinating one's motor activity with a mental picture of the act that is being imitated (Bandura, 1977). Because very young infants do not imitate others, it seems safe to conclude that they either cannot form a mental picture of the act of another or cannot coordinate their motor activities with that picture.

Piaget has studied imitation in infancy extensively and has written a great deal about it (Piaget, 1961). According to his view, infants cannot imagine objects until about the last quarter of the first year of life. Before that, it is possible to get a baby to imitate such responses as opening and closing of the hands, which babies master early in life and can see themselves doing. (Piaget calls this pseudo-imitation.) A student of Piagetian theory has followed the imitation patterns of 12 infants from the time they were four weeks to two years of age. She found that, while these infants indeed did not imitate gestures until after the fourth quarter of the first year, many of them would imitate vocal sounds before that time (Uzgiris, 1971). Other observations indicate that babies do imitate novel actions very early in the first year of life, but that imitation is not as prominent a part of their everyday behavior as it will come to be (Uzgiris, 1972). It seems reasonable to conclude that learning by imitation does not play nearly the role in development during infancy that it will play in later development.

Summary

Let us review the initial questions with which we began the chapter, and see how much progress we have made in answering them. Psychologists are primarily concerned with how the basic processes of perception, memory, and learning occur in infants. We have learned that young infants are likely to notice contour movement; this facilitates their awareness of the objects as distinct from a background. Later, novelty influences their attention: babies pay the most attention to events that are moderately discrepant from familiar events. Habituation occurs in the youngest infants, which indicates that, from the start, babies shift their attention from objects with which they are familiar. The fact that they can habituate also shows that some primitive memory capacity exists even in very young infants. Babies are clearly capable of changing their behavior to "fit" the circumstances they experience in early infancy: they are capable of learning at a very early age. The passive learning that classical conditioning entails occurs less often and takes longer than the operant learning based on consequences of one's own acts. Indeed, stimulation contingent on their own actions appears to be one of the most powerful reinforcers that babies experience. We may speculate that babies who are born helpless also are born with an innate potential to be pleased by "making things happen."

The philosophical nativism vs. empiricism controversy plays an important role in the study of how we come to know the world. If very young infants' views of the physical environment—space, objects, and their interrelations—are similar to those of adults, then probably these world views are inborn. If, on the other hand, infants seem to lack some basic aspects of an adult's perception, one can argue that those aspects are learned and that infants have not yet learned them. Some aspects of the visual world that have been studied in infants are depth perception, distance, and shape

Figure 3-6. *A baby imitates the hand-clapping of her caregiver. (Photo courtesy of Emilio A. Mercado.)*

and size constancy of objects. Young babies seem to have a fair degree of size and shape constancy, but their perception of depth gradually develops during the first six months of life. Their abilities to integrate information coming in from the several senses is present but is not very efficient at birth. Infants may be aware of objects and their motions, but may imagine that the world has many more objects in it than adults see. Although some sense of distance is implied by babies' ability to judge the size of an object at various distances during their early months of life, babies do not have a mature sense of depth.

Caretakers' concerns about perception probably center on the role they should play in providing or regulating "stimulation" for the infant. The main wisdom to be gleaned from the material of this chapter is that babies can and do attend to the details of objects and events in their surroundings. We would not want to install babies in silent, dim places that had few objects or ongoing events to offer. Because babies are most aware of their immediate visual fields, such stimuli as attractive mobiles, crib liners, and wall decorations interest them most. Many caregivers carry their infants about as they go through their daily routines. Thus, the babies can have an opportunity to experience new and varied surroundings. Babies naturally organize the stimulation they receive, so there is no need to structure their experiences for them, although they may be responsive to such sensory "games" as hiding and covering faces in the time-honored "peekaboo" tradition.

The evidence described in this chapter suggests that babies are especially responsive to gamelike stimulation that comes from the personal expressiveness of their caretakers. The faces and voices of familiar caretakers are quite successful at attracting and holding infants' attention. There is no need to self-consciously plan a schedule of stimulation for them.

Chapter 4

Cognitive Development

This chapter is about how babies know the world—the objects in it, their locations in space, and their various properties and potentials for action, as well as events and their causes and consequences. Psychologists use the term *cognition* to designate the acts of knowing, including such processes as sensing and perceiving, thinking, remembering, and problem solving. Adults have an advantage over babies: they can learn about the world through symbolic systems, such as language, whereas infants (as far as we can tell) are unable to use such systems. Babies overcome this "disadvantage," however, by perceiving the world in terms of action. An adult may picture a ball and label it "b-a-l-l," but a baby identifies a ball by how it acts: a ball rolls. Accordingly, I will first discuss how babies learn to use their bodies (motor development) and will then trace their discovery that they can combine a sensation, such as seeing someone's glasses, with an action, such as grasping them (sensory-motor integration). Then I will explain how babies explore the world, what they remember, and how they solve problems.

What questions shall we address through this discussion? Psychologists are interested in how babies think. Do babies, like adults, use concepts to organize what would otherwise be a chaos of perceptions? Do babies experience objects, space, time, and cause-and-effect relations? Do they sense that the walking, talking creatures around them are "people"—beings like themselves—with whom they can form relationships? Psychologists are also interested in the ability of babies to use new information coming in through the senses. Do babies realize that their senses can cue them to adapt to changing situations? For example, when a baby hears his mother come in does he realize that he can expect her to walk to the crib? In general, psychologists want to know how babies process information and how the characteristics of both the individual and the environment influence those capacities. They would also like to know to what extent the early experiences of babies influence the experiences they will have later in life.

A question that has long been of concern to philosophers is whether or not infants can know reality (which, to make matters more difficult, each philosopher may define differently!). Some philosophers, the nativists, believe that humans are born with an innate ability to know the world, whereas others, the empiricists, believe that babies have no such innate ability but must learn to know the world and to make sense of it through continued interaction with the environment. The philosophers' concept of "knowing the world" is roughly synonymous with the psychologists' concept of cognition. Thus, psychological studies of infant cognition may produce some tentative answers for even as philosophical a question as, "How do we *first* know the world?"

Caregivers who wonder what the world may be like from a baby's point of view likely have one of two concerns. One relates to our natural desire for empathy with anyone who is going to share our world—we may wonder whether the baby in our care experiences the same events that we are experiencing. Communication and rapport between adults (or between adults and older children) start from the common ground between them. If we can have a clear picture of how our infants experience the objects, people, and events in their lives, we can develop a common ground out of which communication and care will grow.

Our culture values cognitive skills—both because they are tools to attain other goals and because we like to believe that our minds direct our emotional growth. Thus, in Western society, caregivers are also concerned with fostering the baby's cognitive development. They have questions about how they can arrange the physical environment and organize the day to nurture an infant's developing mental skills. Are there special toys to make, buy, or borrow? Is it good or bad to have lists of activities, a time schedule, and definite locations for things? Is organized stimulation important to a baby's development?

Motor Development and Sensory-Motor Integration

Gross Motor Development

Because newborn babies have poor control of their own movements and have not yet developed much muscular strength, the spontaneous movements they make while lying face up often seem to be merely a random "thrashing" of arms and legs. Before the end of the newborn period, however, a baby lying on her stomach can lift her head from the mattress. Next she can lift her chest, reach, roll over, and sit—at first only with support, but later without help. In a short time she can stand with help, creep, walk with support, and, finally, walk alone. Figure 4-1 shows Shirley's figures for

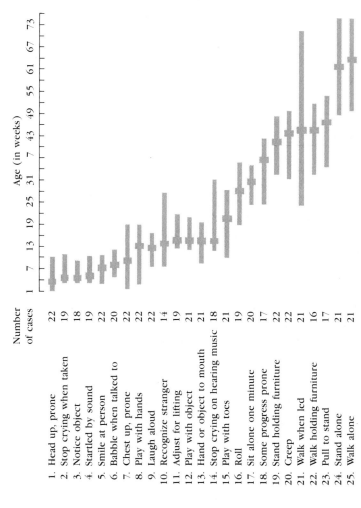

Figure 4-1. *Shirley's schedule of motor development. (From* The First Two Years, *by Mary M. Shirley. Copyright 1933 by the University of Minnesota. University of Minnesota Press.)*

the average age and the range of ages for these landmarks of motor development. Much of the discussion that follows depends on the analysis developed by T. G. R. Bower and presented in his summary of his fascinating research with babies, *Development in Infancy* (1974).

The sequence of landmarks shown in Figure 4-1 is the same for all infants, but babies master these challenges at different ages. The usual explanation for the unchanging sequence of motor behavior is that the baby's normal maturation creates this pattern (Gesell and Ames, 1937). *Maturation* is the process of change over time that is governed by genetic information, which is adapted for the typical environment of a species. Evidence to support the notion that normal maturation determines the observed sequence of events in a baby's development includes several related facts. First, although premature infants are exposed to the postnatal environment at an earlier age and for a longer period of time than full-term infants, premature infants do not raise their heads, sit, stand, or walk earlier than full-term infants when the age for these events is measured from conception. This could mean either that stimulation from the environment does not affect the development of babies or, alternatively, that stimulation is necessary, but only influences their development after they have matured enough first.

A second type of evidence to support the maturational theory relates to the child-rearing practices of various cultures. In some cultures infants' movements are drastically restricted and yet these infants walk at an average age close to that of American and European babies, who are not restricted as much. For example, even though the Hopi Indians of North America swaddle their infants and bind them to cradle boards for at least their first year of life, Hopi children learn to walk at the same age as children who were not swaddled in infancy.

Third, studies of identical twins have suggested that maturation, not training, determines how quickly babies develop their motor skills. Gesell, Thompson, and Amatada (1938) found that at 53 weeks of age the untrained twin climbed stairs quite well, only a little slower than the trained twin who had been "practicing" for eight weeks. Thus, the evidence would seem to make a strong case that maturation, not experience, guides our early motor development.

However, the situation is not as simple as it seems. Consider walking, for example. When babies begin to walk (usually at sixty-some weeks of age), are they exhibiting a completely new kind of behavior or are they doing something that evolved from earlier skills? If walking is an evolved behavior, its development depends upon the earlier development of other motor skills.

There is an early form of walking during the newborn period called the *stepping response* or *walking reflex.* If you support a newborn baby by firmly holding her upright with her feet touching a surface, she will take steps as if

Figure 4-2. *With the help of his mother, and a grassy meadow to cushion him if he falls, a 12-month-old takes his first steps. (Photo courtesy of Bruce Silva.)*

she were actually walking. This reflex disappears in a few weeks and several months pass before true walking begins. Two studies in the literature have demonstrated a relation between getting an infant to practice the walking reflex and the occurrence of true walking at an earlier-than-normal age (Andre-Thomas and Dargassies, 1952; Zelazo, Zelazo, and Kolb, 1972). This relation suggests that true walking arises from the walking reflex. With this evidence, we can revise the straight maturational theory: landmark gross motor abilities are the products of a sequence of behavior changes that began as part of the maturation process, but the rate at which these abilities develop may be influenced by events at various points in the sequence.

Reaching and Grasping

A baby grasping someone's glasses is demonstrating *fine motor behavior,* so called because it involves coordination of some of the smaller muscles. Newborns start grasping by reflex until they gradually learn to coordinate reaching with their whole arm and watching to judge their progress toward the object. Let us examine these developments in detail.

This common but complex process, called *visually directed reaching,* generally develops in the following sequence. First, the infant notices his hand when it happens to move into his field of vision. This interests him and, for a time, he may be engrossed in watching his hand. Sometimes the baby sees objects near his hand, and eventually he may swipe at such objects, but without opening his hand and touching the object. At this point it looks as if the baby needs actually to touch an object before his hand will open.

Soon—perhaps in several weeks—the baby may be seen looking back and forth between his hand and some object, an indication to some psychologists (e.g., White, 1971) that the baby is learning to integrate his looking, reaching, and grasping. We can sometimes see him clasping and unclasping his hands as he stares intently at them. Perhaps he is intrigued by the dawning realization that what he feels while he grasps is also what he sees while he looks at his own hands. In any case, when babies are almost five months old, they usually have mastered the challenge of reaching while watching to direct the endeavor (Field, 1976).

White (1971), in order to verify his view that babies follow this sequence as they combine and coordinate the component behaviors of reaching and grasping, observed 34 infants living in an institution over their first five months. In order to rectify the stimulus-impoverished environment of the institution, White provided some of the infants with a number of interesting stimuli: bright-colored linen, crib stabiles (objects attached to the cribs for the babies to grasp), and patterned crib sides. These things were given to them when the infants were between 37 and 124 days old, during the supposedly critical time for them to begin to develop visually directed reaching. The remaining infants were given much milder stimuli: a pacifier on either side of the crib between days 37 and 68 and a stabile between days 69 and 124.

White clearly expected that babies exposed to the stronger stimuli would exhibit visually directed reaching sooner; they had more interesting objects available to encourage them to reach out. He reasoned that, once babies begin to swipe at objects, further experience should help them organize looking, reaching, and grasping into an efficient and correctly ordered sequence. White also predicted that the babies who were given stabiles from the beginning would be distracted by them and so would not look at their hands as soon as those given only pacifiers at first. The babies given the milder stimuli presumably would take notice of their hands somewhat earlier, and thus should develop a smoothly integrated reach-and-grasp before those given the stronger stimuli.

The results of White's observation showed that both of his groups had their visually directed reaching perfected before the normal time. Although those given stabiles from the outset did indeed look at their hands later than normal, they began to swipe at objects even before they were observed to watch their hands for prolonged periods. Although before it appeared that hand studying triggered swiping, these results indicate this is not necessarily true. Some of the babies in both groups learned smoothly coordinated reaching and grasping without the touch-then-grasp process that White initially considered a necessary beginning. It seems that some of the time for some infants grasping and reaching occur separately, but they may occur together. Their occurrence together does not necessarily depend on their having occurred separately before.

In his very controversial and as yet unreplicated study, Bower (1974) demonstrated that newborns can reach for and grasp objects if they are supported under the arms, a position in which they do not have to use their arms to hold up their bodies and heads as they do when lying on their stomachs. Because of this, Bower suggested that the combined reach-and-grasp may be innate, but that, as babies mature, the combined reach-and-grasp changes into two separate acts. This separation is more adaptive, Bower notes, because it permits us either to reach first and then grasp to secure an object or to grasp first and then reach out to use an object as a tool. The separation of the reach-and-grasp responses also allows us to adjust our grasps without moving our arms, as we must if we do not get a good grip on an object we have reached for. Similarly, if in mid-reach we discover than an object is not quite where we thought it was (perhaps, like a kitten or a ball, it is moving erratically), we can adjust our reach course without necessarily disrupting our grasp. Newborn infants, however, don't make these readjustments if objects they are reaching for move: they will sit with their hands out toward the wrong location rather than redirect them to the right one.

Having separate reaching and grasping reflexes is clearly more adaptive than having the two actions totally integrated. However, although newborns do combine the actions while slightly older babies do not, this one fact is not enough to prove Bower's theory that infants learn to separate the two actions as they mature. Because Bower's work on reaching and grasping has not been replicated by others, we need to observe more babies as they grow before we can make definite statements about how babies develop the "simple" process of reaching and grasping. Bower has begun the task, and he has presented a provocative invitation to others of us to do research on this topic.

After babies develop their visually guided reaching, they still need another series of adjustments in the reach-and-grasp operation. In the early months, infants do not adjust the tension in their arm muscles in anticipation of weights of the objects they intend to grasp. After a baby has an object in hand, however, his arm tension adjusts slightly so that the object will not fall out of his hand. Sometimes you can see a slight tremor in a baby's arm while he makes adjustments to bring an object nearer his face to suck it or look at it.

As babies mature, they continue to improve their ability to adjust their arm muscles to the weight of an object. After having held a particular object just once, many one-year-old babies will make adjustments for its weight before actually touching that object again. But these babies seem to adjust only to particular objects. Given a series of objects varying in size and weight, the babies adjust to those objects that they have already picked up. Apparently, they do not generalize the information about size and weight to the next object in the series.

By 18 months of age infants begin to show that they are able to predict the weight of an object by its size. Shown a set of attractive objects in which size and weight are related, babies reach for them with their arms already tensed correctly for the weight of the objects. However, when Bower gave babies "irregular" objects that were lighter than they looked, he demonstrated that babies use size as the basis for predicting weight, and accordingly can be fooled when size does not relate to weight in the expected manner. Nevertheless, by 18 months, infants have developed their reaching and grasping into a smoothly coordinated sequence. They skillfully manipulate the objects in their environment, and they use them as tools when they want to.

Significance of Motor Development

The hallmarks of motor development that I have described here are often cited as major steps of overall infant development as well. The pediatrician keeps track of sitting, creeping, standing, walking, reaching, and grasping; and any marked delays in the appearance of any of these behaviors is regarded as a danger signal that development is not proceeding as well as it might. Infant tests, which are discussed in the Appendix, are heavily weighted with items that assess how well babies are developing their motor and sensory-motor skills. However, most psychologists do not think of sensory-motor behaviors as being, in themselves, manifestations of intelligence. Instead, we can think of coordinated sensory-motor skills as starting places for the baby's interaction with objects and events in the environment. This interaction and the learning about the environment that results constitute the baby's first cognitive experiences. Thus the baby's motor development and sensory-motor coordinations form the foundation of intelligence, but they are not the same thing as intelligence. In the remainder of this chapter, I will discuss various theoretical views and research findings to clarify further the role of motor development in infant cognition.

Piaget's Theory of Sensory-Motor Intelligence

Jean Piaget, a Swiss psychologist and philosopher, has devoted his career to studying cognition in children and adolescents. Born in Neuchatel in 1896, he grew up in a highly intellectual household where he was encouraged to pursue his early interest in the natural world. After he spent many childhood hours carefully observing birds and animals in their natural habitats, he was rewarded by a position in the local natural history museum and by seeing a series of his own papers on natural history published during his adolescence.

When Piaget was introduced to philosophy during his secondary school years, he was immediately intrigued by *epistemology,* which deals with the nature and origin of knowledge. He was fascinated by various theories about the role the senses play and the way internal factors affect cognition. He continued to read and think about these issues through his years of studying natural sciences at Neuchatel University. After he earned his Ph.D. in biological studies in 1917, he spent several years in Zurich and Paris pursuing a broad range of studies in psychology and philosophy.

During some of this period, Piaget worked in the laboratory of Theophile Simon, who had collaborated with Alfred Binet to develop the first IQ test. Here Piaget began to think seriously about approaching the study of the nature and origin of knowledge by combining the observational and factual approach of his training in science with the analytical approach of his training in structural philosophy and logic. In 1921, he returned to Switzerland as the director of studies at the Rousseau Institute in Geneva, where he began to translate his ideas for a new interdisciplinary approach to the study of cognition into a systematic program of research.

Remaining at Geneva, Piaget devoted his entire career to developing *genetic epistemology,* an interdisciplinary field that examines how we know the world and that is informed by the direct observation of developing children—who, after all, are people coming to know the world for the first time. Because babies are the newest "knowers," Piaget has focused several of his research efforts on babies—most notably his extensive analysis of the cognitive development of his own three children. In *Construction of Reality in the Child* (Piaget, 1954) and *The Origin of Intelligence in the Child* (1963) Piaget presents his basic ideas about infant cognition. Let us examine these ideas.

Assumptions and Essential Ideas

Piaget made three general assumptions about intelligence. (Like the assumptions of any theory, these are untested notions. They reflect Piaget's background and training, and they are a good starting place for us to examine his work.) The most important of these assumptions is that *thought arises from actions*. We come to understand the world as we act on objects and events, which, in turn, respond to us, not by passively absorbing bits of information from the environment. Intelligence is an active process. For example, a four-month-old infant learns something about space and distance when she bats at a proffered doll but does not quite connect with it. Gradually, she acquires more skill with reaching and grasping until she can gather up nearby toys at will. From her *acts* and their modifications she *constructs* her understanding of objects located at distances in space.

Piaget's second assumption was that intelligence is an *adaptive biological process,* a process in the same class with digestive functions, circulation, and the like. Because we can think, we can adjust our actions to the requirements of the environment. The baby who swipes at her toy and misses will continue to be unsuccessful until she changes her actions according to the actual distance between herself and the toy. Rather than continuing her behavior in exactly the same form, she purposely modifies it to fit the environment better. Having done so, she is in a better position to master a variety of similar reach-and-grasp situations.

Piaget gave the name *equilibration* to the process by which a person gradually improves the fit between his acts and environmental realities. Equilibration occurs continually throughout life; but there may be some periods during which our actions and thoughts change more rapidly than usual and others during which little change occurs because prevailing concepts and actions are adequate for dealing with external realities. When confronted by a new situation, you have two adaptational processes to help you understand and master it. According to Piaget, you can either *accommodate*—change your concepts or activities to agree with reality—or *assimilate*—use your present repertoire of concepts and activities to deal with the experience just as you used to deal with earlier ones. For example, when a baby tries to drink from a cup instead of her familiar bottle, she attempts first to assimilate: she sucks the cup as if it were a bottle. Gradually, she accommodates to the cup and learns the new skill of drinking.

Piaget calls the times of relatively little change *stages*. During each stage of development the child fits both his old and his new experiences into his current set of concepts and actions. After he has assimilated as much as possible, some things will still remain intractable to his repertoire of actions and concepts, so the child must accommodate and learn new actions and concepts or modify old ones. When he accommodates more frequently than he assimilates, he is moving between two stages. He completes the transition to his new stage when he has adequately changed his old actions to be able to handle his experiences principally by means of assimilation.

Piaget's third basic assumption is that all *thought has structure*. A central part of Piaget's idea of thought is that it has relatively permanent parts that go together in logically coherent ways. An example of structure in thought would be the organization of classes of objects into more and more inclusive classes such as exists in biological classification systems.

At any stage, the baby adapts using relatively permanent systems of acting on the environment, called *schemes*. Schemes are the basic units of thought structure. For example, using the "scheme" of "reach and grasp an object," a baby can deal with a variety of novel objects at different distances. Our schemes are the basic units of cognitive structure. The simplest schemes are our reflex acts, which allow us even as newborns to assimilate some events from our surroundings.

As development proceeds, babies combine simpler schemes into more complex patterns as they continually organize their experiences and the schemes used to understand them. Organization, a characteristic of cognitive structure, is a basic biological process in all living creatures. Like assimilation and accommodation, organization helps us adapt. For example, as the baby organizes various sensory-motor schemes, he can construct his first broad world view—based on his combined actions on objects seen, heard, and felt in his immediate physical environment. He develops the ideas of object, time, space, and cause as he explores his environment with sensory-motor schemes.

Piaget's followers use "development" rather than "learning" to describe the changes in cognitive processes that occur as the child grows. Development is the sequence of changes that take place as internal factors interact with forces from the environment. Some other theories emphasize one of these components—inborn characteristics or environmental events—at the expense of the other. For instance, a learning theory would emphasize the molding of an essentially passive organism's response by the stimulus events—both reinforcers and distinctions between stimuli—that exist in the environment. A maturational theory, in contrast, would emphasize genetic programming. The developmental view encompasses the interplay between such inborn factors as the processes of equilibration and organization and such external factors as the particular events and objects the child encounters.

Before moving on to the specifics of Piaget's sensory-motor stages, I must briefly comment on his interesting methodology. Piaget based his work largely on extensive observation. His approach was to set up a situation for the child, but then to leave the child free to act within that situation. For example, following Piaget's techniques for children who talk, an observer might prepare a "race course" on a table top with some small wheeled cars and other miniature toys that the child would be free to pick up and move about. The child's play with these toys would be spontaneous, but it might be interrupted by questions that the observer has been trained to ask: "Which one of your cars is going faster? How do you know? What do you think would happen if I moved it back here?" The observer learns to pay close attention to the child's activities in order to be able to direct challenges, questions, and suggestions that are just at the forefront of the child's developmental state.

Piaget's structured, observational approach can go in many directions and the child is not told what response is expected. However, the questions tend to channel the child's attention to the important features of a complex situation and to increase the chances that the child will reflect on these features and their relations. Piaget uses this examining-teaching style to encourage children to think actively. The child's actions are the central basis of her thought, but her reflecting on her own action can improve her understanding. In any case, if activity is the basis of thought, then we need to observe children's actions in order to construct an understanding of their thoughts.

With a nonverbal infant, the interaction of observer and subject must be modified. Instead of having question-and-answer exchanges the observer and infant exchange activities. The examiner offers a toy; the baby reaches for it. When the observer covers the toy with a scarf, the baby is confused. After the observer uncovers the toy, the baby reaches. Through such a sequence, accompanied by careful observation of the baby's facial reactions and behavior, the Piagetian observer can discover many aspects of how the world looks to a nonverbal infant. In the following sections I will describe some of these procedures in more detail.

Cognitive Events of Infancy: Sensory-Motor Intelligence

Infancy is the first major stage in Piaget's theory of cognitive development (which also includes several substages for each stage). During infancy—roughly, the first two years—you can most clearly see that understanding is grounded in activity. At this time understanding *is* sensory-motor activity. Hence Piaget calls his first stage the *sensory-motor* stage. Babies make sense out of their world and its objects through looking, listening, and manipulating, and also by moving their bodies. Too, they focus only on the immediate situation. Piaget argues that infants younger than about eight or nine months do not make mental representations of missing objects and events that are distant in time. They experience only the here and now. Indeed, the end of infancy is marked by the acquisition of the mental symbols such as visual images, other sensory images, and words that we use to remember the recent past and to make predictions about the near future.

The baby masters several important concepts about the nature of the physical world for the first time during the sensory-motor stage. These concepts—of the object, of cause and effect, of space, and of time—are so elementary that we take them for granted and think of them as "givens" in perception. Philosophers have argued for centuries about the basis for our experiencing the perceived world as three-dimensional, as having objects located within it, and as constantly existing through time. Piaget believes that, although we are not born with these concepts already formed, we are disposed by our nature to construct them out of our everyday experiences with objects and events. This is the main business of infancy. Let us look further at these elementary concepts.

The term *object concept* refers to our understanding of tangible, physical objects. Most of us take for granted that our wallets, pencils, handkerchiefs, books, and other possessions continue to exist even when we are not looking at or touching them. But young babies do not realize that objects are permanent, and they only gradually acquire this insight through many experiences with the comings and goings of objects. As we shall see, some controversy exists about exactly when babies discover object permanence. The object concept, when fully present, concerns several other attributes of objects besides permanence. Objects also have substance—that is, they are made of "stuff"; they are somewhere in space; and they move by various causes that most of the time have nothing to do with our behavior toward them.

To clarify some of these ideas further, let us look at some typical behavior of a baby toward an attractive new toy. Assume that you are an indulgent aunt or uncle and that you are visiting the family of your four-month-old niece. You have just offered her a small toy as she sits in her reclining infant chair on the table. She grasps it and looks gleefully at it until, accidentally, it drops to the floor—whereupon she turns unperturbed to some other interesting sight, seemingly totally unconcerned about the previously enchanting new toy. Piaget would argue that she seems unconcerned about the toy because she doesn't realize that it continues to exist when she cannot see it. A few months later, at seven months of age, the same niece will look around for an attractive new toy if it falls and will show great interest in continuing her playtime with it for as long as possible. However, she still will seem unperturbed if the toy is made to disappear under a scarf or some other hiding device. Once out of sight, the toy is out of mind, and she moves on to something else. However, in the next month or two, she will begin to search for a hidden object, which reveals not only that she has come to understand the notion of hiding places, but also that she realizes the permanence of objects.

At first, however, she does not follow the same rules that you or I would follow in searching for a lost object. You can play a game of hide and seek with her to see this for yourself. Hide the toy several times under a scarf. Now move the toy to a new hiding place—say, under a different scarf a few feet away. You find that the baby looks for the toy under the first scarf, even though she clearly saw you put it under the second one. Piaget points out that, rather than coordinating her behavior with the object's "obvious" location in space, she is operating as if she believes that her own searching would somehow reconstitute the lost object. She knows the object still exists, but she doesn't recognize that the object has an identity that is independent of her behavior.

Gradually, through repeated and varied experiences with objects in everyday life, the baby separates her own acts from the objects in her environment and at last searches for lost objects appropriately. She still becomes confused, however, if great demands are placed on her developing ability to use a symbol to represent an object. For example, if the toy is placed in a paper bag, which is then itself hidden in several places in sequence, the baby is baffled again. Finally, at about the age of 18 months, she masters all the intricacies and can systematically search for a lost toy, even one that she may not have seen for a matter of many hours. This shows that she knows the missing toy has substance, permanence, and a location in space, and that its continued existence is independent of her actions. In other words, she has mastered the *object concept.*

Another important development during infancy is *the separation of means and ends (causes and effects).* During the first few months babies show no really deliberate efforts to bring about desired changes in their surroundings. Although many parents and casual bystanders have the impression that young infants are trying to get them to behave in particular ways, no one has ever shown that any behavior in a very young infant meets the criteria of an *intentional* act. Such an act must clearly precede, and be separate from, its results; the actor must be paying attention to the person or object that will produce the desired results; and the actor must modify the act appropriately if the situation changes.

By about four months of age, however, most infants will show some evidence of trying to "make things happen." At first, the baby of four months capitalizes on events that occur spontaneously or accidentally. For example, Piaget cites his daughter's discovery that, when she thrashed her legs and lower trunk, she could cause the cloth dolls dangling from her basinette cover to flutter. Thereafter, she would often thrash her legs, apparently with the intention of starting the fluttering again. Although her behavior definitely showed that she could separate means (thrashing) and ends (fluttering basinette cover), it was an action of relatively limited usefulness: thrashing is an unreliable means of getting things done; that is, the *end* of moving the cover occurs at the same time as the thrashing only once in a while.

A little later in the first year, babies begin to show more varied and more deliberate efforts to cause things to happen. For example, babies will persistently and forcefully try to remove any barrier—such as a book, a hand, or the like—that is placed between them and a favorite toy. The persistence of such efforts while they remain focused on the goal of reaching the toy is a sign of intentionality, showing a clear separation of means (pushing the barrier with the hand) and end (obtaining the toy). Although babies at this stage may make obvious attempts to cause a variety of ends in various situations, their actions are still limited: the means and ends are strongly suggested by the situation and they are not the product of the baby's thought.

About the age of one year, babies may begin to experiment with various means of making things happen. As a common example, babies confined in their playpens or cribs often throw all their toys out one by one, watching with glee as they fall, and seemingly amused by the different sounds that different toys make when they hit the floor. A baby of this age may also go about a room attempting to open various objects. Some objects open, whereas others do not, and the pattern of results appears to be interesting—and occasionally frustrating—to the baby. This active experimentation with a means to discover interesting ends is a much broader and more flexible means–end separation than the baby was able to make at first.

Finally, at about 18 months of age, babies show signs of inventing new means rather than relying solely upon discovery. A baby of this age may pile up a bunch of pillows and try to stand on them to reach a high object. Another might pick up a toy broom and use it as a rake to pull an object from under a piece of furniture. Another baby might be able to get an adult to fetch a desired, but out-of-reach object, cleverly using even other people as a tool. These actions reveal that babies (now really toddlers) are actively thinking and developing plans or ideas about means to various ends. They can represent objects by symbols, an accomplishment that signals that the sensory-motor stage is at an end.

Two concepts related to the object concept and means–end separation are *space* and *time*. As infants gradually gain insight into what objects are like, they also begin to sense space as a "container" for objects. At about the age of four months, when babies first search after fallen objects, their first primitive notions of dimension emerge. They begin to sense that they are searching an area to find an object within it. As they progress to a systematic search for hidden objects, they simultaneously develop a better idea of location, which, of course, means a position in space. Infants need a system to organize their perceptions. They begin to realize that the seen, heard, and felt impressions can all belong to a single object, and that one object (a scarf) can be located in relation to another (the toy). Because the concept of physical space organizes these ideas admirably, Piaget assumed that it is developed jointly with (or perhaps as a by-product of) the object concept.

Although Piaget has written about the concept of time (Piaget, 1966), he has said relatively little about how babies soon develop this concept in the sensory-motor stage. Presumably, as the means–end separation becomes more and more distinct, babies also gain a sense of *before* and *after* as well. Infants show by their behavior that they do anticipate outcomes and that they partially remember past events. Babies probably sense the *order* aspect of time—the recurring sequences of events. This sense of temporal order emerges step by step along with means and ends. Piaget argues that this ordered time concept is one of the cornerstones of the baby's *construction of reality*. At about 18 months of age, most infants have actively created out of their experience a view of the physical world that includes the concepts of *objects, space, time,* and *cause and effect.*

The Role of Play and Imitation in Infant Cognition

Piaget defines play as an example of pure assimilation, whereby novel experiences are fitted into already known modes of action or already known concepts. When a baby repeats (sometimes seemingly endlessly) a newly acquired scheme, such as opening and closing the hand or sucking a piece of blanket, we can see in this that pure means are being repeated without regard to ends. Thus, whatever happens to go on around the baby is assimilated to the one scheme without regard for results. Piaget presumes that such play helps babies perfect their skills and that it therefore ultimately serves an adaptive purpose. Piaget identifies six substages of the sensory-motor stage. As babies pass through these substages, we can distinguish their play more and more easily from their more immediately adaptive assimilation, which is what occurs when they learn to eat solid food, sit up, and the like. Eventually children spend definite periods of their days "just playing."

According to Piaget, imitation, the opposite of play, is pure accommodation. If I imitate your facial expression, I must observe it carefully and move my facial muscles to match yours. At first, when babies are only a couple of months old, they can only "pseudo-imitate." For example, if, after a baby drops a toy, you pick it up and drop it in imitation, he can pseudo-imitate your action by picking up the toy and dropping it again himself. This is not true imitation because the first action must be the baby's. The baby learns to imitate by stages. The first transition is from pseudo to true imitation. The next involves moving from imitating with seen parts of the body to imitating with unseen parts. If when he is a young infant you repeat an action of his that was made with a part of his body that he can see—such as his hands or legs—he can imitate it. Next he can imitate your actions involving parts of his body that he can't see—his face, for instance. Finally, the infant becomes a skilled imitator, and he employs his new abilities to learn useful and entertaining behaviors. Learning through imitation will be a powerful aid to his development from now on.

The Sequence of Substages

Throughout my discussion of the baby's major accomplishments of the sensory-motor period, I have emphasized that these important concepts— of objects, space, time, and cause and effect—develop gradually over roughly the first 18 months of life. Piaget has pointed out that during this time there are some periods of days or weeks when babies change relatively quickly, followed by other periods when they consolidate and "practice" their new gains. There are six periods of consolidation and practice and these make up the six *substages* of the sensory-motor stage. I will describe the characteristics of each substage in the same format. First, I will tell what Piaget singles out as the salient characteristic of the substage; then I will review the baby's gradual mastery of each of the important concepts; finally, I will summarize the baby's characteristic play and imitation activities for the substage. Table 4-1 lists the major events of the substages.

Substage 1 (0–1 month). Exercising Inborn Schemes. During the first month of life, the behavior of infants is largely reflexive, although there are some very brief, irregular, voluntary actions as well. Babies look at objects, and they may briefly shift their gaze to follow moving objects. They suck and grasp things, and they show changes in *state* (see Chapter 2) according to the stimulation they receive. They have no real sense of objects existing apart from themselves, and indeed we may infer that the entire "in here"/"out there" distinction has no meaning for them. As a consequence, babies can't separate means from ends and because they lack a concept of objects or external events, they don't sense space or time. We have defined play as practicing means for their own sakes rather than for particular ends, and the infants who do not separate means from ends cannot be said to play. During the first month of life babies also do not imitate us because they cannot separate themselves from external events, which is the first step of coordinating our actions with an external model. The first substage is primarily a time for babies to organize their inborn, reflex schemes.

Substage 2 (1–4 months). Primary Circular Reactions. After gaining a little experience in the world, babies begin to notice or discover interesting variations in the environmental stimulation they receive. Crib mobiles flutter or hang still; people change their expressions as they talk, look, and smile; intriguing noises abound. Babies now begin to repeat over and over

Table 4-1   Multidimensional View of Development During Sensory-Motor Period

Substage	Developmental Unit	Intention and Means–End Relations	Meaning	Object Permanence
1	Exercising the Inborn Sensory-motor Schemes (0–1 month)			
2	Primary Circular Reactions (1–4 months)		Different responses to different objects	
3	Secondary Circular Reactions (4–8 months)	Acts upon objects	"Motor meaning"	Brief single-modality search for absent object
4	Coordination of Secondary Circular Reaction Schemes (8–12 months)	Attacks barrier to reach goal	Symbolic meaning	Prolonged, multi-modality search
5	Tertiary Circular Reactions (12–18 months)	"Experiments in order to see"; discovery of new means through "groping accommodation"	Elaboration through action and feedback	Follows sequential displacements if object in sight
6	Invention of New Means (18–24 months)	Invention of new means through reciprocal assimilation of schemes	Further elaboration; symbols increasingly covert	Follows sequential displacement with object hidden; symbolic representation of object, mostly internal

SOURCE: From *The Origins of Intellect,* 2d ed., by John L. Phillips, Jr. W. H. Freeman and Company. Copyright © 1975.

Space	Time	Causality	Imitation	Play
			Pseudo-imitation begins	Apparent functional autonomy of some acts
All modalities focus on single object	Brief search for absent object	Acts; then waits for effect to occur	Pseudo-imitation quicker, more precise; true imitation of acts already in repertoire and visible on own body	More acts done for their own sake
Turns bottle to reach nipple	Prolonged search for absent object	Attacks barrier to reach goal; waits for adults to serve him	True imitation of novel acts not visible on own body	Means often become ends; ritualization begins
Follows sequential displacements if object in sight	Follows sequential displacements if object in sight	Discovers new means; solicits help from adults	True imitation quicker, more precise	Quicker conversion of means to end; elaboration of ritualization
Solves detour problem; symbolic representation of spatial relationships, mostly internal	Both anticipation and memory	Infers causes from observing effects; predicts effects from observing causes	Imitates (1) complex, (2) nonhuman, (3) absent models	Treats inadequate stimuli as if adequate to imitate an enactment —i.e., symbolic ritualization or "pretending"

various behavior patterns that they have accidentally associated with interesting results. They may repeatedly open and close their mouths, kick their legs, or turn their heads back and forth. Their repetitive antics impress adults as actions done to accomplish some result. Babies look in order to see, they suck in order to increase the tactile sensations in their mouths, and they kick in order to move the mobiles that hang above their cribs. Piaget calls these repetitive actions *primary circular reactions.* "Primary" means that the repetitive acts involve only the baby's own body.

Although babies in Substage 2 focus on objects as part of their own behavior of seeing, sucking, kicking, and so on, they have no real sense of these objects existing separate from their behavior. Thus Piaget argues that babies at this substage don't have a real sense of object permanence, space, time, or means and ends. However, one component of the object concept, the idea that objects have substance, is present at this point. Babies in this substage will avoid objects coming at them, and they may attempt to reach and grasp objects (White, 1971).

Primary circular reactions are distinguished from earlier reflexes because babies now have more voluntary control over their actions and more ability to organize them. They are now able to use a coordinated look-and-suck, look-and-reach, or look-and-listen pattern. The looking, sucking, reaching, and listening schemes will themselves show more adaptability to objects encountered as well as to the coordinations among them. Babies who have experienced a given pleasant event—say, being picked up by a smiling adult—will show by smiling and vocalizing that they recognize the event as familiar.

In Substage 2 babies still lack ability to distinguish self from nonself. At this stage, if an object disappears, babies immediately focus their attention elsewhere without searching for the lost article. However, because they can recognize recurrent events, they are able to entertain themselves with repetitive cycles of behavior once they have set these cycles in motion. Here we see pseudo-imitation: if you repeat a baby's actions she will repeat her act after you do.

In summary, during Substage 2, babies with their rich repertoire of actions can respond to events much better than they could in Substage 1, but they still do not distinguish themselves from objects. Piaget supposes that babies' sense of self is completely bound up with the results of their own acts. For a baby at this stage, seeing a mobile move is no different from making it move.

Substage 3 (4–8 months). Secondary Circular Reactions.   The important feature of Substage 3 is the beginning of the ability to separate means and ends. Maturation and experience with primary circular reactions make it possible for babies to shift their attention to the objects that play a part in their circular reactions. Thus, the rattle becomes "a thing to be grasped" and "a thing to be listened to." Now babies can separate their own grasping actions from the interesting sound that results. We sense an infant purposefully reaching and grasping before listening, as he plans to cause the sound. This is the first indication that the baby separates the means and the end of an action sequence. Babies now clearly separate means from ends in time and Piaget infers their separation into two separate schemes.

Babies continue their repetitive cycles of activity, but they now focus on the interplay of their own acts and the external environment. Piaget thus labels these circular reactions as *secondary*: they combine the primary physical aspect of the infant using his own body with a secondary environmental aspect as he involves objects around him in his activities. Through his secondary circular reactions, he experiences objects in more positions in space, angles of view, and in a more varied way, and the object concept begins to develop. Substage 3 babies will search for disappearing objects that disappear when they are paying attention to them. They will grope to pick up an unseen toy that they feel with part of their bodies, visually follow the path of a toy dropped from the highchair, or reach and lunge after a toy that is being withdrawn from them by a playful caregiver. At this point they will only use one sense as they try to understand—listening for a sound, rather than looking for its cause. Their primitive search behavior shows that they do partially sense objects as continuing to exist through time and over some short expanse of space, thus indicating the beginnings of the concepts of time and space, as well as the beginnings of the object concept itself.

When objects are stationary, babies in the third substage can focus on them with all their senses. Thus they can turn objects over and over while looking at them intently and listening to their sounds. Now they can repeat a wide variety of complex and interesting "means" actions simply for enjoyment, and thus engage for the first time in what we have identified as play. Increased mastery of those of their own actions that they can see makes them able to reproduce many interesting actions at will. Thus, Substage 3 babies imitate activities modeled by adults, if those activities are to be done with parts of their own bodies that they can see, and if they involve action sequences they already have mastered.

Substage 4 (8–12 months). Coordination of Secondary Circular Reaction Schemes. The principal milestone of Substage 4 is perfecting the separation of means and ends. Babies at this stage will persist if some barrier or frustration intervenes between their acts and the desired end. They will push your hand away to recover the toy you are blocking and they will tug endlessly at your pants leg until you agree to pick them up. Babies' acts now are plainly *intentional,* and they also realize they are involved in situations "out there," someplace external to themselves. Babies now become systematic problem solvers, varying their means in order to produce the desired end. If you take a toy away from a baby of this age, he may attempt to recover it by pushing your hand, by grasping a protruding part of the toy, or by fussing loudly to induce you to release it.

The clear separation of means and ends is accompanied by a more prolonged and systematic search for lost objects, provided that the baby saw them disappear. Babies now realize that objects are permanent: covered objects continue to exist when they cannot see, hear, or touch them. However, the standard procedure for finding a lost object still has some flaws. At this point if you hide a toy several times in a row at place A and then, in full view, hide it at place B, the baby persists in searching at place A, apparently in the belief that the very act of searching for it at location A will simply cause the object to be there. The baby clearly separates the means (the search) from the end (finding the object), but apparently she still doesn't grasp that the location of an object is independent of her behavior. When you lose your keys, you think of them as being somewhere and so you walk around, trying to put yourself in that same place. But when you use a set of keys to play the hiding game with the baby, once the keys are hidden she thinks they will obligingly be at "the spot where I find lost keys," and so she will look in the place where she last found them. In her concept of space, objects have locations assigned to them by her own actions in those places.

Play and imitation both show major changes in this substage. The baby now enjoys frequently (and intentionally) repeating a sequence of interesting and complex actions. The 9- or 10-month-old baby stacks and unstacks pots, pushes and pulls wheel toys with delight, and may drive adults to distraction with repetitive rhythms banged out with a spoon or shovel. The infant can now imitate actions of grownups that he has never done before—even actions with parts of his body he can't see—and he happily expands his repertoire of renditions of the actions of his family.

Substage 5 (12–18 months). Tertiary Circular Reactions.   During Substage 5 babies become capable of more complex behavior, including longer transactions that consist of a repeated back-and-forth exchange with the environment. Babies now become active experimenters, varying both their means to fixed ends (as in Substage 4) and their ends. I always think of a baby happily throwing toys out of her playpen one by one as the prototype of the Substage 5 baby. She wants to see what will happen when she applies the pick-up-and-drop scheme to different objects. Some make noise, others do not; some break, others do not; and so on through the afternoon. Through this experimentation, she may discover new means as well—for example, if she throws a toy down on a pillow, it makes less noise than it does when it is thrown on the floor. Thus, by choosing her target location, she has a means of controlling the noise made by a falling object.

At this substage the baby will systematically search for a lost object, and she will look in its correct hiding place if she has seen it hidden there. Piaget infers that the baby now represents the object with a mental symbol, and that she knows that its location in space is independent from her actions toward it, which implies considerable improvement of her sense of space. Babies can now think about and deal with longer and longer sequences of time. This is shown by their ability to follow you through a fairly long series of hiding an object, first here, and then there, and then somewhere else, and to retrieve it from the last hiding spot.

The baby can now imitate complex and totally new acts such as clowning stunts done by big sister and brother, or opening a book and turning its pages. Her play is also more complex at this state, and she is finally entertaining herself with what looks like play to an adult. Because she imitates the many new actions she sees around her and practices them in play, Piaget believes that the baby now has organized her behavior, skillfully calling on its new flexibility and variety to meet her needs. The organization is apparent both in the purposefulness shown as the baby (now a toddler) gathers materials, arranges space, and pursues a dramatic theme. The flexibility of thought can be seen in her ability to overcome minor frustrations and redirect actions while still maintaining the general goal—say, building an enclosure with blocks, or making a pillow pile.

Substage 6 (18–24 months). Invention of New Means.   The principal advance of Substage 6 is the beginning of *symbolic function,* Piaget's name for the ability to represent experience through mental symbols. Infancy, as I have defined it ends here, for when children can deal with the world through such symbols as images and words, they are no longer confined to the sensory-motor realities of the here and now. A major impact of this is that they can invent new means as they contemplate particular ends. A child of this age can think of the step stool in the bathroom while he studies the out-of-reach toy in the playroom, and he can act on his insight. Clearly, means and ends are totally separate now, and they can be coordinated in more and more effective ways.

Their ability to use symbols also affects babies' behavior with objects. Because babies can keep and change a mental image of a missing toy, they can systematically search for it even if they did not see it hidden, or if it was first placed in an opaque container and then hidden. Encouraged by their now complete concept of objects, they develop a more advanced sense of continuous time and organized space. Their sophistication about space is apparent when they detour around obstacles on the way to a destination. Their visual images of space also help them organize their experiences.

At this point babies' play changes greatly because they can represent situations. They can at last pretend and play out the dramatic moments of daily life. They repeat their experiences endlessly and, according to Piaget, understand them better as they assimilate them into their repertoire of methods for dealing with the world. They become able to imitate increasingly complex and novel sequences of activity *even when the model is no longer present* and, because they frequently imitate family members as they play, imitation also becomes an important tool for learning about the world. Symbolic models on television and in picture books begin to influence the child. The symbolic function truly transforms the baby whose life is "here and now" into a child who deals with the short-term past and future and who thus can plan, remember, and initiate events.

Research Based on Piaget's Theory of Sensory-Motor Intelligence

Several investigators have undertaken to evaluate Piaget's postulated sequence of development in infancy and to chart the ages when most children change from stage to stage. In this section I will report what has been learned from these efforts. In addition, I will discuss the studies that reveal how children's environment can affect their performance on Piagetian tasks. Finally I will review T. G. R. Bower's creative but controversial experiments, which may clarify some details about how babies develop the object concept.

Studies of Developmental Sequence

In an extensive long-term study, Uzgiris (1973, 1976) traced how 12 infants developed six aspects of cognition important to Piaget's theory. To increase the accuracy of the observations, she devised standardized tests to assess the infants' standing on these six achievements of the sensory-motor stage: object permanence, causality, spatial relation between objects, means–end separation, and the babies' imitations of words and gestures. Table 4-2 lists examples of the tasks that the babies did during the study according to the succeeding steps of developing object permanence. The scale coordinates the examples with the average ages at which babies were able to accomplish the tasks. Uzgiris and Hunt found that the babies they tested generally proceed through the steps of their scales in the same order that Piaget's theory predicts (Uzgiris and Hunt, 1975).

Table 4-2   Object Permanence Scale with Items Ordered from First Mastered to Last Mastered

Average Age (months)	Task to Be Accomplished
1	Following a slowly moving object through a 180° arc.
2	Noting the disappearance of a slowly moving object.
4–5	Finding an object that is partially covered.
7	Finding an object that is completely covered with a single screen in two places.
7	Finding an object that is completely covered with a single screen in two places alternately.
7	Finding an object that is completely covered with a single screen in three places.
9–10	Finding an object after successive visible displacements.
13	Finding an object under one of two superimposed screens.
13	Finding an object following one invisible displacement with a single screen.
14	Finding an object following one invisible displacement with two screens.
14	Finding an object following one invisible displacement with two screens alternated.
14	Finding an object following one invisible displacement with three screens.
17	Finding an object following a series of invisible displacements.
21–22	Finding an object following a series of invisible displacements by searching in reverse of the order of hiding.

SOURCE: Data from *Assessment in Infancy,* by I. C. Uzgiris and J. McV. Hunt. Urbana: University of Illinois Press, 1975, pp. 151–164.

A technique for evaluating whether a set of tasks (such as those of Table 4-2) are mastered in a predicted order is *scalogram* analysis. To use this technique, we examine which infants pass and which fail the tests. If the object concept tasks of Table 4-2 always develop in the listed sequence, then an infant who passes an advanced task shouldn't fail a supposedly easier one. Armed with the statistics for how often babies' abilities agree with the order of the tasks, we can judge the degree to which the order of the steps conform to a theoretically predictable sequence.

Several investigators performed scalogram analyses for the object concept. Using the Uzgiris-Hunt scales, Uzgiris (1976) analyzed several groups of infants' records and discovered evidence that strongly supports Piaget's postulated sequences for mastering the six achievements of sensory-motor development. Two other teams of investigators using scalogram analysis to study the object concept had results that were consistent with Piaget's theory (Kopp, Sigman, and Parmelee, 1973; Kramer, Hill, and Cohen, 1975); both of the teams studied the babies over a length of time and observed that they did go through the sequences in the predicted order. Another group of investigators reports longitudinal results for their own version of Piaget's object concept tests that support Piaget (Gratch and Landers, 1971).

However, one investigator team reported negative results for scalogram analysis in which experimental controls ruled out the role of irrelevant cues such as the colors of covers, right vs. left preferences, and the like (Miller, Cohen, and Hill, 1970). It is difficult to know how heavily we should weigh the findings of this study except to note that it employed carefully controlled and standardized procedures and that its results do suggest that the way in which the tests are given probably affects how well the baby performs, a point to which we will return.

After sufficient studies of a Piagetian sensory-motor task, we might expect that babies' skill at one task would match their performance on another to the extent that object concept, means–end relations, and spatial awareness all are different facets of the same underlying cognitive structure. However, Piaget counters our expectations by arguing that babies are surrounded by objects and events that they assimilate at different rates, so at any particular moment their mastery of one task won't match their skill at another. In fact, the few studies that have looked at interrelationships among Piagetian sensory-motor skills do not find much evidence that babies' competence at one skill will reflect their ability at others (Uzgiris, 1976; Kopp, Sigman, and Parmelee, 1973). Babies' various sensory-motor skills may well be influenced by their experiences—a quite strong possibility because sensory-motor intelligence is so immediate, concrete, and unsymbolic. The specific toys that are used, the distracting stimuli, and the tempo of testing are all factors that may change how babies react to testing. Let us look now at the specific evidence we have on this point.

The Effects of Tasks and Procedures

How do the procedure and articles that are part of a task affect an infant's performance with an object? Piaget says that infants become better "finders of hidden objects" as they improve their mental image of them. Presumably, younger babies do not have any mental picture of missing objects. During sensory-motor Substage 4, babies represent the missing object well enough to be encouraged to search for it, but apparently are unable to envision its various movements through space, and instead think of it as being at the place where they last found it. Several investigators have reasoned that our ability to keep a memory image of an object in its correct (most recent) location depends on how long we must hold the image before we use it.

Some of these investigators have varied the time between hiding an object and letting the baby search for it. In all the studies after the researchers hid the object several times in one place (place A), they moved it to a second place (place B), and then had the babies wait various numbers of seconds before searching. When infants of eight or nine months of age were allowed to search in place B immediately they did not make the error common to infants their age of searching at A. However, when the babies waited 3 to 15 seconds they made the error part of the time (Gratch et al., 1974; Webb, Massar, and Nadolny, 1972; Harris, 1973). Babies who are given a second chance when the object is hidden in first one, then another, and finally a third place will search in the third place most of the time (Webb, Massar, and Nadolny, 1972). This fact seems to suggest that children eight or nine months old do hold some memory image over time but that the image may be a blend of the object and their search behavior.

Whatever image of the object babies may have, investigators always face the challenging problem of keeping their attention on the object in the correct location. Indeed, one investigative team noted that a clear result of increasing how long babies waited was that they were correspondingly less interested in the object. Their diminishing interest was in turn reflected by how frequently they made the usual Substage 4 error of looking in the first location (Gratch et al., 1974). Two investigators used a music box for an object because it makes noise even when it cannot be seen. They found that, when the box was playing, the babies could find it, but that, even after several trials in which the babies correctly located the playing box, they could not find it when it was silent (Ginsburg and Wong, 1973). The sound of the playing music box apparently focused their attention on the proper spot. Adults' helpful explanations—such as "that's a cat"—also seem to assist the baby by separating one object from the mass of other stimuli. An interesting study shows that 18- to 22-month-old babies not only prefer and pay more attention to named objects over unnamed objects but also show more object permanence toward named objects (Roberts and Black, 1972).

In general, activities that either lighten the load on a baby's memory image of an object (such as only a short delay before search) or draw his attention to the mental image (giving the object interesting features or a name) will help him successfully search for the hidden object. Given this reasoning, mastery of object permanence is a matter of degree and takes place over a period of time. Perhaps even adults fail to achieve it perfectly when they are distracted by fatigue or confused by drugs. The general rule would seem to be that we become better detectives as we gain greater control over the distribution of our own attention and a greater capacity for mental imagery.

Another way of looking at the sequence of object concept development is in terms of elementary learning principles. In this view, when the baby makes the standard Substage 4 search error, we could conclude that she wants to continue her same actions (searching at A) because she was rewarded by finding the object there in the past. The chances that she will do this increase with each successful search. The likelihood of her making an error increases when the two locations are identical or similar, and thus do not have any characteristics between which she can discriminate other than their spatial location. One study showed that, the more times babies have found the object at A, the greater the chance they will erroneously search there when the object is finally hidden at B (Landers, 1971). Another experimenter varied the number of times babies found the object when they originally searched at place A. The more times they had successfully recovered the object at A, the more often they continued to erroneously choose A after the object was moved to B (Harris, 1973). Apparently, babies do learn to make the response to a situation that is similar to one they have already faced—this is what we call *habit*. This can interfere with babies' using mental images to discover the correct solution. Of course, eventually, when babies repeatedly fail to find the object at A, it encourages them not only to switch to searching at B instead but also, according to the Piagetian view, to reorganize their concept of what the task is. Their task now becomes following a moving object through space, remembering its movements, and coordinating their search with those memory images. According to Piaget, infants' searching is gradually shaped by their many informal experiences with objects and the results they get from their activities with them *and* by their maturation. The few experiments done on the way in which changing the task influences babies to reorganize their concept of it seem to show that their specific learning experiences greatly aid them to "get the right idea" more quickly. Indeed, research done in babies' normal surroundings indicates that their performance on Piagetian tasks is greatly affected by whether other people offer them interesting stimulation and whether they too play a part in the outcome (Paraskevopoulos and Hunt, 1971).

Another factor that might be expected to influence the baby's search for a disappearing toy is the spatial set-up of the search. Piaget points out that one achievement of the sensory-motor period is learning to separate the location of an object from its other properties. One simple study demonstrated that even when the object hidden at B was different from the one hidden at A, nine-month-old babies still searched at A (Evans and Gratch,

1972). Perhaps Substage 4 babies associate certain spatial locations ("this is the spot where lost objects turn up") with the reappearance of all lost objects. This would agree with Piaget's notion that babies do not separate objects into entities that are distinct from the actions of others toward them and from their positions in space.

However, one carefully controlled study used two boxes for "hiding at A" trials and "hiding at B" trials and found that perhaps the confusion between spatial locations and the object itself might not be as great as it first appears. Babies were presented with two boxes side by side for their A trials. Half of the babies found the object in the left-hand box, whereas the other half found it in the right-hand box. For half of the two groups, the B trials simply reversed the location of the object and the babies mistakenly searched in its original location. However, for the other half the two boxes were moved to one side of the babies for the B trials. When the babies had to turn and reach in an entirely new direction to find the object, they looked in the correct box to find the object (Butterworth, 1975). Clearly, babies' perception of space, their physical movements, and the results of their search interact in a fairly complex way to determine how they will perform.

Psychoanalytic theory argues that infants will develop images of the objects that are central to their emotional life earlier than they will form images of other objects (Fraiberg, 1969). If this is so, we would expect babies to regard their parents as solid, independent entities in space sooner than they would accord the same qualities to the toys used in experimental studies. Indeed, evidence indicates that this is true (Bell, 1970; Goiń-DeCarie, 1965). Apparently, babies believe that their mothers continue to exist when they cannot be seen months before they entertain similar beliefs about toys. A crucial part of babies' attachment to their mothers is that they recognize them as permanent; we cannot have a relationship with someone unless we regard that person as existing permanently. Indeed, unless we believe that another person can behave independently of us, there is no need to try to reconcile ourselves to, or maintain a bond with, them, any more than we discuss with our hands whether they are going to remain attached to our bodies. The issue of relationship arises only with our recognition of separateness. We will pursue this topic further when we discuss attachments in Chapter 5.

As you can see, there is ample evidence to suggest that the specific characteristics of activity and procedures influence the way a baby will perform on Piagetian tasks. Our own "mental images" of how babies regard objects are also affected by the means we have of inferring their ideas. Since they can't talk to us, we have to devise clever experimental activities for them that may help us find out what they are thinking. Our assumption is that what they *do* follows from what they *think*. So far I have focused on a task in which a baby must do something obvious and systematic to demonstrate object permanence. In the next section we look at some innovative experiments using subtler behaviors and physiological changes to reveal a baby's understanding of objects. You may find that you have a somewhat modified picture of the younger baby's thought processes.

Bower's Work

T. G. R. Bower has done a series of laboratory experiments in an effort to better understand how young infants perceive the comings and goings of objects. The principal focus of his studies is the nativism-empiricism controversy, which we most recently considered in Chapter 3. Bower has sought to determine which properties of an object and its behavior very young infants understand through inborn methods of perceiving and which they understand only through experience and maturation.

Bower's view of the infant's concept of the object is not wholly opposed to Piaget's; rather, Bower's concern is with creating methods of finding out precisely what babies think about objects. In developing these methods, Bower divides the object concept into specific attributes of objects and then attempts to assess the baby's insight—or lack of insight—into each. His result is to help us understand what babies at various ages do or do not know about objects. With this information, we can evaluate Piaget's view and the information gathered from studies using his tasks. I should note here that some psychologists hesitate to use Bower's results to further their own understanding because thus far they have not been replicated by others. Any set of findings will be strengthened when verified by others, and so I offer this discussion of Bower's work as a start.

In order to evaluate the newborn infant's perception of the *substance* of objects, Bower developed the apparatus shown in Figure 4-3. Using filters and a projector set up behind a baby, he creates an illusory object a few inches in front of the young infant, who is held firmly upright by an adult. When this device creates the visual impression of an object moving rapidly toward the infant's face (looming), the newborn defends himself by closing his eyes and turning his head. This behavior shows that the baby must expect the illusory object to be solid—that is, to have *substance*. Previous work with newborns lying on their backs had indicated that they did not show defensive behavior (e.g., White, 1971) and thus Bower's technique is a valuable contribution. (Of course, his results need further replication by others.) Bower had also found that, when properly supported, very young infants of two weeks would reach out to grasp small illusory objects. When they grasped only air, they acted surprised, again demonstrating that they expected objects to have substance (Bower, 1974).

Figure 4-3. *The apparatus developed by Bower to study the perceptions of infants. Here the infant is seated in a chair rather than held upright by an adult. (From "The Object in the World of the Infant," by T. G. R. Bower. Copyright © 1971 by Scientific American, Inc. All rights reserved.)*

To examine the *permanence* of the object concept, Bower devised a machine that permits the experimenter to move either the object or a screen that can hide it. With the machine, the procedure of hiding and revealing objects could be made standard from one baby to the next. The machine also allowed evaluation of only the perception of the object without requiring the baby to use motor skills. In Piaget's classic procedures babies must smoothly reach for a hidden object while removing a scarf from it. But babies may be unable to do this even if they have a mature object concept if their motor skills are not sufficiently developed. In Bower's experiments, babies sit on their mothers' lap at a table where they look straight at the white screen and small colorful ball.

Sometimes the screen moves while the ball stays fixed. At other times, the ball moves from one side to behind the screen and out the other side. In either instance the ball disappears from sight for varying numbers of seconds. Sometimes the ball is removed during this interval; at other times it is not. Bower measures how much a baby's heartbeat changes as an indicator of surprise. He uses the moving screen device for the following reason: if babies "know" the ball continues to exist when they cannot see it, they will be startled if it has disappeared when the screen is removed. On the other hand, if they think its existence ceases when it is out of sight, they will be surprised if the object *is* there.

The results of Bower's studies using this technique were these: When the ball was covered for only a few seconds, infants as young as two months of age were more surprised when the ball disappeared than they were when it reappeared. We can conclude that these young infants had some fleeting sense of object permanence. But when the ball was hidden for a longer time, the younger infants were no longer as startled if the ball disappeared; instead, they were amazed when it reappeared. Thus, because an essential step of realizing that an object is permanent is remembering it, as babies' memories gradually improve, they are increasingly aware that objects continue to exist (Bower, 1974).

To find out how babies see moving objects in relation to space and to their own actions toward the objects, Bower studied babies watching moving objects with the same general set-up I described above. The objects were small plastic animals that moved from left to right across a table top in front of the baby. During their trip, they would pass behind a screen and reemerge on the other side. Films of the babies' eye movements and reports of observers revealed that most babies shifted their eyes to watch the right edge of the screen when the animal disappeared. Apparently, they realized that the toy traveling in front of them was a single object moving through space that they could watch by shifting their eyes in time with its motion.

What happens when the apparatus stops the toy to the left of the screen so that it doesn't go behind the screen? Babies 12 to 20 weeks of age stop

---

Figure 4-4. *Disappearing train confirms the hypothesis that infants 12 weeks old do not watch a single object when the object is at first stationary, then moves and stops. They do not follow the moving object from place to place but rather apply a cognitive rule that can be stated: "Object disappears at* A; *object reappears at* B." *In the experimental test the infant sat watching a toy train with flashing lights at rest in the middle of the track (a). After 10 seconds the train moved to the left and stopped (b) and remained there for 10 seconds before returning to the center again. The cycle was repeated 10 times. On the next cycle (c, d) the train moved slowly to the right and stopped. If the infant had been following the moving object, he would have looked to the right, but if he had been following the hypothesized cognitive rule, he would have looked to the left in the place where the train had stopped before. (From "The Object in the World of the Infant," by T. G. R. Bower. Copyright ©* 1971 *by Scientific American, Inc. All rights reserved.)*

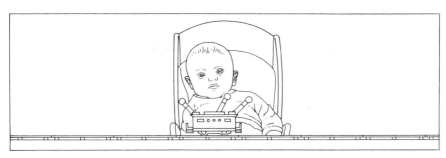

a

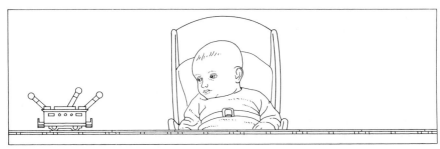

b

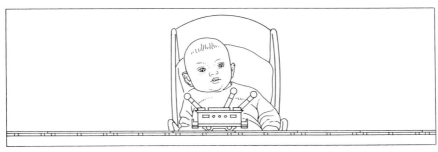

c

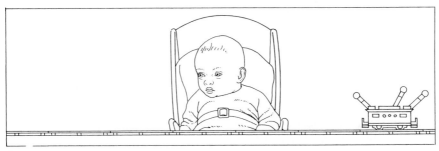

d

momentarily and then still look ahead along the intended path of the toy; they don't grasp yet that an object can move or remain still (Bower, 1974). Infants this age may regard moving and stationary objects as two different entities.

Bower has also used an electric train circling a track to study infants' perceptions of objects that sometimes move and sometimes are stationary. He has found that as infants watch the train slowly travel from point A to point B and slowly back, they follow it with their eyes each time. Then, when the train suddenly switches its direction and moves from A to C, the babies continue to look at B, following the train's previous route. Bower thinks that 12- to 16-week-old infants in this experiment perceive the moving object in front of them as several different objects: the "place A train," the "place B train," and, perhaps, the "moving train." In his view, they do not yet think of a single object located in space that can move through space regardless of where they are looking and completely independent of their looking (Bower, 1974).

Bower's program of researching the various details of how babies make inferences about objects includes more studies as well. The experiments discussed here will serve as a sample of what we can learn about the object concept using such subtle measures as babies' heartbeat, their eye movements, and their startled expressions. What relation does this work have to Piaget's theory? Piaget's basic idea that babies develop the object concept through maturation fits these observations well. If Bower's work on the reactions of newborns to real (rather than illusory) objects is properly replicated, Piaget's theories might have to be modified to reflect that object substance is inborn. Bower's results would agree with Piaget's idea that babies recognize the permanence of objects before they realize that an object's location and movements are independent of their actions. Bower's work clarifies the babies' concept of the permanence of objects by showing that they expect stationary objects to continue to exist before they grant the same property to moving objects. Possibly infants only gradually realize that objects change location by moving through space; instead, they may experience a moving object as several objects that vanish from one spot and reappear in another.

Bower's findings primarily challenge the assigned normal ages at which babies supposedly realize these concepts. Bower's work shows that babies only two months old may realize that stationary objects are permanent, and that by five months of age babies are already unraveling the complexities of how objects move through space (Bower, 1974, p. 204). In Bower's opinion, his results are consistent with Piagetian theory. However, the search tasks devised by Piaget require infants to demonstrate their perceptions through coordinated actions as they reach for and uncover objects and the like, but babies lack the coordination necessary to perform these activities until several months after they have grasped the concepts of object permanence and location.

One of Bower's major contributions is showing that babies' perceptions must be separated from their motor abilities when their concepts about objects are studied. Bower's subtler measures indicate that babies may have more mature notions about objects than is apparent from their motor acts toward them. Piaget's method of studying object permanence requires, not only an understanding of object permanence, but skilled eye-hand coordination, whereas Bower's requires only the former.

Before leaving the topic of Bower's work, I should mention that his interpretations of his results have been criticized on the grounds that he ignores the possibility of babies' learning during the experiments and, presumably, in life as well. One investigator, using a moving object and stationary screen arrangement similar to Bower's, found that the babies dramatically changed their looking patterns as the trials continued. When the infants began they would be looking only roughly in the location of the object, but gradually with experience they would adjust their eye movements to the varying speed of the objects. When the objects sped up while behind the screen, the six- to eight-month-old babies learned to anticipate their reappearance by shifting their eyes rapidly to look steadily at the right of the screen (Nelson, 1974).

Summary of Object Concept Research

In general, research on the development of the object concept supports Piaget's postulated sequence. But both memory and "on the spot" learning affect an infant's performance in active demonstrations like Piaget's searching tasks and in Bower's perception tasks. Bower's work shows that babies gradually understand about objects in several steps. The first objects they see as permanent are those that are stationary; then they come to realize that permanent objects can move steadily through space without "skipping" from one spot to another; and, finally, they coordinate these insights with their own motor acts on objects. Bower's view does not conflict with Piaget's but instead extends and clarifies it.

Bruner's Skill Theory

Jerome Bruner has also written about sensory-motor development in the first year of life. He has paid particular attention to how babies develop fine motor activities that require them to think while they coordinate their eyes and hands. Bruner is interested in these skills partly because the intricate ways in which we can use our hands to wield tools have, until the recent past, been part of the definition of being human. Like Piaget, Bruner explores infants' increasing ability to translate their *intentions*—which are a form of cognition—into detailed and highly organized hand motions.

Bruner describes the three phases of development of a skill such as visually directed reaching. He believes that we are innately prepared or pre-adapted to progress through these phases as we gain experience with objects and space. The first is intention. A baby sees an object he can manipulate and decides he will do so. His behavior reveals his intention. He directs his attention and actions to obtaining the object by one means or another. Once he has it, he stops his efforts. If one means (such as stretching out his arm with his hand closed) fails, he substitutes another (perhaps reaching with his hand open).

In the second phase of skill development the baby refines his techniques for getting objects. He has a loosely organized set of relevant actions—he may stare at the object, open his hands, and tense and extend his arms. However, he may do these actions in the wrong order, or at least may err in his timing. He may open his hand only after touching the object, for example, and thereby knock it down rather than hold onto it.

Soon enough the third phase arrives. The outcome of his experiences encourages the infant to reorganize his techniques until he develops an act that is smooth and correctly sequenced and timed. With a very few repetitions, babies completely master the act and thereafter execute it "unconsciously" in the sense that they can accomplish it while they are directing their attention elsewhere. For example, a baby who is nine months old may be interested in putting a small cube into a coffee mug. To succeed at this, he must concentrate on bringing together two objects—the cup and the cube. Because he does not need to plan to reach and grasp them, he is free to concentrate instead on their location. Thus, once he can manage simple skills without a great deal of conscious effort, he can organize them into the more complex and lengthy sequences that constitute complex skills such as picking up and throwing a ball, pushing about on a "scooter bike," or washing his hands.

Bruner draws a parallel between developing a skill and processing information. Information comes to us from the environment and is processed (worked with mentally) and translated into actions. The results of those actions are feedback that can tell us how to make our actions more successful. By acting and receiving feedback we can rapidly change, which is another indication of the essential human characteristic of *adaptability*. To illustrate this idea, let us compare the development of skills with learning a language. We generally think of mastering a language as simply a matter of learning words and then phrases from being exposed to them. But very young children manage to organize words and phrases quickly into grammatically correct sentences long before they could possibly learn another system of rules for behavior to match the complexity of grammar. Some psychologists disagree with Bruner's notion that we are innately prepared, or preadapted, to organize units of our sensory-motor behavior into skilled actions. To defend his theory, Bruner argues that we develop our skills too rapidly and sporadically for them to be the slow result of elementary learning processes such as reinforcement or modeling. Bruner acknowledges the importance of modeling for learning but questions its ability to account for the acquisition of skills. It could be that we have an inborn ability to translate the actions we see our model do into an intentional act of our own (Bruner, 1973).

Recently, Scarr-Salapatek (1975) proposed a theory similar to Bruner's. She points out that sensory-motor behaviors vary less from one person to another than do the intelligent behaviors that we develop. She suggests that, as human beings evolved, the variations in their motor abilities were reduced because their motor skills were present a longer time: to her, motor skills are the most primitive aspect of human intelligence. Despite the fact that human beings use their hands in similar ways, they learn different complex skills: one child may excel at opening boxes; another, at toy-throwing. According to Scarr-Salapatek, our preadaption simply helps us to quickly organize our hand-skill "units" into novel acts after only brief experiences of following the actions of another. The long period that human infants must spend watching others insures that they will eventually develop a great variety of skills.

In order to evaluate this view of hand skills—which considers both evolution and biology—we would have to train babies in skills new to them by means of ordinary learning techniques. If we discovered that they learn the new hand skills more efficiently than they learn other skills, we would have additional support for Bruner's view that human beings are preadapted to learn hand skills efficiently.

Problem Solving, Exploratory Behavior, and Play

A persistent concern in the theories of sensory-motor development that we have discussed is the way in which babies separate means from ends. Infants have successfully separated means from ends when they can focus all of their attention upon the object for which they are reaching and the position they want to attain while they are acting toward these ends. For example, a baby has achieved means-end separation when he is able to see a drum, decide to make noise, pick up a block, and bang with it on the drum.

When babies learn to separate means and ends, they are able to enjoy several new activities. First they begin solving problems—pursuing a single end using various means to achieve it. The term *exploratory behavior* describes how children vary their means to reach a particular end—as, for example, when a one-year-old child toddles about a room, picking up, shaking, and putting down every toy in turn. Children have learned to *play* when they ignore the distinction between means and ends and exercise the means for its own sake, as when an infant waves her arms just for the fun of it. In the second half of their first year, babies begin to solve problems, to explore, and to play more often.

Problem Solving

After watching infants of six months or so for a few minutes, you will realize that they have many problems to solve. They want to hold distant toys, they want to stand when they are sitting, and their persistence in the pursuit of these goals is often quite dramatic—they sometimes grunt and grimace with exertion. Toward their first birthday and after, babies' goals may take longer to achieve and may be directed toward objects that are out of their sight.

Only a few systematic studies have been done on how infants solve problems. Several experimenters have recreated a typical problem babies face, and the results of their experiments are very informative. In one experiment the researchers put the infant on one side of a room and some attractive toys on the other. Then they placed a plastic screen, or frustration barrier, between the infant and the toys so that the infant could see the toys but could not reach them. The infant could retrieve them by going around the barrier, but would discover this only by examining the barrier with that goal in mind.

One investigator using a small table-top version of the frustration barrier with one-year-old babies found that they reacted in one of three ways. One group of babies, the "winners," did not become upset by the barrier but instead persisted in wanting the playthings and finally went around the barrier to get them. Thus, the winners did not abandon their end, but instead varied their means of reaching it. The second group, the "shifters," forgot their intention to get the toys when they were confronted with the barrier, and became interested in other objects such as the decorations on the wall. Although these babies did not become upset by the barrier, they also were unable to solve a problem that was similar to many frustrations in their normal environment. The third group, the "criers," were very upset by

Figure 4-5.   *A persistent toddler attempts in vain to penetrate the frustration barrier set up by investigator Michael Lewis. (Photo courtesy of Michael Lewis.)*

the barrier, and they abandoned, not only their original end, but all other ends as well (Kramer and Rosenblum, 1970).

Because our Western culture values problem solving, we may be interested in answers to several questions about how infants solve problems. First, do their problem-solving skills reflect the skills they will have throughout life? Next, do certain characteristics of their environment—like the number of problems it presents or how adults interact with the infants—influence how successfully they will solve problems? Third, can babies be taught to solve problems more effectively? Although we have little systematic knowledge about problem solving of infants, we do have some clear findings about differences among individual babies and groups of babies (Kramer and Rosenblum, 1970; Lewis and Wilson, 1972). We also know that the characteristics of a problem can affect a baby's skill at solving it (Kopp, O'Connor, and Finger, 1975). Because this topic is so important for understanding how human beings adjust to the world, it definitely merits further study. Perhaps such study will eventually permit us to present everyday problems so that babies can learn general problem-solving skills from their encounters with them.

Exploratory Behavior

Anyone who has spent time with a newly mobile infant has seen as least one form of exploratory behavior that is characteristic of infants—the endless circling of a room on hands and knees. Babies also explore their surroundings by sitting still and handling toys and objects—they turn them over, look closely at them, put them in their mouths, shake them, and finally discard them. These activities obviously help infants to learn about their environment. They develop their ideas about space by moving through it, and they find out about the potential of objects by manipulating them.

Because exploring is essential to a baby's cognitive development, those characteristics of babies and their environments that foster it are of interest. Many researchers have studied infants' exploratory behavior, but most have related it to other issues such as babies' attention or mother-infant interaction. Here we will briefly review what we know about the characteristics of objects, infants, and situations that promote exploration. I will also briefly examine other topics related to exploring.

We have already discussed contingent stimulation, which is so interesting to babies that they delightedly choose to manipulate an object if it can give it. A magic quality seems to belong to an object that responds to the baby's own actions. For example, objects that make noise or change form because of the babies' activities will likely encourage them to explore—musical toys that they can start and crib mobiles that they can move are very appealing. If

Figure 4-6. *Under the watchful gaze of an adult, infants explore the world at their front steps. (Photo copyright © Suzanne Arms.)*

babies had to choose their favorite contingent stimulation toy, they probably would choose other people, whose facial expressions change in endless ways in immediate response to babies' antics.

Babies' own characteristics may influence their patterns of exploration. Two studies that followed babies through childhood reported that they differed consistently in their overall activity levels (Escalona, 1968; Thomas and Chess, 1977). One study found that these differences predict a baby's preferred style of exploring. Physically active babies move around their environments, but they do not quietly manipulate small objects as much as the less active infants, who more often enjoy sitting and exploring an individual object in detail (Escalona, 1968). These differences must have profound effects upon what the infants learn about the world and upon how they view it. Some evidence shows that female infants are more likely to be the manipulative, visual explorers; male infants, the moving explorers (Maccoby and Jacklin, 1974), a point to which we will return in Chapter 6.

Play

Play in the sense of practicing the skills as means without a situation that requires them begins around six or seven months of age (corresponding to Piaget's sensory-motor Substage 3). First, infants focus their play on actions of their own bodies, such as kicking while they are on their backs, repeatedly changing a neutral expression to a smile, or manipulating their hands. Next, they play with single objects—they bang spoons on the floor, they push or pull a toy along the floor again and again, or they reach and grasp for a series of toys someone else offers them. Later in the second year, babies learn to use two objects: stacking and unstacking two blocks, placing a small trinket in turn into several alternative containers, or connecting and disconnecting two large plastic beads several times. Finally, as the sensory-motor period ends, we see the beginnings of symbolic play, which relies upon mental images. Once he is capable of symbolic play, a baby may gesture to drink from a small cube as if it were a cup, or pretend to take a bath when the subject comes up (Fenson et al., 1976).

Pre-Language Development

Many psychologists define infancy as the period before babies learn language. However, babies' vocalizations, which begin in their first weeks of life, are important forerunners to the language that follows. and they also are significant in themselves. The pre-language babbling of babies relates to the other developments of the babies in the realm of cognition. In this section you will learn about the course of infants' vocalizing and about some of the factors that influence these early sounds.

Babbling

During their third week of life, infants begin to separate their communication into crying and noncrying vocalizations (Wolff, 1969). At first their noncrying sounds are limited compared with the wealth of sounds in the language spoken around them. But gradually, babies begin to make more varied sounds, and usually by their fifth or sixth month they begin to combine them into a series of sounds resembling language, which we call *babbling*. Although the age at which infants start babbling varies widely, most infants babble by the time they are six months of age (Dale, 1976). One set of first-born male infants who were studied over a length of time spent about 20 percent of their awake periods babbling, which indicates that this activity is an important part of infants' repertoire of behavior (Roe, 1969).

A substantial amount of evidence points to the important role the baby's surroundings play in influencing babbling. Usually infants raised in institutions in which they receive little personal attention learn language more slowly, and have various other cognitive problems (Brodbeck and Irwin, 1946; Rutter and Mittler, 1972). However, because institutional care does not slow the development of all babies (e.g., Tizard, Cooperman, and Tizard, 1972), we need to pinpoint what specific conditions of the environment have a positive effect upon vocalization (and other cognitive skills). Several studies based on learning techniques may give us some insight.

Do babies vocalize more when they receive positive responses if they do so? Apparently, this plays an important role. Both in the lab and at home, babies will vocalize more when their sounds are greeted by a response that enables them to interact with people around them. They babble in response to a recording of their mothers' voices (Tomlinson-Keasey, 1972), as well as to being smiled at, spoken to, and stroked (Routh, 1969; Rheingold, Gewirtz, and Ross, 1959; Weisberg, 1963). Because many adults and older children express their pleasure at a baby's communication by smiling at, stroking, or talking to the baby, we can conclude that a positive personal response to vocalization has an important effect on his progress. Indeed, results of one study indicated that if infants whose vocalizing was not proceeding normally received personal responses at home each time they babbled they would dramatically increase their attempts to comunicate with sounds (Wiegernick et al., 1974).

However, the relation between infants' making sounds and adults' making sounds is not as straightforward as it first appears. If an adult starts to talk in the vicinity of a babbling infant, the baby falls silent (Webster, 1969; Barrett, Goldfarb, and Whitehurst, 1973). When babies hear recordings of their own voices, they stop babbling (Belmore et al., 1973). This natural, perhaps inborn, pattern seems to help them to pay attention to the voices of people around them, and it also acquaints them with the talk-listen cycle of conversations.

But adults' talking in the presence of a baby and their talking to the baby have quite different effects. In both instances the infants are likely to stop their own "noise" momentarily; but only when an adult is talking *to* them and in response to their sounds do babies increase their vocalization. We can recall the importance of contingent stimulation to interpret the findings that infants' vocal development is influenced by their social interaction with their mothers. Mothers who assert their own personalities and restrict any activities that their babies initiate tend to have babies who babble less. The mothers of infants who babble often let the babies' apparent interest guide their responses (Beckwith, 1971; Jones and Moss, 1971).

There is another possible interpretation for the relation between adults' talking and infants' vocalization. Do babies model their babbling on the speech they hear? As yet we have little evidence that relates directly to this question. However, apparently infants do not need to hear the speech of others to begin their pre-language babbling: children raised by deaf parents babble as much as those raised by parents who can hear (Lenneberg, Rebelsky, and Nichols, 1965). The results of one series of training trials with three two-year-old children reveal that modeling helps to increase certain sounds in the child's vocalizing but that this influence is much stronger if buttressed by praise for vocalization of certain sounds (Hursh and Sherman, 1973). Very likely, modeling is much more important for language after children have begun to speak than it is during infancy.

Another interesting question about babbling remains: Do these early sounds relate to how well the infant will talk later? Although babbling begins just as babies' sensory-motor development is proceeding at its most rapid pace during the first year (Roe, 1969), babies vary in how much they babble. A fanatic babbler of six months later may talk no more or less than an infrequent babbler. Some evidence shows that the rate of vocalizing in female babies is more predictive of later talking than it is for male babies (Minton, 1969; Kagan, 1969). Perhaps the early sounds of females, who have a longer and more intense interaction with their mothers, are more consistently noticed and encouraged than those of males and, similarly, the quiet female baby is not noticed and is left to her quiet self. The male, having less close interaction with his mother, is encouraged or discouraged from babbling for reasons unrelated to his existing rate of babbling. At this point, we simply do not know why babbling would be more predictable for members of one sex than for members of the other. But the fact does alert us to the possibilities that language development may follow different courses for the two sexes and that important aspects of their environment may be responsible for the difference.

Infants' Perception of Speech

So far our discussion of language has centered upon babies' earliest sounds because they seem to be the first steps toward learning to speak. Of equal interest to most parents and relatives is the question of when they and their baby can begin to communicate by means of language. We know that babies begin exchanging smiles with their caregivers at about two months of age. This gradually evolves into a mutual imitation game, which is a form of communication. But when do babies begin to decode the meaning and pattern of the complicated sounds that are made in the speech that goes on around them? Very young infants apparently can distinguish between the various phonetic sounds which are the universal building blocks of language. For example, if you repeat a phonetic sound to your one-month-old son, you will find that he habituates, or gets used, to it. When you introduce a contrasting sound, his reactions will show that he has noticed the difference (Friedlander, 1970; Dotty, 1972). He can also distinguish between speech sounds and similar, but nonspeech, sounds (Morse, 1972). Of course, we do not know what meaning these distinctions have for babies, but the fact that they can make them suggests to some researchers that human beings have some inborn receptivity to language—related sounds. Perhaps we are prepared at birth to organize the language spoken around us into categories of sounds that correspond to the categories of language— basic sounds, words, and phrases (Dotty, 1974).

At about the same age that they begin to discriminate among speech sounds, babies also begin to prefer listening to the human voice rather than other sounds (Friedlander, 1970). They are especially tuned in to their mothers' voices, which is demonstrated by the fact that they synchronize their bodily movements with the pace and rhythm of their mothers' speech (Condon and Sander, 1974). Babies' special attraction and responses to a familiar voice, together with their ability to discriminate among speech sounds, suggests that they could learn the meaning of language at a very young age.

Adults also do their part to keep communication a two-way exchange. Infant and caregiver pairs have a back and forth "conversation" that consists simply of eye contact. They look at each other, then momentarily away, and then again at each other in a pattern that exactly resembles the one adults use when they are conversing (Jaffe, Stern, and Perry, 1973). It has also been found that adults who talk to a two-year-old toddler adjust the pace, pitch, and length of their conversation to suit the age of the child (Phillips, 1971). If we assume that adults follow this same pattern when they speak to pre-linguistic children, it seems that they are helping the babies decode language by making the relevant distinctions more apparent. Adults also try—with some success—to figure out what babies are communicating through their pre-language sounds (Wasz-Hockert et al., 1964; Mallard and Daniloff, 1973). Infants' ability to detect speech sounds and adults' efforts to communicate with them set the scene for language development.

Theories of Early Language Development

Developmental psycholinguistics is the interdisciplinary field that studies how children acquire language. Because the scope of this book covers children's development before they are old enough to learn language, a thorough discussion of linguistic theory would be out of place here. We will look only briefly at the role infants' babbling and early language discrimination play in their ultimate development of spoken language.

A leading idea in psycholinguistics is Noam Chomsky's notion of an innate *language acquisition device* (LAD). According to his view, infants are born with the capacity to receive and organize language sounds into categories that correspond to those of language. In Chomsky's view we experience either "things" or "processes" that correspond neatly to the nouns and verbs we use in speaking. We are either doers or receivers of actions, which dovetails with the "subject" and "object" roles in sentences. Thus infants' early ability to discriminate phonemes—the basic sounds of language—can be a manifestation of the more general LAD. Perhaps infants' preference for human voices would be one mechanism of the LAD that orients them toward relevant sounds.

Learning theorists hold an alternative view (Skinner, 1957). They argue that, although babies may be born with the tendency to babble, these early sounds are gradually shaped into meaningful language by the way in which those around them respond to the sounds that babies make. People will enthusiastically respond to sounds similar to meaningful words, but they do not react so positively to meaningless babbling. According to the learning theorists, babies learn to associate objects or actions with the correct word label because their other sounds, which are either meaningless or inappropriate, do not receive such an enjoyable response. For example, you probably would be very pleased if your infant daughter responded with the word "cow" upon seeing a cow; you would be much less pleased if she greeted a doting aunt with the same word.

It is difficult to make definite statements about a possible LAD. Neither the equation of LAD with a learning process nor the notion of an innate LAD is entirely satisfactory. Some evidence does suggest that the learning theory approach is not adequate to explain language (Dale, 1976). The evidence for existence of an LAD is largely circumstantial: many descriptive facts, including the ones we discussed in the two previous sections, are consistent with the LAD idea, but the group of facts does not establish the existence of such a device. For example, it has been found that 14-month-old babies express surprise when they see a film of two objects interacting in a manner opposite to the expectations their linguistic categories set up: if a table pushes a man, rather than the reverse, babies are startled. Apparently they expect the man to commit the act and the table to receive it. This is a linguistically organized expectation and one that is difficult to explain on the basis of either a simple nativist or a simple learning theory (Golinkoff, 1975). Perhaps we should regard the LAD as a useful metaphor for organizing our thinking about a set of related facts. We still don't fully understand

now the babbles of a young infant are transformed into the prolific banter of
a three-year-old child.

Memory

Memory is an organism's ability to retain a mental representation of experience over time. Although psychologists are very interested in how much
and how well babies store their experiences for later retrieval, these questions are difficult to study, and little is really known about infants'
memories. We have already discussed the evidence that suggests that
people cannot mentally represent objects and events during infancy as well
as they can later in life. If this is so, babies would be unable to remember
their experiences as clearly as older children can. This in turn would imply
that they cannot completely distinguish familiar experiences from new ones,
which would undoubtedly affect how they explore and thus learn about
their environments.

Memory is generally divided by researchers into several subprocesses.
First, a representation of experience is *stored* out of our immediate awareness in a "location" from which it can later be retrieved. Then we *retrieve* the
event when we remember it. Research on adults' memories suggests that
they store information differently, depending upon how long it must be
remembered (Schank, 1976). For example, adults use *short-term* memory to
recite telephone numbers to the operator, and *long-term* memory to recall
significant childhood experiences. Because babies' memories of objects appear to be fleeting at best, perhaps they have not yet developed their ability
to store long-term memories very well. This explains why we cannot remember the events of those stories that begin "when you were a baby. . . ."
We may have some emotional reactions that date from our infant experiences, but this is not inconsistent with the notion of weak long-term
memories.

Researchers usually employ the habituation procedure described in
Chapter 3 to study memory in infants. They repeatedly present some
stimulus, such as a colorful design poster, to an infant until he is accustomed
to it. Presumably the baby becomes accustomed by creating some representation of the stimulus that reminds him that he has experienced it before.
When the stimulus is completely familiar to the infant, it no longer holds his
attention, and he spends his time looking at some other stimulus the experimenters provide. The difference between how long the baby looks at
the stimulus when it is new and when it is familiar is often used to measure
memory. Using this approach, one investigator found that five- to six-
month-old infants could remember complex stimuli for several hours, but

that they forgot the stimuli more easily if they saw irrelevant stimuli in the meantime (Fagan, 1970, 1971) or if the stimuli were unrealistic distortions of everyday objects such as faces (Fagan, 1972). Infants as young as one week old can be habituated to some stimuli (Fagan, 1970). Thus, if we accept habituation as indicative of a memory process, we would conclude that infants have at least *some* capacity for memory from the first week of life. Their capacity presumably develops with time, improving noticeably when they begin to represent their experiences systematically, first with sensory images and finally with words. Through classical conditioning adults can "recall' early emotional responses, provided they don't experience the originally arousing stimulus often enough later to break the link between the two. However, this influence from the past does not involve *representing* the event; it is not memory in the usual sense.

Influential Factors in Cognitive Development

We have reviewed what is known about the various cognitive processes in infants. Obvious individual and group differences exist in the rate at which infants develop mentally and cognitively. In this section we will look at some factors that influence the cognitive level of a baby's behavior. First, I will present some well-documented differences between sex, race, and socioeconomic groups. I will follow this with a discussion of some environmental factors that influence individual and group differences in cognition. I will not discuss the genetic factors in individual differences in cognition, although evidence shows that they do exist.

Differences Among Groups

A number of studies have provided descriptions of the sensory-motor skills of different socioeconomic and race groups. Measures based on Piaget's theory reveal few socioeconomic differences, and no differences that relate to socioeconomic class have been demonstrated for object concept, means–end relations, or imitating gestures (Golden and Birns, 1968, 1976; Wachs, Uzgiris, and Hunt, 1971). But differences that can be attributed to socioeconomic class start to appear when babies begin to speak and widen as childhood proceeds (Golden and Birns, 1976). Perhaps sensory-motor intelligence does not require specific experiences beyond what is associated with survival. Perhaps all babies build the same set of skills as they exercise their inborn sensory-motor skills. However, the richness of sensory-motor cognition beyond this minimum does seem to relate to socioeconomic class: middle-class infants play and explore more when they are given simple materials than lower-class infants do (Collard, 1971). The extent to which sensory-motor skills predict later IQ is also related to socioeconomic class.

Low scores on the Bayley Infant Intelligence Scales, which examine sensory-motor development (see the Appendix), often herald a low performance on standardized IQ tests at age four for lower-class children. Apparently, more middle-class children who score low on the Bayley scales "recover" by age four (Willerman, 1970). This may be due to differences among socioeconomic classes in nutrition, home environment, child-rearing techniques, daily routines, or some other factors. At this time, we simply do not know.

Results of a number of studies indicate that motor skills of black American infants are superior to those of white American infants (Bayley, 1965; Walters, 1967; King and Seegmiller, 1973). Black infants' motor development is more rapid than white infants' in Africa and Jamaica as well (Ainsworth, 1967; Granthan-McGregor and Bach, 1971). The meaning of these differences between races is not clear. Speculations range from the possibility that blacks are born with more mature sensory-motor skills (Warren and Parkin, 1974) to the theory that black parents enable their infants to practice their motor skills by allowing them to move about their environments (Williams and Scott, 1953). Heredity is a possibility as well. However, we have little solid evidence with which to evaluate these speculations. The few other findings available about ethnic differences suggest that infants in different ethnic groups have different cognitive levels as indicated by their sensory-motor skills. For example, native Mexican infants are apparently slower in developing sensory-motor skills than are American and European infants (Brazelton, 1972). However, we cannot make many conclusions about the importance of isolated differences among groups without a more complete picture of the factors that influence sensory-motor development. Although few studies focus on the possibility that differences in sensory-motor development might relate to sex, the findings in the main body of literature do not point to sex as a reason.

Physiological Factors in Sensory-Motor Development

Scientists have different opinions about the importance of knowledge about the workings of the brain to understanding cognition. They agree, however, that without healthy brain and nervous system tissue and normal development of the nervous system human beings cannot attain their full mental potential. Let us then briefly examine what we know about the effects of early nutrition, birth complications, and prematurity upon early cognitive development.

It is well established that undernourishment during early infancy can lead to retarded cognitive development, indicated by babies' low scores on various tasks such as those we have discussed in this chapter. Children who are undernourished in infancy generally react poorly to events around them and perform poorly on standardized measures of development, as well as on various perceptual motor tasks (Cabak and Najdanvic, 1965; Richardson, Birch, and Hertzig, 1973). Lack of sufficient protein influences cognition primarily because it directly affects the size and number of cells in the developing brain (Kallen, 1971; Brockman and Riciutti, 1971).

Poor nutrition can also affect the cognitive level of a child long after the period when the child was not eating correctly (Richardson et al., 1972), and the effects are difficult, if not impossible, to reverse (Brockman and Riciutti, 1971). Whether the deficiency in diet exists before babies are born, during their first year of life, or both, the effect is very severe. Clearly, babies must have a proper diet of milk and other sources of protein when they are able to digest them.

Complications during childbirth influence a baby's mental functioning. If at the time of delivery a baby's supply of oxygen is cut off for even a few minutes, this can result in permanent impairment of cognitive abilities. One sign that babies received insufficient oxygen during birth is that they do not respond well to stimulation. Years later, a person who received insufficient oxygen during birth may be mentally retarded or may have learning disabilities (Graham et al., 1962).

Lack of oxygen apparently stops the first steps of organizing the brain, which in turn impairs babies' abilities to pay attention and associate events, making them unable to learn well. Experiments with animals have shown the long-lasting effect of an oxygen deficiency during an organism's early interaction with the environment (Windle, 1963; Meier et al., 1960).

Fortunately, complications during childbirth are rare. However, they are more likely to occur when a mother is in poor health or is undernourished, which unfortunately is true among more lower-class mothers than middle-class mothers. Thus, malnourishment and anoxia, which both occur among more babies born to lower-class mothers, may be factors in the differences in the children's mental abilities that appear by their preschool years.

Premature birth is strongly associated with lower levels of cognitive performance. Severely premature babies are those who weigh less than 5½ pounds at birth. There are a greater number of lower scores on preschool IQ tests among severely premature children than among children who had normal birth weights. Too, children who were severely premature do not do as well at school as children with normal birth weights (Arajarui, Keinanen, and Thuneberg 1973; Scarr, 1969; Drillien, 1969; Ehrlich et al., 1973; McKeown, 1960). Prematurity can have such an impact because the infants are not sufficiently prepared at birth for the stresses of the outside world. Their immature nervous systems are further challenged when respiratory problems reduce their oxygen supply. Because of prematurity there may be other complications in the children's mental development that result from their being isolated for intensive care. Such isolation may enhance the caregivers' feelings of separateness from the infants and their perception of them as fragile. Isolation is also a kind of sensory deprivation. These factors were discussed further in Chapter 1.

Stimulation in the Physical Environment

The amount and variety of stimulating events offered by their surroundings greatly affects babies' ultimate cognitive development. It has been found that when infant monkeys grow up in environments with no variety and few interesting objects or events, they perform poorly on learning and problem-solving tasks at maturity (Davenport, Rogers, and Rumbaugh, 1974; Harlow, 1959; Wilson and Riesen, 1966). Monkeys reared in "impoverished" environments, as these monotonous surroundings are called, also explore less than normal and thus can be presumed to learn less about the world around them (Elias and Samonds, 1973; Sackett, 1972). Apparently, one effect of this impoverishment is that the monkeys' brains weigh less than those of monkeys who live in normal surroundings (Rosensweig, 1966). The findings from studies with monkeys have led to the general notion of "stimulus deprivation" as a major factor of the environment that can inhibit cognitive development.

This idea leads naturally to a theory of how to alleviate cognitive deficits by reversing one factor that causes them. Perhaps adding more and more varied stimuli than are usually found in an infant's environment would aid cognitive development. Some evidence indicates that enrichment of the early environment has a positive effect upon the cognitive development of monkeys (Rosensweig, 1966). But are the effects of stimulus deprivation and enrichment the same for human infants as they are for monkeys? To answer this question, researchers have designed "enriched" experiences for infants, have studied their effects upon infants in the laboratory, and have related infants' mental levels to the characteristics of their home environments. In one enrichment experiment, a group of newborn infants were given supplementary stimulation during their hospital stays of several days and they were also given special stimulation each day for the next 30 days at home by their mothers. This group proved to be more efficient learners, more attentive, and more proficient at Piagetian tasks than infants in a control group (Rice, 1977). This finding clearly demonstrates that sensory stimulation in the environment is an important influence on a baby's cognitive growth.

Results of studies on children brought up in orphanages indicate that they don't do as well on a variety of cognitive measures as children who grow up in homes (Langmeier and Matejcek, 1970; Taylor, 1968; Kohen-Raz, 1968;

Stedman, 1964; Provence and Lipton, 1962). An institution is a complex environment in that it has many varied stimuli. However, it differs in many ways from the environment of the average family. For one thing, children raised in orphanages grow up without the influence of a close relationship with a mother (we will discuss this point at length in Chapter 5). Also, infants raised in orphanages ordinarily do not have as much or as varied stimulation as they would if they were raised at home. This is not to say that "institution" is synonymous with "impoverished" and "impersonal." There are institutional environments that are interesting and are full of potential learning situations. Apparently, children who are raised in Israeli kibbutzim have a group environment that is very beneficial to them (Kohen-Raz, 1968). However, such an environment is, in reality, an exception in institutions; the usual outcome of institutional care is that children do not reach the cognitive levels they would have in the care of personal caregivers in a family setting. Also, day care for infants cannot be equated with 24-hour institutional rearing. According to the results of one study, children who are in day-care programs and who receive regular family care when their parents return from work have the same cognitive levels as children who are cared for all day at home (Bradley and Caldwell, 1976). Indeed, the most notable difference between day care and institutional rearing is that good day care does not affect the infant's cognitive development in an adverse way whereas even good institutional rearing does.

Investigators familiar with the literature on institutional rearing have wondered whether the adverse effect upon cognitive development could be observed on a smaller scale in normal families. That is, families are presumed to vary in the amount and type of stimulation they give their children. Two fairly extensive field studies have been done to gather information about the physical and the social aspects of the home environment in relation to babies' cognitive development (Elardo, Bradley, and Caldwell, 1975; Yarrow, Rubenstein, and Pederson, 1975). In these studies, observers visited homes and rated various aspects of the stimulation that infants received during the first year of life. The findings of these studies show that the greater the variety of events and objects available at home, the better infants were at problem solving and the more cognitive development they experienced; this held true during the first year of life and two or three years later when the children took standardized intelligence tests. The relation between the home stimulation and improved cognition levels increased as the children aged: the relation was stronger for the stimulation and preschool scores than for tests given during the first year.

Clearly, a varied and plentiful array of stimulation helps an infant's development. But remember that our previous discussions of babies' interactions with their environments emphasized the importance of contingent stimulation. Perhaps the stimulation can reach a level at which it is difficult for babies to handle because it requires their being able to see a relation between their own behavior and the stimulation. People in a home have a lot to do with organizing and presenting objects and events to a baby. Is the baby simply a bystander in a fast-paced, noisy, and complicated sequence of events, or is she in a situation where she can respond to them and have them respond to her in return? The answer to this question influences how beneficial the effects of stimulation will be. We will now turn to the social aspects of the home environment.

Social Environment

The people who inhabit infants' daily environment have the greatest control over the amount and patterning of stimulation they receive. Family members can move infants about, carry objects to and from them, and, as they become mobile, can encourage or prevent their activities. Families intrigue the baby simply by talking, changing their facial expressions, and going about their daily routines. Their activities are especially important for babies because they engage them in social interactions that babies cannot have with their toys or with other inanimate objects. Because other people influence both the social and nonsocial stimulation the baby receives, we might expect to find a positive relation between the amount and variety of these two categories of stimulation in a home. That is, we might expect homes of animated and responsive people to have a variety of interesting objects and events. Interestingly enough, the two do not seem to be related (Yarrow, Rubenstein, and Pederson, 1975). Perhaps economic factors influence a family to create and maintain a particular environment of objects, physical space, and noise, which contribute nonsocial stimulation, whereas the caregivers who provide the baby with social stimulation are influenced instead by psychological factors in their interactions. The lack of relation between social and nonsocial home stimulation strongly suggests that they have different sources. At this point we do not know what those sources are.

The results of the studies I mentioned also indicated that the infants whose mothers responded more to their vocalizations and behavior made more sounds and tried to accomplish goals more often. Apparently, they also had higher general development scores on the Bayley scales. Two studies reported that this relation between how much the mother responds to her infant in its first year and the infant's development continues to show its effects until the child is three years old (Elardo et al., 1975; Bradley and Caldwell, 1976). In these studies a mother's responsiveness was rated by how often she let the baby take the lead in their interesting exchanges, allowing her actions to be contingent on the baby's. Did she smile at and talk to the baby in response to the baby's smile or expectant look, or did she smile and talk without taking the baby's actions into account? Once more, we see that people have such a powerful influence over babies because, unlike objects, they have the unique capacity to respond to the baby's signals. However, these findings do not indicate that a caregiver who is a slave of an infant dictator is best for promoting the child's development. Indeed, one investigator found that mothers of the most cognitively competent toddlers in his program differed from the other mothers primarily in their skill at making contingent responses "on the run" as they went about their ordinary daily activities (White, 1975). The degree to which responding to a particular infant's signals is feasible can vary greatly from situation to situation. But clearly, caregivers' responsiveness to infants is a significant factor in their cognitive and emotional development. In the debate about what environment is best for infants we need to think about the contingency of social stimulation. Babies have the best opportunity to have people respond to them when they are in the company of other children and an adult who is committed to a caregiving role. But we should also remember that, either because of the overwhelming number of people and events within some families or because the caregiver has other priorities, some homes provide less of the responsiveness a baby needs than would full or partial day care outside the home. Choices among care situations for infants must be made with thought for the needs of all concerned.

Genetic Factors

Genes influence our cognitive development during infancy, and throughout life as well. Researchers frequently study the effect of genes upon development by tracing the development of fraternal and identical twins. The genes of identical twins are the same, but those of fraternal twins match only as closely as those of any brother and sister would. Thus, by comparing the development of identical and fraternal twins, we can get an idea of how important genes are to mental growth. If genes are very important, then identical twins who have the same genes will have cognitive scores much closer together than those of fraternal twins. If the environment is more important than genes, then, because the infants shared the same environments as their twins, the scores will be as close for fraternal twins as for identical twins.

The results of the several studies of infant twin pairs suggest that genetics plays a significant role in infant cognitive development. When eight-month-old identical twins were tested on the Bayley scales, there was a close relation between their scores, whereas relations between the scores of eight-month-old fraternal twins were moderate for males, low for females, and moderate for mixed pairs (Nichols and Broman, 1974). Infants' ratings on the Bayley scales are clearly influenced by their genes. Another investigator found that the timing of "spurts" and "lags" in mental development (measured in a variety of ways) was closely related for identical twins and less closely related for fraternal pairs (Wilson, 1972). A study focusing on Bayley items that were similar to Piaget's tasks also found a pattern of higher correlations for identical twins scored at 3, 6, 9, and 12 months compared with fraternal twins scored at the same ages (Matheny, 1975).

Clearly genetics plays some role in infant cognition. You should be aware that determining the relative importance of genetic and environmental factors in cognitive (and other) development remains one of the central controversies in the history of behavioral science. In the heated debate about the interpretation of data from twin studies, the environmentalists contend that identical twins share environment more closely than do fraternal twins. Similarly, argument abounds about the meaning of the information obtained in field studies that supposedly shows environmental influence. Perhaps infants who differ genetically in turn cause their mothers to behave differently toward them and that is why correlations differ for identical and fraternal twins; this would mean that the environments for the fraternal twins were actually not the same as those for the identical twins.

Most participants in these controversies agree that both heredity and environment play *some* role and, further, that they interact; the importance of one of the two factors is determined in part by the other. Even an ideal environment is not going to benefit infants much if their genetic makeup severely limits their potential. Similarly infants with great potential are not going to develop it in an unstimulating or chaotic environment as well as they could in a better environment. The real challenge for the developmental theorist is to specify exactly how it is that heredity and environment interact. Is timing important? Is one of the factors more significant at one stage than another? Can environmental change affect a sequence of maturation that has been predetermined by heredity and, if so, how? Some attempts to deal with these issues are summarized in the next section.

Is Early Experience Especially Important?

Many parents and professionals believe that the events of a child's first 18 months of life are more important than events that come later for determining the child's ultimate cognitive level (Spock, 1977; Salk and Kramer, 1969). This belief is based partly on the idea that the baby's early learning forms the conceptual foundation on which later learning rests. Also contributing to this idea is the fact that, the younger infants are when their environment changes severely (for example, if a parent or the infant is hospitalized), the more deeply their cognitive abilities seem to be affected

(Rutter, 1972). Whatever the source of this belief, we need to look at the available evidence to evaluate its merit. If early experience is somehow more important than later experience, it should be possible to demonstrate it in experiments with animal infants reared in various environments. We should also find that measures of early cognitive development accurately predict later cognitive development because, if this theory were correct, early development would contribute to all later development.

Experimental work with animals indeed suggests that a crucial early period exists during which environmental influences have an especially important effect. It was found in one study that, when monkeys were reared in isolation for six months, they had difficulty with depth perception and more complex perceptual-motor functioning in adulthood. On the other hand, when the infant monkeys' environments were "enriched" by the addition of specific stimuli to their cage decorations, they performed better at maturity than other monkeys on learning tasks that employed these stimuli (Wilson and Riesen, 1966). Work with rats demonstrates that environmental events—either positive or negative—have a powerful influence on the rats' later abilities to learn mazes if the events occur during the rats' opening weeks of life (Schwartz, 1964; Forgays and Read, 1962; Smith, 1959). Although the animal work clearly demonstrates an effect of early experience on later behavior, most studies do not also test the effects of the occurrence of the same experience later in life, a comparison that is needed to answer the question about whether early experience is somehow more important than later experience.

Many studies compare human beings' performance during infancy (on the Bayley scales or other standardized tests) to their performance on cognitive measures given at later ages. Usually these comparisons attempt to evaluate whether the infant tests can measure some general trait called "intelligence" that is presumed to underlie both the infant measures and the later ones. If the early and later measures actually do assess the same general domain of behavior, then the earlier scores will accurately predict later scores. Or, if we regard the earlier scores as measuring the *results* of early experience that are needed for later development, then the earlier scores should relate to the later ones.

In general infant tests such as the Bayley scales, the Griffiths Inventory, or the Cattell scales do not accurately predict Stanford-Binet IQ scores at preschool age (Bayley, 1968; Ramey, Campbell, and Nicholson, 1973; Lewis, 1973; Lewis and McGurk, 1972). We can make better predictions (although still partially inaccurate) using clinical ratings made in the second year (Escalona and Moriarty, 1961) and various other measures that concentrate on language skills (Moore, 1967; McCall, Hogarty, and Hurlburt,

1972), or neurological indicators used-by physicians (Ireton, Thwing, and Graven, 1970). However, although children's preschool IQs cannot be predicted on the basis of their infant development test scores, they can be predicted from their combined scores on the Hunt-Uzgiris tasks, which rate their performance on Piagetian tasks such as object concept mastery and mastery of means–end relations (Wachs, 1975). In the Appendix I discuss methodological problems of predicting later behavior from earlier behavior.

Does the "special importance" of early experience stand up under these findings? We would have to rule out any simple notion that babies' early development directly determines their later mental abilities. So the close relation between how well they do at Piaget's sensory-motor tasks and their later cognitive status may reflect how well they adapt, which would be more important to their later cognitive level than their success at the specific sensory-motor skills that were part of the infant developmental tests.

Overall, the evidence does not support any straightforward generalization that early experience is more crucial for development than later experience. Our behavior is more flexible than that of lower animals. Like them we are born with certain behaviors, such as reflexes. But using our experiences, we quickly transform our reflexes into modified versions of themselves. Modified behavior helps to influence what happens next—what caregivers do, for example. If a baby sucks poorly or has difficulty rooting (a reflexive means of finding the nipple) a mother might change the way she handles and holds the baby or she might even change from breast to bottle. If your infant son begins to repeat his reflex smiles—for whatever reason—you might respond by holding him out from your body, so that you could see and appreciate the smile.

The aftermath of these changes then influences our progress in an adaptive spiral. At each step in the adaptive spiral the person as well as the environment and its adaptive demands make important contributions. Our earliest experiences may have special importance in that they set the whole series of events into motion. But the evidence of human flexibility argues against any simple model in which an adult's mental level is determined by a particular early experience.

Educational Programs for Infants

Since the 1920s Western countries have used various programs to prepare three- and four-year-olds for their experiences of formal education. During the 1960s Americans made a greater commitment to have children of lower socioeconomic groups also participate in these preschool programs. As part of Lyndon Johnson's "Great Society" plans, operation Head Start was created with the hope that it could eliminate the differences in cognitive skills that had been observed between school-aged minority and poor children and white middle-class children. In the Head Start program, four-year-olds from low-income families participated voluntarily for a year during which they were given paper, crayons, books, and were made participants in activities designed to help them develop fundamental concepts of space, form, and language. Unfortunately, this massive enrichment effort closed the social-class gap in cognitive skills only temporarily. Within a year or two, the poor children who were in Head Start again lagged behind the middle-class children as much as or more than poor children who did not have the Head Start experiences (Jensen, 1969).

Some educators consider this disappointing outcome to be an indication that Head Start intervention comes too late. They argue that infancy is the crucial time for cognitive development because it is the time when human beings first organize and find meaning in the myriad stimuli that constitute their worlds. Some researchers have been working to develop programs to enrich an infant's first experience in the hope of influencing the emerging spiral of interaction between infant and environment that will ultimately lead to the individual's adult cognitive level. Some of these programs take place in the infant's home; others are part of a larger program of group care. The notion of group care concerns many issues about infants' emotional well-being and their ties to their mothers, which we take up in more detail in Chapter 5. Here we consider only the cognitive aspects of these efforts.

Caldwell and her associates in Arkansas have conducted a high-quality day-care intervention program that will serve as our model for what good programs can achieve (Elardo, Bradley, and Caldwell, 1975). In this program infants six months or older are offered a variety of experiences. Their needs for rest, food, and exercise are met regularly. Each day, each infant has one-to-one communication with a caregiver. At these times, the baby can play with an object or with the caregiver and receive immediate and contingent feedback. The babies have times to explore alone and with older children. The care situation offers a lot of stimulation, but the caregivers help the baby to sort out the stimuli and they regulate the stimulation to keep it manageable for the baby. With this program babies from poor families have experienced definite gains in IQ, language, and problem-solving skills—making the difference between them and middle-class children at preschool age much less than it would otherwise be (Golden and Birns, 1976).

Many professionals express concern about the emotional effects on infants of the long daily separations from the mother and father that participation in these day-care programs requires. Agencies giving grants question

Figure 4-7. *Infants' cognitive development may be fostered by enriched day-care programs, in which they have interesting toys and responsive caregivers with whom they can interact. (Photo courtesy of Emilio A. Mercado.)*

whether the money to help disadvantaged children is best spent on these costly programs. For both of these reasons, some efforts have been made to develop programs that can take place in infants' homes. One such program is the extensive one involving over 200 low-income, black mother-infant pairs carried out by Levenstein (Golden and Birns, 1976). Participating families received regular home visits from a program "demonstrator" during children's second and third year. The demonstrator showed mothers ways to use toys and books (provided as part of the program) to spark children's interest and encourage them to respond. Through this program, infants of the families made steady gains, as compared with infants from similar families who had not been visited. At the end of first grade, children who had participated in the program still were more advanced than those children who had not. These long-term gains were the result of a relatively inexpensive program that modified the children's daily routine only slightly. In general, infants' cognitive levels can be improved by enrichment programs that give them interesting experiences, a responsive caregiver, and events that react to their lead.

The longer the infants participate in the programs, the more effective the programs are in producing long-term gains. Differences between the children in the programs and those not in them seem to be greatest after about the middle of the second year of life, which may suggest that most of the long-term effects come from important experiences toward the end of infancy. Clearly, we must see more results of careful research before we can spell out precisely how infant educational programs work and when they work best. We already have a basis to argue that such programs can be very effective in fostering cognitive growth for normal infants, infants in institutions, and infants with low birth weights.

Summary

At the beginning of this chapter, I presented various questions that could be asked about infants' cognition. Let us see which of them have been answered.

Psychologists are often interested in comparing babies' concepts about the world with those of other people. We have seen that babies group events and objects into concepts on the basis of how they perceive and act upon them. To a baby, balls and oranges are alike: one can grasp, roll, and drop both. Infants, through their behavior, show that they are organizing their experience, pigeonholing each object or event into its proper category according to its reactions when they test it in a sensory-motor fashion: opening, tasting, squeezing, or the like.

An infant's sensory-motor developments include visually directed reaching, walking, and, finally, using a coordinated chain of activities to attain a goal. These developments are enough to give the baby a concrete grasp of some elementary features of their immediate physical reality. Babies acquire the *object concept* when they understand that objects are made of "stuff" whose permanence and location in space is independent of their action. One aid to babies discovering the object concept is their gradual separation of goals (ends) from the behavior that leads to them (means). Babies gain a sense of three-dimensional space with their first experiences of moving about on their own, often in pursuit of interesting objects. Infants at first are not aware of the passage of time, but, as they become able to focus their efforts on an end, they begin to perceive an immediate future—when they will pick up the desired toy, set the ring on its peg, or accomplish another goal.

The information that is presented in this chapter outlines babies' changing attitudes toward experiences as they shift from being watchers and listeners to actors by the end of their first year. Babies' concepts of objects and events first depend more on their senses than their physical actions: objects exist only if they can be seen and felt. If any object falls, moves, or is hidden from view, it ceases to exist for babies. This will change, of course, with maturation. The work of T. G. R. Bower indicates that infants are using their perceptual experiences to formulate expectations and ideas about the comings and goings of objects. Their physical inactivity should not be mistaken for mental inactivity. Apparently, infants start by developing some notions about object permanence through their sensory experiences of the behavior of objects. Then, as their motor skills increase, their actions show that they can separate means from ends. Finally, they can also relate the associated object, space, and time.

Because babies lack an organized symbol system, their memory skills are very limited. We have seen that repeated experience with an object perfects a baby's skills at handling it, and that babies indicate that they recognize familiar objects in various ways. Their memories of an object seem to be based on their continued use of their sensory-motor skills in connection with the object. We do not have any evidence that infants remember by using mental representations or that they have any system for long-term storage and later retrieval of information. And, although they do babble and cry, infants are still in a shadowy pre-language period without the accuracy and organization of true language to convey their ideas and desires.

Infants' subjective experience of reality is clearly centered on the *here* and *now*. Without a sophisticated symbol system, babies cannot ponder the philosopher's question of whether appearances are reality. To a baby, appearance and reality are the same. As we have seen, babies' trust in appearances gives them some ideas about reality that differ from ours. Bower has suggested that the world that the baby perceives may contain many more objects than ours: some objects are the "stationary ones" with certain fixed locations in space and others are the "moving ones." The objects with fixed locations may "dissolve" when the moving objects "appear." But babies do not appear to reflect on the reason for this: they simply accept their experiences.

Gradually, as infants get older and develop the concepts of object, means–end separation, space, and time, they become more concerned with any discrepancies between appearance and reality. Older babies' confusion is obvious when they search for an object and find that it is not where it "should" be or that a strange object has taken its place. Even then we need not infer that the baby is engaging in any sophisticated questioning of the reliability of perception. Rather, it seems that the baby is first beginning to separate perception and reality, a division that will be the basis for questioning the reality of what is perceived.

Caregivers are interested in arrangements of the environment that might enhance infants' cognitive development. Piaget has emphasized the importance of events in which the baby has to wait briefly in suspense for the outcome. To develop the object concept, for instance, the infant needs to experience a variety of comings and goings of objects: the handkerchief covers the watch; the handkerchief is lifted; the watch is still there. In the same way, in order to separate means and ends, babies need to have the opportunity to act in a variety of situations so that they can "see what happens." The absence of strong differences attributable to socioeconomic class in infant cognition suggests that most homes offer a range of stimulation that is wide enough to provide babies with a sufficient supply of experiences to foster their basic sensory-motor development. However, because clearly many (but not all) infants in institutions develop only part of their mental potential, we can see that some minimum of early experience is necessary to nurture a baby's cognitive development.

Other evidence reviewed here points to the regulation and organization of stimulation as a key feature in the influence of the environment on cognitive development. In the last chapter, we saw the importance of contingent stimulation. According to Piaget's theory, the development of the concepts of space and object depends upon infants' having the opportunity to act with objects and in space. The records of successful early intervention programs show that if babies are given more opportunities to experiment with objects and to receive individual attention from an adult caregiver who responds to their experimenting, they profit from the experience. Babies' movements and exploration are also related to development. But caregivers need not feel it is essential that they give children a specific set of toys or arrange spaces in a specific way lest they stunt their children's mental growth. Instead, they should simply make sure the baby has plenty of opportunity to handle objects, to move through space, and to observe other people doing these things as well. Also, at least some of the time the baby needs the undivided attention of a caregiver who responds to his actions and who can set up interesting situations with which he can experiment. The generous caregiver, who helps the baby by organizing the stimulation the baby receives, aids the baby to make sense of the challenging world that awaits discovery. Apparently, a relatively small amount of regular and reliably recurring interaction between infants and responsive caregivers will suffice to insure that the babies will develop their cognitive potentials.

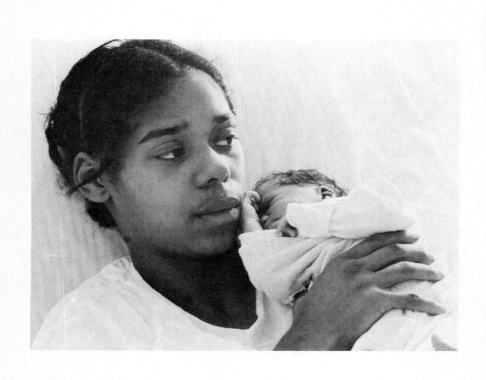

Chapter 5

Attachment and First Social Relations

Who among us does not delight in the smile of a baby who seems to find the utmost joy in our very existence? The earliest relationships between babies and their parents, especially their mothers, have been recognized over the ages as central to the human experience. The attachment between a mother and an infant is apparent in many ways: the mother's concern for the infant's comfort, the infant's responsiveness when she is near, and his smile fading or even becoming a cry when the mother leaves. To some degree, babies show these signs of attachment to other family members and caregivers as well.

Immediately at birth infants appear to have no strong attachment to their families; they seem to be oblivious to the comings and goings of their parents and undisturbed by strangers. Gradually through the first months of life they begin to have slightly different reactions to their mothers than to other people. By four months of age, they may smile and relax when their mothers approach them, but stare soberly at those less familiar to them. By the seventh or eighth month, their negative reactions to strangers may become more intense. Meanwhile, a baby is learning to prolong every contact with his mother by cooing at her, reaching for her, and, when it becomes possible, crawling about the house after her to remain near her. The attempts of babies to stay in contact with their mothers notify onlookers of the strong bond between mother and child, and they tend to insure that babies will receive a fair amount of attention from even the busiest of mothers.

The intensity and course of infants' attachment to their mothers do vary with the circumstances and with the infants' nature. In this chapter, I will discuss the major theories about the special relationship between mother and infant. I will then review what is known about attachment and early social relations from research in homes and laboratories, and consider such issues as alternative arrangements for care of infants and the greater participation of fathers in caring for their children. Last, I will consider some questions about how mothers and their infants interact.

There are many questions we hope to answer in this chapter. Is the mother-infant bond inborn, or is it the product of the particular infant care practices used in various countries? Why do attachment bonds differ in strength and how does the strength of a bond between mother and infant affect the later well-being and development of an infant? Another topic of interest is the causes and consequences of various patterns of parent-infant interaction.

Many of us wonder whether there is a natural bond between one human being and another. Are we by nature social animals who from our earliest relationship with our mothers need contact with one another? No clear answer to this question emerges from all the studies and observations to follow. Nevertheless, the question underlies some of our interest in the first social relations.

There are practical questions as well. Is it desirable for infants to form a strong attachment with their caregivers? Will close bonds foster babies' feelings of security and help them to overcome life's challenges, or will they retard the development of the autonomy and independence that are crucial to their personal growth? Once we discover what the best level of attachment is, we may wonder what arrangements will foster it. Should the baby have one or many caregivers? How about secondary caregivers who come and go for specific events? Should infants be cared for individually or in small groups? These questions and many others are the day-to-day concerns of those who seek to establish the best possible environment for the infants for whom they care.

Theories of Mother-Infant Attachment

A *theory* of attachment is a set of statements about how the bond between mother and infant is formed and the role it plays in the infant's development. In the sections that follow we will consider three of the most important theories of attachment: psychoanalytic theory, ethological theory, and learning theory.

Psychoanalytic Theory

According to psychoanalytic theory, of which Sigmund Freud was the founder, infants at birth are aware only of their own overwhelming feelings and sensations as they undergo the dramatic increase in stimulation that is brought about by their movement from the uterus into the external world. At first, babies make no distinction between their subjective experiences

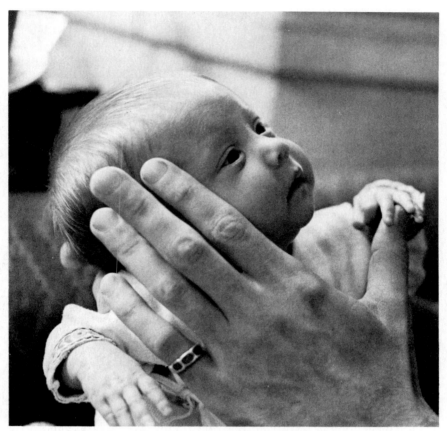

Figure 5-1. *Are there inborn bonds between offspring and their parents? Here an eight-week-old baby responds to the caring touch of his father. (Photo copyright © Suzanne Arms/Jeroboam, Inc.)*

and the reality outside of them. Their feelings are their only reality, according to Freud, because they are in a state of *primary narcissism*. Primary narcissism acknowledges no mother who is apart from the self; thus, because a relationship exists only between two or more people, no issue of relationship arises.

The infant knows only that he feels good or bad. Often when he feels bad and cries, he soon begins to feel good again. To observers it is clear that his feelings of pleasure began when his caregiver changed him, fed him, or otherwise ministered to him. However, he only experiences a connection between his own distress cry and his increased comfort, as if his need—as plaintively expressed by his cry—caused the comfort. He has the sensation, Freud conjectured, of being *omnipotent*.

However, a crying baby is not always comforted immediately, and sooner or later he becomes aware of variations in the timeliness and adequacy of the comfort he receives. These variations in comfort relate to the mother's comings and goings, and gradually the baby begins to be aware of this. Mother's breast, face, and voice come to be associated with comfort, especially the oral gratification of sucking for milk, which is thought by psychoanalysts to be the most important biological comfort during infancy. This association of mother and comfort gradually causes infants to realize their separateness from their mothers, who are not always close by. With this awareness, they become anxious over the loss of comfort and the loss of their control over it. They react by making a frantic struggle to hold onto their mothers: they cling and cry and try to be picked up. This behavior is characteristic of babies in the later months of the first year, and it reveals their first attachment to another human being.

After a time, babies resign themselves to the fact that they are separate beings from their mothers and cannot control them. According to psychoanalytic theory, babies (who by this time are toddlers) identify with their mothers by making their mothers' caregiving activities and other traits a part of their own personalities through a process called *introjection*. Introjection is the adoption of the traits of others as one's own. Once this identification process is begun, children's obvious and strong efforts to control their mothers' whereabouts subside, and they decide to ignore their separation anxiety (their fear of losing their mothers) by not thinking about it—*repressing* it, in Freud's parlance.

Margaret Mahler, a psychoanalyst who works with severely emotionally disturbed children, has written extensively on the process of mother-infant attachment (see Mahler, Pine, and Bergman, 1975). She believes most of her patients' disturbances stem from their failure to separate themselves from their mothers in early infancy. According to Mahler, mothers play active and crucial roles in babies' developing a sense of their separateness. When babies are born, their mothers must accept their total dependency and allow them to experience the relation of their comforts to their needs—an impression that forms the basis of the babies' sense of self. Gradually, mothers must relinquish their control over the infants' experiences and allow their children increasing amounts of control over when and what they are fed, what they look at, and where they go about a room. A mother who is in conflict about dependency either may fail to meet her baby's needs sufficiently or may continue to meet them past the time when the baby could take a stronger role. According to Mahler's view, the disturbances in the delicate balance of control between mother and infant lead to psychotic illness.

Table 5-1   Margaret Mahler's Stages of Infant Ego Development

Approximate Time from Birth (months)	Stage	Characteristics
Before Separation of Self from Mother		
0–1	Normal autistic	The baby does not distinguish him/herself from the mother.
2–2½	Early symbiotic	The baby experiences his/her own activities and feelings but as if they were part of the mother's activities, which are, in turn, experienced as his/her own.
2½–3	Normal symbiotic	A reciprical pattern of mutually interdependent acts—eye gaze exchange, etc.—develops further.
Separation and Individualization		
4–8	Differentiation or "hatching"	The baby becomes aware of his/her separateness and expresses this by pulling back from mother when held or by manipulating her hands, ears, and other body parts as if they were external objects.
8–15	Practicing	The toddler, fully aware of him/herself, moves out into the environment and walks, talks, explores independently.
15–24	Rapprochement	The toddler begins to return to the mother more often—to show her toys and otherwise share independent acts.
24–30	Consolidation of individuality	The toddler develops ways of dealing with separation and separateness and establishes a permanent sense of him/herself as a separate person.

SOURCE: After *The Psychological Birth of the Human Infant,* by M. S. Mahler, F. Pine, and A. Bergman. New York: Basic Books, 1975.

Mahler has recently worked with normal infants and their mothers in a laboratory setting. She has observed mothers and infants interacting from early in the first year through the second year of the infant's life, and sometimes beyond. Based on this work, as well as on her work with disturbed infants, she has developed an outline of the progression of the mother-infant relationship from a psychoanalytic view. The stages of Mahler's theory are summarized in Table 5-1.

During the first stage infants presumably are unaware of themselves as beings that are separate from their mothers. Right after birth they are dimly conscious only of their sensations, a state that corresponds to Freud's primary narcissism. The second, or *early symbiotic,* stage begins when infants are four or five weeks of age and are alert enough of the time to discern that their needs are being met (or not met) by forces outside of themselves. As this stage continues, babies become increasingly aware of external events and stimuli, so that their mothers' role in regulating the amount of stimulation they receive assumes great importance. According to Mahler, babies experience their mothers' ordering of events as their own. But babies still experience themselves and their mothers as being one. The symbiotic stage lasts from approximately one to four months of age.

Between four and eight months of age, babies' increasing awareness of the world and increasing skill in action lead to their awareness of their separation from their mothers. Mahler calls this experience *hatching.* By this time they can reach and grasp an object or call out to get attention. As their crawling and toddling skills emerge at 8 to 15 months, infants' power to create distance between themselves and their mothers increases. They enter what Mahler calls the *practicing* stage, in which they spend most of their time going back and forth between their mothers and some distant (to them) points in the room. In doing so, they are assuming more and more active control over how much contact they and their mothers have.

At some point around the middle of the second year, babies have built a large repertoire of independent actions that often take them into situations where their mothers are not immediately available. These situations develop both because the baby has ventured to try a new activity and because the mother has become more willing to attend to other matters while the baby plays. But, realizing the full extent of their separateness, babies experience true separation anxiety and make an attempt to recover the intimacy that they once had with their mothers. During this *rapprochement* stage, babies engage more frequently in dependent behavior and they attempt to share their activities with their mothers by talking (which they have just learned to do) and showing off. Many children who are in the rapprochement stage develop an intense attachment to some physical object such as a blanket, diaper, or teddy bear. By carrying *transitional objects* (as psychoanalysts call them), children make sure that they always have something familiar nearby to reassure them if need be. These possessions are dependable in that they can be controlled, which is not true of mothers. Results of a study of children's transitional objects indicate that two-thirds of infants have a favorite object to carry, which generally is soft, malleable, and associated with the child's daily experiences since birth (Busch et al., 1973).

Finally, when cognitive growth permits children to maintain a sense of permanent relationship with their mothers without continuous or immediately available contact, the intense attachment behavior of infancy dis-

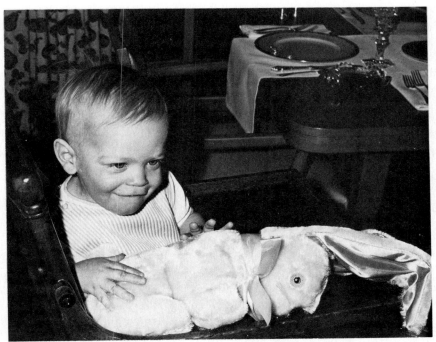

Figure 5-2.   *During the rapprochement stage, many children develop a strong attachment to an object such as a blanket or stuffed animal. By carrying such an object around, they make sure of always having something familiar nearby for reassurance—even at the dinner table. (Photo courtesy of George B. Fry III.)*

appears. The children have gained a sense of themselves as separate entities who can relate at will to others.

Erik Erikson is another psychoanalyst who has given a great deal of attention to the mother-infant relationship. Erikson is particularly interested in the development of such *ego* processes as establishing a sense of self and adapting to the environment of other people. In his pursuit of this topic, he emphasizes the interaction between the role culture plays in creating an individual's personality and the influence individuals have on their culture. Thus, he considers the mutual influence of mother and child upon each other to be partly determined by what the society says about mothering, the place of babies, and the roles people should have in the care of babies.

Like other psychoanalysts, Erikson believes personality develops in a series of stages determined largely by biological growth. However, Erikson considers life to be a series of inevitable conflicts between a maturing person and the reactions of other people to the maturation. Erikson's theory describes eight such psychosocial crises that cover the entire lifespan, but only the first two concern us here.

During the first two-thirds of the first year of life, according to Erikson, babies must deal with the issue of *trust*. They are almost wholly dependent on others, who must bring them food, keep them warm and dry, and care for them in other ways. If these ministrations occur on a reasonably regular schedule in proper relation to babies' needs, babies begin to believe in the world's basic trustworthiness. If, on the other hand, babies find themselves in pain or discomfort much of the time because their needs are not predictably met, they come to see the world as untrustworthy. In Erikson's view, how a culture traditionally cares for infants—through the family or special child-care institutions—strongly influences whether they will develop *trust* or *mistrust* of the world in which they live.

When people trust, they can approach life's challenges with a general expectation of mastery and success, even when they sometimes experience frustration and failure. But mistrust makes it difficult for people to accept experience or to allow others to influence them. Erikson believes that our experience of depending on a caregiver in earliest infancy is the basis for our negotiations of situations in which we must trust others throughout life.

Once their physical development reaches a certain point and they have begun to learn to speak, babies must face the psychosocial issue of their autonomy. Like Mahler, Erikson sees the interplay between the child's emerging autonomy and the continuing need for mothering as the central theme of the toddler period. If children's autonomous acts—acts that they initiate—are positively received, even applauded, by those around them, children embrace the independence of directing themselves and so develop a sense of separate selfhood. But if people restrain them or punish their independent acts harshly or often, they may feel ashamed and may wonder whether further autonomous exploration is worthwhile. Again, the attitude of the surrounding culture toward individuality will influence how parents react to their children's attempts to act independently. A culture that values individuality will have a larger proportion of autonomous people, according to Erikson, than one that does not. In any case, as babies develop a sense of autonomy, their parents' function shifts from one of indulging their dependency to fostering their autonomy by allowing them to experience more of it.

The various psychoanalytic views of the mother-infant bond all assign it a crucial position, and they believe the bond develops out of the mother's role in gratifying the baby's needs. The strength of the bond, at least during infancy, gives the mother the ability to influence the baby's emerging personality in powerful ways. Psychoanalysts suggest that in order to retain some permanent tie with our mothers, we make their characteristics, be-liefs, and values part of ourselves. They believe that our efforts to please our mothers (as we envision them) continue to influence our ethical con-duct and our efforts to work with one another in society.

Ethological Theory

Ethological theory has as its origin the psychoanalytic work that was done with infants who were separated from their parents during World War II. However, this theory draws its basic premises not from psychoanalysis but from the theory of evolution, and John Bowlby of England and Mary Ainsworth of the United States are its leading advocates (Bowlby, 1969; Ainsworth, 1969). Whereas psychoanalytic theory presents the mother-infant relationship as emerging from the dependence of the infant on the mother, in the view of ethological theorists this attachment is a separate, innate, motivational system that is on a par with feeding and sexuality but not dependent upon them. According to this theory, both mother and young infant are motivated to remain physically close. Ethologists cite as evidence the fact that most mothers want to carry their infants about and that they frequently inspect them to make sure of their well-being. Gradu-ally as infants learn to crawl and walk, they assume a more prominent role in keeping the two together by following their mothers about, frequently checking their whereabouts, and, if all else fails, crying and fussing to bring their mothers back to close and reassuring proximity.

   The ethological theorists see the efforts of mother and infant to stay together as adaptive patterns that have evolved to insure that relatively helpless infants remain with a mature adult who can protect them from harm and can meet their needs. Cultural patterns are such that many of the world's infants are near their caregivers much of the time. Thus they are not particularly aware of their attachment need; even a close observer might see little indication of an obvious attachment. Frantic following or crying to attract attention are behaviors that are aroused only when a baby feels a need or senses a threat—as, for example, when parents leave a baby alone in a strange or new situation, so that the baby feels abandoned when he most needs comfort or reassurance.

   Ainsworth has devised a standard laboratory situation in which an ob-server can watch the interactions that reveal the attachment between babies and their mothers. Infant and mother (or other caregiver) are brought to a small, sparsely furnished room—a strange environment that presumably enhances the infant's desire to be protected. Observers (behind a one-way mirror) watch changes in the babies' behavior during a series of three-minute episodes in which they remain, first, alone with mothers; second, with their mothers and a stranger who enters; third, alone with the stranger; fourth, all alone; fifth, with the stranger again; and sixth, with their mothers again. Using this procedure, Ainsworth has been able to measure the increases in babies' efforts to stay near their mothers when a stranger enters or when their mothers are about to leave them. She has also reported that babies explore their environment less when their mothers are gone, thus suggesting that, instead of hindering exploration, attachment promotes it (Ainsworth and Bell, 1970). Researchers testing diverse hypotheses have used variations of the Ainsworth observational situation, and I will report the results of some of their studies in a later section.

Learning Theory and Attachment

Learning theory differs from the psychoanalytical and ethological theories of attachment in that it minimizes inborn factors. To the learning theorist, the attachment between mother and infant is created because the mother has met the baby's needs in the past and thus the baby has come to associate her with the pleasure of being content. Infants enjoy being with their mothers so mothers themselves become a source of gratification or reinforcement. In this theory, babies *learn* attachment. It would follow logically that the strength of the attachment bond would depend entirely upon how much a mother gratified a baby's various needs. If this were true, different child-care arrangements such as a home baby sitter, day care, or group living would cause the child to form more than one attachment relationship and to have relationships of varying strengths. Indeed, the leading advocate of this viewpoint, Jacob Gewirtz, has rejected the usefulness of the idea of *an* attachment bond. Instead he considers separately each of the actions we label "behaviors that indicate attachment." Thus, the circumstances of a baby's care arrangements may lead him to show a strong tendency to follow his mother when she is present, but none at all to cry when she leaves for work each day. Learning theory, then, rejects the concept of "attachment bond" and substitutes a discussion of circumstances that influence specific attachment behaviors. The learning theorist presumes that these circumstances are environmental and that just as surroundings vary widely, so will the ways individual children show their attachments to their caregivers.

Empirical Findings on Attachment

Normative Course

At around five months of age, the majority of infants begin to respond very differently to their mothers than they do to strangers. Mothers receive a smile from them, but strangers receive a neutral stare—a reaction described as "wary" by many researchers. Babies encounter family members and friends less warily but nevertheless not as warmly as they receive their mothers (Emde, Gaensbauer, and Harmon, 1976). As the first year proceeds, many babies come to react more negatively to strange people, which demonstrates, according to some, their special relationship with their mothers. Babies who are not particularly bothered by strangers may nevertheless gradually come to show other signs of attachment such as crawling about to follow their mothers and attempting to keep in contact with their mothers by exchanging looks with them or by babbling. A variety of attachment behaviors commonly become pronounced in babies nine months old and continue to be so through part of the second year (Mahler, Pine, and Bergman, 1975; Ainsworth, 1969).

Relations Among Attachment Behaviors

According to both the psychoanalytic and the ethological theories of attachment, such behaviors of infants as following, clinging, continually looking at their caregivers, vocalizing, and objecting to separation are all facets of a single underlying motive—attachment. To the extent that this is so, some overall relationship should connect them. One would think that infants who have strong attachment needs would show the same strong intensity in all behaviors that are intended to keep their mothers close by, whereas infants who do not need to have their mothers near so much would behave in those ways only rarely. Ainsworth has stressed that babies act to keep near their mothers only when they feel the relationship is threatened, or when they suddenly need the relationship more, perhaps because of hunger (Ainsworth, 1969). Thus, an infant who needs his mother very much will not show attachment if he spends most of his time comfortably near her with little interruption to their interaction. His protests at separation will be observed only if separation occurs.

Ainsworth developed her laboratory situation to create circumstances in which babies would show their need for their mothers because of a series of mildly stressful incidents designed to arouse the attachment motive. The observers would not be able to measure the intensity of all of the baby's attachment behaviors at the same moment because some of them would never occur together: a baby cannot coo for a mother's attention and, at the same instant, cry. But we can ask how these behaviors relate to each other over the entire course of an Ainsworth observation session. If it makes any sense to speak of a "highly attached" infant or one who is "not attached," then the baby should show a high intensity of all various behaviors used to measure this attachment.

In general, various measures of the intensity of children's protests and searching when their mothers are gone are more closely associated than are behaviors that presumably measure attachment to mothers who are physically present—behaviors like following, clinging, and looking. But despite this, all the different studies are not consistent regarding exactly which measures of attachment are significantly associated. Moreover, when infants experience more than one Ainsworth session, their ratings on the measures of attachment do not remain the same through all the sessions (Masters and Wellman, 1974; Coates, Anderson, and Hartup, 1972; Willemsen et al., 1974). If these ratings accurately indicated the strength of babies' relationships with their mothers, they would remain more nearly the same from session to session. Apparently, babies' various ways of keeping in contact with their mothers—trying to be near them, touching them, looking for them, cooing to attract their attention, and the rest—are influenced by the situation and babies' attitudes, not by some single clear characteristic in the infant called "attachment." Harriet Rheingold has pointed out that all studies of infants in the laboratory involve exposure to strange people and situations. Despite this, crying and other kinds of intense attachment behavior are rare (Rheingold, 1974).

Attachment studies based on Ainsworth's techniques do reveal a clear relation between how much babies explore and whether their mothers are present so that they do not feel threatened. When a stranger enters the room in studies modeled after the Ainsworth situation, babies immediately become less active: they don't crawl about or play with toys as much. When their mothers leave, many babies stop their activities entirely (Ainsworth and Bell, 1970; Gershaw and Schwarz, 1971; Willemsen et al., 1974). Looking at their behavior from an ethological point of view may explain it: their mothers are a secure base from which they can venture forth to find out about the world. Without a secure place to retreat if necessary, infants dare not challenge the unknown. Thus, the relationship of protection, comfort, and aid between mothers and infants not only promises infants safety but also encourages them to risk exploring the world and thus influences what they learn about it.

"Attachment" is probably not a single characteristic that impels infants to engage in a variety of behaviors. But there is a type of situation—for example, if a familiar caregiver is close at hand when the circumstances are not so new that they are frightening—that does encourage babies to relax and let curiosity lead them into exploring.

Let us look at some of the factors that influence how infants show their need for their mothers. Some evidence indicates that, whether or not a single attachment characteristic exists, each infant has characteristic attachment *behavior*. Ainsworth has noticed that infants have various patterns of responding to her laboratory situation. Some infants appear not to be strongly attached; they act the same to their mothers as they do to strangers.

A second group shows what we might call "classic" reactions: although they are content with their mothers, they become uneasy when a stranger is present. After a brief separation from their mothers, they cling to them or follow them closely. A third group, who are uneasy even when their mothers are present, are so anxious to keep close to mother that they cannot use her as a secure base from which to go forth to explore. When researchers visited the families, they found that the babies showed the same attachment behavior at home as they did in the lab (Ainsworth, Bell, and Slayton, 1971).

Because the American society sets different standards for how much babies of either sex are allowed to cling and be dependent, we might anticipate that sex differences would abound in this area. Indeed, several studies do find that one-year-old girls keep closer to their mothers and show more distress if separated from them than do one-year-old boys (Brooks and Lewis, 1974a; Goldberg and Lewis, 1969; Bronson, W. C., 1971). However, several other studies find that boys show more distress than girls (Corter, Rheingold, and Eckerman, 1972; Feldman and Ingham, 1975; Marvin, 1971) and the majority of studies find no differences that relate to sex (Maccoby and Jacklin, 1974). Apparently, no overriding sex differences in attachment behavior exist, although perhaps babies of opposite sexes might react differently in situations that have not yet been identified. In a similar vein, several studies on whether attachment behavior is influenced by social class found no differences related to class (Tulkin, 1973a). However, when infants heard a tape recording of their mothers' voices followed by a recording of a stranger's voice, middle-class infants responded differently to the two voices, whereas lower-class infants did not (Tulkin, 1973b).

Babies' behavior may be affected by the identity of the caregiver who accompanies them through a potentially trying experience such as a laboratory session. The identity of the caregiver has crucial theoretical and practical impact. The notion of attachment implies an exclusive relationship in which infants depend on a certain "special" caregiver to meet their needs. The theories of attachment disagree about the extent to which attachment depends upon and grows out of the child's experience of being cared for by a particular person. In many modern families, fathers care for their infants and, even when a father does not help regularly with his infant's care, he is a potential "haven in a storm." What happens in the Ainsworth situation when babies are accompanied by their fathers rather than their mothers? The studies that have sought the answer to this question have found that infants generally do not behave differently with their fathers than they did with their mothers (Lamb, 1977; Willemsen et al., 1974; Ban and Lewis, 1974). Even though infants apparently spend much less time with their fathers than with their mothers (Rebelsky and Hanks, 1971), this finding would seem to say that infants' behavior in the Ainsworth laboratory situation should not be hailed as an infallible measure of the strength of some exclusive bond they have only with their main caregivers. Some studies reveal that, when babies must choose between mother and father for comfort in a strange laboratory situation, they choose their mothers Cohen and Campos, 1974); possibly their choice indicates the strength of the baby's attachment more accurately.

Children probably have multiple attachments, with that to the principal caregiver taking precedence in times of conflict. But what is the nature of the relationship between babies and their regular baby sitters? Very likely, we will find that infants behave toward these secondary caregivers in many of the same ways as they do toward their parents. Indeed one pair of investigators found that two-year-old subjects who were strongly attached to their security blankets relied on the blankets for security in an Ainsworth stranger situation just as much as they relied on their mothers (Passman and Weisberg, 1975.) However, a later follow-up study revealed that in times of great stress the blankets were not as comforting as mothers (Passman, 1977).

The characteristics of the stranger who participates in a laboratory session also seem to influence a baby's reactions. Researchers who use two or more strangers for a study usually find that they evoke different responses, but the exact reason for this difference is hard to disentangle from the effects of other variables (e.g., Willemsen et al., 1974). One study compared an adult female stranger to a preschool child stranger. Interestingly, the infants who were left with the child stranger were not as distressed as infants left with the adult stranger (Lewis and Brooks, 1974). To pinpoint which characteristics of strangers cause the babies' distress and increase their attachment needs, we would have to design studies using as strangers people who varied in specific, observable ways. At the same time, we would have the important and difficult task of separating the baby's responses that were caused by anxiety about the stranger from those caused by being without the mother. Some studies of babies' reactions to strangers are discussed in a later section.

The social context of the stranger's entrance and the mother's departure may influence how babies react: for example, infants generally show less attachment behavior at home than they do in strange laboratory situations (Ainsworth and Bell, 1970), which supports the idea that the strangeness of unknown surroundings arouses an infant's need of a protecting mother. An interesting study showed that when the mothers chatted and played cards with the stranger during the experiment as they might at home the babies did not stop exploring and did not show as much attachment as they did in the standard laboratory situation (Fein, 1975).

How babies react is also influenced by whether they have other means of amusing themselves than interacting with their parents. Babies will play alone longer when they have attractive and complex toys to entertain them (Willemsen et al., 1974). Toys may even attract them away from their parents (Corter, Rheingold, and Eckerman, 1972). Eventually, even with interesting toys, a baby begins to seek the company of an available parent in an experimental situation (Brooks and Lewis, 1974b), but at home this is not the case. We will probably understand the attachment between mother and infant better when we determine the cause of each of the babies' behaviors—for example, trying to be close to the mother, making sounds or searching for her—rather than theorizing about a single quality called attachment.

During our search to understand attachment we can discover interesting facts about it by examining other areas of development. Babies' mental development, which we can measure by how well they have mastered Piaget's object concept (see Chapter 4), relates quite closely to their increasing need for the security of caregivers. Babies who have reached a point in development where they search for an object that is not in sight—perhaps a toy left in the living room or a ball hidden under a blanket—show various signs that could be interpreted as signs of strong attachment to their caregivers. For example, they cry when their parents go away, they try to stay close to them, and they protest when parents stop an activity that they were sharing and enjoying. One investigator did an extensive examination of babies' personal styles of showing their need of caregivers and their ability to understand the object concept. She found that babies begin to be distressed when their caregivers leave—showing that they realize the caregiver is a permanent object—almost always before they also regard nonhuman objects as permanent. Several other investigations have confirmed this sequence (Goiń-DeCarie, 1965). Perhaps because those who care for him are the objects that appear most frequently in an infant's experience, he gives them the honor of being the first permanent objects. Or perhaps the emerging emotional bond between infant and caregiver may mean that the infant pays more attention to this important human object and thus learns more about him or her than about any other object.

Only after babies have experienced sufficient cognitive development to realize objects are permanent will they be aware of the separation and loss that is part of attachment. We can hardly long for the presence of loved ones unless we have some notion that they exist somewhere else when they could be with us. Indeed the deepening bond between children and their mothers reflects infants' increasing awareness of their separateness and, therefore, their vulnerability to being deserted. But the mental growth that inspires this "separation anxiety" also helps babies to overcome their worries. When they repeatedly see that caregivers come back, they soon learn to expect a return, so their dramatic demonstrations of attachment become less intense than they were at nine or ten months of age.

In summary, research with Ainsworth's model proves that many babies seek the continuing presence of familiar adults, and that their seeking usually intensifies when they are in unknown surroundings or with people who are unknown to them. The various behaviors that make the baby's concern apparent—their looks, their protestations upon separation from their parents—seem to depend upon specific qualities of a situation rather than springing from a single feeling of attachment. Babies seek out both fathers and mothers for comfort during stress even though they may not have as much contact with their fathers as with their mothers. When a familiar caregiver is present, babies will generally explore and play more than they will when this person, their "haven," is gone. Applying the all-inclusive label of attachment is a useful means of summarizing the various facets of the protective bond linking the baby and caregiver, but there is little evidence for the existence of an underlying trait that characterizes either the baby or the relationship.

First Communications

Before babies show the clear-cut signs of attachment we have been discussing, they communicate with their caregivers. When they smile, most parents joyously interpret the smile to mean that at last they have received a message from their otherwise enigmatic baby. An exchange of smiles between parents and baby can indeed be a heartwarming experience that may be followed by a cooing and babbling "conversation" and rounds of imitation: baby of parents, parents of baby.

When does the first smile occur and what does it mean? Several studies have charted the normal development of smiling; from them, we see that the meaning of the baby's smile changes over the course of the first year. Newborns smile spontaneously without regard to any particular aspect of the environment simply because their nervous systems are developing (Emde, Gaensbauer, and Harmon, 1976). Before the end of the first month of life, babies smile in definite response to interesting events, such as people's voices, flashing lights, or bright moving objects. At first, babies seem to bestow the same smile on parents that they give to the mobile above their beds but, during the second month, this changes. Two-month-old babies meet people's eyes and recognize the pattern of a human face—anyone's face, be it parent or stranger—with a cheerful equanimity. They continue to smile at other interesting occurrences in the environment, but their responsiveness to human contact continues to stand out for the next several months.

By four months of age, long before more distinctive signs of attachment develop, babies begin to show different reactions to strangers and familiar caregivers. Over the course of the early months the infant, mother, and other intimates have also developed ways of communicating by exchanging glances and facial gestures. The earliest "talk" of this sort consists of an exchange of glances between babies and those around them. Newborn babies do not look directly into the eyes of others, but after several weeks of age they are able to establish direct eye contact.

Inspired by the pleasure of making eye contact with a very young baby, many people increase the pace of their encounters and try to get their babies to smile. You smile. The baby smiles, which delights you enough to make you grin broadly. The baby responds with another smile and off you are to a round of "The Game," as Watson, one investigator, calls it. According to Watson, babies realize that your smile is *in response to* their smiles; this contingency apparently is innately pleasurable. Babies delight in the facial responses of adults because they can control them through their own responses (Watson, 1973).

People who don't belong to the baby's family may not respond as consistently to the baby's antics. Sometimes they may look away toward the adults with whom they are conversing or withdraw into their own thoughts. Babies may respond by assuming a neutral expression because they are unable to get the stranger to respond; perhaps this explains why they treat strangers differently from their parents. Or perhaps babies smile as they recognize or understand an event, and are unable to understand strangers as well as the family members (Zelazo, 1972).

Several interesting investigations have given us insight into the way in which mothers and their young infants have wordless dialogues. In one study, films were made of infants who were one to five months old as they interacted with their mothers (the mothers had been asked to capture their babies' interest). The pairs showed a definite cycle of watching each other momentarily and then looking away for a moment; this then was followed again by mutual attention. The infants apparently signaled their mothers when they were temporarily satiated by averting their gaze. The mother responded by waiting for the baby to indicate renewed interest by meeting her eyes. The mother may help to regulate the interchange by removing distracting stimuli such as her purse or keys and by showing through her demeanor that she expects to communicate (Brazelton, 1974). Some research indicates that the extent to which the mother detects the rather subtle cues of her infant reflects her general attitude toward the infant and her role as a mother. Women who happily looked forward to their approaching motherhood while they were pregnant had better coordinated eye communication with their babies than the women whose attitudes were less positive (Moss and Robson, 1968).

The role of infants in starting and maintaining these exchanges is also important. As I said, they routinely signal their mothers when they have had enough interaction by averting their gaze. Mothers apparently become very adept at interpreting their infants' patterns of watching and looking away (Stern, 1974). The importance of mutual eye contact is most apparent among infants who are born blind because of the effects of its absence. Sylvia Fraiberg has written movingly of her own reactions to holding and looking at small babies who cannot respond to her interest and facial animation. She has admitted feeling a great distance between herself and blind babies and finding it difficult to continue to pay attention to an infant whose expression is impassive. Apparently, many people experience similar feelings, with the result that many blind infants do not have sufficient social encounters with the people around them. Their lack of socialization profoundly affects their development. Fraiberg has made the important discovery that blind infants express their emotional reactions to what they feel and hear by making gestures, using their fingers and hands in definite patterns to convey specific meanings. Once mothers of blind infants are taught to watch their infants' hands, a "dialogue" develops between them that parallels the visual exchanges of sighted infants and their mothers (Fraiberg, 1974).

The wordless dialogue between infants and their mothers and other caregivers is infants' first experience of making things happen regularly. You may recall from Chapter 4 that such experiences are crucial to a baby's mental development. We can infer that, the more opportunity infants have to exchange messages, the better they will develop mentally and emotionally. We can expect infants who communicate with people around them to be more aware of their environment and to be more likely to feel secure enough to risk exploring it.

Reactions to Strangers

The psychoanalytic and ethological theories of infant-mother attachment consider infants' seemingly negative reactions to strangers to be one sign of their special bond with those who care for them most. As we have already discussed, babies' reactions to strangers have causes and consequences that are somewhat different from those of their other attachment behavior. Let us look at reactions to strangers apart from the stressful experience of separation from the mother, which we will examine later. As you read about

Figure 5-3.   *Between two and six months of age most infants become wary of people they do not know. Here a six-month-old infant soberly surveys the stranger who has come to take his picture. (Photo courtesy of Emilio A. Mercado.)*

babies developing negative reactions to strangers, you should keep in mind that many babies do not demonstrate such reactions to any great degree. We will take up individual differences in fear of strangers in a few pages.

The first indication we have that babies are reacting differently to strangers than to those they know comes during their second month: although they will immediately brighten up at the sight of a familiar face, they do not smile at strange faces. Between two and six months of age, most infants gradually become more wary of strangers; they may greet strangers by stopping their activities and staring. By nine months of age, some infants begin to show their distress by crying at the entrance of a stranger. Others continue to have a reaction that is mild but clearly different from the one they show to familiar persons. Their wariness of strangers varies with the situation but continues to some extent throughout their second year. By two or so, most children adapt to the coming and going of strangers and

Table 5-2   A Structured Step-by-Step Approach of Strangers to Infants

Step	Behavior
1	Stranger knocks on the outside of the closed door of the baby's experimental room.
2	Stranger steps into the room and smiles at the baby.
3	Stranger talks to the baby from his or her initial distance away.
4	Stranger moves to a mark on the floor midway between the initial position near the door and the high chair where the baby is.
5	Stranger moves to within one foot of the high chair and smiles and talks to the baby.
6	Stranger takes the baby's hands.

cease to treat it as an event of importance (Mahler, Pine, and Bergman, 1975). In recent years, researchers have studied the impact of various circumstances on a baby's reaction to a stranger. In order to do so, they have designed some standard ways to introduce strangers to babies. In most studies, the stranger approaches the baby in a series of steps that gradually increase the potential threat to the baby. Table 5-2 is an example of such a series of steps. Observers then record the baby's reactions at each step.

Many researchers use this approach because it is suited to a variety of circumstances at home or in the laboratory, and several interesting findings have emerged from their efforts. One is that the babies regard the strangers' systematic behavior to be strange in itself. After asking for their aid, one investigator filmed passers-by on the street as they approached a baby. She found that strangers usually approached a baby in a way that was quite different from the procedure researchers commonly use (Goiń-DeCarie, 1975). These "people in the street" approached continuously and rapidly, but only to a spot within a few feet of the baby's carriage. They did not talk much or gesture to touch the baby as experimental strangers do. Another pair of investigators found that ten-month-old infants would be fearless enough to approach a distant stranger who looked at and talked to them, but would avoid the same stranger if she stared impassively at them (Lewis and Brooks, 1974). Possibly, we have mistakenly interpreted infants' negative reactions in a laboratory as fear of strangers when the babies actually only fear the strangeness of our laboratory procedures. We know quite well that we are frightened by unfamiliar events such as being examined by a new doctor or dentist. This seems to be related to the fact that we can't safely predict what will happen.

The general social context in which babies encounter strangers clearly has an effect on their reaction. Babies not only show less of the other attachment behaviors at home, but also respond less negatively to strangers whom they encounter at home rather than at a laboratory (Stroufe, Waters, and Matas, 1974). When a laboratory situation is made more homelike—if there is living-room furniture and if mothers and strangers interact as friends do—babies abandon nearly all of their negative reactions to strangers (Fein, 1975). The extent to which babies are familiar with the environment seems to be a key variable in how they behave. Some researchers have experimented with this idea and have found that, when babies are allowed to spend a few minutes in a strange environment before being observed there the next day, their distress reactions definitely lessen (Rheingold, 1974). When the mother stays close to her infant in an otherwise strange environment, the infant's reactions to a stranger are much less negative than when she remains at a distance (Morgan and Riciutti, 1969). Clearly the strangeness of the environment, of the new person, and of the new person's behavior all influence the baby's reactions.

One question of obvious practical importance is whether the characteristics of strangers influence babies' reactions to them. It seems logical that they would, but most studies use only one or two strangers, and thus it is difficult to tell whether any of their characteristics have an effect on babies. One study used as strangers several adults and preschool children of each sex, and found that the 8- and 12-month-old babies reacted positively and were not afraid of the child strangers but were wary and distressed with the adult strangers. Twelve-month-old boys were somewhat more negative toward male adult strangers than toward female adults. Otherwise the sex of the strangers did not affect the babies' reactions (Greenberg, Hillman, and Grice, 1973). Two other studies also found that child strangers did not upset babies; their responses depended entirely on whether the stranger was a child or an adult (Lenssen, 1973; Lewis and Brooks, 1974). An additional study used a midget as the stranger and found that the babies were still distressed, which suggested that the babies react positively to both children's age and size, not just their size alone (Brooks and Lewis, 1976). But we can only speculate about why children are less threatening to babies than adults. Perhaps babies identify more closely with children. And we know even less about other characteristics that influence children's reactions to strangers.

Common sense would suggest that babies' responses to strangers might depend on the extent to which they have experienced unfamiliar faces, and, in this case, science seems to support common sense. Babies who have been around many different people apparently tolerate the situation better; they are older before they become wary of strangers (Schaffer, 1966) and they are not as fearful (Willemsen and McTighe, 1977). But even the most experienced babies still show some signs of unease around strangers. Their apparent mistrust is more than just a straightforward response that they have learned by experience. If this were so, then we could simply teach them not to be afraid by insuring that they met only those people with whom they would be comfortable. However, babies may be born with a fear of strangeness (Hebb and Riesen, 1943), which means that they would not lose this fear until they mature to the point at which they are not fearful of unknown qualities.

Any parent or professional caregiver will tell us that different babies react differently to strangers. Indeed, according to several studies, many babies—perhaps even half of all babies—do not react in any definitely negative way to strangers (Bronson, G. W., 1971). Some babies even react positively to strangers in experiments (Eckerman and Whatley, 1975). Apparently, those babies who are most distressed by strangers also are wary of new experiences in general (Paradise and Curcio, 1974). As you will recall, most babies change their reactions to strangers during the second half of their first year. This change, which parallels babies' increasing cognitive abilities, seems to represent some very basic shift in infants' attitudes toward their experiences. Rather than simply going along with circumstances, they stop to examine them. However, babies can be strongly affected by the circumstances in which an experience takes place. Temperament, a part of which is inborn, also plays an important role in the baby's reactions. When a baby about 18 months old starts being upset by strangers, you should consider this a normal sign of his increasing awareness of the details of the environment. As babies learn to interpret the strangeness they encounter, their reactions will cease to be so intense and negative.

The Styles of Interactions Between Babies and Their Mothers

Most research and theory dealing with attachment focuses on the universal patterns of mother-infant interaction. But recently, many American developmental psychologists have begun to study the individual differences in the ways mother-infant pairs interact. The ways in which infants interact with various other people may be equally significant; however, at this point, we haven't studied these other relationships enough to know their impact on babies' development. We will discuss some first efforts to understand babies' relationships with other people as well. In the present section, we will discuss interactions between mothers and infants. Ideally we would like to balance the presentation with as much information about interactions between children and their fathers; but detailed studies of interaction with fathers are just now beginning. So there is still very little such information available.

How Mother-Infant Interaction Can Affect Development

Because in our society most infants and mothers spend most of the day together, common sense suggests that the baby's development will be profoundly influenced by the way in which they spend this time. The ethological theories of attachment argue that the mother is mainly a "secure base" from which the baby can risk exploring alone, safe in the knowledge that aid will be available if necessary. Let us look more specifically at what the "secure base" of mothering consists of. Mothers and infants interact in four ways that influence the pace and development of babies' increasing mental abilities. First, mothers can *regulate stimulation* for their babies: they can move them, can bring objects or people close or take them away, and can subtly direct their infants' attention away from one activity to another. Second, mothers *observe and decide* what stimulation their babies need. Third, mothers *reinforce*: they reward the baby with a smile, a touch, or attention for some actions, but not for others. Finally, mothers are the *models* after which babies can pattern their developing skills.

Babies have their own roles to play. They may pay more or less attention to their mothers' behavior and thus be more or less aware of subtle patterns in it. Their activities and moods may vary in a predictable way, so that their mothers can fairly accurately predict what their needs will be, or their activities and moods may be irregular, so that their mothers will determine their needs only with difficulty. Mothers, babies, and pairs all are different, so researchers try to bring an ordered understanding to these variations by separating the behavior of each from that of the other.

Dimensions of Mothers' Behavior

To study mother-infant interaction, investigators have observed, interviewed, and used standard tests to measure the ways in which mothers' behavior affects interactions with their children. These are listed in Table 5-3. We will consider four of their findings. First, a mother's *attitude* appears to have a strong influence upon her handling of the various activities. Her confidence—or lack of it—about herself and her role as a mother influences the messages she gives her baby. The mother who lacks confidence may carry her infant tentatively. She may frequently change the course of her caregiving activities—feeding, diapering, and the like—because she is unsure what the baby needs. Or, on the other hand, she may inflexibly stick to a particular routine because the routine offers her the security that she otherwise would lack. The self-confident mother who

Table 5-3 The Mother's Part in Various Interactions in Which Mothers and Infants Engage

Type	Interaction
Vocal	Vocalizing
Facial	Smiling
	Laughing
Visual	Intent-looking
	Dull-looking
	Looking away
Manual	Reaching
	Touching
	Holding
	Adjusting
Postural	Moving into line of vision
	Bobbing and nodding
	Leaning forward
	Leaning back
Miscellaneous	Facial gestures of various kinds
	Hand gestures
	Kissing
	Wiping baby's face
	Miscellaneous

SOURCE: After "The Origins of Reciprocity," by T. B. Brazelton, B. Koslowski, and M. Main. In M. Lewis and L. A. Rosenblum (Eds.), *The Effect of the Infant on Its Caregiver,* p. 52.

welcomes motherhood along with her other roles may interact with her infant in a definite way, so the baby will feel reassured that its needs will be satisfied predictably.

Second, *the accuracy of the mother's perceptions* about her baby's characteristics and needs also influences her interactions with the baby. Obviously, the fit between what the mother is doing and what the baby needs will be better if the mother actually knows what the baby needs. Mothers can make mistakes about what their babies need for many reasons—because babies' behavior is sometimes irregular and hard to predict or because some of mothers' perceptions are based more on their own thoughts (especially if they are caring for a baby for the first time) than on the real behavior of their babies. A mother is most likely to understand her baby's needs if she pays careful attention to its behavior and forgets her own preconceptions.

A third important influence upon mothers' interactions with their babies is the *response* they make to their babies' activities. For example, if you react with pleasure and pay more attention when your son makes sounds, looks directly at something, or reaches for a toy, you are rewarding him and thus encouraging him to repeat the behavior: you are reinforcing those actions to which you respond positively. The characteristics of a mother's response that affect the baby's development are, first, the nature of the response—whether positive or negative—and, second, its relation to the baby's own behavior. For example, when a mother's reactions correspond closely to her infant's actions, the infant comes to sense a cause-and-effect relation. Mothers differ in their responses to their infants: some respond whether they are pleased or displeased, some respond only when they are displeased, and some respond not to their babies' behavior but rather to other things. If a mother consistently responds favorably to a baby's actions, she influences the baby's activities to a great extent. If she always greets a certain behavior with an unpleasant reaction, she will succeed in eliminating that particular behavior but will not influence the rest of the baby's actions much. If her reactions have nothing to do with the baby's behavior, they will have either no influence or a rather confusing influence. This is not to say that babies respond only to actions that have a direct connection to their own. They also thrive on large quantities of affection that is not contingent upon their good behavior but rather is simply an expression of their mothers' love. Perhaps the security the child feels at having a mother who has proved her loving concern is the foundation of the "secure base" that Ainsworth and Bowlby discuss.

Finally, mothers can act as *models* of behavior for their infants, who come to watch their every action with interest. Infants who pay attention to their mothers learn a great deal about the world by doing so. The fact that some infants do more of this learning while others do less suggests that some mothers are more effective models than others, but it could also be interpreted to mean that babies differ in their ability to learn through observation.

Aspects of Babies' Behavior

What do babies contribute to their interaction with their mothers? The literature on the subject mentions various aspects of infants' role in their interaction with their mothers, which I have summarized into several classes. First, the interaction between a mother and baby is influenced by the baby's *state* of awareness. Mothers adjust the amount and intensity of their own caregiving activities according to their perceptions of the baby's ability to receive them—as you can well imagine, mothers do not usually talk to a sleeping baby or ignore a fussing one. An apparently receptive, alert baby may inspire a mother to bring objects over for her attention.

Second, infants influence their interaction with their mothers in a conscious way by *signaling*—through vocalizing, touching, and looking—that they want to communicate. Once communication has begun, their continuing touching, looking, and vocalizing help to maintain it, whereas their abruptly stopping these signals tends to bring it to a close. During the early months, the mother rather than the baby often makes these signals; a baby comes to make more signals with age. According to how much babies' efforts to communicate actually reflect their needs, their signals help their mothers to satisfy those needs correctly. As you can see, both parties play important roles in making their shared activities successful.

Apart from making sounds, touching, and looking to signal the mother, babies may influence their mothers' behavior by the *amount of attention they seek*. A baby who is constantly babbling and looking around may get more attention than one who is quiet. But a mother may come to want a respite from that "stimulation," and may retreat into another room, get a sitter, or take other actions that she would not have taken otherwise. On the other hand, some people might interpret the stimulation as a sign of the baby's happiness and therefore might actually spend more time with a noisy baby than they would with the quiet one. In either case the baby's stimulating behavior often has dramatically influenced the mother's behavior.

Finally a relationship between a mother and a baby is influenced by the extent to which the baby *responds* to his mother's ministrations. When a baby is fed, changed, or covered, does he acknowledge that his need has been met? Does the baby who was thrashing restlessly about in his crib before his morning feeding become quiet upon receiving it and look about the room? Does he nestle gently into his mother's arms and coo with satisfaction? Or does he continue thrashing as if he had never been fed? Babies' responsiveness rewards their mothers for smiling, laughing, looking, and holding and in this way is complementary to the mothers' reinforcement of their smiles, looks, laughs, and coos.

Mother-Infant Styles of Relating

When you consider the various aspects of a mother's contributions and those of an infant's contributions, it becomes clear that relationships between mothers and infants can follow any of a number of patterns. Here we identify a few clear-cut patterns that will be helpful in interpreting the research findings. In a relationship of *high mutuality* the infant sends out clear signals that the mother perceives accurately, and both are very responsive to each other. *Failure of mutuality* occurs when the baby does not make clear signals, the mother is inaccurate in her perception of what the baby needs, or neither party is responsive. Failure of mutuality, then, can result from the mother's behavior, the infant's behavior, or the behavior of both. Also, an infant may remain responsive to an unresponsive mother, and a mother may be responsive to an unresponsive infant. When the mother is responsive but the baby behaves as if her actions did not matter, the mother receives little reward for her efforts from the baby and continues them because of other rewards such as self-praise or recognition from friends and family. If the baby is responsive but the mother is not, the baby may not develop the confidence and independence that comes to us with our awareness of our ability to influence events. Such an infant may signal more intensely by fussing and crying more frequently because she has found that only by making enough noise can she at last get results.

The Effect of Styles of Interaction on Development: Evidence from Research

As infants develop, several characteristics of their development are influenced by how their mothers interact with them. For instance, babies' mental and perceptual development is at least as strongly affected by their interactions with their mothers as is their social and emotional development. Young infants' early memory skill and general alertness to events around them are linked to their interaction with their mothers—especially to the mothers' general responsiveness and abilities to interpret their babies' signals (Lewis and Goldberg, 1969; Stern et al., 1969). Babies' general developmental progress, measured by how well they do at perceptual-motor tasks and developmental tests, also is related to their mothers' behavior (Yarrow, 1963; Robertson, 1962). Indeed one long-term study found that the child's IQ at 10 was partly predictable from the mother's interaction style during the child's first year of life. Responsive and sensitive mothers had infants who would at 10 years of age have higher IQs than infants of less responsive and sensitive mothers (Yarrow, Rubenstein, and Pederson, 1975).

We might expect that babies' general moods and reactions to their surroundings would be related to their mothers' interaction with them and indeed the babies' general "outlook" and their mothers' interaction are related. Infants who have relationships of mutuality with their mothers are more likely to be interested in their surroundings and to be less fretful than babies who have less satisfactory relationships with their mothers (Rubenstein, 1967; Bell and Ainsworth, 1972; Beckwith, 1972; Lewis and Wilson, 1972). Various measures of general well-being—for example, how much babies smile and look at the people around them—correspond to mothers' caregiving style. Babies' apparent interest in events and their crying patterns are also related to mothers' style.

What about the behavior of these mothers seems to help or hinder their infants' development? Unfortunately, we don't have a clear, uniform standard by which to evaluate the complex interchanges between mothers and babies because investigators have used slightly different techniques. Nevertheless, some apparent trends stand out. Again and again results of studies have indicated that the mother who is responsive to the baby's communications tends to have a more alert, cognitively mature, and happy baby than does the less responsive mother. *Responsiveness* in this instance means reacting when the baby signals for attention. Going to a crying baby, smiling back at a smiling baby, and looking with interest at a babbling baby are all responsive acts. When mothers respond in this fashion, they improve not only their babies' mental development (Robertson, 1962; Yarrow, 1963; Stern et al., 1969; Lewis and Goldberg, 1969), but also their generally good moods (Lewis and Wilson, 1972; Bell and Ainsworth, 1972). The infants who have had the assurance of being responded to respond in turn, as we can see their joyous interchanges with their mothers and with others. Also, the infants of more responsive mothers tend to obey their mothers' requests more readily than those of less responsive mothers (Stayton, Hogan, and Ainsworth, 1971).

The mother's general attitude toward the mothering role moderately relates to the baby's development in somewhat the same way that her responsiveness to the baby does (Stayton et al., 1971). And to some extent, how accurately the mother knows what the baby's needs are is also related to the baby's development (Lytton, 1971).

Because all of the statistical measures of relationship employed in these studies relate only moderately, many individual cases will not fit the patterns I am describing. Undoubtedly, some unresponsive mothers have alert and intelligent babies who are not unhappy. Most assuredly, some involved, caring mothers also have infants who are slow to develop. Although evidence indicates that a mother's behavior influences her infant's development, her behavior is by no means the only influence. In other chapters I have described some other influences. No one can be expected to respond to a baby's signals all of the time. Probably the key influence is the extent to which a baby's signals receive a response. Babies who receive 20 minutes of concentrated attention from mothers who are devoting this time exclusively to them each day may receive more responsiveness than a baby whose mother spends more time with him but is not very responsive.

How does a mother's responsiveness help her baby's development? The correlational studies we are discussing do not directly address this question, but they do give some clues. Infants who have frequent stimulating social exchanges with their mothers explore novel objects and open space more than other infants (Lytton, 1971). Perhaps the responsive mother provides a more "secure base," and thus encourages her infant to learn more about the world.

Or the comfort of the "secure base" relationship may be based on infants' experiences that most of their actions will get a response. The mother who accurately reads her child's signals and makes a response to them gives her child the experience of "making things happen." (This is the "contingent stimulation" phenomenon we discussed in the last chapter.) One study team found that, when children have been deprived of interesting experiences and have suffered severe developmental delays, they can be helped by a program of visits from therapists who give them social responses that are contingent on their activity.

Although much of what I have said in this section suggests that infants' development is fostered through attentive and responsive social interaction, there are limits to how much stimulation you should give a baby. A baby will feel engulfed by an overly attentive mother. Constant attention deprives infants of the self-enhancing experience of "making something happen" and also makes them feel helpless in the face of inescapable bombardment of activity. Indeed, when infants are older they need to move about on their own and explore. For this, mothers must allow them space—both physical and psychological—to govern their own actions. A responsive mother retreats when she thinks the baby needs it, and involves herself when the baby is receptive.

The Effects of Infants on the Interaction: Evidence

Babies contribute to the pattern of mother-baby interaction. Some babies seem to want a large amount of close body contact and intense social dialogue, whereas others who are highly active physically want to be at some distance from the mother and to be able to move about (Schaffer and Emerson, 1964). A mother will act to "protect" a fussy infant more than she would an apparently content one. Babies who respond to being touched—who smile, coo, and laugh when picked up or talked to—may receive more attention than infants who seem impassive (Bell, 1974).

Some evidence shows that babies' sex influences the amount of stimulation mothers give them. White female infants are talked to more than male infants, whereas the reverse is true for black mother-infant pairs (Moss, 1967; Korner, 1974; Brown et al., 1975). Perhaps this is because mothers respond simply to the sex of their infant in response to cultural norms, or perhaps there are differences in infants' behavior that are attributable to sex. If children in a particular cultural group tend to be more irritable, sleep less soundly, and move their limbs more, as is true for white male infants (Ball, 1969), then maybe the mothers are changing how they care for children so that it is appropriate to their needs. It is clear that when infants are obviously different—for example, if they are severely handicapped—their mothers behave differently toward them than toward normal infants (Buinun, Rynders, and Turnure, 1974).

Babies' general characteristics—sex, size, and the like—and their behavior convey information about their needs and capabilities. One theorist has suggested that the ways in which babies signal adults have a single theme: that of increasing their proximity. Most adults accept all of the baby's activities within a certain range with a mental, "That's O.K., nothing to worry about." When the child's behavior falls within limits that are acceptable to us we continue with our own activities. But if a baby is far too active or noisy *or* is far too inactive or quiet we *do* something: we increase the amount of attention and care we give to the child. Either crying or total silence will bring us running (Bell, 1974).

Mothers gradually develop more skill at "reading" their babies' signals. As babies get older, their mothers respond more accurately to their needs (Escalona, 1973). Toddlers who begin an activity they want their mothers to share are more successful at getting their mothers to follow their lead than younger babies are (Bronson, 1974). The pair's interaction seems to develop in a regular sequence. First, the babies adapt their biological rhythms—eating, sleeping, waking up—to the mothers' caregiving routines. Gradually, babies take a more active role, signaling *their* opinions for "more of this, but not so much of that." As time goes on, babies begin their own activities more often. A clear example of this step of the sequence and an obvious sign of the baby's attachment is when a baby stops an activity and looks to check his mother's whereabouts. After acting independently babies at this stage want to share the activity with their mothers. Finally, when they become toddlers they will even oppose their mothers' wishes if they disagree with them (Sander, 1969). With age, babies also improve their skill at anticipating their mothers' behavior. Apparently the "mutuality" of their relationship—how well the two respond to each other—improves as the mother and baby come to know each other.

Several studies with monkeys have dramatically illustrated how infants contribute to their own care. When baby monkeys are temporarily unable to move after an injection of a paralyzing drug, their mothers protect and care for them more by shielding their bodies, grooming them, and staying near them (Rosenblum and Youngstein, 1974). When the situation is reversed and the mothers are temporarily unable to move, their infants act confused for a time and they increase their efforts to signal their mothers to care for them (Rosenblum, 1971). Results of the animal studies offer important insights that can be related to the behavior of human beings. Two psychologists have developed a method to make detailed observations to clarify how both the mother and infant cause and influence the other's actions as they share everyday activities (Lewis and Lee-Painter, 1974). We now know that both mother and child influence their interaction, which in turn profoundly affects the baby's development. How exactly does this influence occur?

Determinants of Mothers' Interaction Styles

Because our personalities and style of interacting affect our relationships with others, we would expect these same characteristics to color our interactions with babies as well. We would assume that people's personalities in turn reflect the culture. Very little systematic study has been made of the relation between how a mother cares for her child and her other characteristics. However, some evidence does indicate that the mothers of infants who are having difficulties adjusting to a feeding and sleeping schedule lack confidence in themselves and may have had mothers who did not meet their needs adequately (Frommer and O'Shea, 1973; Brown, 1961).

One team of investigators has looked extensively at the difference in how white middle-class mothers and white working-class mothers interact with their 10-month-old infants at home. They found that mothers in both classes showed the same warmth and affection for their children but that they cared for their babies differently. Children of working-class mothers were talked to much less than middle-class babies and they were also given less opportunity to move about and explore things. The investigators learned that the primary reason for this variation was that the two groups had different beliefs about what babies are like. Working-class mothers believed that because the babies couldn't think or understand language the mothers didn't need to talk to them or give them freedom to explore. Some working-class mothers were under the mistaken impression that babies cannot see or hear very well, and this colored their behavior. Middle-class mothers believed that babies are capable of some form of communication, and thus they were ready to participate as partners in communication (Tulkin and Kagan, 1972).

Cross-cultural studies from other countries reveal a great variety of ways in which children are raised. One major difference is in the freedom allowed to infants. Caregivers also have various methods for holding and talking to children that are dependent upon culture as well. Some cultures emphasize the importance of physical contact between mother and child, whereas in others, such as middle-class America, mothers talk to as well as touch their children. After considering the universality of our sensory-motor skills (we all learn to walk, talk, and understand the world in the same sequence) and the variations in interactions of mothers and babies from culture to culture, it seems clear that mother and infant interactions don't need to follow a specific pattern to allow babies to develop their sensory-motor skills.

The Baby and Other People

All this discussion of babies and their mothers will surely have aroused the indignation of some of my readers. What about fathers? Brothers and sisters? Grandparents? And all of those people other than mothers, who care for babies? As I have said, we do not know very much about babies' relationships with people other than their mothers because investigators have concentrated on studying the mother-infant relationship. Only recently have we started to find out more about babies and their fathers, and it seems that we will soon know much more (e.g., Lamb, 1976). There are good reasons for researchers' interest in mothers: for one thing, most babies spend most of their time with their mothers until they are at least two years old. Too, many researchers think that, regardless of where babies spend their time, the relationship between mother and child is the primary one. A factor that has been allowed to influence studies perhaps more than it should is that investigators have found it difficult to arrange extended observations of babies interacting with the various other people who are significant in their lives. Cultural patterns are changing rapidly, and, with them, investigators are changing their attitudes about what information is significant. But let us look at the information we now have.

Fathers

Freda Rebelsky and a student made some startling findings about fathers and their babies when they studied 10 babies from the time they were two weeks old until they were three months old. For 24-hour periods during that time, the investigators attached tape recorder microphones to the babies' clothing to find out who was communicating with the baby and for how long. They discovered that fathers spoke to their babies an average of 2.7 times a day. Further, the 10 fathers spent an average of 38 seconds with their infants each day (Rebelsky and Hanks, 1971). The mothers in this study all stayed with their babies during the day while the fathers all worked at demanding jobs outside the home.

Many couples are now questioning this traditional division of roles, and more fathers are making an effort to spend time with their children. Undoubtedly many fathers spend more than 38 seconds a day with their children, especially given the change in attitudes that has occurred in the years since the study was done. But in Western countries infants spend much more time with their mothers than they do with their fathers, even when their mothers have full-time careers.

When researchers study a father's relationship with his child, they usually ask the father to attend a carefully designed laboratory observation session

Figure 5-4. *Investigators know little about the relationships between babies and members of their families other than their mothers. Here children interrupt a birthday party to play with a six-month-old baby, who happily acknowledges the attention. (Photo copyright © Suzanne Arms/Jeroboam, Inc.)*

such as the Ainsworth sessions. As I mentioned earlier, one-year-old babies who participate in sessions with their fathers react just as they do with their mothers. Taken by itself, this fact tells us little about how fathers and babies interact under ordinary circumstances. Furthermore, these highly planned laboratory sessions are not the best way in which to detect special patterns of interaction that may characterize one relationship more than another. These structured situations exert a tremendous influence on both the parents' and children's behavior; they may behave differently from the way they normally would. We need more detailed observational studies of father-child interaction in the family's usual surroundings. One such study indicates that fathers have a definite pattern of interacting with infants that differs from that of mothers (Lamb, 1976).

Studies of infants interacting with other relatives, sitters, and peers are almost nonexistent, although a few interesting studies have been made of older toddlers and their peers (Lewis and Rosenblum, 1975). One study of the interactions between two infants in group sessions revealed definite patterns of communication. Babies who had never met before frequently exchanged looks, smiles, and babbles. When a toy was available, one infant would generously offer it to the other as part of their new relationship; struggles over possession of a toy were uncommon (Eckerman, Whatley, and Katz, 1975). Because more mothers work, and infants are being cared for with groups of their peers, we probably will know more about their interactions shortly. Infants have been cared for by various relatives, neighbors, and friends for some time now, but researchers have studied little about their interaction.

Literature exists on studies comparing infants who frequently are separated from their mothers for regular lengths of time with those who are not separated. So we have some factual basis on which to make general statements about how infants are affected or not affected by the absence of their mothers, but it tells us very little about the effects of the care they receive. This is because many studies of children whose mothers work do not consider aspects of the alternative care environment. Without forgetting the insufficiency in information, let us look at the studies of children who are regularly separated from their mothers.

Separation of Infant and Mother

The central role the infant's mother plays in many cultural practices, in developmental theories, and in popular conceptions of infancy makes any separation of mother and baby seem to be a tragedy. Indeed, infants who are permanently separated from their mothers become unhappy and withdrawn; many become very ill despite sufficient physical care. Also, as we have just seen, between 9 and 24 months of age many infants are distressed when they are temporarily separated from their mothers in unfamiliar situations. These two forms of separation are sometimes considered to be different versions of the same basic experience: separation with a capital "S."

During World War II many children in Europe were abruptly separated from both of their parents during evacuations of population centers or for other reasons. In England, many city children were sent to live in nurseries in the countryside.

These children developed many psychological problems that we will discuss shortly. Following the war, John Bowlby (who, as you will recall from our earlier discussion, later developed the ethological theory of attachment) summarized the observations of English and displaced continental psychoanalysts who worked in these British nurseries. In a monograph he wrote for the World Health Organization, Bowlby reported that separation from their mothers was the most stressful experience the disturbed children had known. He argued forcefully for social programs to enable the mothers of infants and young children to stay at home with their babies (Bowlby, 1969).

Many professionals who write about this subject and who, like Bowlby, have been influenced by medical and psychoanalytic training, describe mother-infant separations as if all separations were psychologically the same phenomenon as wartime separations. Mothers frequently encounter newspaper columns or books of advice that counsel them not to leave their children (although in the care of someone else) while they go to work or on a vacation trip. They are advised that when separations are essential, as when the mother is hospitalized, they must maintain actual or symbolic contact with their infants (e.g., Salk, 1970; Spock, 1976).

Repeated Separation for a Regular Period: The Employed Mother

The climate of rapid social change of the late 1960s and 1970s has led many more young couples to develop alternative lifestyles. The particulars of these lifestyles are as varied as the people who have them, but one characteristic of most of them is that mothers and children are regularly separated while the mothers work. An analysis of the effect of this upon infants will be accurate only if it is based on careful observations of various arrangements for their care that take into account the circumstances that made the care necessary or desirable. Are both parents working, or traveling, or has a sudden unpredictable emergency occurred that will be stressful for parents or their babies? These circumstances almost certainly have different effects upon babies.

Until a short time ago, we had little of the information that we need to properly analyze the impact upon children of being away from their mothers. We had a fairly extensive literature of clinical case histories and professional observations from residential care and foster homes for infants who were orphaned, abused, or neglected (e.g., Bowlby, 1969; Rutter, 1972; Robertson, 1962). A few studies had compared the behavior and temperament of children of employed mothers in America and England with groups of children of similar backgrounds whose mothers were unemployed (Hoffman and Nye, 1975). But the children of employed mothers were cared for in various ways and, because the researchers often did not separate the children they studied according to what type of care they had received, it is difficult to isolate the exact causes of any differences among groups. Recently, more reports from group-care programs for infants (and older children) have been published. Most of them compare the infants to groups of infants who were cared for at home by their mothers. and although the reports lack the scientific controls that are desirable, they do give us some useful information.

With these observations, we can now trace how mothers' working during their children's infancy affects the children's behavior at preschool age (three to five years). We can compare the infants in group day care with those who remain at home. We do not have a sufficiently reliable basis for comparing the effect of various alternative care arrangements upon the infant's behavior. Few, if any, studies exist of infants who are cared for by individual baby sitters in their own or the sitter's home. But let us see what we can learn from the information we do have.

Field Studies of Day Care

A number of studies of university-based day-care centers have been published in recent years (Robinson and Robinson, 1971; Fowler, 1972; Braun and Caldwell, 1973; Riciutti, 1974; Schwarz, Strickland, and Krolik, 1974; Blehar, 1974; Ragozin, 1976). These centers serve many types of families, usually because the staff has tried to encourage the participation of families from diverse backgrounds. Although the specifics of the programs may differ, they have some features in common. Babies are cared for in small groups, and a caregiver is assigned to each infant younger than two years old. This caregiver changes and feeds the infant and is trained to enliven these routines by communicating and sharing with the infant during them. Often during the day this same caregiver takes an infant for a few minutes to show him things and invite him to react. If infants can crawl they are free to move about and explore in an area reserved and made safe for that purpose.

The care centers are brightly painted and decorated. Many people come and go—students, resident doctors, visiting scholars, parents of other children—so the atmosphere is lively, but all activities follow a familiar routine and take place in the presence of a familiar caregiver. Most university centers have separate rooms for observers so that babies are not uncomfortably aware of being watched by strangers.

The studies on university-based day care have looked at a number of characteristics that can be divided into two broad categories: first, sensory-motor and cognitive development as measured by standard tests for infants or by standard IQ tests given when the babies reach the appropriate age, and second, babies' attachment to their parents and caregivers as measured by their emotional reactions and exploration in Ainsworth-type situations. These two facets of development have been singled out deliberately for intensive study in the day-care facilities because infants who have been permanently separated from their mothers and have grown up in institutions are usually deficient in them: their perception and cognitive abilities are retarded, and they cannot form or sustain attachments to caregivers or others later in life. Day care for children of employed parents has aroused the concern of professionals on the grounds that perhaps similarly devastating effects will occur. The day-care directors of university faculties wanted to address these concerns.

Hal and Nancy Robinson at the University of North Carolina at Chapel Hill compared the Bayley developmental scores and subsequently the Stanford-Binet IQ scores of poor rural black children who attended their university's center with those of infants who did not attend the center but who had similar backgrounds. The comparison began when the children were six months old and continued until they were four years old. In the day-care program at North Carolina babies received medical attention, proper nutrition, and visits at home from a social worker as well as the basic program. The mental abilities of black infants from poor families did not decrease during the time they received group care; on the contrary, the average developmental scores of the black infants were much higher than those of children who hadn't been in the day-care program. Ordinarily, for a variety of complex reasons, the Stanford-Binet IQ scores of black children are significantly lower than those of white children, but the children who participated in the North Carolina program while they were infants not only surpassed the black children who didn't participate in it, but also significantly surpassed the average of children in general. Clearly the program did not slow the children's cognitive development (Robinson and Robinson, 1971).

The day-care program at the University of Arkansas includes a regular schedule of observations and caregiver assessments by students and professionals for each child. Cognitive, social, and medical aspects of the child's development are measured regularly.

Psychologists seem to agree that, in general, day-care children and home-care children do not behave differently (Braun and Caldwell, 1973). Two studies of private day-care centers in university communities also did not find any differences between the groups (Schwarz, Strickland, and Krolick, 1974; Hakansson, Horneman, and Leidholm, 1973). Most recently, the Harvard Day-Care Group reported as well that the personalities of day-care children were similar to those of home-care children (Kagan, Kearsley, and Zelazo, 1978).

Day-care children have patterns of attachment behavior that are different from those of home-care children. Blehar, who studied one-year-old children with Ainsworth, also observed two- and three-year-olds several months after they started day care. She found that the toddlers showed what she interpreted as distress signals: the day-care infants cried more on their mothers' departure, were upset longer by strangers, and more frequently acted negatively toward their returning mothers than did home-care infants. These reactions were particularly strong among infants who had started day care when they were three instead of at an earlier age (Blehar, 1974). In Blehar's study none of the children had been in day-care programs during their first year of life. The findings suggest that the children were having difficulty with the change from their previous daily pattern, in which they were with their mothers all of the time.

In another study set in a laboratory systematic procedures were used to observe infants who had been in day care since the first several months of life. Observers compared the babies' reactions as a stranger approached them in three situations: when they were alone, when they were with their mothers, and when they were with their caregivers. It was found that babies reacted the same way to the departure of mother and regular caregiver and that both of these women could comfort them when they were upset. Only a few of the babies were more distressed by the stranger in the regular caregiver's presence than in the mother's presence. This study indicates that the babies derived a feeling of security from their working mothers, but formed relationships that we usually describe as "attachment" to both their mothers and their caregivers (Riciutti, 1974).

These field studies of programs in university communities clearly demonstrate that group care for infants does not in itself destroy their attachment to their mothers or hinder their mental and emotional growth. Children raised at home show more dependency and attachment behavior than those that attend high-quality day-care centers. Infants in these day-care facilities usually will form one or more attachment relationships there, enabling the caregivers as well as their mothers to help them to develop.

But let us consider the differences between the university-based day-care centers studied for these reports and the day care that average working couples might be able to find. Few centers in the country have the staff and the commitment to match the quality of these "demonstration" programs. True, many commercially operated day-care centers have competent, knowledgeable staff and ample, well-organized space, but many more day-care centers do not. The demonstration programs indeed demonstrate something: it is possible to provide group care for infants that, rather than harming them, will aid their social, emotional, and intellectual development. In order to make this possibility into a reality, many more centers run by professionally trained, committed staff members who are concerned with the development of babies (as well as that of the older children who would also be there) are needed. Americans differ in their opinions about who should be responsible for creating and supporting child-care programs. Many people oppose any publicly supported care for young children (just as many used to oppose public education) because they fear that it would allow the government to have too much control over the family. Many well-educated, upper-middle-class couples would prefer to have a system of nongovernmental, self-supporting day-care centers that would incorporate the superior aspects of the university programs but would be controlled in large part by the families who use them. However, poorer working families could not afford to maintain superior centers; this inequality is one of the stumbling blocks to the establishment of an entirely private system for day care. It is beyond the scope of this book to analyze alternative funding plans, but you should know that "high-quality day care" is not readily available in most communities. How easily it could be made available is a matter of much debate.

Comparisons of Infants of Employed Mothers and Those of Unemployed Mothers. If a mother is employed, does her employment harm her baby in any demonstrable way? Since 1959, several studies that compare the characteristics of offspring of employed mothers with those of unemployed mothers have been published. Unfortunately, none of these studies measured the offspring while they were infants. Therefore, our knowledge is based on the personality traits, the behavior, and the school records of children and adolescents whose mothers were employed during their early years. In general, few differences in personality can be attributed to the mother's employment (Etaugh, 1974; Wallston, 1973). A series of studies done in England showed that the fact that some children of employed mothers were poorly adjusted reflected the instability of their alternative care. Children who were shifted frequently and irregularly from one caregiver and care location to another reportedly were much more likely to exhibit disturbed personality patterns than those who received reasonably stable care (Rutter, 1972). Children's adjustment is also affected by their mothers' attitudes about working. Offspring of mothers who work with reluctance, as well as those of mothers who remain at home reluctantly, reportedly experience more difficulties than those of mothers who are content with their employment status (Hoffman and Nye, 1975). More research focused on the infants of working mothers is needed. But the existing evidence demonstrates that a mother's employment in itself does not harm her infant.

Lengthy and Unpredictable Separations from Family

When some event removes mothers from their infants abruptly, the separation deeply affects the infants. They may cry continually, they kick and thrash when strangers pick them up, and their eating, sleeping, and elimination rhythms are disrupted. If mothers return after a few days, they may find that their babies are not pleased to see them.

If separation continues for more than a few days, infants stop their fussing and agitated crying, and they begin to withdraw their interest from their surroundings. They no longer look expectantly at new objects and events and they seem to stop reacting to stimulation. Instead, they suck their fingers, rock, and in other ways become more preoccupied with their own bodies than with the outside world. They even may seem to lose the sensory-motor ability they once had. They are suffering from what some psychologists call the *maternal deprivation syndrome,* so named because it is the consequence of an infant's truly being deprived of a mother. This section is about these severe reactions to separations that are not part of a normal family routine.

Clinical Case Studies.   Most of our understanding about the effects of being deprived of a mother is based on clinical treatments of people who have psychological problems related to being separated from their mothers during childhood. Descriptive studies have also been made of the characteristics of children who live in particular residential institutions for orphaned children. Both clinical records and studies of children who live in institutions indicate that when infants are separated from their mothers for a long time they experience the maternal deprivation syndrome (Dennis and Najarian, 1957; Bowlby, 1969). How does this process work?

What happens to infants separated from their mothers has much to do with how the separation will affect them. Most infants who are separated from both parents are taken to institutions, many of which are understaffed and organized upon principles of efficient physical care rather than effective psychological care. Infants may be placed on their backs in drab cribs from which they cannot see their surroundings. Because their caregivers are busy, they may receive attention from a responsive caregiver only rarely, and may never be given the opportunity to exert any influence on the people or things around them. This common institutional set-up promotes their withdrawal from the world.

The Robertsons specialize in foster care for children in England. They emphasize the role that the caregiving environment plays in maternal deprivation. They care for children in a family setting where each child receives some personal attention each day. Having found that many of their foster children did not have the severe reactions of grief that most children in institutions experience, they concluded that the institutional environment, not the separation from the mother, causes the deep unhappiness of babies who are deprived of a mother (Robertson and Robertson, 1971). Other evidence suggests that the physical environment of the infants also plays a role (Dennis and Najarian, 1957).

In summary, the maternal deprivation syndrome is more properly identified as the response to an impersonal institution because the characteristic withdrawal and apathy of these infants is caused, not by the separation in itself, but by the lack of affection and cognitive and perceptual stimulation. I do not mean to suggest that mothers are like standardized parts that can be replaced by a measure of stimulation, or that if we disappear our infants can just get somebody else and remain unaffected. But in times of separation the proper care can prevent the most severe and pathological damage that occurs to babies in institutions. Even with the most enlightened foster care, infants who have lost their mothers will be upset initially and may be profoundly affected by the separation. But their development need not be permanently impaired. Instead, they can be helped to recover from their grief (if separation is permanent) and to regain their interest in the world.

Evidence from Animal Research.   To more fully understand the effects of separations from the mother, experimenters have studied the response of animals to separations of various lengths of time. Controlled experimental separations have been done with the nearest relatives of the human being, the monkey. Harry Harlow has made this research famous with his initial work on "motherless monkeys." Harlow raised several Rhesus monkeys from birth without mothers but with terrycloth objects, called cloth mothers, that had distinctive faces. Harlow found that the infant monkeys, who had never experienced real mothering, could use their terrycloth mothers as "secure bases" the way human infants do with their own mothers. The monkeys spent hours clinging to these substitutes even though, unlike real mothers, the substitutes did not give them food. The infants generally gave the impression that they were comforted by the close body contact with the substitute mothers.

However, as Harlow's monkeys matured toward reproductive age they demonstrated more and more pathological characteristics. They could not function sexually and did not engage in normal play. Instead, they sat and rocked, bit themselves, and otherwise withdrew from their surroundings. If forced to interact with another monkey at close quarters, they were extremely aggressive and were unable to guide their own behavior according to what the other animal was doing. Clearly, being raised without a real mother or other live companion had devastating effects on these monkeys (Harlow, 1959).

Harlow and other researchers have continued this research to answer the following questions: Can these profound effects be reversed by any special care short of restoring the mother? Are the effects different if the mother and infant are together for a while before being separated? If so, how do the timing and duration of separation affect the results of it?

Variations in how the monkeys were reared indicate that the first six months of life may be a critical period for infant monkeys to form social relationships. Rhesus monkeys who are reared in complete isolation until some time after they are six months old show severe social and sexual inadequacy and cognitive retardation. When the infant is placed with a companion or companions before six months, these effects do not become as severe and they are reversed as time goes on (Harlow and Harlow, 1962).

Researchers have also found that even the most severe effects of being raised in isolation until after they are six months of age can apparently be reversed in monkeys. A team of investigators housed severely withdrawn monkeys who had been reared in isolation with younger infant monkeys who exhibited normal social behavior. During this time the younger infants chased, touched, and even groomed the isolates. Gradually over the weeks, the isolates began to respond to their antics. At maturity, their social and sexual behavior was near normal (Novak and Harlow, 1975).

Other evidence corroborates the importance of peers in developing the normal social behavior of monkeys. Monkeys who are raised without a mother but with monkeys their own age have normal sexual and maternal behavior, and they have fully developed repertoires of social behavior, although they are somewhat less aggressive than animals reared with mothers and peers (Harlow and Harlow, 1962). On the other hand, monkeys reared with their mothers but without peers tend to be more aggressive. For monkeys, continuous interaction with their peers while they are infants can make up for inadequate mothering, but mothering cannot counter the effects of not sharing activities with peers (Harlow and Harlow, 1962). Experiments with monkeys gathered into artificial nuclear families (consisting of a mother, father, and child who are not related) have demonstrated that when the children were allowed to play together every day for an hour they were not as aggressive as the monkeys without peers (Harlow, Harlow, and Suomi, 1971). When the young monkeys played with only one peer, they also became less aggressive (Harlow, Harlow, and Suomi, 1971). Apparently, the depressions created in the monkeys by these experimental separations are less severe and more readily reversible than those the monkey experiences after being isolated from birth.

A note of caution is in order if we reflect on the implications of these important contributions from animal research to our understanding of human infants. Differences have been observed among the various nonhuman primate species in how infants and mothers interact and in how infants react to separation from their mothers (Rosenblum, 1971). And members of the same species can have very different responses to being apart from their mothers (Hinde and Spencer-Booth, 1970). According to one suggestion, perhaps the flexibility of behavior is greater at higher evolutionary stages (Cairns, 1979). If this is so, we might expect that the adaptability of human infants to the trauma of maternal separation would be generally better than that of Harlow's monkeys.

These precautionary comments have some important implications about the usefulness of experiments with animals. First, the animal experiments are useful because they allow us to control the monkey's separation from and relationship with the mother. By changing only certain variables in the experiments we discover which are important. For instance, these experiments have shown the significance of the length of the monkey's separation from its mother, its age at separation, and the effect of other companions. They have also revealed that the effects of maternal deprivation are reversible. But before we can draw firm conclusions about how these variables affect human infants, or about the proper therapy for human infants who are separated from their mothers, we have to study them.

Experimental Studies of Infant-Initiated Separation in Humans

Few researchers would even dream of deliberately separating human infants from their mothers for a long time, given the potential damaging effects of such a course of action. However, several experiments have given the infants an opportunity to leave their mothers for a few moments and researchers have been able to study the effects of this. They have found that, when attractive spaces and objects tempt infants to explore, most infants not only will endure separation but will instigate it and enjoy brief episodes of it (Rheingold and Eckerman, 1970). The traumatic impact of brief separations in real life seems to arise from their unpredictability and lack of relation to the infant's own behavior. When children are separated from families for a longer time, they suffer the damaging effects of permanently having no one to respond to their activities and involve them with other people. They come to explore much less because they do not have the security of a familiar caregiver who assures them of aid, protection, and concern as they risk discovering a world away from what they have known. Brief daytime separations for definite periods—when the parents are working or when the infant chooses to explore alone for a few moments—do not harm the infant. As yet, we don't have research sufficient to enable us to determine whether separations of intermediate length—for trips or illness—have any harmful effects on infants. In both brief (a few minutes or a few hours) and intermediate length (one or two weeks) separations, how the baby is cared for during the time of separation is probably more significant than the separation itself. In very lengthy or permanent separations, the loss of a relationship and the consequent "separation" may be more significant.

The Question of Imprinting

The literature on the reactions of animal infants when they are separated from their mothers has sometimes been discussed in the context of imprinting, which, as you may recall, is the phenomenon whereby the young of many species begin to follow, cling to, or otherwise stay near the first moving object they encounter during a *critical period* of time shortly after birth. Many researchers who study animals think that the preferences young animals show for their own mothers over other adult females is the result of imprinting rather than of an inborn or developed attachment.

One might immediately wonder whether human infants are imprinted on their mothers and whether this might be the basis for the formation of all later attachments. One point of view is that because a definite period of time (8 to 12 months) exists during which the existence of a regular caregiver to "mother" the child has profound effects, the bonds that are formed during that time have profound effects on the child's capacity to relate (Bowlby, 1969). However, as we have discussed, human infants are much more flexible—both in the number of persons with whom they can form relationships and in the time during which they do so—than birds, rodents, and ungulates. There is some evidence that the time immediately after birth is an important period in which infants form relationships with their mothers (Korner, 1973), but when mother and child are separated just after birth because of hospital procedures, babies certainly still form attachments later. The notion of imprinting refers to a process more definite and inflexible than the diverse patterns of interaction of human infants and their mothers.

Summary

According to all the theories we have reviewed, the relationship between infant and mother has central importance in the child's first two years of life. This relationship insures infants' survival despite their biological immaturity because it assures that their mothers will probably be close at hand when need arises. Their relationships with their mothers may give infants a secure base from which they can explore their environments and gradually develop independence. However, the notion of attachment as a controlling force in a baby's life may not be as helpful as the theorists first thought it would be because the behaviors grouped under the label "attachment" seem to have diverse and independent influences. Instead it seems to make sense to think of babies' relationships with their mothers as being individualistic and ever changing.

Despite the variations in circumstances and individuals, there are certain almost universal characteristics of attachment. Most babies demonstrate some special relationship with their mothers, and, if the mothers are not available, with another person. When both parents are available, many babies show a greater attachment to their mothers than to their fathers. Apparently, babies form many attachment relationships that adjust to the caregiving arrangements. Indeed, infants show their need for security in "attachment behavior" appropriately, according to the unfamiliarity of the circumstances in which they find themselves.

Many, perhaps most, babies react differently to strangers than to their parents by the time they are eight months old; some become very curious, whereas others feel wary or even afraid. The babies who respond to strangers with curiosity seem to be those who have a secure relationship with their mothers (which fosters their independence); the fearful babies seem to have a mother-centered relationship. Both babies' characteristics and the situation also influence their reaction to strangers. Characteristics such as socioeconomic class and sex do not seem to relate to attachment behavior or anxiety around strangers in any demonstrable way.

The studies of mothers and infants interacting in their own homes and in laboratories has revealed several interesting facts. First, mothers control the stimulation their babies receive; some do so in response to babies' cues and others follow their own notions about what their babies need. The relation—or lack of relation—that babies sense between their own signals and the mother's response influences not only their control over the amount of stimulation they receive but their development in other areas as well. Second, infants' cognition, perceptual skills, emotional state, and exploratory behavior have all been found to depend upon how much their mothers respond to their signals. Babies whose mothers show them non-contingent love also develop better than those whose mothers do not. Apparently, mothers can help their babies' development by responding to the babies' cues, while at the same time showing acceptance and love, regardless of what the babies are doing.

Although it seems clear that the relationship between infant and mother is of central importance (at least in Western culture, where the mother is assigned the role of caring for children), a relationship between the two apparently is not changed drastically by alternative caregiving arrangements. Infants in group care show the same attachment to their natural mothers that those cared for at home do, and they also form attachment relationships to their other caregivers. Indeed, the attachment patterns of babies with their fathers and with their employed mothers demonstrate that long periods of waking time together are not the material from which the strong ties of affection between family members and the infant are formed.

Other studies with middle-class infants in high-quality group care show that these infants are not very different in any way from similar infants who were cared for at home. Infants from lower socioeconomic classes who receive high-quality day care score substantially higher on standard cognitive tests and motivational measures than those who are cared for at home. Although much remains to be known about day care, clearly it is not the damaging experience that many have feared it to be.

However, unpredictable separation of mother and infant over a long period, as happens when the infant or the mother is ill, can be very damaging. Many infants who live in foster homes are held back from their full cognitive and emotional development by the lack of stimulation and affection. Babies who suffer this sort of deprivation are generally apathetic and uninterested in their environments and do not perform well on sensory-motor tasks. When infants who have experienced sudden and lengthy separation from their families have been cared for in a responsive family setting, these devastating results have not occurred.

The question of whether mother-infant attachment is natural may be tentatively answered, "Yes, but so is attachment to other regular caring individuals such as fathers or professional caregivers." Attachment is not an exclusive bond that is made only with a mother, as myth would have us believe. Because the simple label of "attachment" is too broad, research has not focused on a single cause for it. Instead, researchers examine the effect of various child-care arrangements and home atmospheres upon the way in which children show their need for security and the way in which they explore. In general the child's actions are more readily influenced by such situational factors as toys, adult behavior, and spatial arrangements than by the care arrangements as such.

We must wait for the results of future research to answer the important, and yet unstudied, question of whether infants' interaction with their caregivers causes them to adopt a particular style of showing their attachment. Another unstudied question is how the different styles of attachment influence a child's later development. So although psychologists know a great deal about the reactions of infants to experimental attachment situations, much remains to be known about how their reactions relate to the rest of their lives.

Those who wonder whether we are "social beings" from birth can be more readily satisfied. Evidence seems to say we are. Early in the first year of life babies prefer to listen to and look at human beings rather than inanimate objects, and they continue to be attracted to people even though some wariness toward strangers emerges later in the first year. The parent-infant relationship seems to be a central social relationship, but many infants form close bonds with other caregivers as well. In fact, infants' abilities to form bonds with the people who care for them and to use these relationships as secure bases for development may be the earliest evidence of our strongly social nature. The important role peers play in monkeys' development suggests that this social nature may be part of our evolutionary past. In any case, we are social beings from the start.

Finally, in answer to those who wonder whether it is desirable for infants to form strong attachments to their caregivers, it seems that babies rarely form only a single strong attachment bond. When infants have a familiar caregiver with them, they can direct their attachment behaviors toward the caregiver and not only satisfy their need to be safe but also gain the courage to explore. As yet, we do not have definite information about how attachment patterns in infancy relate to independence later in life. Because various events throughout our lives are known to influence our independent behavior, it is wrong to assume that a child who has a strong need for affection and security will automatically become a dependent adult. Instead, it seems more sensible to think (and future research may support common sense) that an affectionate relationship between caregiver and infant, which gives the infant reassurance and an opportunity for emotional interactions, will help the child develop into an independent human being. No one should hesitate to experience the affection and closeness that both baby and adult seem to want.

Chapter 6

Infant Personality

In earlier chapters, we have discussed much of what is known about babies' abilities to perceive, think, remember, and learn. We have concentrated on the basic psychological processes that are shared by all human beings as members of the same species. You may think that, thus far, we have left out something very important: our individuality as unique human beings. *Personality,* as psychologists call this uniqueness, is the topic of this chapter. We will consider both theories of and evidence about infant personality.

What questions do you have about babies' personalities? Every parent wants to believe that his or her child is a unique human being with whom a special relationship may be established, however different it may be from a relationship with an older child or an adult. So, parents might ask: "Who is our baby?" "What is she like?" "Can we tell now what sort of person she will grow up to be?" "Does she recognize us and is she responding to us as she seems to be?"

On the other hand, psychologists have come to question the idea of a fixed personality in which definite, enduring characteristics may be identified. If there is such a thing as a fixed personality, are the characteristics apparent in infancy? Will an infant's characteristics foretell those that will be a part of the adult's personality?

This last question requires two brief cautionary notes. Because the number and variety of possible behaviors increase dramatically after early infancy, it is difficult to demonstrate that the behavior of older children has an antecedent infant behavior. This problem is inherent in all developmental psychology. Several investigations have been able to draw exact parallels between earlier and later behavior, so the task is by no means impossible.

A related problem is that consistency may be in the eye of the beholder. People generally attribute more consistency to others' behavior than can be demonstrated (Mischel, 1976). A consideration of uniqueness could not be made without some knowledge of what babies have in common. So we may ask whether there is a basic nature that all humans share. If there is, is it made up of characteristics that are inborn? This last question is simply a restatement of the question of *nativism vs. empiricism,* which we have addressed before in relation to perception.

Concepts of Personality

Psychologists use the term *personality trait* to describe the qualities of a person's behavior that reappear in many situations. For example, if I am impatient with people who want me to make decisions for them at home, at the university where I teach, and in my community work, you are likely to conclude that I am intolerant of dependency. That is, you will attribute a personality trait to me to explain this behavior. However, if I were impatient only with some of my students, you might conclude that something about their behavior toward me is making me act as I do. To be considered a trait a behavior must occur consistently. When we consider all the ways in which a person acts consistently, we have outlined his personality. In "personality" we sense both what differentiates the way in which one person behaves from the way in which others behave and the similarity in behavior of a given person from one situation to the next.

Theories of Infant Personality

Three prominent theories of personality make statements about personality in infancy: classical Freudian psychoanalytic theory; Erik Erikson's modified psychoanalytic theory, which focuses on human identity as it develops during life; and the social learning theories of Albert Bandura and others.

As you may recall from our earlier discussion, the Freudian view is that infants are dominated at birth by common biological instincts. All newborns are quite similar in their psychological functioning. Although their drives differ in intensity, each infant has only so much psychological energy to expend in development. No mother can sense an infant's needs perfectly or meet them instantaneously; young infants have to come to terms with the discrepancy between what they want and what they can have. According to Freudian theory, as the infants accept the fact that they depend on their mothers, they develop a method of dealing with the realities of the environment by forming an ego. *Ego* includes the actions babies use to adapt to their surroundings, which are less than the perfectly pleasurable ones babies would prefer. Egos differ more from one baby to another than do the largely reflective innate behaviors. Some child psychoanalysts name the babies' early ego patterns the *basic core,* presumably of personality (Weil, 1970). The basic core is made up of an infant's needs, the patterns of behavior by which they are exhibited, the mother's responses, and the patterns of those responses. Thus, this early ego is shared by infants and their mothers. Indeed, according to this view, the most profound mental illnesses—the schizophrenias—have their origins in the failure of a mother-infant pair to separate their functions. Normally, infants' developing motor and language skills gradually separate them from their mothers. Their increasing independence and their awareness of it gradually brings them to the realization that they are separate entities from their mothers. As the development of toddlerhood proceeds, the infants adopt a stable pattern of adaptive behavior: their ego.

Classic psychoanalytic theory emphasizes the regular sequences of interaction between the self and the environment during the first five years. Infancy makes a major contribution to this interaction because during this period our egos are born and we establish a lasting style of interaction with our mothers. Although behavior undergoes changes after infancy—notably the development in preschool years of a *superego* to dictate right and wrong—the groundwork laid down in infancy has long-lasting consequences. Our ways of meeting frustration throughout our lives and of interacting with those who love us or have authority over us are said to date back to our earliest experiences with these same issues. Thus psychoanalytic theory would expect our personalities as infants to be quite stable and to shape our later character.

Erikson, another psychoanalytic theorist, agrees that biological drives are the primary forces that set personality development in motion. However, he disagrees with Freudian theory in several important ways. First, he assigns a very significant role to the cultural institutions that set down the framework of customary social behavior guiding a child's development. For Erikson, there is an important mutual influence between the developing child and cultural institutions. According to him, children the world over develop the basic elements of their personalities in the same sequence of stages because all cultures, despite different practices, pose certain issues for them. These issues generally arise in a certain order: first, adjusting to the family, then to peers, then a larger group, then to parenthood, and so on. The social institutions of family, government, school, and church allow us to meet our basic needs for emotional attachment, some degree of independence, and opportunities to make things happen. In turn, the cultural institutions can continue to function only because the personalities needed to sustain them have formed within the culture: societies will not have parenthood or schools or other institutions unless their members are trained to value them.

Let's look at an example of the mutual influence between personality and culture in relation to early infancy. According to Erikson's theory of personality development, the first need of infants is trust, because their biological helplessness requires that they depend on others for care in order to survive. Will the caregivers be dependable and will infants' needs be met? If so, they will gradually begin to trust the world and others in it. The family insures that babies will receive regular care, so in fact most do develop trust. In turn, the existence of many people within a culture who have the capacity to trust—and thus experience faith—allows the society to have the institution of religion. So because the culture leads individuals to develop trust, they in turn lead the culture to establish and maintain an institution—religion. This example of trust and religion illustrates the theme of *reciprocity* between components of individuals' personalities and components of the social order that is such a major one in Erikson's version of psychoanalytic theory.

A second difference between Erikson's view of personality and the classical Freudian view is his idea that our personalities continue to develop throughout our lives. Erikson, like other psychoanalysts, considers infancy a crucial stage that strongly influences how we will develop our individuality later. However, Erikson sees the interaction between culture and personality as a never-ending one. The issues of infancy—trust versus mistrust and autonomy versus shame and doubt—will reverberate through all of our life experiences. However, if we successfully resolve these conflicts of our infancy, we will develop egos strong enough to help us negotiate the subsequent crises. In Erikson's view, our infancy continues to have an important influence on the rest of our lives, but we also have other opportunities to resolve these fundamental issues. Our personalities develop "best" when we resolve each of a series of eight psychosocial issues or "crises" in its appropriate time in our lives. Thus, infancy is the best time to resolve issues of trust, and resolutions made for the first time at a later age are not quite so satisfactory.

Much of Erikson's theory is in agreement with classical psychoanalytic assumptions: the belief that the basic conflicts and issues with which we must deal as infants are posed for us by biology, the notion of an adaptive personality core, or ego, and the idea that we possess only so much psychological energy to use as we develop. However, his major differences with Freud—those that concern the role of cultural institutions and our development over our whole lives—lead him to make different predictions about the stability of our personalities.

Erikson's theory leaves room for fairly major shifts in personality over time if, at any point, a person becomes dissatisfied with the social roles or cultural circumstances in which he finds himself. According to Erikson's theory, a person living in a fairly constant situation would have a fairly stable personality throughout life. But this stable personality could change quite a bit if the person's familiar environment underwent a major shift, especially one that removed an institution upon which he depended. For example, if an infant was cared for by someone other than his parents, he would not necessarily immediately start wondering whether he could trust the world, but if the institution of caregiving suddenly crumbled, and he was left without anyone to meet his needs regularly, he might begin to lose his trust.

Social learning theorists take a view of personality that contrasts sharply with that of Erikson; in fact, they question the whole notion of personality. They explain our behavior as the outcome of influences from our situation—whom we model ourselves after, whether we receive positive or negative results from our actions, and our vicarious experiences that are the result of observing what happens to other people in various situations. Until recently, this theory has disregarded the notion of development; changes in behavior following a systematic sequence that relates to age were not thought to occur.

Bandura, a leading proponent of this view, has recently written a revision of this theory that takes development into account: he acknowledges that infants do not have the cognitive skills that they would need to change their behavior according to the social learning process (Bandura, 1977). Very young infants are not prepared to change their behavior by imitating models or learning secondhand from the experiences of others. Most of the patterns we see in infants' behavior either are inborn or are adopted because of the responses to previous behavior.

According to social learning theory, individual differences among infants come about through differences in their temperaments, which are inborn, and the variations in their surroundings.

The social learning viewpoint does not predict that behavior will be consistent throughout life. Instead, the social learning theorist believes that human beings tailor their various behaviors to fit the situation more effectively as they develop and become able to master more complex discriminations. When a certain child's behavior does stay the same, this is because the situation that shaped the behavior also remained the same over time. For example, according to social learning theorists, if you consistently are told that aggressive behavior is unacceptable, then you are likely to behave unaggressively in most circumstances.

Only classical psychoanalytic theory considers personalities to be consistent year after year. However, "personality" implies a consistency in behavior, so if the term is to make sense it would have to be established, first, that one baby will behave the same in various circumstances and, second, that other babies will behave differently from the first child in various situations. Is there such evidence that personality exists?

Dimensions of Infant Personality

Thomas, Chess, and Birch conducted a large-scale study of infant personality at New York University that addressed these two issues: Will infants have individual responses to each circumstance, and will they respond consistently in various circumstances (Thomas and Chess, 1977)? Also of interest was the question of whether personal styles of behavior in infancy could predict later characteristics in childhood and beyond. The investigators interviewed 141 parents about the behavior of their infants. There are problems with using parent interviews as a data source, but Thomas, Chess, and Birch attempted to overcome them by phrasing their questions very specifically, referring to behavior instead of to traits. Parents were asked questions about the babies' reactions to feeding, bathing, and other concrete events. The research staff then analyzed the parents' reports of their infants' behavior.

Nine of the characteristics accurately described the infants' behavior in many situations. These characteristics are summarized in Table 6-1. Let's begin by defining these descriptive terms. Notice that the investigators have called these characteristics *temperamental qualities,* which means that they see the traits as innate tendencies that adapt in certain ways to demands that are made of babies by their environments.

Consider the quality "activity level" as an example. Very active young infants seem to squirm a lot when they are fed, changed, or carried. They give you the feeling you might drop them, and they make you aware of the opposition between your own actions and theirs. They will become toddlers who are very inquisitive and hard to manage. By the preschool years, they will be wiggle-worms who do not like to sit still for long car trips or lesson times at nursery school. As adults, they may be active, busy people who engage in strenuous hobbies or sports.

In contrast, infants who have a low activity level respond to the environment by taking it in through their senses rather than by acting on it. They may appear relatively placid to the person who changes and feeds them, and as they get older, they may enjoy quieter activities such as puzzles, books, and board games. As adults, their lower activity level may show itself in their focus on a few activities that give them the opportunity to put their concentration to its best advantage.

When I write about the "high active" and the "low active" person in this way, I am assuming that these classifications have some significance that endures through many situations. What is the evidence for such an assumption? Generally, to defend the idea that something like activity level is an enduring personal characteristic, we look at several relations. First, we see whether an individual's activity level in a wide variety of contexts tends to be more or less the same—always high, low, medium, or whatever. Next, we see whether ratings made at different points in time tend to agree. Thus when Thomas, Chess, and Birch list activity level as a characteristic (or dimension) of infant temperament, this means that they have found significant consistencies among their subjects' activity level ratings in various situations and over time.

In a similar manner, stable individual differences have been demonstrated for the other eight characteristics listed in Table 6-1. Because it has been shown that the traits are identifiable as early as two months of age and stable over at least the first 10 years, we can say that they constitute infant personality characteristics.

The investigators took one additional step to summarize what they learned to make it more useful in counseling new mothers. After each infant had been rated on the nine characteristics, they examined the patterns of interrelationship among them. Some of the traits tended to cluster together, so that a baby at one end of one characteristic also tended to be at a particular end of another. This analysis produced three basic clusters, which are summarized in Table 6-2.

The "easy babies" are so labeled because they best coordinate their own behavior with that of their caregivers, and they generally have positive reactions to people and events. This makes caring for them easy. The relationship between these infants and their caregivers is likely to be one of mutual pleasure and attachment, and this in turn may affect both the infants' personal development and the caregivers' sense of competence and success in their role. This initial interaction may leave its legacy long after infancy in a smooth and mutually gratifying relationship between child and caregiver. About 40 percent of the babies studied were classed as "easy babies."

"Difficult babies" are those who have irregular sleeping and eating patterns, and who experience more than an average amount of upset or frustration over new and challenging events. Although only 10 percent of the infants studied fell into this category, a disproportionately high percentage of those who later developed serious adjustment patterns came from this group. Perhaps the initial mismatch between the caregivers' ministrations and the babies' irregular reactions play a role in this, as well as the babies' inherent patterns of adjustment. If mothers, fathers, and other caregivers are more aware of inborn differences in the temperaments of infants, perhaps having "difficult" babies will cause fewer feelings of inadequacy, and thus the relationship between caregiver and infant will be improved. Such improvement may go a long way to mitigate permanent adjustment problems that a developing child experiences.

The remainder of the babies who were studied either fell into a type called "slow to warm up" or were unclassifiable. The large number of un-

Table 6-1 Nine Characteristics of Infant Temperament Found to Remain Relatively Stable from Infancy Through the Tenth Year of Life

Temperamental Quality	Rating	2 Months	6 Months
Activity Level	High	Moves often in sleep. Wriggles when diaper is changed.	Tries to stand in tub and splashes. Bounces in crib. Crawls after dog.
	Low	Does not move when being dressed or during sleep.	Passive in bath. Plays quietly in crib and falls asleep.
Rhythmicity	Regular	Has been on four-hour feeding schedule since birth. Regular bowel movement.	Is asleep at 6:30 every night. Awakes at 7:00 A.M. Food intake is constant.
	Irregular	Awakes at a different time each morning. Size of feedings varies.	Length of nap varies; so does food intake.
Distractibility	Distractible	Will stop crying for food if rocked. Stops fussing if given pacifier when diaper is being changed.	Stops crying when mother sings. Will remain still while clothing is changed if given a toy.
	Not Distractible	Will not stop crying when diaper is changed. Fusses after eating, even if rocked.	Stops crying only after dressing is finished. Cries until given bottle.
Approach/ Withdrawal	Positive	Smiles and licks washcloth. Has always liked bottle.	Likes new foods. Enjoyed first bath in a large tub. Smiles and gurgles.
	Negative	Rejected cereal the first time. Cries when strangers appear.	Smiles and babbles at strangers. Plays with new toys immediately.
Adaptability	Adaptive	Was passive during first bath; now enjoys bathing. Smiles at nurse.	Used to dislike new foods; now accepts them well.
	Not Adaptive	Still startled by sudden, sharp noise. Resists diapering.	Does not cooperate with dressing. Fusses and cries when left with sitter.

SOURCE: From "The Origin of Personality," by Alexander Thomas, Stella Chess, and Herbert G. Birch. Copyright © 1970 by Scientific American, Inc.

1 Year	2 Years	5 Years	10 Years
Walks rapidly. Eats eagerly. Climbs into everything.	Climbs furniture. Explores. Gets in and out of bed while being put to sleep.	Leaves table often during meals. Always runs.	Plays ball and engages in other sports. Cannot sit still long enough to do homework.
Finishes bottle slowly. Goes to sleep easily. Allows nail-cutting without fussing.	Enjoys quiet play with puzzles. Can listen to records for hours.	Takes a long time to dress. Sits quietly on long automobile rides.	Likes chess and reading. Eats very slowly.
Naps after lunch each day. Always drinks bottle before bed.	Eats a big lunch each day. Always has a snack before bedtime.	Falls asleep when put to bed. Bowel movement regular.	Eats only at mealtimes. Sleeps the same amount of time each night.
Will not fall asleep for an hour or more. Moves bowels at a different time each day.	Nap time changes from day to day. Toilet training is difficult because bowel movement is unpredictable.	Food intake varies; so does time of bowel movement.	Food intake varies. Falls asleep at a different time each night.
Cries when face is washed unless it is made into a game.	Will stop tantrum if another activity is suggested.	Can be coaxed out of forbidden activity by being led into something else.	Needs absolute silence for homework. Has a hard time choosing a shirt in a store because they all appeal to him.
Cries when toy is taken away and rejects substitute.	Screams if refused some desired object. Ignores mother's calling.	Seems not to hear if involved in favorite activity. Cries for a long time when hurt.	Can read a book while television set is at high volume. Does chores on schedule.
Approaches strangers readily. Sleeps well in new surroundings.	Slept well the first time he stayed overnight at grandparents' house.	Entered school building unhesitatingly. Tries new foods.	Went to camp happily. Loved to ski the first time.
Stiffened when placed on sled. Will not sleep in strange beds.	Avoids strange children in the playground. Whimpers first time at beach. Will not go into water.	Hid behind mother when entering school.	Severely homesick at camp during first days. Does not like new activities.
Was afraid of toy animals at first; now plays with them happily.	Obeys quickly. Stayed contentedly with grandparents for a week.	Hesitated to go to nursery school at first; now goes eagerly. Slept well on camping trip.	Likes camp, although homesick during first days. Learns enthusiastically.
Continues to reject new foods each time they are offered.	Cries and screams each time hair is cut. Disobeys persistently.	Has to be hand-led into classroom each day. Bounces on bed in spite of spankings.	Does not adjust well to new school or new teacher; comes home late for dinner even when punished.

(continued)

Table 6-1 *(continued)*

Temperamental Quality	Rating	2 Months	6 Months
Attention Span and Persistence	Long	If soiled, continues to cry until changed. Repeatedly rejects water if he wants milk.	Watches toy mobile over crib intently. "Coos" frequently.
	Short	Cries when awakened but stops almost immediately. Objects only mildly if cereal precedes bottle.	Sucks pacifier for only a few minutes and spits it out.
Intensity of Reaction	Intense	Cries when diapers are wet. Rejects food vigorously when satisfied.	Cries loudly at the sound of thunder. Makes sucking movements when vitamins are administered.
	Mild	Does not cry when diapers are wet. Whimpers instead of crying when hungry.	Does not kick often in tub. Does not smile. Screams and kicks when temperature is taken.
Threshold of Responsiveness	Low	Stops sucking on bottle when approached.	Refuses fruit he likes when vitamins are added. Hides head from bright light.
	High	Is not startled by loud noises. Takes bottle and breast equally well.	Eats everything. Does not object to diapers being wet or soiled.
Quality of Mood	Positive	Smacks lips when first tasting new food. Smiles at parents.	Plays and splashes in bath. Smiles at everyone.
	Negative	Fusses after nursing. Cries when carriage is rocked.	Cries when taken from tub. Cries when given food she does not like.

1 Year	2 Years	5 Years	10 Years
Plays by self in playpen for more than an hour. Listens to singing for long periods.	Works on a puzzle until it is completed. Watches when shown how to do something.	Practiced riding a two-wheeled bicycle for hours until he mastered it. Spent over an hour reading a book.	Reads for two hours before sleeping. Does homework carefully.
Loses interest in a toy after a few minutes. Gives up easily if she falls while attempting to walk.	Gives up easily if a toy is hard to use. Asks for help immediately if undressing becomes difficult.	Still cannot tie his shoes because he gives up when he is not successful. Fidgets when parents read to him.	Gets up frequently from homework for a snack. Never finishes a book.
Laughs hard when father plays roughly. Screamed and kicked when temperature was taken.	Yells if he feels excitement or delight. Cries loudly if a toy is taken away.	Rushes to greet father. Gets hiccups from laughing hard.	Tears up an entire page of homework if one mistake is made. Slams door of room when teased by younger brother.
Does not fuss much when clothing is pulled on over head.	When another child hit her, she looked surprised, did not hit back.	Drops eyes and remains silent when given a firm parental "No." Does not laugh much.	When a mistake is made in a model airplane, corrects it quietly. Does not comment when reprimanded.
Spits out food he does not like. Giggles when tickled.	Runs to door when father comes home. Must always be tucked tightly into bed.	Always notices when mother puts new dress on for first time. Refuses milk if it is not ice-cold.	Rejects fatty foods. Adjusts shower until water is exactly the right temperature.
Eats food he likes even if mixed with disliked food. Can be left easily with strangers.	Can be left with anyone. Falls asleep easily on either back or stomach.	Does not hear loud, sudden noises when reading. Does not object to injections.	Never complains when sick. Eats all foods.
Likes bottle; reaches for it and smiles. Laughs loudly when playing peekaboo.	Plays with sister; laughs and giggles. Smiles when he succeeds in putting shoes on.	Laughs loudly while watching television cartoons. Smiles at everyone.	Enjoys new accomplishments. Laughs when reading a funny passage aloud.
Cries when given injections. Cries when left alone.	Cries and squirms when given haircut. Cries when mother leaves.	Objects to putting boots on. Cries when frustrated.	Cries when he cannot solve a homework problem. Very "weepy" if he does not get enough sleep.

Figure 6-1. *An active infant crawls out of her backyard swimming pool—a dishpan.*
(Photo courtesy of Gary Head.)

classifiable cases—about one-third—shows the limitations of an over-simplified scheme that takes into account only three types. What we gain from such an approach is an increased awareness that, like the rest of us, babies are individuals and need to be treated as such.

What other evidence is there of the individuality of infants? Several investigators have found evidence of reliable individual differences in var-

Figure 6-2. *Will this placid 12-month-old baby grow up to be an adult who enjoys quiet activities? Long-term studies have been conducted in an attempt to discover whether behavior in infancy can predict behavior throughout life. (Photo courtesy of Gary Head.)*

ied groups of infants (Thomas, Chess, and Birch, 1970). Activity level is one of the most frequently identified characteristics of infant individuality (Escalona, 1968).

Sometimes personality theorists are interested in differences among groups of infants as well as between individual infants. If certain characteristics are systematically associated with membership in a given group, then perhaps something about their experience or genetic background will help us understand how the characteristic comes about. For example, sex differences may have important implications for how developing infants will come to see themselves and to be seen by others. Elsewhere in the book, you have seen that there are relatively few regularly observed sex differences in infancy. A recent major review of the literature on sex differences confirmed that although the basic characteristics of infant personality have been studied, no reliable and repeatedly observed sex differences have been discovered. Occasionally a study finds higher activity level in boys or a more

Table 6-2   Characteristics of Categories of Temperament

	Activity Level	Rhythmicity	Distractibility	Approach/ Withdrawal
Type of Child	The proportion of of active periods to inactive ones.	Regularity of hunger, excre- tion, sleep, and wakefulness.	The degree to which extraneous stimuli alter behavior.	The response to a new object or person.
"Easy"	Varies	Very Regular	Varies	Positive Approach
"Slow to Warm Up"	Low to Moderate	Varies	Varies	Initial Withdrawal
"Difficult"	Varies	Irregular	Varies	Withdrawal

ready response to tactile stimulation in girls. However, these observations do not hold firm when compared with results of other similar studies (Maccoby and Jacklin, 1974).

Differences among infants of different social classes have been found by many researchers. As you may recall from our earlier discussion, mother-infant interaction patterns vary with socioeconomic class, as does the pattern of physical stimulation. These differences may have important long-term implications for our development of cognition. However, little is known about the effects of socioeconomic class differences upon personality traits. Probably infants from all backgrounds vary in a fashion similar to the one described by the New York University group. Reactions of the caregivers to these patterns may, however, differ a great deal according to socioeconomic class. This may be one reason why babies come to differ according to class by the end of infancy.

In sum, researchers have not yet studied systematically group differences other than sex differences in young infants' personalities or temperaments. One reason for this lack of systematic study is psychologists' attitudes. Many psychologists view the individual differences among very young infants as reflecting variations in inborn biological processes for adaptation. They do not believe that the differences tell us much about the interaction of the person and the environment and, since such interaction is the main theme in much psychological theory, these investigators see the differences as irrelevant to psychology. In any case, a more extensive sampling of babies from the racial and social-class groups in our society would give us a more complete picture.

Adaptability	Attention Span and Persistence	Intensity of Reaction	Threshold of Responsiveness	Quality of Mood
The ease with which a child adapts to changes in his environment.	The amount of time devoted to an activity, and the effect of distraction on the activity.	The energy of response, regardless of its quality or direction.	The intensity of stimulation required to evoke a discernible response.	The amount of friendly, pleasant, joyful behavior as contrasted with unpleasant, unfriendly behavior.
Very Adaptable	High or Low	Low or Mild	High or Low	Positive
Slowly Adaptable	High or Low	Mild	High or Low	Slightly Negative
Slowly Adaptable	High or Low	Intense	High or Low	Negative

Common Ground Among Infants

I have mentioned the psychoanalytic concept of the basic core, supposedly the most central component of the emerging ego. Although the idea of personality is based upon the existence of differences among people, it also requires some commonality among people in the central issues of life to which they are responding in different ways.

What are the basic adaptive issues for developing infants? Four are reflected in the theoretical writings on infancy. First, infants face the task of establishing biological rhythms—those of sleep, eating, respiration, arousal, activity, and so forth. Second, infants need some basic skills for dealing with the potentially overwhelming influx of information from their environments. Third, as babies react to this stimulation from the environment, they must establish some voluntary control over their own activity. Fourth, they need to practice and refine the adaptive skills they are acquiring (Wolff, 1963). All babies react to these basic issues, but they react in different ways. Thus, their emerging individuality can be seen as a product of their approaching a set of common issues.

Let's look further at the relation between the common issues and emerging differences through an example: the development of fear. According to Hebb, a leading motivational theorist, stimulation from the environment increases the general arousal level of the organism— in our context, a baby (Hebb, 1943). We feel "fear" when so many new aspects of the environment demand to be dealt with that we cannot deal with them all. Thus, fear of the very strange (and sudden) event is innate. We do not fear events of "intermediate strangeness" because our brains can process them, and we can so readily process familiar events that they arouse little emotion.

How do babies react to strange or new events? The interesting fact is that young infants do not react much at all. By nine to ten months, most infants show some definite emotional reactions to new experiences. When they encounter a new event that is accompanied by toys, people, and events that are familiar, babies usually respond with interest and pleasure (Schaffer, Greenwood, and Parry, 1972). Extremely new events, on the other hand, frighten babies, who try to withdraw by looking away, fussing, and the like (Bronson, 1968). Although a new event may initially arouse anxiety and stress, it brings laughter and pleasure when the infant comes to master it (Rothbart, 1973). Indeed, children's automatic reaction of wariness or fear to strange events wanes as they apparently learn to expect that they will eventually be able to deal with whatever faces them. Adults can be frightened by sudden and totally strange environments, but the range of situations that frighten them is definitely smaller than that of a one-year-old infant.

All infants encounter an environment full of potential stimulation, and, because the whole world is a surprise to them, dealing with new and different information is inevitable. However, as evidence shows us, babies deal with stimulation in very different ways (Scarr and Salapatek, 1970). Some babies are more fearful of moving objects, others of strange persons, and still others of heights or other physical dangers. Some babies stop what they are doing when they are afraid; others become more active. Some avert their gaze to shut off stimulation whereas others fuss in hopes of being rescued.

These individual ways of reacting to a common issue are one illustration of a principle. Our biological nature seems to set up a core of issues long before we are born, and from birth each of us has particular ways in which to react to them. Individuality is an essential characteristic of our humanity.

Stability and Change

The fact that individual uniqueness exists from our earliest weeks brings us to our second question: How accurately can we predict an individual's personality in later childhood or adulthood from information about that person's infancy? Will a very active infant become a very active and athletic adult? Will sensitive, easily overstimulated babies choose quiet lifestyles to limit their stimulation in later life?

To seek answers to these questions we must compare people's behavior as adults with their behavior as infants. Such comparisons are fairly straightforward for such physical measures as height, heart rate, and proportion of body fat. However, when we compare people's behavior at various periods of their lifespans we run into certain difficulties. Infants are not as integrated into their society as 10-year-olds, 16-year-olds, or adults. Thus, an infant who is frustrated by an overabundance of stimulation may fuss and cry, whereas an adult who has the same problem may become quiet and retire into fantasy. Conversely, although adults do cry, they often do so in response to entirely different circumstances than do babies. So we will learn little by comparing certain behaviors at different ages unless we consider the circumstances in which they occur. This is the central methodological problem of developmental psychology, and I will not attempt a complete analysis of it here. Suffice it to say that the search for behavior in older children and adults that can be considered parallel in meaning to their behavior as infants is a difficult one that few investigations have made successfully.

The New York University investigations followed their subjects through childhood and adolescence and now are following them during adulthood. With the thought that each trait represented a transaction between a person and the surroundings, the researchers traced corresponding behaviors at later ages. For instance, the baby who is slow to respond to strange people and toys may become a 10-year-old who hesitates at first to try new games, athletic endeavors, or mathematical principles. The one-year-old baby who energetically forages through her toybox (and perhaps her parents' cupboards) to find a toy may become the 10-year-old who cannot sit still in a classroom and needs active experience in order to learn.

The New York group found a moderately high degree of stability between individual differences observed in infancy and those observed at age 10. This means that children's traits tended to be in the same position in the study group when they were 10 that they had been in when they were infants. Not surprisingly, this stability in behavior was more characteristic of those who as infants were classified as slow to warm up, difficult, or easy, than it was of those who were unclassifiable.

Although not all the characteristics this group studied have been used in other research, "activity level" is a clear exception. Several studies have examined both changes in children's activity level and environmental and genetic factors that relate to their activity level. Evidence indicates that activity level has at least some genetic component because higher and lower levels of activity seem to run in families (Willerman, 1973; Willerman and Plomin, 1973). Because different circumstances call for different responses, the pattern of environments children experience will gradually modify their innate dispositions. But we can divide people into those who understand their world through action in it and those who do so through perceiving and organizing these perceptions. Only a few characteristics show resemblance among family members that is strong enough to show up when we study children from varied backgrounds (Willerman, 1973).

How many such characteristics are there? The New York investigators use the term "temperament" to describe most basic aspects of our responses to change. Temperamental characteristics are thought to be largely innate: to be genetic in nature or caused during gestation or birth. At this time, we do not know how many temperamental characteristics exist or the extent to which they influence our reactions to change. But you should recall the massive evidence we have already reviewed in this book about the effect of environment upon an infant's responses. The number, sensory properties, and responsiveness of objects in children's environments clearly affect their interest in and manipulation of them. The suddenness, speed, and unfamiliarity of a new event influence whether children will respond with curiosity or fear. The number of objects and events that are competing for an infant's attention will influence his reaction to a particular event.

Because environment and inborn temperament both play important roles and because they often interact, how can we explain the stability we have seen in infants' characteristics? Such stability can reflect the continuing influence of genetics, but it may also reflect a stable environment. From this discussion, we have gathered some essential facts: infants have very definite personality characteristics, and these characteristics can be identified so early in infancy that the idea that they are part of our inborn temperaments must be seriously considered. These characteristics are stable enough over time to support a claim that our personalities as infants will be similar in some ways to our personalities as adults, an idea that has great popular appeal. The obvious role of our environments, however, should lead us to balance these generalizations with caution. The apparent individuality of young infants should not be interpreted as a fixed and already determined personality. Human beings are highly flexible. Although genes and prenatal and birth-related events affect much of our development, much of our personality also remains to be molded by our experiences.

Summary

Although the personalities of infants have not been as thoroughly studied as their cognition, perception, and social behavior, some general ideas about them have been established. There are certain temperamental characteristics that are inborn, and, while many influences may operate to modify these through time, there is some stability from infancy to age 10 or so in personality traits. Psychoanalytic theory has emphasized the important and central role played by infancy in our total development. Erikson's modification of psychoanalytic theory—with its emphasis on sociocultural factors—seems more consistent with the real complexities of development than the less flexible Freudian version. The brevity of this chapter serves to emphasize the fact that much more information will be needed about infant characteristics and their stability over time before we can develop a deeper and more satisfactory understanding of individuality in infants.

Appendix

Techniques for Studying Infants

The information about babies discussed in this book is based on the careful observations of researchers, and so I include here a discussion of the techniques they used to compile these data. I have several reasons for doing this. First, it will enable you to understand the difficulties they encountered while tracking down the facts and to recognize why some answers still elude them. Second, it will enable you to evaluate their findings better. Third, if you deal with babies—either in a clinical, practical, or research relationship—you may want to know how to observe them as carefully as these researchers did in order to find out as much about them as you need to. You may wish to use these techniques to keep a record—perhaps a notebook—of your baby's behavior. This record will help you be aware of the baby's personality, needs, and development. And when the baby grows older, you will be able to show him a record of what he was like in his early days.

However, the beginner who has never confronted the jargon and methods that researchers use might be daunted by the seeming density of the subject. Therefore, I have divided the material into sections. If you have a specific question—for example, if your baby was tested using the Bayley scale and you want to know what it is and what the results mean—you can simply look over the titles until you find the appropriate section. Because this chapter is meant to help you acquire a professional attitude about observing, the sections are organized for someone who is planning to observe babies seriously.

The chapter has eight sections. In the first two sections, I describe recording systems and their various applications. In Section 3, I discuss how reliably these systems measure behavior. Section 4 focuses on the standardized infant test that evaluates babies in relation to their peers in a precisely defined situation. Then, in the fifth section, I explain how some of the baby's physical responses, like heart rate and sucking, indicate a subjective experience—fear or attention, for example. In Section 6, I show the relation between the setting where observations are made and how the observations should be used. Because age is an especially important aspect of the study of infant development, I treat it separately in Section 7. In the final section, I discuss some of the difficulties of choosing a representative sample. How can we select a group of babies whose reactions will allow us to judge how the babies we did not include would also respond to the situation? In this section, I also suggest ways in which you can make informal observations of the babies with whom you are in close contact.

1. Recording Ongoing Behavior for Research

Characteristics of Recording Systems

How does one record babies' behavior? There are many ways. All of the systems discussed in this section apply to a situation in which behavior is continuous and spontaneous in the environment you are observing. The systems to be presented differ in four ways: (1) the number and type of categories into which behavior and events are classified; (2) the way in which time is recorded; (3) the method, if any, of counting or rating behavior numerically; and (4) whether classification (coding) is done while behavior occurs or later.

Coding Categories

Why use coding categories? Faced with the task of making a complete and accurate record of complex behavior, many of us would scorn pencil and tablet as too slow and imprecise. Why not make a film or videotape of the behavior that is being studied and run through it at your leisure? Sometimes this procedure is helpful, but there are some problems with having a file cabinet full of videotaped play sessions. For example, suppose the purpose of your study is to describe how the activity level of a seven-month-old girl who is sitting on the floor of a small playroom full of toys might be expected to change during 10 minutes. You examine the videotape you have made of each of the 24 babies you are studying. Some babies seem very active as they crawl about the floor. Others cannot crawl, but they sit and twist their bodies in an effort to reach toys. Still others appear to be able to crawl but rarely do so. Some infants seem to become more active as time goes on, whereas others appear to tire and to become less active.

But what summary statements can you make? At some point you are going to have to reduce the complexity of the videotape record to a simpler, less complex form. You are also going to have to group similar behaviors so that you can list them in a manageable number of descriptive categories. This classification process is called *coding.* Babies' behavior is divided into events, or *units,* each of which can be said to belong to one or more categories. A unit might be everything that goes on in a 30-second interval, or babies' responses to a flashing light stimulus, or their behavior in some caregiving transaction such as diapering.

Coding behavior not only simplifies the process of description, but also enables an observer to look for patterns and relationships. For example, we might want to determine whether babies of opposite sexes are engaged by different types of activities. Or we might want to record the change in babies' activities that takes place when their mothers move away from them. We might want to compare the activities we have observed with other characteristics of the babies, such as age, birth circumstances, or aspects of their physical growth.

Table A-1 is a set of coding categories suitable for describing the activities of seven-month-old infants from 10-minute videotape records. A unit of behavior in this example is defined as whatever occurs in a 15-second interval; this means there will be 40 units to be coded. Notice that the categories in this example are not mutually exclusive—for instance, if an infant is looking at an object that he is holding (manipulating) and laughing at the same time, his behavior would be coded into two categories: "Behavior with Toy" and "Expression of Emotion." To compare the frequency of occurrence of the various behaviors, we count the number of marks in each behavior category and compare the totals. We can also compare the average behavior of the children studied with that of individual subjects.

How many coding categories should be used? What kinds should they be? In deciding these things, investigators must weigh several interacting considerations—a complicated process. Their most important concern is to devise sufficient categories so that they can list most of the behavior that occurs in the situations they are observing. For example, if we were to make the mistake of using the categories of Table A-1 to observe three-year-old children instead of seven-month-olds, we might find them inadequate. Three-year-olds walk, rather than creep or crawl, and they might never examine the toys. Although they might cry, whine, laugh, or smile, they could just as well spend all their time talking to their mothers, which is not listed in Table A-1. Almost all the observed behavior might only apply to a "none of the above" category, and we would be left without an accurate description of the children's activity.

A coding system can be inappropriate for other reasons as well. What if we placed our seven-month-olds in a feeding table so that they could not reach the toys or their mothers, and they could not move around the room? We would again find that all of their behavior applied to one category—

Table A-1   Coding Categories for Describing the Play Activities of Seven-Month-Old Babies

Locomotor Behavior	Behavior in Relation to Mother
Crawls on hands and knees	Looks at mother
Scoots on tummy without supporting weight on knees	Moves closer to mother
	Touches mother
Behavior with Toy	Expression of Emotion
Manipulates toy with hands	Laughs
Throws toy	Smiles
Looks at or examines toy	Cries
	Whines

perhaps "crying" or "whining." Therefore, the observer must design coding categories that correspond to the range of behavior that takes place—including enough categories to reasonably describe what transpired and yet few enough to summarize similar forms of behavior.

A coding system must enable the observer to make the distinctions required by it in the time available. If there are too many categories, an observer will be unable to distinguish them reliably and will be left with an inaccurate summary. When this problem arises, you can solve it either by decreasing the number of categories, by increasing the time interval, or by dividing the categories among more than one observing team. These choices are discussed further in subsequent sections.

If you use coding categories that resemble those that others have used to study the same sort of behavior, you can more easily compare your findings with other work that has been done. So before you begin an investigation you should read what others have found out. Observational codes can be adapted to suit a unique situation, but before adapting them, you should consider the problem of comparing your findings with those of others.

Many investigators develop coding categories by trial and error. For example, they might film several sample sessions, and then view them over and over while experimenting with different coding schemes until they design a coding scheme that is sufficiently reliable and adequately descriptive.

Duration is an important aspect of behavior and therefore it is necessary to record time in some way. The simplest plan is to take *continuous* notes describing the behavior as it occurs and making notations of the time every minute or so. Table A-2 is an example of this kind of continuous record. Such a record, called a *narrative record,* enables observers to make rough estimates of the duration of the behavior they are studying. In Table A-2 the baby stared at the ceiling for about three minutes.

Table A-2   Example of Narrative Record with Time Notations

Time	Comments
	Three-month-old Marie (lying supine in her crib) stares up at the ceiling where father is shining his
10:01	flashlight. Her hands open and close while her forearms move up and down, sharply hitting
10:02	the mattress. She starts to grimace and breaks into a wide grin. Grin continues. Marie continues staring
10:03	but she quiets body. Her legs and arms go
10:04	limp. She laughs and looks at her father.
Interpretation:	Marie notices the spot of light on the ceiling and it interests her. Her focusing of attention on the light spot is evident from her smile of recognition and the quieting of her motor activity.

Obviously, these rough estimates must be abandoned when you desire greater accuracy. Electronic equipment can be used for more precise measurements, provided that it does not distract the baby: you can dictate a running account of behavior into a tape recorder while recording the clicks of a timer to mark off time intervals. The clicks can be set for each minute, each half-minute, every 15 seconds, or whatever interval you wish.

Instead of recording all the behavior that you observe, you can also use a procedure called *time sampling,* in which you list the categories of behavior you are investigating, and then divide recording space for the categories into time intervals. At the end of each time interval, you make a check in the appropriate columns on your chart for the behaviors that occurred during the interval. For example, to obtain a time-sampling measure of a baby's interaction with her mother, you might use a record sheet such as Table A-3.

All of the behaviors that are listed are continuous—they can last throughout a 10-second interval or for just part of it. However, this system only records whether or not each behavior occurred during each of the 10-second intervals. When the session is over, we can score each behavior by counting the number of time intervals in which it took place. We can then compare the behaviors and get a picture of their relative durations.

But if a given behavior is repeated within our set time interval, its resulting score will be misleading. Consider what would happen if we measured heart rate by a time-sampling procedure with 1-second intervals, for four minutes. Table A-4 is a section of the record of two subjects whose heart rates are very different from each other's. Subject A's is 60 beats per minute and thus his record divides neatly into 1-second intervals with one beat per

Table A-3   Record Sheet for the Time Sampling of Attachment Behaviors

Behavior Category	First 10 sec.	2nd 10 sec.	3rd 10 sec.	4th 10 sec.	5th 10 sec.	6th 10 sec.	7th 10 sec.	8th 10 sec.	9th 10 sec.	10th 10 sec.	11th 10 sec.	12th 10 sec.	Total
Looks at Mother													
Touches Mother													
Smiles at Mother													
Moves Closer to Mother													
Shows Toy to Mother													

Table A-4 Time-Sampling Record of Heart Rate for Two Subjects

	Time								
10: 10:05	06	07	08	09	10	11	12	13	Total
Subject A's time-sample record	x	x	x	x	x	x	x	x	8
Subject A's actual beats	x	x	x	x	x	x	x	x	
Subject B's time-sample record	x	x	x	x	x	x	x	x	8
Subject B's actual beats	x	x x	x	x	x x	x	x	x	

interval. However, Subject B has a rate of 75 beats per minute, so sometimes he has two beats in an interval and sometimes only one. Though their heart rates are quite different, both Subjects A and B receive time-sampled scores of 8, which would indicate that their heart rates are identical. Time sampling is not the appropriate method to use if you are measuring a series of clearly defined events that may occur more than once during an interval. For such studies, it is better simply to count the number of occurrences, as we do with heartbeats.

Let us look back at Table A-3 to consider another aspect of the time-sampling procedure. As you are busily dashing down check marks, you cannot also be observing, so you find that you miss a certain amount of information. You can deal with this problem in two ways. One is to divide the time interval into two subintervals, one for looking and listening and one for recording information. Thus a 15-second interval might be divided into 5 seconds of observation and 10 seconds of writing, Another solution is to separate the time sampling from the observing process altogether. You can use a time-marked tape and dictate a continuous observational record. A coder then listens to the tape and fills out time-sampling sheets like those illustrated in Table A-3. I will discuss this method further later.

We have seen that observers record time either by noting it on a continuous narrative or by using preset intervals of time. If you need a precise picture of how behavior is distributed through time, then you can use very small intervals in time sampling. Electronic equipment, while not essential, increases the accuracy of time measurement.

Quantitative Aspects. So far we have discussed observation in qualitative terms: the classifying of behavior into different categories. However, when the observed data are interpreted, many of the analyses are facilitated if you can summarize your observations with a numerical score. One of the simplest ways to do this has already been illustrated in the preceding section. In time sampling, the numerical score received by a subject for a given behavioral category is simply the total number of time intervals in which that behavior occurred. Note that within each time interval, you are recording a quality of the behavior, but by adding all the time intervals, the quantity of the behavior emerges. This procedure essentially amounts to counting and so, from now on, I will refer to it as *counting* to distinguish it from *rating,* which we will discuss next.

Ratings are used when you want to convey the intensity of behavior. For example, a rating of 5 on a 5-point scale of aggression means that a behavior—whether one or several acts—was extremely aggressive. Like counting, rating also assigns a numerical score, but it means something different.

Observers may rate a characteristic immediately at the end of an observation period, or the score may be assigned later by someone else on the basis of the observational record. In either case the rating is a summary of behavior that may occur over some extended period of time. Ratings are generally done on scales that have from 3 to 10 points; using more than 10 points puts too great a burden upon the observers, who cannot reliably distinguish a greater number of degrees. Table A-5 is an example of a 7-point rating scale that might be used to describe the activity level of an infant who can crawl but cannot walk.

How well do ratings represent the behavior they are meant to summarize? Although it is beyond the scope of this book to discuss all the measurement and statistical considerations that determine the accuracy of ratings, two general comments are in order. First, the criteria used to describe each point on the scale must be carefully worded. If these criteria are clear, unambiguous, and related to the behavior being observed, then the resulting ratings will be reliable. Second, ratings are summaries of behavior; they are not intended to give detailed descriptions of a sequence of events. For instance, activity level may vary quite a bit from one minute to the next within a 15-minute session and this variance may not be reflected in a summary rating. Ratings are best used when the overall level of some behavior is of more interest than its pattern.

Immediate vs. Delayed Coding.   We have already seen that behavior can be coded into categories either immediately as it occurs, or later, by use of a narrative record of the behavior. Two considerations favor waiting before assigning a rating. First, you can manage the task better if you don't have to alternate your attention between observing and coding. In fact, immediate ratings are practical only if the number of coding categories is small.

Table A-5   Example of a 7-Point Rating Scale for Activity Level of Crawling Infants

Rating	Criteria for Assignment
7	Very much vigorous movement that consists of locomotion and movement of arms, legs, and torso.
6	Much vigorous movement that consists of locomotion and movement of arms, legs, and torso.
5	More than an average amount of movement of arms and legs plus some locomotion.
4	Average amount of movement—some locomotion and movement of arms, legs, and torso.
3	Little locomotion and some movement of arms, legs, and torso.
2	No locomotion and little movement of arms, legs, and torso.
1	No locomotion and very little movement of arms, legs, and torso.

Second, the delayed coding system removes one type of bias. An observer at the scene, working with a small set of categories, tends to "see" behavior as being appropriate for these categories and to think in terms of them. A second observer is usually present, so by comparing their reports, the observers can detect any bias that exists. But, if there is a significant disagreement between observers, it is impossible to go over the behavior again to resolve the discrepancies. However, the delayed coding system allows the raters to go back over the behavior (on videotape, typed transcript, or dictated record) again and again if necessary as they refine their criteria. Also, if those who designate the appropriate categories and those who observe and record behavior are different people, observers are free to concentrate on recording the events accurately.

Location of the Observer.   Where should an observer be stationed in order to work most effectively? Where the observer works is not strictly part of the definition of the observation system. Nevertheless, your location can influence your findings and you should be acquainted with the various possibilities. When babies are brought into laboratories or clinics, usually they are in one room while the observer is in another. The two rooms are separated by a large window of one-way glass that is a mirror on the babies' side and an ordinary, transparent window on the observer's side. Sound is transmitted electronically between the two rooms. Studies done in the home typically proceed with the observer stationing himself in an unobtrusive spot from which he can observe both caregiver and baby. In still other studies, the observer shares some activity with the baby, such as a medical examination. The extent to which an observer intrudes upon a situation may affect the resulting observations in important ways. However, no one has made controlled experimental investigations of this question with infants.

Commonly Used Systems

The characteristics of observational systems that we have been discussing can be combined in numerous ways. Here we will consider five commonly used combinations.

In *time sampling with immediate recording using behavior codes,* observers are given a set of behavior categories such as those in Table A-1 that they commit to memory. Each category is represented by a symbol that the observers record whenever they see an instance of the category in the behavior they are observing. When watching for very few categories—say five or fewer—they might use a check sheet such as Table A-3. To handle a greater number of categories, the observer can work with symbols or abbreviations for the category names, recording on a sheet ruled in columns for the time intervals. Thus, the category "Manipulates Toy" might be represented by the symbol MT. Table A-6 is an example of a record sheet for this observational system.

The principal advantage of this system is its great efficiency. When an observation session is over, you simply count the symbols and thus have scores that can be analyzed. When the behavior that interests you is clearly covered by the categories used, and when scoring is reliable (see Section 3), then the efficiency of this system recommends it. But in practice, this system is effective only when the categories have been set up after extensive experience with similar behavior and a similar situation. This insures that the categories are probably relevant and the observations reliable.

But the virtue of this system is also its flaw: the only permanent record of the behavior is the code sheet. If questions arise later about some aspect of the baby's behavior or the circumstance that is not coded, you cannot go back to a complete record of the behavior and find answers. Also, if observers' records disagree, there is no other record that can serve as a basis for resolving these disagreements.

Clearly, the decision to use this system depends on how much confidence an investigator has that the coding categories cover the important aspects of the behavior he is studying. If there are a substantial number of other investigations in the same field that have defined the behavior well, this confidence might be justified. If, on the other hand, the investigation is in a new and unexplored area, using one of the systems with delayed coding would give better results.

The system of *time sampling with immediate recording of numerical ratings* is similar to the system we have just discussed, but instead of checking off or

Table A-6   Check Sheet for Time Sampling with Immediate Coding: Play Activities
of Seven-Month-Old Babies

Subject ID _____ Observer _____

Codes (taken from Table A-1):

	Cr	Crawls	MT	Manipulates Toy
	Sc	Scoots	TT	Throws Toy
			LT	Looks at Toy
			ET	Examines Toy
	LM	Looks at Mother	L	Laughs
	MM	Moves Closer to Mother	S	Smiles
	TM	Touches Mother	C	Cries
			W	Whines

Time On _____   Time Off _____

end ½ min.	_____
1 min.	_____
1½ min.	_____
2 min.	_____
2½ min.	_____
3 min.	_____
3½ min.	_____
4 min.	_____
4½ min.	_____
5 min.	_____

writing down category codes, the observers rate the intensity of the behavior. Thus for example, instead of entering C for "cries," the observer might enter "2" to indicate that the baby is crying "moderately" on a scale of crying that goes from 1 to 3. In this system, the completed sheet would look much like Table A-6 but would contain numbers instead of letters. The division of each interval to allow time for looking and time for writing might have to be modified to allow more time for writing because a numerical rating system requires more judgment than a system that consists of a qualitative code.

The advantage and disadvantage of this recording system are basically the same as those of the previously discussed system: the complex judgment that is required would try the reliability of the observers even more, but otherwise the same considerations apply. If reliability is good, and the behavior being studied can be clearly rated, this is a highly efficient system. To obtain a numerical score, we would first add the ratings of a behavior for all the time intervals and then divide by the number of time intervals to get an average intensity of the behavior for the total time observed. For example, if a baby cried for a minute at intensity 3, a minute at 2, and a minute at 1, his crying over the three minutes would average to a 2 rating. This score can then be used in an analysis of the behavior.

Continuous recording with delayed use of time-sampled behavior codes is the most commonly used observational system. The fact that the recording process is divided into two parts gives the system several advantages. First, observers can record a narrative of all of the essential ongoing behavior of the infant while it occurs. Many observers use a tape recorder to do this because it permits them to keep their eyes on the action and because time intervals can be recorded on the tape automatically. For example, using this system one could dictate a fairly detailed account of what a baby is doing with her hands.

Later, after the observation session, a typed transcript of the session is prepared, from which the coders can work. The coders then read through the transcript with record sheets similar to Table A-6 in hand. The behavior on the transcript for each time interval is classified into the various coding categories and total scores are counted, as they were in the system in which behavior is coded immediately. However, the narrative transcript allows this coding process to be examined any number of times. If the observers' records differ, then the transcript can be reviewed. When observers have clarified their disagreement and criteria have been refined, the coding can be done over again until it accurately reflects the behavior.

This system also allows the observers to make the initial taped narratives without knowing the hypotheses or questions under investigation. Their instructions can consist simply of concrete activities to observe ("note any movement through space") rather than in theoretical terms ("note any proximity seeking"). Although we cannot avoid the fact that all observational records select only some behavior from among all that occurs, at least we can minimize the problem of systematic bias that influences observers to see behavior that matches the codes that they have devised.

Another advantage of this system is that the coding system can be modified after the observation sessions. If a session suggests new, interesting categories of behavior, they can be added to the original categories when the coding is done.

In more general terms, this two-stage process has the principal advantage of flexibility and the drawback of expense in time and, inevitably, money. At least four people—two observers and two coders—are required for it, as well as the minimal electronic equipment and the clerical work. Also, for observational work in the subjects' real-life settings, the dictating can sometimes be disruptive. But because many of the scores derived from this system are very reliable the question is whether a less costly system is as effective. Of course, for some research problems in which only a few behaviors are of interest, this two-stage system is really unnecessary.

The system of *continuous recording with delayed use of quantitative ratings,* like the previous system, is a two-stage process. The observer dictates the narrative record at the scene of the action as before. In this system, however, the coder reads (or listens to) the entire transcript before making any decisions. Finally, the coder makes numerical ratings of the information that is relevant to the research topic. Thus the assigned number represents a summary of all of the behavior relevant to certain aspects appearing in the transcript.

What are the advantages and disadvantages of this system? This system, like the previous one, allows great flexibility because recording and coding are done in two stages. But because the ratings are summaries of many behaviors, it is more difficult for two raters to agree. However, when the observers are well trained and reliable, this system has the same advantages as the previous one. A principal drawback is that ratings usually do not provide a picture of how behavior responds to events in the environment or how it changes over time. Coders may assign ratings on the basis of one or two salient kinds of behavior, disregarding much of what happens. This problem is compounded by the fact that often we cannot determine whether influential events are being overlooked. The extent to which this problem poses a serious disadvantage depends on the questions that are being investigated and how subtle the important influences are.

The system of *continuous recording with delayed use of time-sampled ratings* is similar to the previous system except that the ratings are not summaries. The behavior is recorded on a tape that has time intervals marked off. Then coders later rate the behavior for *each* time interval, and the average of these ratings for each aspect of behavior becomes the final score for that aspect. For example, a baby might be rated for "arousal" for each of twelve 15-second intervals. His final arousal score would be the average of the twelve scores. This modification insures that noticeable but infrequent events do not influence the final scores out of proportion to their actual significance. Thus, if our example baby cries briefly for only one of the twelve intervals, her arousal score will be low. Although this system is a logical one, and suited to certain research questions, it is seldom used. As a general rule, investigators use time sampling that examines the behavior according to a length of time in conjunction with a *counting* score, and reserve quantitative ratings that record the behavior according to its intensity for use with transcripts that are not divided into time intervals.

2. Clinical Records of Infant Behavior

The observational systems I have described are appropriate for the research situations in which more than one baby is to be observed. Pediatricians, social workers, child-care workers, and others who deal with individual babies and their needs also use observational records, which, when they are properly focused on the behavioral information that is truly relevant to the questions clinicians want answered, can be an invaluable tool. One way behavioral records are used in clinical work is to describe a person's general behaviors, and thus serve as a basis for a diagnosis of any medical condition or developmental difficulty that is shown by behavioral signs or symptoms. For example, if a clinician wants to evaluate an infant's coordination, he must have several observations of the infant dealing with objects.

Records also chart long-term changes in babies, which may be subtle and gradual. Sometimes these changes escape notice in one examination or play sessions, but can be discerned by a look through the records. For instance, the normal gradual lessening of certain reflexes of newborns is apparent in the records kept by doctors of their routine behavioral examination of infants that takes place at the times of medical check-ups. Without written notes, however, an observer might fail to notice such change, whose absence is a sign of abnormal development.

Clinicians can also use behavioral records as "facts" when they discuss the baby with colleagues and parents. Often when people are discussing their ideas about a given baby, they find that they have very different perceptions of the baby's actions. Indeed, their basic conceptions of the baby may differ dramatically. But it is difficult to explain or to reconcile such different reactions if there is no means to relate the ideas to specific behavior. With a behavioral record at hand, one can see that perhaps a particular behavior is given different meaning by two different people, or perhaps one person places greater emphasis on one behavior while the other person emphasizes another. When the sources of perceptions are tentatively identified in this way, the dialogue can deal with the issues clearly.

Behavioral records can also help in programs to train clinicians by giving them guidelines of expected behavior. Although clinical work depends heavily on the unlearned intuitive skills and empathetic capacity of the clinicians, clinical training programs can teach them to be more successful practitioners by following some general principles. For example, many directors of programs for babies believe that allowing plenty of freedom for exploring and discovering the environment is important to a baby's development, and the innumerable incidents that occur between adults and babies in day-care centers, clinics, and private homes seem to confirm this idea. A teacher can use these incidents as examples, creating a factual basis for discussion. When students share these events with each other, they begin to develop a picture of what behavior is typical at certain ages. Many an inexperienced student working for the first time with infants has been excited by an instance of discovery and communication between baby and caregiver, only to face the frustrating experience of being unable to find the right words to report the event. True, these special moments are difficult to capture in words; nonetheless we should attempt to find the right phrases to communicate these experiences lest the discoveries we make be wasted. By sharing our observations and our feelings about them with others, we can also realize that the same experiences can have a different meaning for them.

Types of Clinical Records

The fortunate babies who live in homes where their caregivers are enlightened about children's health needs usually receive frequent medical examinations. The case records on their developmental progress are mainly concerned with physical growth and they do not mention their behavior. However, our discussion will focus on the behavioral records that clinicians use when they want a record of behavior. Typically these professionals interact with either the baby, the caregiver, or both during the time that the baby is at the office or examining room. These people certainly cannot and should not take the role of the detached observer. So the notes and summaries they use are less structured than those I described in Section 1.

Anecdotal Record.   Anecdotal records are used very commonly by clinicians: as soon after a session with the baby (or caregiver) as possible, the clinician simply writes a summary of the events that occurred. The clinician must be able to interpret these events for their possible emotional meaning and developmental significance while also clearly separating the actual behavior (what the baby did and what others did and said) from the interpretation of that behavior, perhaps by using a two-column sheet such as Table A-7. This vital separation of behavior and interpretation clarifies the relation between them. For example, looking at Table A-7, we can see that the observer first described the baby's behavior objectively: "he . . . began to giggle and thrash his legs on his mother's lap. . . . " Then the observer interpreted the behavior: "The bright lights are interesting . . . ."

When people who were not present during this incident read the anecdotal record, they can suggest other interpretations or inquire for further details about the behavior from the person who made the record. However, if the behavior and interpretation were not separated, it would be impossible to react independently to the interpretation. The report would then be a statement of the clinician's private experience; perhaps this would enhance our understanding of him, but it would give us little insight about the baby. Separating behavior and interpretation is also useful because the clinician

Table A-7   Two-Column Record Sheet for Making an Anectodal Record

Observational Narrative	Interpretations
The baby bounced in his mother's lap and looked all around the room. Suddenly, he noticed the bright overhead lights and began to giggle and thrash his legs on his mother's lap. The mother shifted around in her seat to reach for a magazine, and the baby began to fuss and push against his mother's body with his straightened arms.	Active baby. Interested in new things, especially the lights. The bright lights are interesting to the baby. The baby is frustrated by being cut off from the interesting sight.

can discover instances where seemingly identical behaviors were perceived differently at various times; this might give him an important clue to the meaning of that behavior.

Anecdotal records of behavior can be made following medical examinations, psychological testing, or play sessions arranged for the purpose of observation. They are invaluable tools for charting changes and for fostering productive exchange among professionals who are working together with a particular baby.

Interview with a Parent.   Another source of information about babies' behavior is a parent interview. You may wonder about the accuracy of the information that parents give about their children. Some clinicians are skeptical about the validity of a parent's perceptions. However, some evidence shows that parents' opinions are accurate: one study used information from mothers about their infants and predicted correctly which children would have psychiatric problems by their fourth year (Broussard and Hartner, 1970). Parents can offer very useful information about their babies' behavior if they can remember it and accurately describe it. The clinicians can ask separately about the baby's behavior and the parents' opinions about the baby's behavior, thus helping to keep the two separate.

An interview is a complex process that is influenced by many interacting factors. Although it is beyond the scope of this book to discuss completely the techniques of giving and interpreting interviews, the questions that are asked and the general atmosphere of the situation definitely influence what is said.

Experienced clinicians learn to compare the picture they get of a child from parent interviews with other sources such as anecdotal records and their own direct clinical contact. The pattern of these combined sources is often more meaningful than any one would be.

All of the information about a given baby is then organized and interpreted in an integrated report, a *case study*. Along with other information, such a study might include the baby's medical history, pertinent facts about the family's circumstances, summaries of the anecdotal records of clinical sessions with an interpretive summary, descriptions of the parents and of their perceptions of the baby based on interviews, and any scores from formal tests. Many clinics also require staff members to explain why they are treating the baby and what the specific goals for treatment are.

However, when members of a clinical staff are part of a research program and are studying babies, they must strive to keep more uniform records, perhaps using a coding system like those I described before. Otherwise their observations have little utility except to themselves.

3. *Observer Reliability*

Rationale

In all research that employs observers it is crucial to know whether the observers are recording what is actually happening. If they are, then they are said to be *reliable*. But if their records are inaccurate, then the research findings will be invalid as well. One way in which to test the accuracy of observers' data is to compare the records of two or more independent observers who have used identical procedures and have experienced the same situation. As you can imagine, these two conditions are never perfectly met because people understand procedures differently and notice different details. However, researchers try to see that the two conditions are satisfied as nearly as possible.

How can one make the procedure identical for many observers? First, investigators carefully define what behavior the observers should notice and also explain how to record it. Second, the investigators train all the observers at the same time so that all of them have received the same information. But how can we be sure that the observers experience the same situation when they are recording? After all, our perceptions of the world are extremely subjective and individualistic. However, when the situation is fairly simple and the observers are watching for events that have clear beginnings and endings—like the trials in experiments—they will probably be aware of the same events. But as the situation becomes complex, the observers will pay attention to different aspects, so they will have different perceptions. In practice, the assumption that the observers are experiencing the same situation stands unchallenged; perhaps it is impossible to regulate perceptions.

A general rule of the scientific method says that someone must be able to duplicate an observation for it to be considered accurate. But instead of repeating an observation with first one and then another observer, many studies of infant development simply use two observers, who work simultaneously.

The private, intuitive, hard-to-articulate impression does not find its way into observational research data, although clinicians often find these private, subjective impressions to be important clues about the outlook for their clients. As a result, some clinicians are skeptical about the relevance of research findings to important human problems because researchers exclude any unshared impressions from their data. Meanwhile, the researchers are skeptical about clinicians' insights when they cannot be verified by a second observer.

I believe that this mutual skepticism is unfortunate and unnecessary. When behavior and one's interpretation of it can be separated, then it is possible to specify, at least tentatively, how the two are related. When a clinician can identify the behavior to which he or she is responding, then we can see whether a second observer can also perceive that behavior. We then have the basis for comparison. We can discuss the interpretation and develop a coding scheme if research is involved. But when research is not involved, we do not need exact agreement, although people sharing and reconciling their observations is still important. Shared reality is certainly not the only reality, but it may provide the only basis for discovering and teaching about regular patterns in human behavior.

How to Measure Interobserver Reliability

How can we measure the extent to which two observers are agreeing in their observations? Most investigators use one of two common indexes. First, the percentage of observed units (time units, behavior categories, etc.) in which the two observers classified or rated the behavior in the same way can be calculated. This is called the *percent agreement* and it may be calculated as follows:

$$\text{Percent agreement} = 100 \times \frac{2 \text{ (number of units classified the same by both)}}{\text{Total number of units}}$$

The second index is commonly used for numerical data such as ratings. The *correlation coefficient* (a measure of how strongly associated two sets of scores are) can be calculated between the first observer's ratings and the second observer's ratings.

Table A-8 illustrates the calculation of percent agreement for a hypothetical coding scheme with five codes and 10 intervals. Table A-9 illustrates the

Table A-8 Calculation of Percent Agreement for One Code in Sets of Time-Sampled Codes

Time Interval	Observer A	Status of ET Code	Observer B	Status of ET Code
1	Cr, MM, S	Absent	Cr, MM,	Absent
2	S, ET	Present	M, ET	Present
3	ET, LM	Present	LM	Absent
4	ET, L	Present	EM, L	Present
5	ET, S	Present	M	Absent
6	Cr	Absent	Cr	Absent
7	MT, ET	Present	MT, ET	Present
8	ET, L	Present	ET, S	Present
9	MT, L	Absent	MT, L	Absent
10	ET	Present	ET	Present
11	Cr, MM	Absent	Cr, MM	Absent
12	MM, TM	Absent	MM	Absent

Percent agreement for code ET

$$= (100) \frac{2 \times (\text{number of intervals showing either both present or both absent})}{\text{Number of intervals coded by A} + \text{number of intervals coded by B}}$$

$$= \frac{2 \times 10}{12 + 12} = (100) \frac{20}{24} = 83\%$$

calculation of a Pearson Product Moment Correlation for Agreement among two sets of ratings made from the scale in Table A-5.

If data are found to be unreliable, the scores must be abandoned. Researchers also must abandon the behavior category altogether or revise their definitions, training procedures, or scoring systems until they are able to obtain reliable results. Unfortunately, because there is no universally accepted standard to judge how accurate data should be to be considered usable, researchers use data that vary widely in reliability. Authors should report their reliability figures so that readers may take them into account in evaluating the research. As a broad rule of thumb, one should be slightly skeptical of counting-based scores with less than 75 percent agreement between observers. Correlations between two sets of numerical ratings should exceed .8. In the next section, I explain some of the many factors that influence the reliability of observations.

Variables That Affect Agreement Between Observers

Should observers be monitored for accuracy? It probably will not surprise you to learn that when observers are aware that their records are being

Table A-9   Calculation of a Correlation for Agreement Among the Sets of Ratings Based on Table A-5

Time Interval	Observer A	Observer B
1	5	6
2	4	6
3	3	4
4	4	4
5	3	3
6	3	2
7	2	3
8	2	3
9	1	1
10	2	2
11	3	4
12	2	3
13	3	2
14	4	3
15	3	4
16	3	5
17	2	4
18	1	1
19	2	2
20	4	4
Sums	56	65
Sums of squares	178	249
Sum of products	204	

$$r = \frac{20(204) - (56)\,(65)}{\sqrt{20(178) - (56)^2}\ \sqrt{20(249) - (65)^2}} = \frac{440}{565.7937} = .78$$

a reasonably good overall agreement

compared to those of other observers, their observations agree more (Jones, Reid, and Patterson, 1975). Some investigators train their observers in groups to some preset criterion of agreement (say 80 percent) and then, assuming they are reliable, allow them to observe alone when they are gathering the data for the actual study. Reid has demonstrated that, when observers believe they are not being monitored, the number of instances in which they agree drops radically and thus their observations are less accurate (Reid, 1970). However, if observers are informed that random samples of their data will be compared with those of other observers, their work becomes more accurate and this drop does not occur (Taplin and Reid, 1973). Thus it would seem desirable for investigators to employ more than one observer for all observational work so that the observers will know that they must be accurate because their records will be checked for agreement.

Observers' agreement, and thus their accuracy, are influenced by their understanding of their task. If I tell you to observe a baby's "exploratory behavior," you may record a set of behaviors that differs from those recorded by a second observer. You may record instances in which the baby moves about the room and initiates activities, while your partner may disregard the movement and only record instances in which the baby looks at and handles objects.

The problem is that you and your partner don't agree on the definition of exploratory behavior. Before you could agree, I would have to be much more explicit—I might give you both a list of types of actions that you are to record as "exploratory behavior." You both would obtain information that was even more accurate if I listed all "exploratory behaviors" specifically, saying you should look for moving about, looking at toys, handling toys, initiating activities, and thus leaving no doubt in your minds about what to look for. Given that you and your partner had made similar and reliable observations, I could determine an overall "exploratory behavior" score that was based on the average of your separate scores.

How does *training* affect agreement between observers? There is wide variation in the kind and amount of training observers receive before they participate in a study. Training is generally accomplished by showing observers the situation and the observational system and discussing the definitions in the coding system with them. The discussion is crucial because all the observers must define the behavior they are to observe as the investigator does. One study has demonstrated that self-training and being trained by another person were equally effective (Wildman, Erickson, and Kent, 1975). Although these findings need to be verified by other studies as well, we may conclude that the most important training components are experience with the system and clarification of definition through discussion.

Reliability of observers is also influenced by the instructions they receive. Instructions create expectations in the observers' minds about what they are going to see, so they must be clear and carefully worded. If I tell you that I am interested in mothers' rewarding dependency, you may see every act of the mother as rewarding dependency. Or if I tell you that the infant you are watching has been frustrated before the start of the session, you may see frustration reactions more often than you would if I had not told you this. Results of one study verify that receiving information before an observation session decreases an observer's reliability (Mash and Makohoniuk, 1975). The best instructions are those that clearly define the behavior to be observed but add no unnecessary information about the subjects or the situation.

Reliability is affected by the predictability of the behavior that is being observed. If a baby tends to repeat some pattern of behavior, the observer may come to expect that behavior to recur. Expectations created in this way have the same undesirable effects as those created by instructions. Because it is not always possible—or even desirable—to control the predictability of the subjects' behavior, one should try to minimize this influence by making observers conscious of the problem.

Reliability is influenced by the environment in which the observations are made. An observer who is bombarded by background noise and confusion must struggle to focus on the subject of the observation and those aspects of behavior that are being observed. Two observers may record impressions different from each other's when they channel their attention in a complex situation. However, because it is important to observe real-life situations, many of which are complex, observers must learn to block out background confusion and concentrate on behavior to be studied.

How to Resolve the Discrepancies in Observations

Investigators typically work with their observation system until they are satisfied that the observers agree. However, unless the observers agree perfectly, they sometimes will record different things. When the scores are quantitative ratings, the investigator usually averages the discrepant ratings and uses that average score. If the system requires counting the number of times a behavior occurred, the investigator has two possible solutions when the observers disagree. He can toss a coin to decide whether the behavior should be rated as "present" or "absent" in each instance or he can take the observers' totals, average them, and use the average as the subject's score. If the investigator has many discrepancies to resolve, both approaches would yield the same results, but if the number of discrepancies is small, he should average the total counts for the most accurate results. The following are two ways of resolving the discrepancies that appear in Table A-8.

1. A coin is tossed for interval 3, in which a discrepancy occurred, and for interval 5, in which another discrepancy occurred. This results in the baby being given a "present" for interval 3 and also for interval 5.
2. We note that Observer A has given the "ET" code "present" in 7 intervals and Observer B has given it as present in 5 intervals. We average the 7 and the 5 and enter a "6" as the total number of ET codes scored for this baby.

The Use of Apparatus to Increase Reliability

How can we increase the reliability of our findings? Sometimes it is helpful to use equipment that has capabilities that we do not have: for example, researchers sometimes use an eye camera to record a baby's eye movements. Thus instead of relying on an observer's judgment of what the baby is looking at, they can examine a film frame by frame and see what is reflected in the baby's cornea. Another example is the stabilometer crib, which is set onto springs fitted with electronic switches that automatically record the baby's body movements. There are many other kinds of equipment that can decrease the subjectivity that always colors human perceptions. But some researchers believe that subjectivity is important. They argue that they are studying how adults perceive babies' behavior and that only unaided observers can record these impressions. Others value the greater accuracy of observations that use of equipment assures.

4. Structured Assessment of Infants

The term *assessment* means the use of psychological tests to measure characteristics. The tests rest on the assumption that people possess relatively enduring traits that influence them to behave in certain ways. Most psychological tests are *standardized:* stimuli are presented to all those who are tested, the *respondents,* in the same manner and in a certain planned sequence. Or tests can be said to be standardized if all respondents are placed in a situation at the same time. Because the structure of the test is identical, the different results reflect the personal differences of the respondents rather than different situations.

How are psychological tests given and what are their uses? In psychological tests for older children and adults, interviewers ask questions and sometimes use picture puzzles and other materials. These tests, which examine a wide variety of personality and intellectual characteristics, are used primarily because they make it easier to compare individuals and to evaluate the degrees of individual differences.

The most commonly measured psychological characteristic is intelligence. Several standardized tests yield an *intelligence quotient,* or IQ score, which may become part of a child's school records, or an adult's file if he or she is a mental patient. But a great deal of controversy has arisen in recent years over the proper interpretation of these IQ scores, and many professionals question the value of IQ tests. Nevertheless, IQ tests are widely used for testing children—beginning at about 2½ years of age—and for adolescents and adults. Because IQ tests are verbal questions, children younger than 2½ cannot understand an interviewer's questions well enough to take the tests.

However, researchers have argued that if the label "intelligence" can be applied to some basic characteristic that is partly inherited, then we should be able to test how much of this characteristic infants have. Inspired by this notion, some infant specialists have developed standardized tests of infant development in hopes of finding some aspect of development that will predict how babies will score on IQ tests when they are older.

The several infant tests that exist differ in their underlying assumption about how intelligence is manifested in early infancy. Some regard intelligence as a unitary trait, whereas others see it as involving more than one trait. Many infant-test builders see sensory-motor coordinations as the principal manifestation of intelligence in infancy, whereas others see social behavior and emotional responses as relevant too. All the tests face the problem of developing a set of stimuli that can be presented to all babies in more or less the same way. They typically look for simple coordinations and adaptive responses such as an infant's ability to put a cube into a cup. These behaviors have little obvious resemblance to the more abstract and verbal skills that appear in IQ tests. Thus, it is not surprising that infant tests do not usually predict later IQ scores (Thomas, 1967).

In the remainder of this section we will discuss examples of two common infant tests: the Gesell Developmental Scales and the Bayley Scales of Infant Development (BSID). Very possibly, if your baby is tested by a doctor or researcher, the examination will include items from these two tests. In fact, the tests are so frequently used that they have furnished much of the data on the normal course of infant development.

The Gesell Test

Arnold Gesell is known primarily for the large body of information that he began collecting in the 1920s about the growth and behavior of children. All of his work was done at the Yale University Clinic of Child Development. Gesell stressed "maturation" as the most important aspect of development. He believed that babies develop by a biological timetable, so that their behavior must change as they age; thus children will behave in a predictable way. Predictable behaviors characteristic of a given age are called *developmental norms*. The developmental norm for a behavioral change—say, the disappearance of the reflex grasp—is the age at which this change occurs in most babies.

Gesell's test uses developmental norms to evaluate the baby's abilities in four categories: (1) motor ability, (2) adaptive behavior, (3) language, (4) personal-social behavior. For example, a baby would be evaluated for behavior considered appropriate for the average baby of her age. A developmental quotient can be calculated from the scores in a manner similar to that used to determine IQ in other tests. Basically, a developmental quotient is the ratio of the baby's chronological age (in weeks) to the average chronological age of all babies who perform similarly. If she passes the tests, she will be presented with increasingly harder tests that are designed for older babies, until she reaches a point at which she can't pass any. Testing also proceeds in the opposite direction: the baby is presented increasingly easier tests until she passes all those for an age group.

Table A-10 consists of examples from the Gesell test appropriate for the range of 4 to 56 weeks of age. Some of these examples—like the reflex behaviors—simply show the babies' physical maturity. Others test complex coordinated responses that are not merely based on physical growth, although their precise origins are unknown. The Gesell test produces reasonably reliable scores according to the customarily accepted standards, but it does not reliably predict later IQ scores (Thomas, 1967). The Gesell test is significant because it was the earliest infant test and because it established useful tests that have been borrowed liberally by other, more systematic, test constructors.

The Bayley Scales

Nancy Bayley and her colleagues developed the Bayley scales while they were measuring characteristics of a group of children living in Berkeley, California. The researchers first studied the children in the early 1930s and over the years gathered the information now known as the Berkeley Growth Study, which has told us much about the development of intelligence throughout the childhood years and into adulthood (Bayley and Oden, 1955). The original purpose of these scales for infants was to judge babies' developmental progress and thus predict their scores on conventional IQ tests that they would take later in childhood. But the relations between this and other infant scales and later IQ were never well established. However, when the Bayley scales are used in research, they do predict how infants will perform on some laboratory tasks (Lewis and McGurk, 1972). As you may recall from Chapter 1, low Bayley scores can warn us that babies need medical treatment because they are not developing properly. Today, the Bayley scales are used primarily for research and diagnostic screening.

The items on the Bayley scales are divided into three parts: the mental scale, the motor scale, and the behavior record. The mental scale measures the baby's perceptions, senses, memory, learning, problem solving, and ability to make sounds that resemble language. The motor scale assesses the baby's coordination. The behavior record, filled out by the examiner after the testing, measures the baby's reactions to both the impersonal and the social environments during the examination.

Table A-11 gives six examples from the mental and motor scales. Some, such as "stacking cubes" and "picking up a cube," are borrowed from the Gesell test. Notice that many motor skills are included in the mental scale.

Table A-10 Example Items from the Gesell Test

Age	Motor	Adaptive	Language	Personal-Social
4 weeks	Lifts head momentarily (when prone)	Diminishes activity when bell sounds	Throaty noises	Stares at examiner's face, diminishes activity
8 weeks	Head erect when held in sitting position	Follows moving ring with eyes through prolonged trajectory	Vowel sounds	Follows moving person with eyes
16 weeks	Hands clasp each other when baby supine	Looks at a rattle which she herself holds	Laughs aloud	Makes spontaneous social smile
28 weeks	Sustains large fraction of own weight when held by examiner	Transfers objects from one hand to the other	Polysyllabic vowel sounds	Reaches for and pats mirror image
36 weeks	Grasps small cube with thumb opposition	Hits one cube with another in play	Imitates sounds	Feeds self cracker
12 months	Walks if one hand held by examiner	Puts one cube in cup; tries to do so in narrow bottle but fails	Several simple words	Cooperates in dressing
18 months	Walks fast and runs stiffly	Imitates examiner's stroke with crayon on paper	Points to picture of objects named by examiner	Carries or hugs doll
24 months	Walks up and down stairs alone	Puts square piece into square slot (on test puzzle)	Uses sentences of three or more words	Imitates familiar domestic events

SOURCE: From *The First Five Years of Life: A Guide to the Study of the Preschool Child*, by Arnold Gesell et al. Copyright 1940 by Arnold Gesell. By permission of Harper & Row, Publishers, Inc.

Table A-11   Examples of Items on the Bayley Scales

Age	Mental Scale Items	Motor Scale Items
Newborn	Baby quiets when picked up.	Baby makes a postural adjustment when examiner puts her to his shoulder.
2 months	When examiner presents two objects above infant in crib, she glances back and forth from one to the other.	Baby holds her head steady when being carried about in vertical position.
5 months	Baby is observed to transfer object from one hand to the other during play.	When seated at a feeding-type table and presented with a sugar pill out of reach, baby attempts to pick it up.
8 months	When object in plain view of baby (on table) is covered by a tissue, baby removes tissue to recover toy.	Baby raises herself to a sitting position.
12 months	Baby imitates words when examiner says them.	When asked by the examiner, baby stands up from a position lying on her back on the floor.
16 months	Baby builds a tower with three small cubes after demonstration by examiner.	Baby stands on her left foot alone.

Items defined as "mental" require the babies to coordinate what they sense with moving their hands, moving both hands together, or using more than one skill.

The examiner rates the infants' behavior on the "Infant Behavior Record" scales listed in Table A-12. These scales take account of problems such as fatigue, irritability, distraction, and interruptions.

The ratings of behavior are summary scores assigned after a session ends. The mental and motor scales are administered systematically. The examiner begins with the baby's chronological age and proceeds to give items for younger ages until the baby passes all items at some age level. This is called the baby's *basal level.* The examiner then continues with successively more difficult items until the baby fails all items at some age level—the baby's *ceiling level.*

The Bayley mental scale consists of 163 items; the Bayley motor scale has 81. The examiner scores the baby as passing or failing each item, calculates a "total passed" score, and then consults statistical tables to interpret these

Table A-12   Infant Behavior Record Scales from the Bayley Scales

Name	Possible Points
Social orientation:	
Responsiveness to persons	9
Responsiveness to examiner	5
Responsiveness to mother	5
Cooperativeness	9
Fearfulness	9
Tension	9
General emotional tone	9
Object orientation:	
Responsiveness to objects	9
Plays imaginatively?	Yes, No
Persistent attachment to any specific toy?	Yes, No
Goal directedness	9
Attention span	9
Endurance	9
Activity level	9
Reactivity	9
Sensory areas of interest:	
Sights	9
Producing sounds	9
Listening to sounds	9
Banging hands or toys or throwing toys	9
Manipulating with hands	9
Body motion	9
Mouthing:	
Thumb or fingers	9
Pacifier	9
Toys	9

scores. The tables compare a baby's score to the averages of babies who took the test when it was developed.

In general, the test scores are reliable indicators of development: the baby's performance is tested consistently over many items, and two independent observers of the examination usually give identical scores. Although the reliability of the Bayley scales is high and certainly reaches an acceptable level in many studies, I should note that it is not as high as the reliability of IQ tests that are given to older children.

Are the Bayley scales and Gesell tests IQ tests? The *validity* of any psychological test is determined by its ability to measure accurately the trait it claims to measure. Thus, if the Bayley scales are to be considered IQ tests, we have to check their ability to predict what scores the children will get on IQ tests when they are older. In general, these scales do not predict later IQ scores (Thomas, 1970); consequently, it does not seem justified to call any of them an infant IQ test. The Bayley scales have, however, been successful in identifying children who, according to other evidence, are developing more slowly than average. So the Bayley scales scores of infants can validly serve as a basis for selecting infants to use in research studies and for assigning them to appropriate groups.

Other Infant Tests

Several other tests for infants are available. The Cattell Infant Intelligence Scale, intended to extend the Stanford-Binet test to younger ages, yields an IQ-like score that has reasonably good reliability (consistency and inter-tester agreement), but is not very successful at predicting IQ after age 3. The Griffiths Mental Development Scale, which is used in England, has several subscales that yield the useful descriptive details needed in clinical practice. The Griffiths and the Cattell tests both draw heavily on the Gesell test's item pool and therefore overlap with it somewhat in content. Graham has developed a device to screen newborns for various birth traumas, but it has not proven to be reliable. If you would like to read further about research with these tests and others as well, I recommend an excellent review article by Hoben Thomas (1967).

Summary of Infant Tests

As you can see, a number of tests can be used to evaluate the development of infants. Most of them contain entries that are taken from the Gesell test or are very similar to them, and therefore they share, at least in part, Gesell's rationale: that if babies are developing like other babies their age, they are maturing normally. Of the standardized tests, the Bayley Scales of Infant Development are the most extensively researched, and therefore they best enable clinicians to evaluate a baby's rate of development. Researchers are accumulating evidence on the relation between behavior on the Bayley scales and behavior in research situations. This evidence will probably help explain why individual babies react differently from one another to research situations.

5. Indicator Responses

In some kinds of research the investigator is interested in a behavior or mental experience that is not directly observable. For example, psychological processes such as attention, expectation, surprise, curiosity, and pleasure are not manifested directly in behavior. In studies of adult subjects, we can sometimes simply ask them to tell us about their perceptions. For example, we might show them a complex visual array of designs and ask them to describe what they see. When one adult begins to describe a red triangle, we infer that he is paying attention to the shape and color of one of the designs. In a similar fashion, we might use an adult's answer to "How happy are you about your current life?" as an indication of her feelings.

So quite conveniently, researchers can frequently use adults' verbal responses to indicate some less observable psychological process. This procedure is acceptable when the verbal response accurately reflects the process being studied. Thus, for adults, words can be *indicator responses*—reactions that indicate that an unobservable situation is occurring. But these convenient verbal responses are not available to researchers working with babies and thus other, more behavioral, responses are needed to indicate a baby's perceptions. In the remainder of this section, I will present five examples of indicator responses commonly used in research work with infants.

Examples of Indicator Responses Used with Infants

All of us who have suddenly noticed something interesting or have been surprised by the unexpected appearance of a friend know that our heart rate changes when we shift our attention or are startled. In infants past the newborn period, the momentary slowing of heart rate signals that they are aware of a new experience. Researchers use this change as evidence that babies are paying special attention to a new situation. We call the slowing of heart rate an indicator response because it indicates that the more subjective attention-paying process is going on. Heart-rate acceleration in these infants has been associated with potentially frightening stimuli such as sudden noises. Accordingly, researchers interpret it as an indication that the baby is afraid. However, newborn infants often have quicker heartbeats when they are in a new situation so the interpretation of a change of heart rate in infants is open to controversy (Woodcock, 1971).

But we are not going to resolve this controversy here. Instead, I simply note that many studies use heart-rate deceleration to indicate that infants past newborn age are paying attention and use heart-rate acceleration to indicate that the infants are afraid. But with newborns the meaning of these heart-rate changes is ambiguous, so some skepticism about what heart rate indicates in newborns would seem appropriate.

Another indicator response that researchers sometimes use to measure attention is the interruption of sucking behavior (e.g., Semb and Lipsitt, 1968). Infants who are sucking on their bottles or pacifiers will often cease to do so momentarily when a new situation (a novel stimulus) occurs. The researchers can use the interruption of sucking to determine whether a baby pays attention to various experimental stimuli. Like heart-rate changes, the interruption of sucking appears to be a highly variable and unstable response in newborns (Kaye, 1963, 1966). So anyone investigating attention and other subjective nonobservable responses should probably use more than one indicator response. Kagan has used this approach of "multiple indications" to advantage (Kagan, 1972) in his study of the responses infants give when they are paying attention.

A third indicator response is the degree of preference an infant shows for looking at one stimulus instead of another. Stimulus preference is used to study infant attention when infants have a limited number of objects at which to look. For example, an investigator puts an infant in a reclining chair inside a specially created chamber (like, for example, the Fantz looking chamber; see p. 53). Then, using a rear slide projector, he presents a slide show on the roof of the chamber. When the baby looks at a slide, a reflection of it appears on the surface of his eye. This reflection can be recorded by a human observer or by a camera. Either way, it is widely used to indicate visual attention.

An infant's expectations are also unobservable and subjective phenomena. Many studies of what infants understand require that we have some way to know what babies expect because of their experience with objects and events. For example, if I take an interesting toy from a baby girl and hide it from her under a cloth, will she expect it to remain there even though she can no longer see it? If she does expect it to remain, she might be startled or at least surprised to find it gone when I remove the cloth. If, on the other hand, she does not expect it to remain in the same place when she cannot see it, she might be startled or surprised to find it there. Therefore, researchers use a baby's reactions of surprise to indicate that the baby expected something else to happen.

Charlesworth has developed a rating procedure that observers can use to evaluate the degree of surprise that a baby reveals (Charlesworth, 1966). His procedure has been employed by several investigators in the study of infants' understanding of the qualities of objects (their *object concept*) (LeCompte and Gratch, 1972; Bower, 1972). Bower has also used heart-rate acceleration as an indicator of surprise. One outcome of using indicator responses was the modification of our understanding of how babies learn about the characteristics of objects as they develop. If we judge babies' interest in the things around them by seeing when they actively search for a lost object, we get the impression that they do not realize that objects are permanent until they are eight or nine months of age. However, when we consider their surprise to be a measure of their expectations about the coming and going of objects, we see that object permanence emerges in some preliminary form as early as two months after birth. You can now understand the central role that our methods play in determining the conclusions we reach.

6. *Studying the Relations Among Variables*

Thus far I have described the various procedures for obtaining data. The observational techniques and coding methods I have described ultimately result in qualitative or numerical scores for particular characteristics of each baby studied. Usually, researchers compile these scores with some specific purpose in mind. Often, they seek to discover how different characteristics relate to one another or to test some theory about an already established relation.

There are several research strategies for accomplishing these things. Although it is not the purpose of this book to discuss research methodology in detail, I will briefly survey them so that you can identify them when you read studies in which they are used.

The Experiment

What techniques are best to study particular behaviors? Although in everyday speech, we use *experiment* to refer to any test in which we are changing a situation to see what happens, a scientist uses the term more precisely. For a scientist, designing an experiment is controlling one facet of a situation to establish how it affects another facet. Suppose we want to test the folk wisdom that rocking will quiet a crying baby. Our first step is to separate the *variables* in the situation—in this instance, rocking and crying. A factor that supposedly causes another to occur is called the *independent variable.* In our example the independent variable is rocking, which influences our *dependent variable,* how much the baby cries.

The key to the experimental process is that the investigator can control the independent variable to see whether it does affect the dependent variable.

In our example the investigator can have some crying babies rocked and others left alone. We could arrange this in a hospital nursery by instructing nurses that all babies in cribs marked with a certain tag are to be rocked when they cry until, for example, 10 episodes of crying have occurred and that those without tags are not to be rocked. The measure of quieting might be simply the number of seconds that passed after the babies began crying until they stopped; low scores would indicate that they stopped quickly and high scores would indicate that they took much longer to stop. We could then see whether, on the average, the rocked babies quieted faster than those who were not.

There are variables other than rocking that affect how quickly a baby will quiet. An experimenter usually tries to insure that these other variables—such as temperature, time since feeding, and background noise—are kept the same for all babies or, at least, that on the average the two groups have equivalent experiences with respect to them. This is called *controlling extraneous variables,* and the success of the experiment often depends on how well this is accomplished. Sometimes experiments are carried out in private homes or noisy day-care centers where it is hard to control all the extraneous variables. If this is so, it may be hard to demonstrate a clear relation between the two variables that interest us. Nevertheless, we are conducting an *experiment* because in our investigation, we are controlling the independent variable and can assign subjects to groups in which they will only experience it if we choose for them to.

Correlational Strategies

Whenever we measure both variables in a relation but do not control either variable, we are using a *correlational strategy.* The problem discussed above in the context of the experiment could also be studied by the correlational strategy, but in this case, we would be observing a relation, not testing for cause and effect. If we interviewed mothers or observed mothers and newborns interacting, we could measure both the amount of rocking and how quickly the baby stopped crying. We would then look at the rocking and crying to estimate how closely the two variables are related. Basically, correlational statistics are employed when we know the degree of one variable and want to predict the degree of the second variable: if babies are rocked, how quickly do they become quiet?

The correlational strategy is used in a wide variety of settings. One reason is that it is sometimes undesirable to exert experimental control over a variable because we fear we will alter the situation until it no longer reflects the issues we want to study. Another reason to call on this strategy is that much research—especially with infants—is still in such early stages that we do not have firm hypotheses about cause and effect. A third reason is that it would be unethical to control some variables. For instance, it would be wrong to deliberately frighten babies severely, to expose them to an environment that might inhibit their cognitive development, or to impose a heavy burden of frustration on them. So we use a correlational strategy to investigate these variables.

Naturalistic Field Studies

A *naturalistic field study* is a correlational strategy that investigators commonly use with infants. The adjective "naturalistic" indicates that the observations are made in the baby's natural setting—usually the family home—in the course of normal, everyday events. The field study may employ any one of the observational systems described in Section 2 and any number of variables (within the limits of what observers can do reliably). Occasionally, investigators bring a special apparatus or toy to the study, which means that they are introducing some control over the situation. Whenever investigators control a variable but do this in "the field" (outside of the lab), they are conducting a *field experiment*.

The crucial distinction between the experimental and correlational strategies thus does not depend on where the observations are made or on the observational system used. Instead this distinction is made on the basis of whether the investigators control one (or more) of the variables. If they do control variables, they are conducting an experiment and the investigator-controlled variable is called the independent variable and the other is called the dependent variable. If they do not influence the two (or more) variables, the variables are equivalent in status and the study is correlational.

You should realize that no investigation in which an observer is observing from a subject's natural environment is completely free of investigator control. Whenever we go into someone's home, we are creating conditions that undoubtedly differ from those that would exist if we were not there. This fact implies a number of questions about methods that are too specialized and extensive for inclusion here. I simply want to note that intrusion does not really make the study an experiment. Instead, it is one of those extraneous variables whose influence is regulated by its being the same for all subjects.

7. *Age as a Variable*

As you probably know, developmental psychology is the branch of psychology concerned with changes in behavior and experience that occur as a human being ages. In this book we are specifically concerned with the many and dramatic changes that take place during infancy. Until recently, developmental psychology was concerned with simply *describing* the changes that accompany changes in age and did not attempt to explain these changes. Describing and classifying are important in the early stages of any new discipline because it cannot go further without a clear idea of the phenomena to be explained.

From the 1890s to the 1940s, the literature in the field was filled with charts and graphs showing how vocabulary, motor skills, memory skills, attention span, and many other characteristics differed in children of different ages. Some of these tables and charts appear in this book. When you examine them briefly, you can easily make the mistake of thinking that babies' other characteristics are all dependent variables that shift because of their age. But this impression is wrong. Age is merely a number that indicates how much time has elapsed since a person's birth. *The mere passage of time does not by itself cause any change.* Therefore developmental psychology does not study how age causes changes. Instead, it studies factors that bring about relations between age and psychological characteristics. Indeed "development" means change related to time or age in this context. Theories of development postulate mechanisms of change to account for the observed changes that occur with age. One type of research investigation tests the predictions of the theories about these mechanisms. Another type of research investigation charts how some characteristic changes with age and leaves the question of why the changes occur to be answered at a later date. Thus many investigations, including many cited in this book, just report the basic descriptive information that is the starting place of developmental psychology. In this section I discuss the various strategies for studying these changes in behavior that occur at certain ages.

How to Study Changes in Behavior Related to Age

The three common approaches to collecting data for charting age-related changes are cross-sectional, longitudinal, and cross-sequential.

Cross-Sectional Design. In the cross-sectional research plan, data are gathered about individuals of different age groups at the same time. Thus, for example, if I wanted to describe the development of very early language, I might select a cross section of age by observing ten 6-month-olds, ten 12-month-olds, and ten 18-month-olds. This design is represented in Table A-13 by the column headed "July 1979." In the month of July 1979, 10 subjects from each age in months 6, 12, and 18 are being observed. By comparing the language behavior of these three groups of babies we can get a rough idea of how language changes with age.

I say "rough idea" with good reason. The main disadvantage of the cross-sectional plan is that, in it, any comparison of two ages can only be made by studying two groups of babies. Suppose the 6-month-olds babble a lot whereas the 12-month-olds do not. We might conclude that between 6 and 12 months of age babies begin to develop more complex language to replace babbling. But it is also possible that the 10 babies who exhibit the babbling behavior have always done so whereas those who do not never will. This latter possibility may seem implausible to you but a cross-sectional design cannot rule it out. This is because the cross-sectional design allows age differences and group differences to become mixed together. Therefore

Table A-13 Designs for Measuring Change in Behavior in Relation to Age

Groups	Test Score July 1978	Test Score January 1979	Test Score July 1979	Test Score January 1980	Test Score July 1980
Cohort I Born January 1978 (n=10)	X	X	X		
Cohort II Born July 1978 (n=10)		X	X	X	
Cohort III Born January 1979 (n=10)			X	X	X

A longitudinal comparison: age and time varied, cohort constant.

A cross-sectional comparison: age and cohort varied, time of testing constant.

A cohort comparison: age constant, cohort and time of test varied.

we cannot tell to what extent the group differences are due to age and to what extent, to other things.

Despite this limitation the cross-sectional design is widely used because, by taking all measurements at once, it saves time. If you only want a quick, rough idea about how some behavior changes with age, you should use the cross-sectional design and save time. If a behavior changes little with age, it would be foolish to spend costly research efforts to discover the source of the changes. If, using the economical cross-sectional design, you discover that there are many age-related changes in a behavior, then the cautious approach would be to repeat the tests with a new sampling or to turn to a *longitudinal design,* which I will now explain.

Longitudinal Design.   In the longitudinal plan, a single group of subjects is observed again and again over some extended period of time. Thus, to study early language you could observe a group of babies at 6, 12, and 18 months of age for a total of three observations. In Table A-13 each row represents a separate longitudinal study with 10 subjects. The principal advantage of the longitudinal approach is that there are no group differences with which to contend because the same group of babies is used.

The main problem with the longitudinal approach is that it takes a long time to gather data to cover any lengthy developmental period. Results of a few pioneering longitudinal studies of personality development are the major information in the field about changes in personality over time (Bayley and Oden, 1955; Kagan and Moss, 1962; Terman, 1947). But this drawback does not really apply to infant development because many of the significant and exciting developmental sequences of infancy occur over a period of weeks, not years. Longitudinal following of a single sample over these weeks is really quite feasible and, in fact, it is often done.

But longitudinal studies cannot be used to predict how all of babies' characteristics will influence their personalities in later years. Traits that one might think should stay the same over the years may take radically different forms at different ages. For instance, if a baby girl has a very active disposition, she will move her body vigorously and enjoy crawling. As an adult, she might express that same energy in her thinking and perhaps might exhibit a general lack of patience. But she probably won't translate her desire to be active into direct physical movement as often as she did in babyhood. Some developmental theorists report that they have discovered adult characteristics that express earlier infant characteristics, but we have no way to test their assertions directly.

Cross-Sequential Design.   I have not mentioned one interesting cause of discrepancies that are found in age comparisons: sometimes findings vary because the subjects lived in different historical periods and thus had different experiences. Thus, in cross-sectional age comparisons, differences may be inherent in the groups, may be real age differences, or may arise from the fact that the groups grew up at times in which they experienced entirely different influences. Suppose that in January and February of 1975, a nationally televised and highly publicized series of television specials on infants emphasized the importance of giving them opportunities to look at, reach for, and grasp a variety of objects. Many parents might have been influenced to alter the environments of their infants to increase the amount of reaching they did, in hopes of speeding their progress at learning to reach. If they were, we could not be sure whether changes that occurred after the television shows were caused by some process inherently connected with age or, instead, were influenced by the shows. Using a longitudinal study we could not disqualify one of these two possible explanations. To satisfy our curiosity about whether the television show did influence our findings, we would have to use a *cross-sequential* design that would compare groups born on different dates that, for this reason, developed their reaching during different periods. In Table A-13, each row is a complete longitudinal study, each column of the table is a cross-sectional study covering some of the ages within the range being studied, and the diagonals of the table represent comparisons among groups of babies of a given age (say, 1-month-olds) that were born on different dates. Changes along the diagonal represent changes that are due to historical change but not age. For instance, if the hypothetical television show of January and February 1975 was truly influential, then the 1-month-olds observed in March and April of 1975 would differ from those who were observed earlier.

Researchers prefer to use the cross-sequential design to study how psychological characteristics relate to age because by this means they can separate group membership, age, and historical time—which they cannot do with the cross-sectional or longitudinal design. It is more expensive and time-consuming than the other alternatives, but the cross-sequential design is a more effective means by which to answer certain questions about infants.

8. Sampling

This book, like scientific research, makes generalizations that rest on the assumption that the babies who are studied accurately represent babies in general. Scientists continually face the problem of choosing a group of "average" subjects, a *sample*. Researchers usually try to discover basic facts that will hold true for some broader group of people known as the *population*. In this section I will discuss briefly some of the considerations that are involved in the sampling process and will use babies as examples.

Elementary Ideas of Sampling

Consider the statisticians' fantasy of a perfect sample. They first choose some large population of babies that a research team plans to study. This population might be as broad as "all human infants who are between one and two months of age," but more likely it would be "all urban infants born at tax-supported general hospitals," or "all babies whose mothers receive aid to families with dependent children," or even "all babies whose births were registered in a city newspaper during a given week." After they thus identify the population, statisticians choose an ideal sample. They select babies one by one at random from this defined population until a sample of the desired size is attained. When every baby in the population truly has a chance of inclusion in the sample equal to that of every other baby in the population, a sampling is said to be random. For example, our happy statisticians could write the name of every baby in a given population on a cardboard square, mix the squares in a huge urn, and then select one, continuing the process until they had as many subjects as they needed for the study.

Of course, statisticians' fantasies are not very much like what really goes on in research. In practice, investigators study babies whose mothers (or fathers or sitters) are able and willing to cooperate. They often study babies who are on the enrollment lists of an outpatient pediatric clinic, a private practice in pediatrics, or someone's caseload in social service. In these instances parents give their permission before the researchers start their programs, but those babies who are included in the final sample all have one characteristic in common: they all are part of the enrollment lists. Investigators also frequently obtain samples by telephoning every family to whom a baby was born in a certain hospital during a given span of time. Here the people in the sample share a different characteristic: all of them are willing to cooperate on the basis of such a call. Thus, most samples of babies studied in research are either a captive group—they are clientele of a particular service—or they are unusually well informed and cooperative about scientific activities.

This is not as bad from a scientific viewpoint as it might appear. The babies studied in any given piece of research represent some population. Most researchers in the behavioral sciences describe the socioeconomic and ethnic characteristics of the sample and also explain how they chose the sample. But researchers do not always tell how many families of potential subjects declined to cooperate or broke their appointments for one reason or another. Readers of the research literature are left to estimate what population is in fact being sampled by the investigators' procedures. In the next part, I discuss some factors that you should consider as you make these estimations.

Special Sampling Problems in Research with Babies

All of us who deal with babies know that their activities and attention spans are much more variable than those of older children and adults. Babies are also more surprised by a laboratory research environment than are older children because it is totally new for them. These considerations plague the infant researcher's daily professional life. Babies fall asleep just when the most exciting stimuli are being offered for their attention. They fuss and cry when put into infant seats or other contraptions devised by research technicians. They giggle and coo in delight over the shiny screws in the experimenter's glasses and ignore the shiny, brightly striped experimental stimulus.

It is delightfully reassuring that babies do all these individualistic and very human things. It helps keep scientists in line by reminding us that babies are people after all. It also challenges us to devise more creative ways of observing them that will be less disruptive. But their unpredictability does create a sampling problem, especially for experimental projects. Experimental projects end up having as their participants babies who are especially comfortable in the experimental environment, who stay awake for sufficiently long intervals of time, and who are more likely than average to pay attention to the main stimuli. Customarily, babies who fuss a lot or who fall asleep are sent home, or their data are taken but later abandoned.

Unfortunately, I have no solution to offer for these problems. However, here are some implications you can draw from what I've said about these sampling problems. First, you should recognize that much of the research literature on infants contains information about a certain type of baby—the adaptable, alert infant whose mother is favorably inclined toward research. Undoubtedly, these babies have many of the same characteristics as other types of babies who are not present, but equally undoubtedly, they have many characteristics that are fundamentally different.

A second implication follows: students of child development should try to bring unrepresented groups of babies into research samples. One way to do this is to devise more and better ways to obtain the observations we need in the regular environments of the babies. Another way is to insist that the experimenters be more patient: they should wait for babies to wake up or let them return on another day that is more convenient to the caregiver. Finally, researchers should study how research environments affect different babies. This work would help us to modify the research environments so that they would be less likely to cause unusual behavior.

Animal Infants as Subjects

A large and growing literature on the importance of early experience is made up largely of studies with animal subjects. Animals are used for ethical reasons: we would not want to subject human infants to environments with little stimulation, inadequate diet, or the lack of a stable caregiver. But to give babies the best care, we must know how infants are affected by the environment and people around them. Controlled experimentation involving the manipulation of factors in the animal infant's environment is a primary route to this crucial information. So we devise experiments where we control these factors in an animal infant's environment and thus learn vital information to help us with human babies. Harry Harlow's work with infant monkeys (Harlow, 1970) as well as that of others (see, for example, Lewis and Rosenblum, 1974) has given us valuable insights about the causes and treatment of depression.

But many people wonder whether we can accurately apply findings about animals' behavior to human babies. Those who favor doing research with animals argue that the basic processes of behavior—learning, perception, etc.—are similar at all levels of the evolutionary scale. Our human behavior differs only because it is more complicated. They point out that complex behaviors are built up out of simpler behaviors like those seen in animals. Those against animal research argue that the various species are fundamentally different and that findings from work with chimpanzees, cats, dogs, and rats cannot apply to humans. Still others argue a compromise position: species close to humankind, like other primates, can provide proper bases for generalization, but that "lower" animals cannot.

In my opinion, applying findings from animals to humans requires that the generalizations we make about humans based on animal studies must be consistent with findings from nonexperimental, correlational field studies and clinical work with humans. For example, the findings from Harlow's experiments with monkeys raised from birth without constant mothering has been compared with research and clinical work with humans who experienced early separation from their mothers. In this particular case the conclusions from both sources are remarkably consistent (Harlow, 1970), and thus one tends to trust Harlow's findings. On other occasions, when the conclusions are not consistent, the phenomenon under study might be fundamentally different in different species. In my view, it would surely be a mistake to ignore the vast source of information and new hypotheses represented by studies with nonhuman species. However, I do believe some skepticism might be healthy when we evaluate what such generalizations imply about human infants.

Informal Observations by Caregivers, Devoted Relatives, and Bystanders

Any caregiver of infants can verify that caregivers are not in a position to make detached, "objective" observations of their charges. Nor would this

enterprise be particularly useful, because the techniques of detached observation usually are intended to make generalizations that can be applied to
many babies, while caregivers are concerned with particular babies. By
carefully noting the details of babies' behavior, their caregivers become
more attuned to their individuality, to the current level of their knowledge,
and to what they are perceiving in the world around them.

It is useful for you as a caregiver occasionally to jot down some notes
describing behavior you have observed that seems to you to have psychological significance. One purpose of this book is to acquaint you with
behavior of "psychological significance." The anecdotal record is an approxi-
mate model of the brief behavior summary you can use. A spiral notebook—a handy object—keeps these notes in one place. This notebook can
then serve, along with photographs, as an interesting record of children's
infancies which will bring them and their families pleasure in the future.
The notebook can also be useful when you discuss the baby's development
with other caregivers and with the baby's physician.

A few guidelines may help you to make your notebook record as useful as
possible. First, like the research observer, the caregiver-observer should try
to distinguish behavior itself from interpretations he or she puts on the
behavior. Notes should reflect this separation. First the entries should describe behavior itself, as, for example: "She focused her eyes on the bracelet
I was holding, and she swiped toward it with her right hand." After an
incident has been described in terms of behavior, the observer can go back
over it and note a tentative interpretation such as "She wanted my bracelet
and attempted to reach out to get it." Second, a caregiver can profit from
trying to classify the baby's behavior into some sort of coding scheme such
as those described in Section 1. Although the results of this coding process
will not necessarily be used further, the process itself makes the observer
more aware of details and nuances in the baby's behavior which she or he
would otherwise overlook. Third, it is often enlightening to talk over one's
observations with a second person who also spends time with the baby.
When both people clarify their ideas about the baby, they understand each
other and the baby better. They also share a feeling of mutual responsibility
for the baby that is important for father and mother as well as for a professional caregiver.

Summary

Congratulations! You have just finished reviewing a difficult facet of scientific procedure: how to observe a situation in detail and accurately. When
you read the research about babies referred to in this book, you will be able
to evaluate the methods the investigators used when they (1) developed the

categories to list behavior, (2) recorded time, (3) quantified the episodes, and (4) coded the behavior into the appropriate category either immediately or afterward.

Also you can make your own narrative records if you want. You know the pitfalls and values of rating systems, which should summarize behavior accurately. You know how to determine whether the observers were reliable (and what to do if they were not).

You also know the purpose of clinical records. You now have facts to clear up your questions about the standardized infant test like the Bayley scales and Gesell's test.

The gap between the baby's experiences and the researchers' data sheet is bridged by indicator responses, which show, for example, when the baby is excited or drowsy.

You can now use "experiment" in its scientific sense: an investigation where a researcher influences an independent variable to establish its effect on the dependent variables in a situation. You can identify correlational studies where the researcher measures a relationship without changing any factors. You also have seen how developmental psychologists investigate age-related changes using longitudinal (one group over time) and cross-sectional (several groups at a single time) and cross-sequential (several groups studied at different times) studies.

You also are forewarned about the hazards of sampling: are the babies you are studying representative of all babies?

References

Chapter 1

Alexandrowiz, M. K. The effect of pain relieving drugs administered during labor and delivery on the behavior of the newborn: A review. *Merrill-Palmer Quarterly,* 1974, *20,* 121–140.

Apgar, V. A proposal for a new method of evaluation of the newborn infant. *Current Research in Anesthesia and Analgesia,* 1953, *32,* 260–267.

Apgar, V., and Beck, J. *Is my baby all right?* New York: Pocket Books, 1974.

Barrett, T. E., and Miller, L. K. The organization of non-nutritive sucking in the premature infant. *Journal of Experimental Child Psychology,* 1973, *16,* 472–483.

Beach, F. A.; Noble, R. G.; and Orndoff, R. K. Effects of a perinatal androgen treatment on responses of male rats to gonadal hormones in adulthood. *Journal of Comparative and Physiological Psychology,* 1969, *68,* 490–497.

Bench, J., and Parker, A. Hyper-responsivity to sounds in the short-gestation baby. *Developmental Medicine and Child Neurology,* 1971, *13,* 15–19.

Braine, M. D. S.; Heimer, C. B.; Wortis, H.; and Freedman, A. M. Factors associated with impairment of the early development of prematures. *Monographs of the Society for Research in Child Development,* 1967, *31* (4, Whole No. 106).

Cutler, R.; Heimer, C. B.; Wortis, H.; and Freedman, A. M. The effects of prenatal and neonatal complications on the development of premature children at age 2½ years. *Journal of Genetic Psychology,* 1965, *107,* 261–276.

Davids, A.; Holden, R. H.; and Gray, G. B. Maternal anxiety during pregnancy and adequacy of mother and child adjustment eight months following childbirth. *Child Development,* 1963, *34,* 993–1002.

Dennenberg, V. H., and Whimbley, A. E. Behavior of adult rats is modified by the experiences their mothers had as infants. *Science,* 1963, *142,* 1192–1193.

Dreyfus-Brisac, C. Organization of sleep in prematures: Implications for caregiving. In Lewis, M., and Rosenblum, L. A. (Eds.), *The effect of the infant on its caregiver.* New York: Wiley, 1974.

Drillien, G. M. *The growth and development of the prematurely born infant.* Baltimore: Williams and Wilkins, 1964 (summary).

Dubignon, J., and Campbell, D. Intraoral stimulation and sucking in the newborn. *Journal of Experimental Child Psychology.* 1968, 6, 154–166.

Dubignon, J., and Campbell, D. Sucking in the newborn during a feed. *Journal of Experimental Child Psychology,* 1969, 7, 282–298.

Eisenberg, R. B.; Coursin, D. B.; and Rupp, N. R. Habituation to an acoustic pattern as an index of differences among human neonates. *Journal of Auditory Research,* 1966, 6, 239–248.

Emde, R. N.; McCartney, R. D.; and Harmon, R. J. Neonatal smiling in REM states IV: Premature study. *Child Development,* 1971, 42, 1657–1661.

Engleson, G.; Rooth, G.; and Tornblom, M. A follow-up study of dysmature infants. *Archives of Disease in Childhood,* 1963, 38, 62–65.

Frank G., and Chase, J. Sleep rhythms in premature infants. *Psychophysiology,* 1968, 5, 227.

Goldie, L.; Svedson-Rhodes, U.; Easton, J; and Robertson, N. R. The development of innate sleep rhythms in short gestation infants. *Developmental Medicine and Child Neurology,* 1971, 13, 40–50.

Katz, V. Auditory stimulation and developmental behavior of the premature infant. *Nursing Research,* 1971, 20, 196–201.

Kornetsky, C. Psychoactive drugs in the immature organism. *Psychopharmacologia,* 1970, 17, 105–136.

Lehrman, D. S. Interaction of hormonal and experiential influences on development of behavior. In Bliss, E. L. (Ed.), *Roots of behavior.* New York: Harper, 1962.

Lewin, R. Nutrition and brain growth. In Lewin, R. (Ed.), *Child alive.* New York: Anchor, 1975.

Lubchenco, L. O.; Horner, F. A.; Reed, L. H.; Hix, I. E., Jr.; Metcalf, D.; Cohig, R.; Elliot, H. C.; and Bourg, M. Sequelae of premature birth. *American Journal of Diseases of Children,* 1963, 106, 101–115.

MacMahon, B., and Feldman, J. J. Infant mortality rates and socio-economic factors. National Center for Health Statistics, U.S. Public Health Service, 1972.

Mussen, P. H.; Conger, J. J.; and Kagan, J. *Child development and personality.* 4th ed. New York: Harper, 1974.

Ottinger, D. R., and Simmons, J. E. Behavior of human neonates and prenatal maternal anxiety. *Psychological Reports,* 1964, 14, 391–394.

Rice, R. D. Neurophysiological development in premature infants following stimulation. *Developmental Psychology,* 1977, 13, 69–76.

Rosenbaum, A. L.; Churchill, J. A.; Shakhashiri, Z. A.; and Moody, R. L. Neurophysiologic outcome of children whose mothers had protein uria during pregnancy: A report from the collaborative study of cerebral palsy. *Obstetrics and Gynecology,* 1969, 33, 118–123.

Rothschild, B. F. Incubator isolation as a possible contributing factor to the high incidence of emotional disturbance among prematurely born persons. *Journal of Genetic Psychology,* 1967, *110,* 287–304.

Scarr-Salapatek, S., and Williams, M. L. The effects of early stimulation on low-birth-weight infants. *Child Development,* 1973, *44,* 94–101.

Schulman, C. A. Effects of auditory stimulation on heart rate in premature infants as a function of level of arousal, probability of CNS damage, and conceptional age. *Developmental Psychobiology,* 1969, *2,* 172–183.

Smith, N.; Schwartz, J. R.; Mandell, W.; Silberstein, R. M.; Dalack, J. D.; and Sacks, S. Mothers' psychological reactions to premature and full-size newborns. *Archives of General Psychiatry,* 1969, *21,* 177–181.

Solkoff, N.; Taffe, S.; Weintraub, D.; and Blase, B. Effects of handling on the subsequent developments of premature infants. *Developmental Psychology,* 1969, *1,* 765–768.

Sontag, L. W.; Steele, W. G.; and Lewis, M. The fetal and maternal cardiac response to environmental stress. *Human Development,* 1969, *12,* 1–9.

Sterman, M. B., and Hoppenbrouwers, T. Development of a rest-activity cycle in the human fetus. *Psychophysiology,* 1968, *5,* 226.

Thompson, W. R. Influence of prenatal maternal anxiety on emotionality in young rats. *Science,* 1957, *125,* 698–699.

Werner, E. E., and Smith, R. S. *Kauai's children come of age.* Honolulu: University of Hawaii Press, 1977.

Wiener, G. Scholastic achievement at age 12–13 of prematurely born infants. *Journal of Special Education,* 1968, *2,* 273–250.

Wortis, H.; Heimer, C. B.; Braine, M.; Redlo, M.; and Rue, R. Growing up in Brooklyn: The early history of the premature child. *American Journal of Orthopsychiatry,* 1963, *33,* 535–539.

Zamenhof, S.; Van Marthens, E.; and Gravel, L. DNA (cell number) in neonatal brain: Second generation (F_2) alteration by maternal (F_0) dietary restriction. *Science,* 1971, *172,* 850–851.

Chapter 2

Anders, T. F., and Roffwarg, H. P. The relationship between infant and maternal sleep. *Psychophysiology,* 1968, *5,* 227–228.

Apgar, V. A proposal for a new method of evaluation of the newborn infant. *Current Research in Anesthesia and Analgesia,* 1953, *32,* 260–267.

Ashton, R. State and the auditory reactivity of the human neonate. *Journal of Experimental Child Psychology,* 1971a, *12,* 339–346.

Ashton, R. The effects of the environment upon state cycles in the human newborn. *Journal of Experimental Child Psychology,* 1971b, *12,* 1–9.

Bartoshuk, A. K. Human neonatal cardiac acceleration to sound: Habituation and dishabituation. *Perceptual and Motor Skills,* 1962a, *15,* 15–27.

Bartoshuk, A. K. Response decrement with repeated elicitation of human neonatal cardiac acceleration to sound. *Journal of Comparative and Physiological Psychology,* 1962b, *55,* 9–13.

Bartoshuk, A. K. Human neonatal cardiac responses to sound: A power function. *Psychonomic Science,* 1964, *1,* 151–152.

Bee, H. *The developing child.* New York: Harper, 1975.

Bell, S. M. The development of the concept of object as related to infant-mother attachment. *Child Development,* 1970, *41,* 292–311.

Bell, S. M., and Ainsworth, M. D. Infant crying and maternal responsiveness. *Child Development,* 1972, *43,* 1171–1190.

Bench, J. Some effects of audio-frequency stimulation on the crying baby. *Journal of Auditory Research,* 1969, *9,* 122–128.

Berg, W. K.; Adkinson, C. D.; and Strock, B. D. Duration and frequency of periods of alertness in neonates. *Developmental Psychology,* 1973, *9,* 434.

Bernal, J. F. Night waking in infants during the first 14 months. *Developmental Medicine and Child Neurology,* 1973, *15,* 760–769.

Boring, E. G. *A history of experimental psychology.* New York: The Century Co., 1929.

Bosack, T. N. Effects of fluid delivery on the sucking response of the human newborn. *Journal of Experimental Child Psychology,* 1973, *15,* 77–85.

Bower, T. G. R. The visual world of infants. *Scientific American,* 1966, *215,* 80–92.

Brackbill, Y. Continuous stimulation and arousal level in infants: Additive effects. *Proceedings, 78th Annual Convention, American Psychological Association,* 1970, *5,* 271–272.

Brackbill, Y. Continuous stimulation and arousal level in infancy: Effects of stimulus intensity and stress. *Child Development,* 1975, *46,* 364–369.

Bridger, W. H. Sensory habituation and discrimination in the human neonate. *American Journal of Psychiatry,* 1961, *117,* 991–996.

Brown, J. States in newborn infants. *Merrill-Palmer Quarterly,* 1964, *10,* 313–327.

Campos, J. J., and Brackbill, Y. Infant state: Relationship to heart rate, behavioral response and response decrement. *Developmental Psychobiology,* 1973, *6,* 9–19.

Clifton, R. K.; Meyers, W. J.; and Solomons, G. Methodological problems in conditioning the headturning response of newborn infants. *Journal of Experimental Child Psychology,* 1972, *13,* 29–42.

Clifton, R.; Siqueland, E. R.; and Lipsitt, L. P. Conditioned headturning in human newborns as a function of conditioned response requirements and states of wakefulness. *Journal of Experimental Child Psychology,* 1972, *13,* 43–57.

Connolly, K., and Stratton, P. An exploration of some parameters affecting classical conditioning in the neonate. *Child Development,* 1969, *40,* 431–444.

Crowell, D. H. Patterns of psychophysiological functioning in early infancy: A preliminary analysis with autonomic lability scores. *Merrill-Palmer Quarterly,* 1967, *13,* 37–53.

Dayton, G. D., Jr.; Jones, M. H.; Giu, P.; Rawson, R. H.; Steele, B.; and Rose, M. Developmental study of coordinated eye movements in the human infant: I-visual activity in the newborn human: a study based on induced auto-kinetic nystagmus recorded by electrooculography. *Archives of Ophthalmology,* 1964, *71,* 865–870.

Desor, J. A.; Maller, O.; and Turner, R. E. Taste in acceptance of sugars by human infants. *Journal of Comparative and Physiological Psychology,* 1973, *84,* 496–501.

Dubignon, J., and Campbell, D. Sucking in the newborn in three conditions: Non-nutritive, nutritive and a feed. *Journal of Experimental Child Psychology,* 1968, *6,* 335–350.

Dubignon, J., and Campbell, D. Sucking in the newborn during a feed. *Journal of Experimental Child Psychology,* 1969, *7,* 282–298.

Eisenberg, R. The organization of auditory behavior. *Journal of Speech and Hearing Research,* 1970, *13,* 461–464.

Elder, M. S. The effects of temperature and position on the sucking pressure of newborn infants. *Child Development,* 1970, *41,* 95–102.

Emde, R. N.; Harmon, R. J.; Metcalf, D.; Koenig, K. L.; and Wagonfeld, S. Stress and neonatal sleep. *Psychosomatic Medicine,* 1971, *33,* 491–497.

Emde, R. N., and Metcalf, D. R. Behavioral and EEG correlates of undifferentiated eye movement states in infancy. *Psychophysiology,* 1968, *5,* 227.

Engen, R.; Lipsitt, L. P.; and Kaye, H. Olfactory responses and adaptation in the human neonate. *Journal of Comparative and Physiological Psychology,* 1963, *56,* 73–77.

Engen, T.; Lipsitt, L. P.; and Peck, M. B. Ability of newborn infants to discriminate sapid substances. *Developmental Psychology,* 1974, *10,* 741–744.

Fantz, R. L. Pattern vision in newborn infants. *Science,* 1963, *140,* 296–297.

Feinberg, I., et al. EEG sleep patterns as a function of normal and pathological aging in man. *Journal of Psychiatric Research,* 1967, *5,* 107–144.

Field, H., et al. Responses of newborns to auditory stimulation. *Journal of Auditory Research,* 1967, *7,* 271–285.

Fisichelli, V. R.; Karelitz, S.; and Haber, A. The course of induced crying activity in the neonate. *Journal of Psychology,* 1969, *73,* 183–191.

Flavell, J. *The developmental psychology of Jean Piaget.* Princeton: Van Nostrand, 1963.

Formby, D. Maternal recognition of infant's cry. *Developmental Medicine and Child Neurology,* 1967, *9,* 293–298.

Freedman, D. G., and Freedman, N. C. Behavioral differences between Chinese-American and European-American newborns. *Nature,* 1969, *224,* 1227.

Friedman, S. Habituation and recovery of visual response in the alert human newborn. *Journal of Experimental Child Psychology,* 1972, *13,* 339–349.

Friedman, S.; Bruno, L. A.; and Vietze, P. Newborn habituation to visual stimuli: A sex difference in novelty detection. *Journal of Experimental Child Psychology,* 1974, *18,* 242–251.

Friedman, S., and Carpenter, G. C. Visual response decrement as a function of age of human newborn. *Child Development,* 1971, *42,* 1967–1973.

Friedman, S.; Carpenter, G. C.; and Nagy, A. N. Decrement and recovery of response to visual stimuli in the newborn human. *Proceedings, 78th Annual Convention, American Psychological Association,* 1970, *5,* 272–274.

Friedman, S.; Nagy, A. N.; and Carpenter, G. C. Newborn attention: Differential response decrement to visual stimuli. *Journal of Experimental Child Psychology,* 1970, *10,* 44–51.

Gaensbauer, T. J., and Emde, R. N. Wakefulness and feeding in human newborns. *Archives of General Psychiatry,* 1973, *28,* 894–897.

Greenman, G. W. Visual behavior of newborn infants. In Solnit, A. J., and Provence, S. A. (Eds.), *Modern perspectives in child development.* New York: Hallmark, 1963.

Haith, M. M. The response of the human newborn to visual movement. *Journal of Experimental Child Psychology,* 1966, *3,* 235–243.

Haynes, H.; White, B. L.; and Held, R. Visual accommodation in human infants. *Science,* 1965, *148,* 528–530.

Hess, E. H. Imprinting in birds. *Science,* 1964, *146,* 1128–1139.

Hilgard, E.; Atkinson, R. C.; and Atkinson, R. L. *Introduction to psychology.* New York: Harcourt Brace Jovanovich, 1975.

Hott, S. J.; Hott, C.; Lenard, H. G.; Bernvth, H. V.; and Montjewerff, W. J. Auditory responsivity in the human neonate. *Nature,* 1968, *218,* 888–890.

James, W. *The principles of psychology.* New York: Henry Holt, 1890.

Kagan, J. The determinants of attention in the infant. *American Scientist,* 1970, *58,* 298–306.

Kahn, E., and Fisher, C. Some correlates of rapid eye movement sleep in the normal aged male. *Journal of Nervous and Mental Disease,* 1969, *148,* 495–505.

Kales, A., et al. Measurements of all-night sleep in normal elderly persons: Effects of aging. *Journal of the American Geriatric Society,* 1967, *15,* 405–414.

Kaye, H. The effects of feeding and tonal stimulation on non-nutritive sucking in the human newborn. *Journal of Experimental Child Psychology,* 1966, *3,* 131–145.

Kaye, H., and Levin, G. R. Two attempts to demonstrate tonal suppression of non-nutritive sucking in neonates. *Perceptual and Motor Skills,* 1963, *17,* 521–522.

Kearsley, R. B. The newborn's response to auditory stimulation: A demonstration of orienting and defensive behavior. *Child Development,* 1973, *44,* 582–591.

Keen, R. E.; Chase, H. H.; and Graham, F. K. Twenty-four hour retention by neonates of an habituated heart rate response. *Psychonomic Science,* 1965, *2,* 265–266.

Kenn, R. Effects of auditory stimuli on sucking behavior in the human neonate. *Journal of Experimental Child Psychology,* 1964, *1,* 348–354.

Kobre, K. R., and Lipsitt, L. P. Negative contrast effect in newborns. *Journal of Experimental Child Psychology,* 1972, *14,* 81–91.

Korner, A. F. Visual alertness in neonates: Individual differences and their correlates. *Perceptual and Motor Skills,* 1970, *31,* 499–509.

Korner, A. F. Individual differences at birth: Implications for early experience and later development. *American Journal of Orthopsychiatry,* 1971, *41,* 608–619.

Korner, A. F. State as variable, as obstacle, and as mediator of stimulation in infant research. *Merrill-Palmer Quarterly,* 1972, *18,* 77–94.

Korner, A. F., and Benson, L. M. Association of two congenitally organized behavior patterns in the newborn: Hand-mouth coordination and looking. *Perceptual and Motor Skills,* 1972, *33,* 115–118.

Korner, A. F., and Grobstein, R. Visual alertness as related to soothing in neonates: Implications for maternal stimulation and early deprivation. *Child Development,* 1966, *37,* 867–876.

Korner, A. F., and Thoman, E. B. Visual alertness in neonates as evoked by maternal care. *Journal of Experimental Child Psychology,* 1970, *10,* 67–78.

Korner, A. F., and Thoman, E. B. The relative efficacy of contact and vestibular-proprioceptive stimulation in soothing neonates. *Child Development,* 1972, *43,* 443–453.

Kron, R. E. Instrumental conditioning of nutritive sucking behavior in the newborn. *Recent Advances in Biological Psychiatry,* 1966, *9,* 295–300.

Levin, G., and Kaye, H. Work decrement and rest recovery during non-nutritive sucking in the human neonate. *Journal of Experimental Child Psychology,* 1966, *3,* 146–154.

Lewis, M. State as an infant-environment interaction: An analysis of mother-infant interaction as a function of sex. *Merrill-Palmer Quarterly,* 1972, *18,* 95–121.

Lewis, M.; Bartels, B.; and Goldberg, S. State as a determinant of infants' heart rate response to stimulation. *Science,* 1967, *155,* 486–488.

Lewis, M.; Dodd, C.; and Harwitz, M. Cardiac responsivity to tactile stimulation in waking and sleeping infants. *Perceptual and Motor Skills,* 1969, *29,* 259–269.

Ling, D. Acoustic stimulus duration in relation to behavioral responses of newborn infants. *Journal of Speech and Hearing Research,* 1972, *15,* 567–571.

Lipsitt, L. P.; Engen, T.; and Kaye, H. Developmental changes in the olfactory threshold of the neonate. *Child Development,* 1963, *34,* 371–376.

Lipsitt, L. P., and Kaye, H. Conditioned sucking in the human newborn. *Psychonomic Science,* 1964, *1,* 29–30.

Lodge, A.; Armington, J. C.; Barnet, A. B.; Shanks, B. L.; and Newcomb, C. N. Newborn infants' electroretinograms and evoked electro-encephalographic responses to orange and white light. *Child Development,* 1969, *40,* 267–293.

Maccoby, E. E., and Jacklin, C. N. *The psychology of sex differences.* Stanford: Stanford University Press, 1974.

Minard, J.; Coleman, D.; Williams, G.; and Ingledne, E. Cumulative REM of three to five day olds: Effects of normal external noise and maturation. *Psychophysiology,* 1968, *5,* 232.

Moreau, T.; Birch, H. G.; and Turkewitz, G. Ease of habituation to repeated auditory and somesthetic stimulation in the human newborn. *Journal of Experimental Child Psychology,* 1970, *9,* 193–207.

Moss, H. A. Sex, age, and state as determinants of mother-infant interaction. *Merrill-Palmer Quarterly,* 1967, *13,* 19–36.

Munsinger, H., and Kessen, W. Uncertainty, structure, and preference. *Psychological Monographs,* 1964, *78,* whole no. 586.

Nagera, H. Sleep and its disturbances approached developmentally. *Psychoanalytic Study of the Child,* 1966, *21,* 393–447.

Papousek, H. Conditioning during early postnatal development. In Brackbill, Y., and Thompson, G. G. (Eds.), *Behavior in infancy and early childhood.* New York: Free Press, 1967.

Papousek, H., and Bernstein, P. The functions of conditioning stimulation in human neonates and infants. In Ambrose, A. (Ed.), *Stimulation in early infancy.* New York: Academic Press, 1969.

Porges, S. W.; Stamps, L. E.; and Walters, G. F. Heart rate variability and newborn heart rate responses to illumination changes. *Developmental Psychology,* 1974, *10,* 507–513.

Prechtl, H. F. R. Neurological sequelae of prenatal and paranatal complications. In Foss, B. M. (Ed.), *Determinants of infant behavior,* Vol. 1. New York: Wiley, 1961.

Rice, R. D. Neurophysiological development in premature infants following stimulation. *Developmental Psychology,* 1977, *13,* 69–76.

Richmond, J. B.; Lipton, E. L.; and Steinschneider, A. Autonomic function in the neonate: V. Individual homeostatic capacity in cardiac response. *Psychosomatic Medicine,* 1962, *24,* 66–74.

Roffwarg, H. P.; Muzio, J. N.; and Dement, W. Ontogenetic development of the human sleep-dream cycle. *Science,* 1966, *152,* 604–619.

Rovee, C. K. Psychophysical scaling of olfactory response to the gliphatic alcohols in human neonates. *Journal of Experimental Child Psychology,* 1969, *7,* 245–254.

Salapatek, P. Visual scanning of geometric figures by the human newborn. *Journal of Comparative and Physiological Psychology,* 1968, *66,* 247–258.

Sameroff, A. J. Changes in the nonnutrituve sucking response to stimulation during infancy. *Journal of Experimental Child Psychology,* 1970, *10,* 112–119.

Sameroff, A. J. Can conditioned responses be established in the newborn infant? *Developmental Psychology,* 1971, *5,* 1–12.

Sameroff, A. J. Learning and adaptation in infancy: A comparison of models. In Reese, H. W. (Ed.), *Advances in child development and behavior,* Vol. 7. New York: Academic Press, 1972.

Sameroff, A. J. Nonnutritive sucking in newborns under visual and auditory stimulation. *Child Development,* 1967, *38,* 443–452.

Schacter, J.; Williams, T. A.; Khachaturian, F.; Tobin, R. K.; and Kerr, J. Heart rate responses to auditory clicks in neonates. *Psychophysiology,* 1971, *8,* 163–179.

Self, P. A.; Horowitz, F. D.; and Paden, L. Y. Olfaction in newborn infants. *Developmental Psychology,* 1972, *7,* 349–363.

Semb, G., and Lipsitt, L. P. The effects of acoustic stimulation on cessation and initiation of non-nutritive sucking in neonates. *Journal of Experimental Child Psychology,* 1968, *6,* 585–597.

Siqueland, E. R. Reinforcement patterns and extinction in human newborns. *Journal of Experimental Child Psychology,* 1968, *6,* 431–442.

Sostek, A. M.; Sameroff, A. J.; and Sostek, A. J. Evidence for the unconditionability of the Babkin reflex in newborns. *Child Development,* 1972, *43,* 509–519.

Spitz, R. A.; Emde, R. N.; and Metcalf, D. R. Further prototypes of ego formation: A working paper from a research project on early development. *Psychoanalytic Study of the Child,* 1970, *25,* 417–441.

Spock, B. *Baby and child care.* New York: Pocket Books, 1976.

Steinschneider, A. Sound intensity and respiratory responses in the neonate. *Psychosomatic Medicine,* 1968, *30,* 534–541.

Steinschneider, A.; Lipton, E.; and Richmond, J. B. Auditory sensitivity in the infant: Effect of intensity on cardiac and motor responsivity. *Child Development,* 1966, *37,* 233–252.

Stone, L. J., and Church, J. *Childhood and adolescence.* New York: Random House, 1973.

Stratton, P. M. The use of heart rate for the study of habituation in the neonate. *Psychophysiology,* 1970, *7,* 44–56.

Thomas, H. Unfolding the baby's mind: The infant's selection of visual stimuli. *Psychological Review,* 1973, *80,* 468–488.

Tulkin, S. R., and Kagan, J. Mother-child interaction: Social class differences in the first year of life. *Proceedings, 78th Annual Convention, American Psychological Association,* 1970, *5,* 261–262.

Turkewitz, G.; Birch, H. G.; and Cooper, K. K. Patterns of response to different auditory stimuli in the human newborn. *Developmental Medicine and Child Neurology,* 1972a, *14,* 487–491.

Turkewitz, G.; Birch, H. G.; and Cooper, K. K. Responsiveness to simple and complex auditory stimuli in the human newborn. *Developmental Psychobiology,* 1972b, *5,* 7–19.

Turkewitz, G., et al. Effect of intensity of auditory stimulation on directional eye movements in the human neonate. *Animal Behavior,* 1966, *14,* 93–101 (abstract).

Vietze, P.; Friedman, S.; and Foster, M. Non-contingent stimulation: Effects of stimulus movement on infants' visual and motor behavior. *Perceptual and Motor Skills,* 1974, *38,* 331–336.

Webster, R. L.; Steinhardt, M. H.; and Senter, M. G. Changes in infants' vocalizations as a function of differential acoustic stimulation. *Developmental Psychology,* 1972, *7,* 39–43.

Wolff, P. H. The causes, controls, and organization of behavior in the neonate. *Psychological Issues,* 1966, *5* (1), 7–11.

Wolff, P. H. Stereotypic behavior and development. *Canadian Psychologist,* 1968, *9,* 474–484.

Chapter 3

Abrahamson, D.; Brackbill, Y.; Carpenter, R.; and Fitzgerald, H. E. Interaction of stimulus and response in infant conditioning. *Psychosomatic Medicine,* 1970, *32,* 319–325.

Aronson, E., and Rosenbloom, S. Space perception in early infancy: Perception within a common auditory-visual space. *Science,* 1971, *172,* 1161–1163.

Ball, W., and Tronick, E. Infant responses to impending collision: Optical and real. *Science,* 1971, *171,* 818–820.

Bandura, A. *Social learning theory.* Englewood Cliffs, N.J.: Prentice-Hall, 1977.

Banikiotes, F. G.; Montgomery, A. A.; and Banikiotes, P. G. Male and female auditory reinforcement of infant vocalizations. *Developmental Psychology,* 1972, *6,* 476–481.

Barrett, T. E., and Miller, L. K. The organization of non-nutritive sucking in the premature infant. *Journal of Experimental Child Psychology,* 1973, *16,* 472–483.

Barten, S., and Ronch, J. Continuity in the development of visual behavior in young infants. *Child Development,* 1971, *42,* 1566–1571.

Bell, S. M., and Ainsworth, M. D. Infant crying and maternal responsiveness. *Child Development,* 1972, *43,* 1171–1190.

Berg, W. K. Habituation and dishabituation of cardiac responses in 4-month-old, alert infants. *Journal of Experimental Child Psychology,* 1972, *14,* 92–107.

Berg, W. K. Cardiac orienting responses of 6- and 16-week-old infants. *Journal of Experimental Child Psychology,* 1974, *17,* 303–312.

Bloom, K. Eye contact as a setting event for infant learning. *Journal of Experimental Child Psychology,* 1974, *17,* 258–263.

Bond, E. K. Perception of form by the human infant. *Psychological Bulletin,* 1972, *77,* 225–245.

Bower, T. G. R. Stimulus variables determining space perception in infants. *Science,* 1965a, *149,* 88–89.

Bower, T. G. R. The determinants of perceptual unity in infancy. *Psychonomic Science,* 1965b, *3,* 323–324.

Bower, T. G. R. *Development in infancy.* San Francisco: W. H. Freeman and Company, 1974.

Bower, T. G. R., and Paterson, J. G. Stages in the development of the object concept. *Cognition,* 1972, *1,* 45–55.

Bowlby, J. *Attachment and loss,* Vol. 1: *Attachment.* New York: Basic Books, 1969.

Brackbill, Y. Developmental studies of classical conditioning. *Proceedings, 75th Annual Convention, American Psychological Association,* 1967, *2,* 155–156.

Brackbill, Y. Continuous stimulation reduces arousal level: Stability of the effect over time. *Child Development,* 1973, *44,* 43–46.

Brennan, W.; Ames, E. W.; and Moore, R. W. Age differences in infants' attention and patterns of different complexities. *Science,* 1966, *151,* 354–356.

Bronson, G. The postnatal growth of visual capacity. *Child Development,* 1974, *45,* 873–890.

Brossard, L. M., and Goiń-DeCarie, T. G. A comparative reinforcing effect of eight stimulations on the smiling response of infants. *Journal of Child Psychology, Child Psychiatry and Allied Disciplines,* 1968, *9,* 51–59.

Brotsky, S. J., and Kagan, J. Stability of the orienting reflex in infants to auditory and visual stimuli as indexed by cardiac deceleration. *Child Development,* 1971, *42,* 2066–2070.

Brown, C. J. The effects of preference for visual complexity or habituation of visual fixation in infants. *Child Development,* 1974, *45,* 1166–1169.

Brown, J. States in newborn infants. *Merrill-Palmer Quarterly,* 1964, *10,* 313–327.

Cairns, R. *Social development: The origins and plasticity of interchanges.* San Francisco: W. H. Freeman and Company, 1979.

Campos, J. J.; Langer, A.; and Krowitz, A. Cardiac responses on the visual cliff in prelocomotor human infants. *Science,* 1970, *170,* 196–197.

Caron, A. J.; Caron, R. F.; Caldwell, R. C.; and Weiss, S. J. Infant perception of the structural properties of the face. *Developmental Psychology,* 1973, *9,* 385–399.

Caron, R. F.; Caron, A. J.; and Caldwell, R. C. Satiation of visual reinforcement in young infants. *Developmental Psychology,* 1971, *5,* 279–289.

Carpenter, G. C. Visual regard of moving and stationary faces in early infancy. *Merrill-Palmer Quarterly,* 1974, *20,* 181–194.

Charlesworth, W. R. Persistence of orienting and attending behavior in infants as a function of stimulus-locus uncertainty. *Child Development,* 1966, *37,* 473–491.

Clifton, R. K., and Meyers, W. J. The heart-rate response of four-month-old infants to auditory stimuli. *Journal of Experimental Child Psychology,* 1969, *7,* 122–135.

Cohen, L. B. Attention-getting and attention-holding processes of infant visual preferences. *Child Development,* 1972, *43,* 869–879.

Cohen, L. B. A two process model of infant visual attention. *Merrill-Palmer Quarterly,* 1973, *19,* 157–180.

Cohen, L. B.; DeLoache, J. S.; and Rissman, M. W. The effect of stimulus complexity on infant visual attention and habituation. *Child Development,* 1975, *46,* 611–617.

Collins, D.; Kessen, W.; and Haith, M. Note on an attempt to replicate a relation between stimulus unpredictability and infant attention. *Journal of Experimental Child Psychology,* 1972, *13,* 1–8.

Cornell, E. H. Infants' discrimination of photographs of faces following redundant presentations. *Journal of Experimental Child Psychology,* 1974, *18,* 98–106.

Cornell, E. H., and Strauss, M. S. Infants' responsiveness to compounds of habituated visual stimuli. *Developmental Psychology,* 1973, *9,* 73–78.

Eimas, P. D.; Siqueland, E. R.; Jusczyk, P.; and Vigorito, J. Speech perception in infants. *Science,* 1971, *171,* 303–306.

Erikson, Erik. *Childhood and society.* New York: Norton, 1950.

Etzel, B. C., and Gewirtz, J. L. Experimental modification of caretaker-maintained high-rate operant crying in a 6- and a 20-week old infant (Infans tyrannotearus): Extinction of crying with reinforcement of eye contact and smiling. *Journal of Experimental Child Psychology,* 1967, *5,* 303–317.

Fagan, J. F., III. Infant recognition memory: Studies in forgetting. *Child Development,* 1977, *48,* 68–78.

Fantz, R. L. Visual perception from birth as shown by pattern selectivity. *Annals of the New York Academy of Sciences,* 1965, *118,* 793–814.

Fantz, R. L., and Fagan, J. F., III. Visual attention to size and number of pattern details by term and preterm infants during the first six months. *Child Development,* 1975, *46,* 3–18.

Fantz, R. L., and Miranda, S. B. Newborn infant attention to form of contour. *Child Development,* 1975, *46,* 224–228.

Fenson, L.; Sapper, V.; and Minner, D. C. Attention and manipulative play in the one-year-old child. *Child Development,* 1974, *45,* 757–764.

Fitzgerald, H. E. Autonomic pupillary reflex activity during early infancy and its relation to social and nonsocial visual stimuli. *Journal of Experimental Child Psychology,* 1968, *6,* 470–482.

Fitzgerald, H. E.; Lintz, L. M.; Brackbill, Y.; and Adams, G. Time perception and conditioning an autonomic response in human infants. *Perceptual and Motor Skills,* 1967, *24,* 479–486.

Fitzgerald, H. E., and Porges, S. W. Infant conditioning and learning research. *Merrill-Palmer Quarterly,* 1971, *17,* 79–117.

Foster, M; Vietze, P.; and Friedman, S. Visual attention to non-contingent and contingent stimuli in early infancy. *Proceedings, 81st Annual Convention, American Psychological Association,* 1973, *8,* 93–94.

Giacoman, S. L. Hunger and motor restraint on arousal and visual attention in the infant. *Child Development,* 1971, *42,* 605–614.

Gibson, E. J. *Principles of perceptual learning and development.* New York: Appleton-Century-Crofts, 1969.

Gibson, E. J., and Walk, R. D. The visual cliff. *Scientific American,* 1960, *202,* 64–71.

Gratch, G. A study of the relative dominance of vision and touch in six-month-old infants. *Child Development,* 1972, *43,* 615-623.

Greenberg, D. J. Accelerating visual complexity levels in the human infant. *Child Development,* 1971, *42,* 905–918.

Greenberg, D. J., and Blue, S. F. Visual complexity in infancy: Contour or numerosity? *Child Development,* 1975, *46,* 357–363.

Greenberg, D. J., and O'Donnell, W. J. Infancy and the optimal level of stimulation. *Child Development,* 1972, *43,* 639–645.

Greenberg, D. J.; O'Donnell, W. J.; and Crawford, D. Complexity levels, habituation, and individual differences in early infancy. *Child Development,* 1973, *44,* 569–574.

Greenberg, D. J., and Weizmann, F. The measurement of visual attention in infants: A comparison of two methodologies. *Journal of Experimental Child Psychology,* 1971, *11,* 234–243.

Haith, M. M. Visual scanning in infants. Paper read at the regional meeting of the Society for Research in Child Development, Clark University, March 1968.

Harlow, H. The development of learning in the rhesus monkey. *American Scientist,* 1959, *47,* 459–479.

Haugan, G. M., and McIntire, R. W. Comparisons of vocal imitation, tactile stimulation, and food as reinforcers for infant vocalizations. *Developmental Psychology,* 1972, *6,* 201–209.

Hershenson, M., Munsinger, H.; and Kessen, W. Preferences for shapes of intermediate variability in the newborn human. *Science,* 1965, *147,* 630–631.

Hillman, D., and Bruner, J. S. Infant sucking in response to variations in schedules of feeding reinforcement. *Journal of Experimental Child Psychology,* 1972, *13,* 240–247.

Horowitz, A. B. Habituation and memory: Infant cardiac responses to familiar and discrepant auditory stimuli. *Child Development,* 1972, *43,* 43–53.

Horowitz, F. D. (Ed.). Visual attention, auditory stimulation, and language discrimination in young infants. *Monographs of the Society for Research in Child Development,* 1974, *39* (5 and 6).

Hunt, J. M. Attentional preference and experience: I. Introduction. *Journal of Genetic Psychology,* 1970, *117,* 99–107.

Hutt, C. Effects of stimulus novelty on manipulatory exploration in an infant. *Journal of Child Psychology, Child Psychiatry and Allied Disciplines,* 1967, *8,* 241–247.

Jones-Molfese, V. J. Individual differences in neonatal preferences for planometric and stereometric visual patterns. *Child Development,* 1972, *43,* 1289–1296.

Kach, T. Conditioned orienting reactions in two-month-old infants. *British Journal of Psychology,* 1967, *58,* 105–110.

Kagan, J. On the meaning of behavior: Illustrations from the infant. *Child Development,* 1969, *40,* 1121–1134.

Kagan, J. The determinants of attention in the infant. *American Scientist,* 1970, *58,* 298–306.

Kagan, J. Discrepancy, temperament, and infant distress. In Lewis, M., and Rosenblum, L. A. (Eds.), *The origins of fear.* New York: Wiley, 1974.

Kalnins, I. V., and Bruner, J. S. The coordination of visual observation and instrumental behavior in early infancy. *Perception,* 1973, *2,* 307–314.

Karmel, B. Z. Complexity, amounts of contour, and visually dependent behavior in hooded rats, domestic chicks, and human infants. *Journal of Comparative and Physiological Psychology,* 1969a, *69,* 649–657.

Karmel, B. Z. The effect of age, complexity, and amount of contour on pattern preferences in human infants. *Journal of Experimental Child Psychology,* 1969b, *7,* 339–354.

Karmel, B. Z. Contour effects and pattern preferences in infants: A reply to Greenberg and O'Donnell (1972). *Child Development,* 1974, *45,* 196–199.

Karmel, B. Z.; Hoffmann, R. F.; and Fegy, M. J. Processing of contour information by human infants evidenced by pattern-dependent evoked potentials. *Child Development,* 1974, *45,* 39–48.

Koch, J. Conditional orienting reactions in two-month-old infants. *British Journal of Psychology,* 1967, *58,* 105–110.

Lang, A. Perceptual behavior of 8- to 10-week-old human infants. *Psychonomic Science,* 1966, *4,* 203–204.

Lester, B. Cardiac habituation of the orienting response to an auditory signal in infants of varying nutritional status. *Developmental Psychology,* 1975, *11,* 432–442.

Leuba, C., and Friedlander, B. Z. Effects of controlled audio-visual reinforcement on infants' manipulative play in the home. *Journal of Experimental Child Psychology,* 1968, *6,* 87–99.

Levison, C. A., and Levison, P. K. Operant conditioning of head turning for visual reinforcement in three-month-old infants. *Psychonomic Science,* 1967, *8,* 529–530.

Lewis, M.; Bartels, B.; Campbell, H.; and Goldberg, S. Individual differences in attention: The relation between infants' condition at birth and attention distribution within the first year. *American Journal of Diseases of Children,* 1967, *113,* 461–465.

Lewis, M., and Goldberg, S. Habituation differences to tactile stimulation for waking and sleeping infants. *Psychophysiology,* 1968, *4,* 498–499.

Lewis, M., and Johnson, N. What's thrown out with the bath water: A baby? *Child Development,* 1971, *42,* 1053–1055.

Lewis, M.; Kagan, J.; Campbell, H.; and Kalafat, J. The cardiac response as a correlate of attention in infants. *Child Development,* 1966, *37,* 63–71.

Lipsitt, L. P.; Engen, T.; and Kaye, H. Developmental changes in the olfactory threshold of the neonate. *Child Development,* 1963, *34,* 371–376.

Lipsitt, L. P.; Pederson, L. J.; and DeLucia, C. A. Conjugate reinforcement of operant responding in infants. *Psychonomic Science,* 1966, *4,* 67–68.

McCall, R. B. Smiling and vocalization in infants as indices of perceptual-cognitive processes. *Merrill-Palmer Quarterly,* 1972, *18,* 341–347.

McCall, R. B. Encoding and retrieval of perceptual memories after long-term familiarization and the infant's response to discrepancy. *Developmental Psychology,* 1973, *9,* 310–318.

McGurk, H. The role of object orientation in infant perception. *Journal of Experimental Child Psychology,* 1970, *9,* 363–373.

McGurk, H. Infant discrimination of orientation. *Journal of Experimental Child Psychology,* 1972, *14,* 151–164.

McKenzie, B., and Day, R. H. Operant learning of visual pattern discrimination in young infants. *Journal of Experimental Child Psychology,* 1971, *11,* 45–53.

McKinnon, C.; Koepke, J. E.; and Apland, R. The effect of social reinforcement on the performance of 1-year-old children. *Psychonomic Science,* 1971, *23,* 313–315.

Melson, W. H., and McCall, R. B. Attentional responses of five-month-old girls to discrepant auditory stimuli. *Child Development,* 1970, *41,* 1159–1171.

Mendel, M. I. Infant responses to recorded sounds. *Journal of Speech and Hearing Research,* 1968, *11,* 811–816.

Mendelson, M. J., and Haith, M. M. The relation between non-nutritive sucking and visual information processing in the human newborn. *Child Development,* 1975, *46,* 1025–1026.

Meyers, W. J., and Cantor, G. N. Infants' observing and heart period responses as related to novelty of visual stimuli. *Psychonomic Science,* 1966, *5,* 239–240.

Meyers, W. J., and Cantor, G. N. Observing and cardiac responses of human infants to visual stimuli. *Journal of Experimental Child Psychology,* 1967, *5,* 16–25.

Millar, W. S. A study of operant conditioning under delayed reinforcement in early infancy. *Monographs of the Society for Research in Child Development,* 1972, *37,* 1–44.

Millar, W. S., and Schaffer, H. R. Visual-manipulative response strategies in infant operant conditioning with spatially displaced feedback. *British Journal of Psychology,* 1973, *64,* 545–552.

Miller, D. J. Visual habituation in the human infant. *Child Development,* 1972, *43,* 481–493.

Miller, D. J.; Cohen, L. B.; and Hill, K. T. A methodological investigation of Piaget's theory of object concept development in the sensory-motor period. *Journal of Experimental Child Psychology,* 1970, *9,* 59-85.

Miller, D. J.; Turnure, C.; and Cohen, L. B. Habituation of visual fixations in human infants in a retroactive paradigm. *Proceedings, 78th Annual Convention, American Psychological Association,* 1970, *5,* 277–278.

Miranda, S. B. Visual abilities and pattern preferences of premature infants and full-term neonates. *Journal of Experimental Child Psychology,* 1970, *10,* 189–205.

Miranda, S. B., and Fantz, R. L. Visual preferences of Down's syndrome and normal infants. *Child Development,* 1973, *44,* 555–561.

Mischel, W. *Introduction to personality.* New York: Holt, Rinehart and Winston, 1976.

Moffitt, A. R. Stimulus complexity as a determinant of visual attention in infants. *Journal of Experimental Child Psychology,* 1969, *8,* 173–179.

Moffitt, A. R. Consonant cue perception by twenty- to twenty-four-week-old infants. *Child Development,* 1971, *42,* 717–731.

Moffitt, A. R. Intensity discrimination and cardiac reaction in young infants. *Developmental Psychology,* 1973, *8,* 357–359.

Morse, P. A. The discrimination of speech and nonspeech stimuli in early infancy. *Journal of Experimental Child Psychology,* 1972, *14,* 477–492.

Moss, H. A., and Robson, K. S. The relation between the amount of time infants spend at various states and the development of visual behavior. *Child Development,* 1970, *41,* 509–517.

Mussen, P. H.; Conger, J. J.; and Kagan, J. *Child development and personality.* 4th ed. New York: Harper, 1974.

Nelson, K., and Kessen, W. Visual scanning by human newborns: Responses to complete triangle, to sides only, and to corners only. *Proceedings, 77th Annual Convention, American Psychological Association,* 1969, *4,* 273–274.

Pancratz, C. N., and Cohen, L. B. Recovery of habituation in infants. *Journal of Experimental Child Psychology,* 1970, *9,* 208–216.

Perry, M. H. Infant wariness and stimulus discrepancy. *Journal of Experimental Child Psychology,* 1973, *16,* 377–387.

Piaget, J. *Play, dreams and limitation in childhood.* London: Heinemann, 1961.

Porges, S. W.; Arnold, W. R.; and Forbes, E. J. Heart rate variability: An index of attentional responsivity in human newborns. *Developmental Psychology,* 1973, *8,* 85–92.

Porges, S. W.; Stamps, L. E.; and Walters, G. F. Heart rate variability and newborn heart rate responses to illumination changes. *Developmental Psychology,* 1974, *10,* 507–513.

Ramey, C. T.; Hieger, L,; and Klisz, D. Synchronous reinforcement of vocal responses in failure-to-thrive infants. *Child Development,* 1972, *43,* 1449–1455.

Ramey, C. T., and Ourth, L. L. Delayed reinforcement and vocalization rates of infants. *Child Development,* 1971, *42,* 291–297.

Ross, H. S.; Rheingold, H. L.; and Eckerman, C. O. Approach and exploration of a novel alternative by 12-month-old infants. *Journal of Experimental Child Psychology,* 1972, *13,* 85–93.

Ross, H. S. The influence of novelty and complexity on exploratory behavior in 12-month-old infants. *Journal of Experimental Child Psychology,* 1974, *17,* 436–451.

Ruff, H. A., and Birch, H. G. Infant visual fixation: The effect of concentricity, curvilinearity, and number of directions. *Journal of Experimental Child Psychology,* 1974, *17,* 460–473.

Ruff, H. A., and Turkewitz, G. Developmental changes in the effectiveness of stimulus intensity on infant visual attention. *Developmental Psychology,* 1975, *11,* 705–710.

Salapatek, P. Visual scanning of geometric figures by the human newborn. *Journal of Comparative and Physiological Psychology,* 1968, *66,* 247–258.

Salapatek, P. The visual investigation of geometric pattern by the one- and two-month-old infant. Paper presented at meetings of the American Association for the Advancement of Science, Boston, December 1969.

Salapatek, P., and Kessen, W. Visual scanning of triangles by the human newborn. *Journal of Experimental Child Psychology,* 1966, *3,* 155–167.

Sameroff, A. J. Respiration and sucking as components of the orienting reaction in newborns. *Psychophysiology,* 1970, *7,* 213–222.

Sameroff, A. J.; Cashmore, T. F.; and Dykes, A. C. Heart rate deceleration during visual fixation in human newborns. *Developmental Psychology,* 1973, *8,* 117–119.

Schaffer, H. R., and Perry, M. H. Perceptual-motor behavior in infancy as a function of age and stimulus familiarity. *British Journal of Psychology,* 1969, *60,* 1–9.

Schaffer, H. R., and Perry, M. H. The effects of short-term familiarization on infants' perceptual-motor co-ordination in a simultaneous discrimination situation. *British Journal of Psychology,* 1970, 61, 559–569.

Schwartz, A. N.; Campos, J. J.; and Baisel, E. J. The visual cliff: Cardiac and behavioral responses on the deep and shallow sides at five and nine months of age. *Journal of Experimental Child Psychology,* 1973, *15,* 86–99.

Sheppard, W. C. Operant control of infant vocal and motor behavior. *Journal of Experimental Child Psychology,* 1969, *7,* 36–51.

Shultz, T. R., and Zigler, E. Emotional concomitants of visual mastery in infants: The effects of stimulus movement on smiling and vocalizing. *Journal of Experimental Child Psychology,* 1970, *10,* 390–402.

Silverstein, A. Secondary reinforcement in infants. *Journal of Experimental Child Psychology,* 1972, *13,* 138–144.

Silverstein, A., and Lipsitt, L. P. The role of instrumental responding and contiguity of stimuli in the development of infant secondary reinforcement. *Journal of Experimental Child Psychology,* 1974, *17,* 322–331.

Simmons, M. W. Operant discrimination learning in human infants. *Child Development,* 1964, *35,* 737–748.

Siqueland, E. R. Operant conditioning of head turning in four-month-old infants. *Psychonomic Science,* 1964, *1,* 223–224.

Siqueland, E. R. Further development in infant learning. Paper presented at the 19th International Congress of Psychology, London, July 1969.

Siqueland, E. R., and DeLucia, C. A. Visual reinforcement of nonnutritive sucking in human infants. *Science,* 1969, *165,* 1144–1146.

Sostek, A. M., and Anders, T. F. Effects of varying laboratory conditions on behavioral state organization in two- and eight-week-old infants. *Child Development,* 1975, *46,* 871–878.

Spears, W. C. Assessment of visual preference and discrimination in the four-month-old infant. *Journal of Comparative and Physiological Psychology,* 1964, *57,* 381–238.

Spears, W. C. Visual preference in the four-month-old infant. *Psychonomic Science,* 1966, *4,* 237–238.

Stechler, G. A longitudinal follow-up of neonatal apnea. *Child Development,* 1964, *35,* 333–348.

Stechler, G.; Bradford, S.; and Levy, H. Attention in the newborn: Effect on mobility and skin potential. *Science,* 1966, *151,* 1247–1248.

Thomas, H. Visual-fixation responses of infants to stimuli of varying complexity. *Child Development,* 1965, *36,* 629–638.

Thomas, H. Some problems of studies concerned with evaluating the predictive validity of infant tests. *Journal of Child Psychology, Child Psychiatry and Allied Disciplines,* 1967, *8,* 197–205.

Thomas, H. Unfolding the baby's mind: The infant's selection of visual stimuli. *Psychological Review,* 1973, *80,* 468–488.

Todd, G. A., and Palmer, B. Social reinforcement of infant babbling. *Child Development,* 1968, *39,* 591–596.

Trehub, S. E. Infants' sensitivity to vowel and tonal contrasts. *Developmental Psychology,* 1973, *9,* 91–96.

Uzgiris, I. C. Patterns of vocal and gestural imitation in infants. Paper presented at the first symposium of the International Society for the Study of Behavioral Development, University of Nijmegen, Netherlands, July 1971. In abbreviated form in Monks, F., and Hartup, W. (Eds.), *Proceedings of the symposium on genetic and social influences on psychological development: Methodological approaches and research results.* Basel: Karger, 1972.

Vietze, P.; Friedman, S.; and Foster, M. Non-contingent stimulation: Effects of stimulus movement on infants' visual and motor behavior. *Perceptual and Motor Skills,* 1974, *38,* 331–336.

Walk, R. D. Monocular compared to binocular depth perception in human infants. *Science,* 1968, *162,* 473–475.

Walk, R. D., and Dodge, S. H. Visual depth perception of a 10-month-old monocular human infant. *Science,* 1962, *137,* 529-530.

Watson, J. S. Perception of object orientation in infants. *Merrill-Palmer Quarterly,* 1966, *12,* 73–94.

Watson, J. S. Operant fixation in visual preference behavior of infants. *Psychonomic Science,* 1968, *12,* 241–242.

Watson, J. S. Operant conditioning of visual fixation in infants under visual and auditory reinforcement. *Developmental Psychology,* 1969, *1,* 508–516.

Watson, J. S. Smiling, cooing, and "The Game." *Merrill-Palmer Quarterly,* 1973, *18,* 323–339.

Watson, J. S., and Danielson, G. An attempt to shape bidimensional attention in 24-month-old infants. *Journal of Experimental Child Psychology,* 1969, *7,* 467–478.

Watson, J. S., and Ramey, C. T. Reactions to response-contingent stimulation in early infancy. *Merrill-Palmer Quarterly,* 1972, *18,* 219–227.

Weisberg, P. Social and non-social conditioning of infant vocalization. *Child Development,* 1963, *34,* 377–388.

Weisberg, P. Operant procedures for the establishment of stimulus control in two-year-old infants. *Journal of Experimental Child Psychology,* 1969, *7,* 81–95.

Weizmann, F.; Cohen, L. B.; and Pratt, R. J. Novelty, familiarity, and the development of infant attention. *Developmental Psychology,* 1971, *4,* 149–154.

Wetherford, M. J., and Cohen, L. B. Developmental changes in infant visual preferences for novelty and familiarity. *Child Development,* 1973, *44,* 416–424.

Wilcox, B. M., and Clayton, F. L. Infant visual fixation on motion pictures of the human face. *Journal of Experimental Child Psychology,* 1968, *6,* 22–32.

Wolff, P. H. The development of attention in young infants. *Annals of the New York Academy of Sciences,* 1965, *118,* 815–830.

Yarrow, L.; Rubenstein, J. L.; and Pederson, F. A. *Infant and environment: Early cognitive and motivational development.* New York: Wiley, 1975.

Zelazo, P. R., and Komer, M. J. Infant smiling to nonsocial stimuli and the recognition hypothesis. *Child Development,* 1971, *42,* 1327–1339.

Chapter 4

Ainsworth, M. D. S. *Infancy in Uganda: Infant care and the growth of love.* Baltimore: Johns Hopkins Press, 1967.

Andre-Thomas, U., and Dargassies, St. A. *Etudes neurologiques sur le nouveau-nel et le jeune nourrison.* Paris: Masson, 1952. Cited in Bower, T. G. R., *Development in infancy.* San Francisco: W. H. Freeman and Company, 1974, p. 143.

Arajarui, T.; Keinanen, T.; and Thuneberg, C. Aspects of development of small prematurely born infants. *Psychiatria Fennica, 1973, 189,* 202 (abstract).

Barrett-Goldfarb, M. S., and Whitehurst, G. J. Infant vocalizations as a function of parental voice selection. *Developmental Psychology, 1973, 8,* 273–276.

Bayley, N. Comparisons of mental and motor test scores for ages 1–15 months by sex, birth order, race, geographical location, and education of parents. *Child Development, 1965, 36,* 379–412.

Bayley, N. Behavioral correlates of mental growth: Birth to thirty-six years. *American Psychologist, 1968, 23,* 1–17.

Beckwith, L. Relationships between infants' vocalizations and their mothers' behaviors. *Merrill-Palmer Quarterly, 1971, 17,* 211–226.

Bell, S. M. The development of the concept of object as related to infant-mother attachment. *Child Development, 1970, 41,* 292–311.

Belmore, N. F.; Kewley-Port, D.; Mobley, R. L.; and Goodman, V. E. The development of auditory feedback monitoring: Delayed auditory feedback studies on the vocalizations of children aged six months to 19 months. *Journal of Speech and Hearing Research, 1973, 16,* 709–720.

Bower, T. G. R. *Development in infancy.* San Francisco: W. H. Freeman and Company, 1974.

Bradley, R. H., and Caldwell, B. M. Early home environment and changes in mental test performance in children six to thirty-six months. *Developmental Psychology, 1976, 12,* 93–97.

Brazelton, T. B. Implications of infant development among the Mayan Indians of Mexico. *Human Development, 1972, 15,* 90–111.

Brockman, L. M., and Ricciuti, H. N. Severe protein-calorie malnutrition and cognitive development in infancy and early childhood. *Developmental Psychology, 1971, 4,* 312–319.

Brodbeck, A. J., and Irwin, O. C. The speech behavior of infants without families. *Child Development, 1946, 17,* 145–156.

Bruner, J. S. Organization of early skilled action. *Child Development, 1973, 44,* 1–11.

Butterworth, G. Object identity in infancy: The interaction of spatial location codes in determining search errors. *Child Development, 1975, 46,* 866–870.

Cabak, V., and Najdanvic, R. Effect of undernutrition in early life on physical and mental development. *Archives of Disease in Childhood, 1965, 40,* 532–534.

Collard, R. R. Exploratory and play behaviors of infants reared in an institution and in lower and middle-class homes. *Child Development, 1971, 42,* 1003–1015.

Condon, W. S., and Sander, L. W. Neonate movement is synchronized with adult speech: Interactional participation and language acquisition. *Science,* 1974, *183,* 99–101.

Dale, P. *Language development.* New York: Holt, Rinehart and Winston, 1976.

Davenport, R. K.; Rogers, C. M.; and Rombaugh, D. M. Long-term cognitive deficits in chimpanzees associated with early impoverished rearing. *Developmental Psychology,* 1974, *9,* 343–347.

DeHirsch, K.; Jansky, J.; and Langford, W. S. Comparisons between prematurely born and maturely born children at three age levels. *American Journal of Orthopsychiatry,* 1966, *36,* 616–628.

Dotty, D. Infant speech perception: Report of a conference held at the University of Minnesota June 20–22, 1972. *Human Development,* 1974, *17,* 74–80.

Drillien, C. M. School disposal and performance for children of different birthweight born 1953–1960. *Archives of Disease in Childhood,* 1969, *44,* 562–570.

Ehrlich, C. H.; Shapiro, E.; Kimball, B. D.; and Huttner, M. Communication skills in five-year-old children with high-risk neonatal histories. *Journal of Speech and Hearing Research,* 1973, *16,* 522–529.

Elardo, R.; Bradley, R.; and Caldwell, B. M. The relation of infants' home environments to mental test performance from six to thirty-six months: A longitudinal analysis. *Child Development,* 1975, *46,* 71–76.

Elardo, R.; Bradley, R.; and Caldwell, B. M. A longitudinal study of infants' home environments to language development at age three. *Child Development,* 1977, *48,* 595–603.

Elias, M. F., and Samonds, K. W. Exploratory behavior of cobus monkeys after having been reared in partial isolation. *Child Development,* 1973, *44,* 218–220.

Escalona, S. *The roots of individuality: Normal patterns of development in infancy.* Chicago: Aldine, 1968.

Escalona, S., and Moriarty, A. Prediction of school age intelligence from infant tests. *Child Development,* 1961, *32,* 597–605.

Evans, W. F., and Gratch, G. The stage IV error in Piaget's theory of object concept development: Difficulties in object conceptualizations or spatial localization? *Child Development,* 1972, *43,* 688–682.

Fagan, J. F. Memory in the infant. *Journal of Experimental Child Psychology,* 1970, *9,* 217–226.

Fagan, J. F. Infants' recognition memory for a series of visual stimuli. *Journal of Experimental Child Psychology,* 1971, *11,* 244–250.

Fagan, J. F. Infants' recognition memory for faces. *Journal of Experimental Child Psychology,* 1972, *14,* 453–476.

Fenson, C.; Kagan, J.; Kearsley, R. B.; and Zelazo, P. R. The developmental progression of manipulative play in the first two years. *Child Development,* 1976, *47,* 232–236.

Field, J. An adjustment of reaching behavior to object distance in early infancy. *Child Development,* 1976, *47,* 304–308.

Forgays, D. G., and Read, J. M. Crucial periods for free-environmental experience in the rat. *Journal of Comparative and Physiological Psychology,* 1962, *55,* 816–818.

Fraiberg, S. Libidinal object constancy and mental representation. *Psychoanalytic Study of the Child,* 1969, *24,* 9–47.

Friedlander, B. Z. Receptive language development in infancy. *Merrill-Palmer Quarterly,* 1970, *16,* 7–51.

Gesell, A., and Ames, L. B. Early evidence of individuality in the human infant. *Scientific Monthly,* 1937, *45,* 217–255.

Gesell, A.; Thompson, H.; and Amatwda, C. S. *The psychology of early growth.* New York: Macmillan, 1938.

Ginsburg, H. J., and Wong, D. L. Enhancement of hidden object search in six-month-old infants presented with a continuously sounding hidden object. *Developmental Psychology,* 1973, *9,* 142.

Goiń-DeCarie, T. G. *Intelligence and affectivity in early childhood.* New York: International Universities Press, 1965.

Golden, M., and Birns, B. Social class and cognitive development in infancy. *Merrill-Palmer Quarterly,* 1975, *21,* 183–195.

Golden, M., and Birns, B. Social class and infant intelligence. In Lewis, M. (Ed.), *The origins of intelligence.* New York: Plenum, 1976.

Graham, F. K.; Ernhart, C. B.; Thurston, D.; and Craft, M. Development three years after perinatal anoxia and other potentially damaging newborn experiences. *Psychological Monographs,* 1962, *76,* whole no. 522.

Granthan-McGregor, S. M., and Bach, E. H. Gross motor development in Jamaican infants. *Developmental Medicine and Child Neurology,* 1971, *13,* 79–87.

Gratch, G.; Appel, K. J.; Evans, W. F.; LeCompte, G. K.; and Wright, N. K. Piaget's Stage IV object concept error: Evidence of forgetting or object conception? *Child Development,* 1974, *45,* 71–77.

Gratch, G., and Landers, W. F. Stage IV of Piaget's theory of infants' object concepts: A longitudinal study. *Child Development,* 1971, *42,* 359–372.

Harlow, H. The development of learning in the rhesus monkey. *American Scientist,* 1959, *47,* 459–479.

Harlow, H. F. Early social deprivation and later behavior in the monkey. In Abrams, A.; Garner, H. H.; and Toman, J. E. P. (Eds.), *Unfinished tasks in the behavioral sciences.* Baltimore: Williams and Wilkins, 1964.

Harris, P. L. Perseverative errors in search by young infants. *Child Development,* 1973, *44,* 28–33.

Hursh, D. E., and Sherman, J. A. The effects of parent-presented models and praise on the vocal behavior of their children. *Journal of Experimental Child Psychology,* 1973, *15,* 328–339.

Ireton, H.; Thwing, E.; and Gravem, H. Infant mental development and neurological status, family socio-economic status, and intelligence at age four. *Child Development,* 1970, *41,* 937–945.

Jaffe, J.; Stern, D. N.; and Peery, J. C. "Conversational" coupling of gaze behavior in prelinguistic human development. *Journal of Psycholinguistic Research,* 1973, *2,* 321–329.

Jones, S. J., and Moss, H. A. Age, state, and maternal behavior associated with infant vocalizations. *Child Development,* 1971, *42,* 1039–1051.

Kagan, J. On the meaning of behavior: Illustrations from the infant. *Child Development,* 1969, *40,* 1121–1134.

Kallen, D. J. Nutrition and society. *Journal of the American Medical Association,* 1971, *215,* 94–100.

King, W. L., and Seegmiller, B. Performance of 14- to 22-month-old black firstborn male infants on two tests of cognitive development: The Bayley Scales and the Infant Psychological Development Scale. *Developmental Psychology,* 1973, *8,* 317–326.

Kohen-Raz, R. Mental and motor development of kibbutz, institutionalized, and home-reared infants in Israel. *Child Development,* 1968, *39,* 489–504.

Kopp, C. B., and Shaperman, J. Cognitive development in the absence of object manipulation during infancy. *Developmental Psychology,* 1973, *9,* 430.

Kopp, C. B.; Sigman, M.; and Parmelee, A. H. Ordinality and sensory-motor series. *Child Development,* 1973, *44,* 821–823.

Kramer, J. A.; Hill, K. T.; and Cohen, L. B. Infants' development of object permanence: A refined methodology and new evidence for Piaget's hypothesized ordinality. *Child Development,* 1975, *46,* 146–155.

Kramer, Y., and Rosenblum, L. A. Responses to "frustration" in one-year-old infants. *Psychosomatic Medicine,* 1970, *32,* 243–257.

Landers, W. F. Effects of differential experience on infants' performance in a Piagetian Stage IV object-concept task. *Developmental Psychology,* 1971, *5,* 48–54.

Langmeier, J., and Matejcek, Z. Mental development of children in families and in infants' homes. *Social Science and Medicine,* 1970, *4,* 569–577.

Lenneberg, E. H.; Rebelsky, F. G.; and Nichols, I. A. The vocalizations of infants born to deaf and hearing parents. *Human Development,* 1965, *8,* 23–27.

Lewis, M. Infant intelligence tests: Their use and misuse. *Human Development,* 1973, *16,* 108–118.

Lewis, M., and McGurk, H. Evaluation of infant intelligence: Infant intelligence scores—true or false? *Science,* 1978, *178,* 1174–1177.

Lewis, M., and Wilson, C. D. Infant development in lower-class American families. *Human Development,* 1972, *15,* 112–127.

Maccoby, E. E., and Jacklin, C. N. *The psychology of sex differences.* Stanford: Stanford University Press, 1974.

Mallard, A. R., and Daniloff, R. G. Glottal cues for parent judgment of emotional aspects of infant vocalizations. *Journal of Speech and Hearing Research,* 1973, *16,* 592–596.

Matheny, A. P. Twins: Concordance for Piagetian equivalent items derived from the Bayley Mental Test. *Developmental Psychology,* 1975, *11,* 224–227.

McCall, R. B.; Hogarty, P. S.; and Hurlburt, N. Transitions in infant sensorimotor development and the prediction of childhood IQ. *American Psychologist,* 1972, *27,* 728–748.

McKeown, T. Prenatal and early postnatal influences on measured intelligence. *British Medical Journal,* 1970, *3,* 63–67.

Meier, G. W.; Bunch, M. E.; Nolan, C. Y.; and Scheidler, C. H. Anoxia, behavioral development, and learning ability: A comparative experimental approach. *Psychological Monographs,* 1960, *74,* No. 1.

Miller, D. J.; Turnure, C.; and Cohen, L. B. Habituation of visual fixations in human infants in a retroactive inhibition paradigm. *Proceedings, 78th Annual Convention, American Psychological Association,* 1970, *5,* 277–278.

Minton, C. Sex differences in generality and continuity of verbal responsivity. *Proceedings, 77th Annual Convention, American Psychological Association,* 1969, *4,* 263–264.

Moore, T. Language and intelligence: A longitudinal study of the first eight years. *Human Development,* 1967, *10,* 88–106.

Morse, P. A. The discrimination of speech and nonspeech stimuli in early infancy. *Dissertation Abstracts International,* 1972, *32,* 7349.

Nelson, K. E. Infants' short-term progress toward one component of object permanence. *Merrill-Palmer Quarterly,* 1974, *20,* 3–8.

Nichols, P. L., and Broman, S. H. Familial resemblance in infant mental development. *Developmental Psychology,* 1974, *10,* 442–446.

Paraskevopoulos, J., and Hunt, J. McV. Object construction and imitation under differing conditions of rearing. *Journal of Genetic Psychology,* 1971, *119,* 301–321.

Phillips, J. R. Formal characteristics of speech which mothers address to their young children. *Dissertation Abstracts International,* 1971, *31,* 4369–4370.

Piaget, J. *The construction of reality in the child.* New York: Basic Books, 1954 (reprint of earlier edition).

Piaget, J. *The origin of intelligence in the child.* New York: Norton, 1963 (reprint of earlier edition).

Piaget, J. Time perception in children. In Fraser, J. T. (Ed.), *The voices of time.* New York: Braziller, 1966.

Provence, S., and Lipton, R. C. *Infants in institutions: A comparison of their develop-*

ment with family reared infants during the first year of life. New York: International Universities Press, 1962.

Ramey, T. T.; Campbell, F. A.; and Nicholson, J. E. The predictive power of the Bayley Scales of Infant Development and the Stanford-Binet Intelligence Test in a relatively constant environment. *Child Development,* 1973, *44,* 790–795.

Rheingold, H.; Gewirtz, J. L.; and Ross, H. W. Social conditioning of vocalizations in the infant. *Journal of Comparative and Physiological Psychology,* 1959, *52,* 68–73.

Rice, R. D. Neurophysiological development in premature infants following stimulation. *Developmental Psychology,* 1977, *13,* 69–76.

Richardson, S. A.; Birch, H. G.; Grabie, E.; and Yoder, K. The behavior of children in school who were severely malnourished in the first two years of life. *Journal of Health and Social Behavior,* 1972, *13,* 276–284.

Richardson, S. A.; Birch, H. G.; and Hertzig, M. E. School performance of children who were severely malnourished in infancy. *American Journal of Mental Deficiency,* 1973, *77,* 623–632.

Roberts, G. C., and Black, K. N. The effect of naming and object permanence on toy preferences. *Child Development,* 1972, *43,* 858–868.

Robinson, H. B., and Robinson, N. M. Longitudinal development of very young children in a comprehensive day care program: The first two years. *Child Development,* 1971, *42,* 1673–1683.

Roe, K. V. A longitudinal study of infant vocalizations. *Dissertation Abstracts International,* 1969, *29,* 3472.

Rosenzweig, M. R. Environmental complexity, cerebral change, and behavior. *American Psychologist,* 1966, *21,* 321–332.

Routh, D. K. Conditioning of vocal response differentiation in infants. *Developmental Psychology,* 1969, *1,* 219–226.

Rutter, M. *Maternal deprivation reassessed.* Harmondswood, Middlesex, England: Penguin, 1972.

Rutter, M., and Mittler, P. Environmental influences on language development. In Rutter, M., and Martin, J. A. M. (Eds.), *Young children with delayed speech.* London: Heinemann, 1972.

Sackett, G.P. Exploratory behavior of Rhesus monkeys as a function of rearing experiences and sex. *Developmental Psychology,* 1972, *6,* 260–270.

Salk, L., and Kramer, R. *How to raise a human being: A parents' guide to emotional health from infancy through adolescence.* New York: Random House, 1969.

Scarr, S. Effects of birth weight on later intelligence. *Social Biology,* 1969, *16,* 249–256.

Scarr, S., and Salapatek, S. Genetics and the development of intelligence. In Horowitz, F. D. (Ed.), *Review of child development research,* Vol. 4. Chicago: University of Chicago Press, 1975.

Schank, R. C. The role of memory in language processing. In Cofer, C. (Ed.), *The structure of human memory*. San Francisco: W. H. Freeman and Company, 1976.

Schwartz, S. Effect of neonatal cortical lesions and early environmental factors on adult rat behavior. *Journal of Comparative and Physiological Psychology*, 1964, *57*, 72–77.

Skinner, B. F. *Verbal behavior*. New York: Appleton-Century-Crofts, 1957.

Smith, C. J. Mass action and early environment in the rat. *Journal of Comparative and Physiological Psychology*, 1959, *52*, 154–156.

Spock, B. *Baby and child care*. New York: Pocket Books, 1976.

Stedman, D. J., and Eichorn, D. H. A comparison of the growth and development of institutionalized and home-reared mongoloids during infancy and early childhood. *American Journal of Mental Deficiency*, 1964, *69*, 391–401.

Taylor, A. Institutionalized infants' concept formation ability. *American Journal of Orthopsychiatry*, 1968, *38*, 110–115.

Thomas, A., and Chess, S. *Temperament and development*. New York: Brunner-Mazel, 1977.

Tizard, B.; Cooperman, O.; and Tizard, S. Environmental effects on language development: A study of young children in long-stay residential nurseries. *Child Development*, 1972, *43*, 337–358.

Tomlinson-Keasey, C. Conditioning of infant vocalizations in the home environment. *Journal of Genetic Psychology*, 1972, *120*, 75–82.

Uzgiris, I. C. Patterns of cognitive development in infancy. *Merrill-Palmer Quarterly*, 1973, *19*, 181–204.

Uzgiris, I. C. Organization of sensorimotor intelligence. In Lewis, M. (Ed.), *Origins of intelligence*. New York: Wiley, 1976.

Uzgiris, I. C., and Hunt, J. McV. *Assessment in infancy*. Urbana: University of Illinois Press, 1975.

Wachs, T. D. Relation of infants' performance on Piaget scales between twelve and twenty-four months and their Stanford-Binet. Performance at thirty-one months. *Child Development*, 1975, *46*, 929–935.

Wachs, T. D.; Uzgiris, I. C.; and Hunt, J. M. Cognitive development in infants of different age levels and from different environmental backgrounds: An explanatory investigation. *Merrill-Palmer Quarterly*, 1971, *17*, 283–317.

Walters, C. E. Comparative development of Negro and white infants. *Journal of Genetic Psychology*, 1967, *110*, 243–251.

Warren, N., and Parkin, J. M. A neurological and behavioral comparison of African and European newborns in Uganda. *Child Development*, 1974, *45*, 966–971.

Wasz-Hockert, O.; Patanent, T.; Vuorenkoski, V.; Valanne, E.; and Michelsson, K. Effect of training on ability to identify preverbal vocalizations. *Developmental Medicine and Child Neurology*, 1964, *6*, 393–396.

Webb, R. A.; Massar, B.; and Nadolny, T. Information and strategy in the young child's search for hidden objects. *Child Development,* 1972, *43,* 91–104.

Webster, R. L. Selective suppression of infants' vocal responses by classes of phonemic stimulation. *Developmental Psychology,* 1969, *1,* 410–414.

Wiegernick, R.; Harris, C.; Simeonson, R.; and Pearson, M. E. Social stimulation of vocalizations in delayed infants: Familiar and unfamiliar novel agent. *Child Development,* 1974, *45,* 866–872.

Weisberg, P. Social and nonsocial conditioning of infant vocalizations. *Child Development,* 1963, *34,* 377–388.

White, B. L. *Human infants: Experience and psychological development.* Englewood Cliffs, N.J.: Prentice-Hall, 1971.

White, B. L.; Castle, P.; and Held, R. Observations on the development of visually-directed reaching. *Child Development,* 1964, *35,* 349–364.

Willerman, L.; Borman, S. H.; and Fiedler, M. Infant development, preschool I.Q., and social class. *Child Development,* 1970, *41,* 69–78.

Williams, J. R., and Scott, R. B. Growth and development of Negro infants: IV. Motor development and its relationship to child rearing practices in two groups of Negro infants. *Child Development,* 1953, *24,* 103–121.

Wilson, R. S. Twins: Early mental development. *Science,* 1972, *175,* 915–917.

Wilson, P. D., and Riesen, A. H. Visual development in rhesus monkeys neonatally deprived of patterned light. *Journal of Comparative and Physiological Psychology,* 1966, *61,* 87–95.

Windle, W. F. Neuropathology of certain forms of mental retardation. *Science,* 1963, *140,* 1186–1189.

Wolff, P. H. The natural history of crying and other vocalizations in early infancy. In Foss, B. M. (Ed.), *Determinants of infant behavior,* Vol. 4. London: Methuen, 1969.

Yarrow, L.; Rubenstein, J. L.; and Pederson, F. A. *Infant and environment: Early cognitive and motivational development.* New York: Wiley, 1975.

Zelazo, P. R.; Zelazo, N. A.; and Kolb, S. "Walking" in the newborn. *Science,* 1972, *176,* 314–315.

Chapter 5

Ainsworth, M. D. Object relations, dependency, and attachment: A theoretical review of the infant-mother relationship. *Child Development,* 1969, *40,* 969–1025.

Ainsworth, M. D., and Bell, S. M. Attachment, exploration, and separation: Illustrated by the behavior of one-year-olds in a strange situation. *Child Development,* 1970, *41,* 49–67.

Ainsworth, M. D.; Bell, S. M.; and Slayton, D. J. Individual differences in strange-situation behavior of one-year-olds. In Schaffer, H. R. (Ed.), *The origins of human social relations.* London: Academic Press, 1971.

Ball, B. C. Some relationships among infant preference for tactile stimulation, infant developmental level, and maternal behaviors. *Dissertation Abstracts International,* 1969, *29,* 4838.

Ban, P. L., and Lewis, M. Mothers and fathers, girls and boys: Attachment behavior in the one-year-old. *Merrill-Palmer Quarterly,* 1974, *20,* 195–204.

Beckwith, L. Relationship between infants' social behavior and their mothers' behavior. *Child Development,* 1972, *43,* 397–411.

Bell, R. Q. Contributions of human infants to caregiving and social interaction. In Lewis, M., and Rosenblum, L. A. (Eds.), *The effect of the infant on its caregiver.* New York: Wiley, 1974.

Bell, R. S., and Ainsworth, M. D. Infant crying and maternal responsiveness. *Child Development,* 1967, *38,* 1171–1190.

Blehar, M. C. Anxious attachment and defensive reactions associated with day care. *Child Development,* 1974, *45,* 683–692.

Bowlby, J. Note on Dr. Lois Murphy's paper. *International Journal of Psycho-Analysis,* 1964, *46,* 44–46.

Bowlby, J. *Attachment and loss,* Vol. 1: *Attachment.* New York: Basic Books, 1969.

Braun, S., and Caldwell, B. M. Emotional adjustment of children in day care who enrolled prior to or after the age of three. *Early Child Development and Care,* 1973, *2,* 13–21.

Brazelton, T. B. Effect of maternal expectations on early infant behavior. *Early Child Development and Care,* 1973, *2,* 259–273.

Brazelton, T. B.; Koslowski, B.; and Main M. The origins of reciprocity. In Lewis, M., and Rosenblum, L. A. (Eds.), *The effect of the infant on its caregiver.* New York: Wiley, 1974.

Bronson, G. W. Fear of the unfamiliar in human infants. In Schaffer, H. R. (Ed.), *The origins of human social relations.* London: Academic Press, 1971.

Bronson, W. C. The growth of competence: Issues of conceptualization and measurement. In Schaffer, H. R. (Ed.), *The origins of human social relations.* London: Academic Press, 1971.

Bronson, W. Mother-toddler interaction: A perspective on studying the development of competence. *Merrill-Palmer Quarterly,* 1974, *20,* 275–287.

Brooks, J., and Lewis, M. Attachment behavior in thirteen-month-old opposite-sex twins. *Child Development,* 1974a, *45,* 243-247.

Brooks, J., and Lewis, M. The effect of time on attachment as measured in a free play situation. *Child Development,* 1974b, *45,* 311–316.

Brooks, J., and Lewis, M. Infants' responses to strangers: Midget, adult, and child. *Child Development,* 1976, *47,* 323–332.

Brown, J. V.; Bakeman, R.; Snyder, P. A.; Frederickson, W. T.; Morgan, S. T.; and Helper, R. Interactions of black inner-city (Atlanta) mothers with their newborn infants. *Child Development,* 1975, *46,* 677–686.

Brown, M. Attitudes and personality characteristics of mothers and their relation to infantile colic. *Dissertation Abstracts International,* 1961, *22,* 319.

Buinun, N.; Rynders, J.; and Turnure, I. Early maternal linguistic environment of normal and Down's syndrome language-learning children. *American Journal of Mental Deficiency,* 1974, *79,* 52–58.

Busch, F.; Nagera, H.; McKnight, R.; and Pezzarossi, G. Primary transitional objects. *Journal of the American Academy of Child Psychiatry,* 1973, *12,* 193–214.

Cairns, R. *Social development: The origins and plasticity of interchanges.* San Francisco: W. H. Freeman and Company, 1979.

Caldwell, B. M. The effects of psychosocial deprivation on human development in infancy. *Merrill-Palmer Quarterly,* 1970, *16,* 260–277.

Coates, B.; Anderson, E. P.; and Hartup, W. W. Interrelations in the attachment behavior of human infants. *Developmental Psychology,* 1972a, *6,* 218–230.

Coates, B.; Anderson, E. P.; and Hartup, W. W. The stability of attachment behaviors in the human infant. *Developmental Psychology,* 1972b, *6,* 231–237.

Cohen, L. J., and Campos, J. J. Father, mother, and stranger as elicitors of attachment behaviors in infancy. *Developmental Psychology,* 1974, *10,* 146–154.

Corter, C. M.; Rheingold, H. L.; and Eckerman, C. O. Toys delay the infant's following of his mother. *Developmental Psychology,* 1972, *6,* 138–145.

Dennis, W., and Najarian, P. Infant development under environmental handicap. *Psychological Monographs,* 1957, *71,* 1–13.

Eckerman, C.O., and Whatley, J. L. Infants' reactions to unfamiliar adults varying in novelty. *Developmental Psychology,* 1975, *11,* 562-566.

Eckerman, C. O.; Whatley, J. L.; and Katz, S. L. Growth of social play with peers during the second year of life. *Developmental Psychology,* 1975, *11,* 42–49.

Emde, R. N.; Gaensbauer, T. J.; and Harmon, R. J. Emotional expression in infancy. *Psychological Issues,* 1976,-10 (1).

Emde, R. N.; McCartney, R. D.; and Harmon, R. J. Neonatal smiling in REM states: IV. Premature study. *Child Development,* 1971, *42,* 1657–1661.

Escalona, S. Basic modes of social interaction: Their emergence and patterning during the first year of life. *Merrill-Palmer Quarterly,* 1973, *10,* 205–232.

Etaugh, C. Effects of maternal employment on children: A review of recent research. *Merrill-Palmer Quarterly,* 1974, *20,* 91–98.

Fein, G. G. Children's sensitivity to social contexts at 18 months of age. *Developmental Psychology,* 1975, *11,* 853–854.

Feldman, S. S., and Ingham, M. E. Attachment behavior: A validation study in two age groups. *Child Development,* 1975, *46,* 319–330.

Fowler, M. A developmental learning approach to infant care in a group setting. *Merrill-Palmer Quarterly,* 1972, *18,* 145–176.

Fraiberg, S. Blind infants and their mothers: An examination of the sign system. In Lewis, M., and Rosenblum, L. A. (Eds.), *The effect of the infant on its caregiver.* New York: Wiley, 1974.

Frommer, E. A., and O'Shea, G. Antenatal identification of women liable to have problems in managing their infants. *British Journal of Psychiatry,* 1973, *123,* 149–156.

Gershaw, N. J., and Schwarz, J. C. The effects of familiar toy and mother's presence on exploratory and attachment behavior in young children. *Child Development,* 1971, *42,* 1662.

Goiń-DeCarie, T. Manifestations, hypotheses, data. In Goiń-DeCarie, T. (Ed.), *The infant's reaction to strangers.* New York: International Universities Press, 1974.

Goiń-DeCarie, T. Manifestations, hypotheses, data. In Goiń-DeCarie, T. (Ed.) *The infant's reaction to strangers.* New York: International Universities Press, 1974.

Greenberg, D. J.; Hillman, D.; and Grice, D. Infant and stranger variables related to stranger anxiety in the first year of life. *Developmental Psychology,* 1973, *9,* 207–212.

Goldberg, S., and Lewis, M. Play behavior in the year-old infant: Early sex differences. *Child Development,* 1969, *40,* 21–31.

Hakansson, B.; Horneman, G.; and Leidholm, M. Attachment in infancy as a function of experience. *Goteborg Psychological Reports,* 1973, *3,* 15 (abstract).

Harlow, H. F. Love in infant monkeys. *Scientific American,* 1959, *200,* 68–74.

Harlow, H. F. Early social deprivation and later behavior in the monkey. In Abrams, A.; Garner, H. H.; and Toman, J. E. P. (Eds.), *Unfinished tasks in the behavioral sciences.* Baltimore: Williams and Wilkins, 1964.

Harlow, H. F. Social rehabilitation of isolate monkeys. Talk to the National Academy of Science reported in *Mainly Monkey,* 1970, *1,* 12.

Harlow, H. F., and Harlow, M. K. Social deprivation in monkeys. *Scientific American,* 1962, *207,* 136–146.

Harlow, H. F., Harlow, M. K., and Suomi, S. J. From thought to therapy: Lessons from a primate laboratory. *American Scientist,* 1971, *59,* 538–549.

Hebb, D. O., and Riesen, A. H. The genesis of irrational fears. *Bulletin of the Canadian Psychological Association,* 1943, *3,* 49–50.

Hinde, R. A., and Spencer-Booth, Y. Individual differences in the responses of rhesus monkeys to a period of separation from their mothers. *Journal of Child Psychology, Child Psychiatry and Allied Disciplines,* 1970, *11,* 159–176.

Hoffman, L. W., and Nye, I. *Working mothers.* San Francisco: Jossey-Bass, 1975.

Kagan, J., Kearsley, R. B., and Zelazo, P. R. *Infancy: Its place in human development.* Cambridge: Harvard University Press, 1978.

Korner, A. F. Early stimulation and maternal care as related to infant capabilities and individual differences. *Early Child Development and Care,* 1973, *2,* 307–327.

Korner, A. F. The effect of the infant's state, level of arousal, sex, and ontogenetic stage on the caregiver. In Lewis, M., and Rosenblum, L. A. (Eds.), *The effect of the infant on its caregiver.* New York: Wiley, 1974.

Lamb, M. Interactions between eight-month-old infants and their fathers and mothers. In Lamb, M. (Ed.), *The role of the father in child development.* New York: Wiley, 1976.

Lamb, M. Father-infant and mother-infant interaction in the first year of life. *Child Development,* 1977, *48,* 167–181.

Lamb, M. E. Twelve-month-olds and their parents: Interaction in a laboratory playroom. *Developmental Psychology,* 1976, *12,* 237–246.

Lenssen, B. G. Infants' reactions to peer strangers. *Dissertation Abstracts International,* 1973, *33,* 6062.

Lewis, M. Cross-cultural studies of mother-infant interaction: Description and consequence: introduction. *Human Development,* 1972, *15,* 73–76.

Lewis, M., and Brooks, J. Self, other, and fear: Infants' reactions to people. In Lewis, M., and Rosenblum, L. A. (Eds.), *The origins of fear.* New York: Wiley, 1974.

Lewis, M., and Goldberg, S. Perceptual-cognitive development in infancy: A generalized expectancy model as a function of the mother-infant interaction. *Merrill-Palmer Quarterly,* 1969, *15,* 81–100.

Lewis, M., and Lee-Painter, S. An interactional approach to the mother-infant dyad. In Lewis, M., and Rosenblum, L. A. (Eds.), *The effect of the infant on its caregiver.* New York: Wiley, 1974.

Lewis, M., and Rosenblum, L. A. (Eds.) *Friendship and peer relations.* New York: Wiley, 1975.

Lytton, H. Observation studies of parent-child interaction: A methodology review. *Child Development,* 1971, *42,* 651–684.

Maccoby, E. E., and Jacklin, C. N. *The psychology of sex differences.* Stanford: Stanford University Press, 1974.

Mahler, M. S.; Pine, F.; and Bergman, A. *The psychological birth of the human infant.* New York: Basic Books, 1975.

Marvin, R. S. Attachment and communicative behavior in two-, three-, and four-year-old children. Unpublished doctoral dissertation. University of Chicago, 1971. Cited in Maccoby, E. E., and Jacklin, C. N. (Eds.), *The psychology of sex differences.* Stanford: Stanford University Press, 1974, p. 534.

Masters, J. C., and Wellman, H. M. The study of human infant attachment: A procedural critique. *Psychological Bulletin,* 1974, *81,* 218–237.

Morgan, G. A., and Riciutti, H. N. Infants' responses to strangers during the first year. In Foss, B. M. (Ed.), *Determinants of infant behavior,* Vol. 4. New York: Wiley, 1969.

Moss, H. A., and Robson, K. S. Maternal influences in early social visual behavior. *American Journal of Orthopsychiatry,* 1967, *37,* 394–395.

Moss, H. A., and Robson, K. S. Maternal influences in early social visual behavior. *Child Development,* 1968, *39,* 401–408.

Novak, M. A., and Harlow, H. F. Social recovery of monkeys isolated for the first year of life: I. Rehabilitation and therapy. *Developmental Psychology,* 1975, *11,* 453–465.

Paradise, E. B., and Curcio, F. Relationship of cognitive and affective behaviors to fear of strangers in male infants. *Developmental Psychology,* 1974, *10,* 476–483.

Passman, R. H. Providing attachment objects to facilitate learning and reduce distress: Effects of mothers and security blankets. *Developmental Psychology,* 1977, *13,* 25–30.

Passman, R. H., and Weisberg, P. Mothers and blankets as agents for promoting play and exploration in a novel environment: The effects of social and non-social attachment objects. *Developmental Psychology,* 1975, *11,* 170–177.

Ragozin, A. S. Attachment behavior of day care and home reared children in a laboratory setting. Paper read at the biennial meetings of the Society for Research in Child Development, New Orleans, 1977.

Rebelsky, F., and Hanks, C. Fathers' verbal interaction with infants in the first three months of life. *Child Development,* 1971, *42,* 63–68.

Rebelsky, F. First discussant's comments: Cross-cultural studies of mother-infant interaction: Description and consequence. *Human Development,* 1972, *15,* 128–130.

Rheingold, H. General issues in the study of fear. In Lewis, M., and Rosenblum, L. A. (Eds.), *The origins of fear.* New York: Wiley, 1974.

Rheingold, H. L., and Eckerman, C. O. The infant separates himself from his mother. *Science,* 1970, *168,* 78–83.

Rheingold, H. L., and Samuels, H. R. Maintaining the positive behavior of infants by increased stimulation. *Developmental Psychology,* 1969, *1,* 520–527.

Rheingold, H. L.; Stanley, W. L.; and Cooley, J. A. Method for studying exploratory behavior in infants. *Science,* 1962, *136,* 1054–1055.

Riciutti, H. N. Fear and the development of social attachments in the first year of life. In Lewis, M., and Rosenblum, L. A. (Eds.), *The origins of fear.* New York: Wiley, 1974.

Robertson, J. Mothering as an influence on early development: A study of Well-Baby Clinic records. *Psychoanalytic Study of the Child,* 1962, *17,* 245–264.

Robertson, J., and Robertson, J. Quality of substitute care as an influence on separation responses. *Journal of Psychosomatic Research,* 1972, *16,* 261–265.

Robinson, H. B., and Robinson, N. M. Longitudinal development of very young children in a comprehensive day care program: The first two years. *Child Development,* 1971, *42,* 1673–1683.

Rosenblum, L. A. Infant attachment in monkeys. In Schaffer, H. R. (Ed.), *The origins of human social relations.* London: Academic Press, 1971.

Rosenblum, L. A., and Alpert, S. Fear of strangers and specificity of attachment in monkeys. In Lewis, M., and Rosenblum, L. A. (Eds.), *The origins of fear.* New York: Wiley, 1974.

Rosenblum, L. A., and Youngstein, K. P. Developmental changes in compensatory dyadic response in mother and infant monkeys. In Lewis, M., and Rosenblum, L. A. (Eds.), *The effect of the infant on its caregiver.* New York: Wiley, 1974.

Rubenstein, J. Maternal attentiveness and subsequent exploratory behavior in the infant. *Child Development,* 1967, *38,* 1089–1100.

Rutter, M. *Maternal deprivation reassessed.* London: Penguin, 1972.

Salk, L. The critical nature of the post-pártum period in the human for the establishment of the mother-infant bond: A controlled study. *Diseases of the Nervous System,* 1970, *31,* 110–116.

Sander, L. W. The longitudinal course of early mother-child interaction: Cross-case comparison in a sample of mother-child pairs. In Foss, B. M. (Ed.), *Determinants of infant behavior,* Vol. 4. London: Methuen, 1969.

Schaffer, H. R. The onset of fear of strangers and the incongruity hypothesis. *Journal of Child Psychology and Psychiatry,* 1966, *7,* 95–106.

Schaffer, H. R., and Emerson, P. E. The development of social attachments in infancy. *Monographs of the Society for Research in Child Development,* 1964, *29* (3, Whole No. 94).

Schwarz, J. C.; Strickland, R. G.; and Krolik, G. Infant day care: Behavioral effects at preschool age. *Developmental Psychology,* 1974, *10,* 502–506.

Spock, B. *Baby and child care.* New York: Pocket Books, 1976.

Stayton, D. J.; Hogan, R.; and Ainsworth, M. D. Infant obedience and maternal behavior: The origins of socialization reconsidered. *Child Development,* 1971, *42,* 1057–1069.

Stern, D. N. Mother and infant at play: The dyadic interaction involving facial, vocal, and gaze behaviors. In Lewis, M., and Rosemblum, L. A. (Eds.), *The effect of the infant on its caregiver.* New York: Wiley, 1974.

Stern, G. G.; Caldwell, B. M.; Hersher, L.; Lipton, E. L.; and Richmond, J. B. A factor analytic study of the mother-infant dyad. *Child Development,* 1969, *40,* 163–181.

Stroufe, L. A.; Waters, E.; and Matas, L. Contextual determinants of infant affective response. In Lewis, M., and Rosenblum, L. A. (Eds.), *The origins of fear.* New York: Wiley, 1974.

Tulkin, S. R. Social class differences in attachment behaviors of ten-month-old infants. *Child Development,* 1973a, *44,* 171–174

Tulkin, S. R. Social class differences in infant's reactions to mother's and stranger's voices. *Developmental Psychology,* 1973b, *8,* 137.

Tulkin, S. R., and Kagan, J. Mother-child interaction in the first year of life. *Child Development,* 1972, *43,* 31–41.

Wallston, B. The effects of maternal employment on children. *Journal of Child Psychology, Child Psychiatry and Allied Disciplines,* 1973, *14,* 81–95.

Watson, J. S. Smiling, cooing, and "The Game." *Merrill-Palmer Quarterly,* 1973, *18,* 323–339.

Willemsen, E.; Heaton, C.; Flaherty, D.; and Ritchey, G. Attachment behavior in one-year-olds as a function of mother vs. father, sex of child, session, and toys. *Genetic Psychology Monographs,* 1974, *96,* 305–324.

Willemsen, E. W., and McTighe, M. J. N. Stranger anxiety in nine-month-old infants as a function of the mother-infant relationship. Unpublished manuscript, University of Santa Clara, 1977.

Yarrow, L. J. Research in dimensions of early maternal care. *Merrill-Palmer Quarterly,* 1963, *9,* 101–114.

Yarrow, L.; Rubenstein, J. L.; and Pederson, F. A. *Infant and environment: Early cognitive and motivational development.* New York: Wiley, 1975.

Zelazo, P. R. Smiling and vocalizing: A cognitive emphasis. *Merrill-Palmer Quarterly,* 1972, *18,* 349–365.

Chapter 6

Bandura, A. *Social learning theory.* Englewood Cliffs, N.J.: Prentice-Hall, 1977.

Bronson, G. W. The development of fear in men and other animals. *Child Development,* 1968, *39,* 409–431.

Escalona, S. *The roots of individuality: Normal patterns of development in infancy.* Chicago: Aldine, 1968.

Hebb, D. O., and Riesen, A. H. The genesis of irrational fears. *Bulletin of the Canadian Psychological Association,* 1943, *3,* 49–50.

Lodge, A.; Armington, J. C.; Barnet, A. B.; Shanks, B. L.; and Newcomb, C. N. Newborn infants' electroretinograms and evoked electroencephalographic responses to orange and white light. *Child Development,* 1969, *40,* 267–293.

Maccoby, E. E., and Jacklin, C. N. *The psychology of sex differences.* Stanford: Stanford University Press, 1974.

Mischel, W. *Introduction to personality.* New York: Holt, Rinehart and Winston, 1976.

Rothbart, M. K. Laughter in young children. *Psychological Bulletin,* 1973, *80,* 247–256.

Scarr, S., and Salapatek, P. Patterns of fear development during infancy. *Merrill-Palmer Quarterly,* 1970, *16,* 53–90.

Schaffer, H. R.; Greenwood, A.; and Parry, M. H. The onset of wariness. *Child Development,* 1972, *43,* 165–175.

Thomas, A., and Chess, S. *Temperament and development.* New York: Brunner-Mazel, 1977.

Thomas A.; Chess, S.; and Birch, H. G. The origin of personality. *Scientific American,* 1970, *223,* 102–109.

Weil, A. P. The basic core. *Psychoanalytic Study of the Child,* 1970, *25,* 442–460.

Willerman, L. Activity level and hyperactivity in twins. *Child Development,* 1973, *44,* 288–293.

Willerman, L., and Plomin, R. Activity level in children and their parents. *Child Development,* 1973, *44,* 854–858.

Wolff, P. H. Observations on the early development of smiling. In Foss, B. M. (Ed.), *Determinants of infant behavior,* Vol. 2. New York: Wiley, 1963.

Appendix

Bayley, N., and Oden, M. The maintenance of intellectual ability in gifted adults. *Journal of Gerontology,* 1955, *10,* 91–107.

Bower, T. G. R. Object perception in infants. *Perception,* 1972, *1,* 15–30.

Broussard, E. R., and Hartner, M. S. Maternal perception of the neonate as related to development. *Child Psychiatry and Human Development,* 1970, *1,* 16–25.

Charlesworth, W. R. Persistence of orienting and attending behavior in infants as a function of stimulus-locus uncertainty. *Child Development,* 1966, *37,* 473–491.

Harlow, H. Social rehabilitation of isolate monkeys. Talk to the National Academy of Science reported in *Mainly Monkeys,* 1970, *1,* 12.

Kagan, J. Do infants think? *Scientific American,* 1972, *226,* 74–82.

Kagan, J., and Moss, H. *From birth to maturity.* New York: Wiley, 1972.

Lewis, M., and McGurk, H. Evaluation of infant intelligence. *Science,* 1972, *178,* 1174–1177.

Lewis, M., and Rosenblum, L. A. (Eds.), *The effect of the infant on its caregiver.* New York: Wiley, 1974.

LeCompte, G. K., and Gratch, G. Violation of a rule as a method of diagnosing infants' levels of object concept. *Child Development,* 1972, *43,* 385–396.

Lipsitt, L. P., and Kaye, H. Conditional sucking in the newborn. *Psychonomic Science,* 1964, *1,* 29–30.

Lipsitt, L. P., and Kaye, H. Enhancement of neonatal sucking through reinforcement. *Journal of Experimental Child Psychology,* 1966, *4,* 163–168.

Mash, E. J., and Makohoniuk, G. The effects of prior information and behavioral predictability on observer accuracy. *Child Development,* 1975, *46,* 513–519.

Reid, J. B. Reliability assessment of observation data: A possible methodological problem. *Child Development,* 1970, *41,* 1143–1150.

Semb, G., and Lipsitt, L. P. The effects of acoustic stimulation on cessation and initiation of nonnutritive sucking in neonate. *Journal of Experimental Child Psychology,* 1968, *6,* 585–597.

Taplin, P. S., and Reid, J. B. Effects of instructional set and experimenter influence on observer reliability. *Child Development,* 1973, *44,* 547–554.

Terman, L. M. *The gifted child grows up.* Vol. 4 of *Genetic studies of genius.* Stanford: Stanford University Press, 1947.

Thomas, H. Some problems of studies concerned with evaluating the predictive validity of infant tests. *Journal of Child Psychology, Child Psychiatry and Allied Disciplines,* 1967, *8,* 197–205.

Wildman, B. G.; Erickson, M. T.; and Kent, R. N. The effect of two training procedures on observer agreement and variability of behavior ratings. *Child Development,* 1975, *46,* 520–524.

Woodcock, J. M. Terminology and methodology related to the use of heart rate responsivity in infancy research. *Journal of Experimental Child Psychology,* 1971, *11,* 76–92.

Index

Abnormality, 11–20
Abortion, 11
Accommodation, 122
Activity level, 230, 232, 237, 238, 241
Adaptation, 37, 122, 148, 232, 239
Adrenalin, 18
Alcohol, 14, 15
Age:
  gestational, 21
  and object permanence, 146
  as variable, 278–282
AINSWORTH, M., 185, 186, 187, 188, 189, 190, 192, 201, 204, 209, 213, 214
Alert inactivity, 39, 40, 42, 45, 46, 56, 58, 64, 68, 71, 72, 84, 89
Amniocentesis, 11
Amniotic fluid, 6
Amniotic membrane, 5
Anecdotal record, 259–260, 286
Anemia, 14
  sickle-cell, 12
Anoxia, 16, 19–20, 23, 162
Anxiety, 19, 27
APGAR, V., 8
Apgar test, 34, 85
Approach/withdrawal, 232, 238
Assessment, 267
Assimilation, 122, 128
At-risk concept, 26–27, 28
Attachment, 95, 141, 175–223
  mother–infant, 178–186
  multiple, 190
  sex differences in, 189
Attachment bond, 186
Attention, 76–86
  indicators of, 51–52

organization of, 107
stimulators of, 52–54
visual, 51–54, 78–80
Attention span, 234, 239
Autonomy, 178, 184

Babbling, 154–156, 173
Babkin reflex, 34
BANDURA, A., 107, 226, 229
Basal level, 271
Basic core, 226
BAYLEY, N., 269
Bayley scale, 14, 161, 165, 166, 167, 168, 213, 268, 269, 271–273, 281, 287
BEE, H., 63, 64
Behaviorism, 31
Berkeley Growth Study, 269
BINET, A., 121
Binocular parallax, 103, 106
Biological adaptation, 33–34
Biological drive, 31, 227
BIRCH, H. G., 230, 231, 234n, 237, 238n
Birth, 8–11, 19–20, 32
  complications during, 65, 162
Blanket, 182, 183, 190
Blastocyst, 5, 6
BLEHAR, M. C., 214
Blind infant, 194
Blinking, 36
BOWER, T. G. R., 102, 103, 104, 106, 116, 119, 120, 142–147, 173, 275
BOWLBY, J., 98, 185, 201, 211, 212, 216, 220
Brain damage, 18, 20, 47
Brain wave, 44, 78
Brazelton scale, 25